PUBLIC MANAGEMENT SYSTEMS

Monitoring and Managing
Government Performance

JAMES E. SWISS
North Carolina State University

D1531325

Prentice Hall
Upper Saddle River, New Jersey 07458

Library of Congress Cataloging-in-Publication Data

SWISS, JAMES EDWIN.
  Public management systems : monitoring and managing government
performance / James E. Swiss.
    p.   cm.
  Includes bibliographical references.
  ISBN 0-13-737545-X
    1. Public administration. 2. Management information systems.
  I. Title.
  JF1411.S83 1991
  350—dc20   90-30981
                                                            CIP

Editorial/production supervision and
  interior design: Mary Anne Shahidi
Cover design: Patricia Kelly
Manufacturing buyer: Robert Anderson

*To my parents,
Edwin and Mary Swiss*

 © 1991 by Prentice-Hall, Inc.
Simon & Schuster / A Viacom Company
Upper Saddle River, New Jersey 07458

Printed in the United States of America
10 9 8 7 6 5 4 3 2

ISBN 0-13-737545-X

Prentice-Hall International (UK) Limited, *London*
Prentice-Hall of Australia Pty. Limited, *Sydney*
Prentice-Hall Canada Inc., *Toronto*
Prentice-Hall Hispanoamericana, S.A., *Mexico*
Prentice-Hall of India Private Limited, *New Delhi*
Prentice-Hall of Japan, Inc., *Tokyo*
Simon & Schuster Asia Pte. Ltd., *Singapore*
Editora Prentice-Hall do Brasil, Ltda., *Rio de Janeiro*

Contents

Contents

SECTION 4   *LINKING MANAGEMENT SYSTEMS
               TO OTHER SYSTEMS*

    Systems   202

    Introduction   202
    The Role of Budgets   203
    Budget Formats   204
    Should Management Systems Be Tightly Linked
       to the Budget System?   223
    Internal Political Effects of Budgetary Systems   229
    Summary   230
    Review Questions   231
    Case   232
    Suggested Further Reading   233
    Appendix—A Detailed Example of ZBB   233
    Endnotes   242

8   Connecting Rewards to Management Systems   247

    Introduction   247
    Behavior and Motivation   248
    At What Level Should Performance Be
       Rewarded?   250
    Focusing on the Individual: Management Systems
       and Personnel Systems   251
    Money as an Extrinsic Motivator: Individual
       Rewards   258
    Money as an Extrinsic Motivator: Group
       and Organization-Wide Rewards   263
    An Overview: Linking Management Systems
       to Other Systems   265
    Summary   267
    Review Questions   269
    Cases   269
    Suggested Further Reading   271
    Endnotes   272

9   Structure as a Management Tool: Links to Management
    Systems   281

    Introduction   281
    The View from the Top: Structure as a Political
       Tool   282

Preface

This book is about management systems. Such Systems track the performance of an organization on a regular, short-term basis. They are essential tools for directing large, complex organizations. This has long been realized in the private sector, and there are many books on private sector management systems. But only during the relatively recent past have many public sector managers come to the same realization. Many government programs that have seemed sound in principle have failed when implemented, and thus attention has naturally shifted to improving the implementation process. Improved management systems are an important step toward improved implementation.

This book is directed at current and future managers of public organizations. It is based on six premises:

1. A government organization is very different from a business organization, and management techniques cannot be imported from the business sector without very extensive modification.
2. The government sector is above all political. In a democracy, this is a positive statement. Nonetheless, politics must be considered in every step of government agency management, as this book demonstrates.
3. Inflated promises are often the greatest enemy of government management systems. In the past thirty years many new government policy-making or

management techniques have been introduced—including planning program-ming budgeting systems (PPBS), management by objectives (MBO), and zero-based budgeting (ZBB). In each case these techniques were strikingly oversold; often they were accompanied by promises that they would supplant politics and finally make public management "rational." Of course no system can live up to such promises, and in the inevitable backlash, all such systems were sometimes dismissed as empty fads. A number of observers lost sight of the fact that some systems, under some circumstances, can make extremely useful contributions. This book emphasizes these potential contributions without falling into the trap of extravagant promises.

4. The perfect is often the enemy of the good. Management systems are generally undeveloped in the public sector. Public managers who wait until they can institute a system that has the sophistication and comprehensiveness of the best business systems will wait forever. This book accordingly emphasizes sturdy systems that can survive the more rough and tumble world of public management—which necessarily involves sacrificing some of the precision of business systems.

5. Most students of public management have had relatively little training in management information systems or accounting, and they are unlikely to handle these areas on a day-to-day basis themselves. Thus this book discusses what public managers should ask from their co-workers and subordinates who do handle these areas, and how to interpret the information that results. Both accounting and MIS affect management systems, but management systems are far broader than either.

6. Management systems are used for much more than controlling. As will be discussed in greater detail in Chapter One, the management systems discussed in this book are usually termed *management control systems* by business texts. Although I have no objection to the term if it is construed loosely, such terminology is misleading to most public managers. It is necessary to emphasize that management systems are as important for the information they provide managers for new, wide-reaching, and sometimes innovative decisions as they are for "control."

I would like to thank a number of people for their help. Charles Coe read several early chapters and recommended a number of useful changes. Elizabethann O'Sullivan used a draft of this book in her class and provided many helpful suggestions. She also wrote Case 2-2. Saul Abreu, a graduate student, wrote the initial drafts of Cases 2-3 and 7-1. Donald F. Kettl, University of Wisconsin, and Hal G. Rainey, The University of Georgia, suggested a number of helpful improvements. Finally, Alois Chalmers very efficiently typed a draft of all the chapters.

On the assumption that techniques are best learned through applica-tions, I have included review questions, problems, and one or more short fic-tional cases at the end of each chapter, thus allowing the reader to apply the concepts there explained.

chapter one

An Overview of Public Management Systems

MANAGEMENT AND MANAGEMENT SYSTEMS

Each month, newspapers and television publicize additional stories of government failures—public hospitals that provide scandalously inferior health care, job-training agencies that teach skills no employers want, and public housing agencies that allow their apartments to deteriorate into seedy slums. Yet at the same time that these stories are commanding headlines, most government agencies are consistently and competently performing their duties. With little or no outside attention, they continue to generate social security checks, teach children, and compassionately care for the mentally retarded.

What distinguishes the successful government agencies from the failures? A number of factors are of course important, but almost all consistently successful agencies share one characteristic: well-working management systems. *A management system is a tool for monitoring the performance of an organization on a regular short-term basis.*[1] (Most management systems track performance on either a quarterly or a monthly basis.) This book is about ways to construct and use such management systems. We will begin by briefly examining the reason for such systems: management.

Management Defined

Management is the coordination of people and resources in order to achieve policy objectives. Thus a manager is any organizational member who attempts to achieve the organization's goals through other people. In large organizations there are often several levels of managers, and a manager may simultaneously be the subordinate of a higher-ranking manager and the superior of yet other managers.

Management's Relation to Operations and Strategic Planning. Management links an organization's strategic planning to its operations.[2] *Strategic planning* sets the overall policies and goals for an organization. It involves deciding such issues as who the organization's clients are, in what ways they should be served, and how the organization should adapt to major changes in its environment. At the other extreme of the continuum, an organization must carry out day-to-day tasks; it must treat patients, teach pupils, pick up garbage, or patrol a beat. This mode of activity is termed *operations*.[3] Management is the connector; that is, management links strategic planning to operations by taking the broad policies set by the strategic planning process and turning them into more specific decisions that direct the organization's operations.

Most public and private organizations are arranged in a hierarchy: The top of the organization is concerned primarily with strategic planning; the middle, with management; and the lower level, with operations. This hierarchy of tasks is often a useful shorthand way of thinking about organizational processes, but it cannot be taken too literally. Some newer organizations are not very hierarchical, and all members are expected to share these tasks. Even in the more traditional hierarchical organizations, these functions overlap. Top-level administrators are often involved in all three activities, and the lower-level workers often influence management. So although the three functions are separable in the abstract, they often overlap in real organizations.

This realization of an overlap is a relatively recent development. For many decades theories of public organizations followed the lead of Woodrow Wilson, a noted public administration theorist who later became president. Wilson suggested that policy making (which we are calling *strategic planning*) could be separated from administration (carrying out the policy, which we have termed *management and operations*).[4] Policy, said Wilson, should be determined by the political leaders of public organizations such as the president or governor, the legislature, and the departmental secretaries. Policy making would be based on political considerations, but once these policies were determined, they could be carried out by the lower-level workers efficiently and automatically without politics intervening.

It has been clear for several decades that such a clear-cut line between policy and administration exists only in books. In public management, judgment (and thus politics) suffuses all levels of an organization, although it is often stronger at the upper levels than at the very lowest.[5]

Management Systems

This book is about public sector management systems. As indicated, they can be defined as tools for monitoring (and eventually improving) organizational performance. Management systems allow managers to set goals for their organization and to judge their performance in terms of these goals. To manage effectively, managers must know, first, where they want to go and, second, whether they are getting there.

A management system is a *feedback system*. Any feedback system has three steps:

1. *Setting initial standards.* Using policy directives from above as guidelines, the manager sets the organizational goals for the period covered, whether it is a week, a month, a quarter, or a year—for example, "to process 5,000 patients this quarter." (Some authors distinguish among broad *goals,* narrower *objectives,* and yet narrower *standards.* Because this distinction often breaks down, and is rarely crucial, we will simply treat all three words as synonyms.)

2. *Collecting information on progress.* During the period for which goals have been established, the manager collects information on how the organization is performing—for example, "Have 5,000 patients been processed?"

3. *Taking remedial action.* This third step is not always necessary. But if step 2 reveals that organizational goals are not being attained, the manager will take remedial action to correct the shortfall. To use the preceding example, if 5,000 patients have not been processed by the end of the quarter, the manager determines the reason. If there is a staff shortage, more doctors and nurses may be hired. If not enough patients are coming in, outreach efforts can be started.

Any feedback system has as its implicit model the thermostat. On a thermostat, a standard is set (say, 72°); then the thermostat monitors the environment to determine the temperature; and finally, if the temperature deviates from the goal, the thermostat takes remedial action by triggering the heater or air conditioner.[6] Managing a complex public organization is obviously not quite this simple. When a thermostat finds a shortfall, the decision (turning on the air conditioner or heater) is automatic. In an organization, a shortfall often demands a creative, unstructured response by the manager. Nonetheless this basic feedback model captures the heart of management. To direct their organization, managers must know where they would like to go and then gather information about how they are progressing.

In gathering this information, managers may sometimes use management information systems (MIS), which are processes for generating structured data. Usually, though not always, an MIS processes the data with computers. The MIS data usually concern operational control as well as management matters. As we will discuss later, an MIS can be *part* of a management system; that is, it can sometimes help provide the information for feedback step 2, determining whether current performance is meeting the standards. But management systems include much more than information from an MIS. Management systems involve setting standards in the first place and then taking action if there is a shortfall. In addition, some of the most important management systems, such as management by objectives (MBO), are run by hand and there is no electronic data-processing component. So an MIS is at most only one small part of a management system.

This book will emphasize the use of management systems to track the *output* of an organization. It will begin with a brief look at financial management systems, which enable administrators to monitor organizational input. We then turn to the more important area of output, examining two output-oriented management systems: MBO systems, which enable administrators to plan and track major organizational projects, and performance monitoring systems (PMS), which enable administrators to plan and track progress on routinized activities. Later chapters of the book will examine how these output-oriented management systems can be connected to other systems, such as budgeting and personnel. The final chapter will discuss ways in which management systems can be installed.

The Two Uses of Management Systems

Most large organizations have a number of management systems operating simultaneously, such as financial management systems that track the money and other systems that track nonfinancial outputs. There are likely to be systems that are used primarily at the organization's upper levels and others used primarily at the lower levels.

However they may vary, all management systems are tools for making an organization more efficient and effective. Moreover, all management systems do this by collecting and structuring information for two primary uses: first, to provide a basis for managerial decision making and, second, to provide incentives for all organizational members to pursue the organization's goals. Some management systems emphasize using their information for *decision making;* others emphasize *behavior-influencing incen-*

tives; but all systems at least partially serve both purposes. We will consider each in turn.

Incentives for Workers' Behavior. All management systems inevitably influence behavior. To return to the earlier example, if one of a system's objectives is "to process 5,000 patients in the next quarter," the knowledge that this objective is being monitored will probably provide an incentive for employees to emphasize processing patients.

Management systems are often called *management control systems.* This term is widely used and understood in the business world, but this book will usually avoid it because it has misleading implications. *Control* suggests coercion and robotlike restrictions, but even management systems designed primarily to influence behavior do not function in such coercive ways. A well-working management system is flexible. Rather than attempting to channel everyone into one rigid behavioral pattern, it provides incentives for workers to find new and better ways of achieving the organization's goals.

Decision Making. Once a management system establishes a goal or objective, the objective serves double duty. At the same time that an objective is influencing behavior, it is also providing the manager with information about how well the organization is functioning. If the organization does better or worse than the objective, the manager will reexamine his or her assumptions and make decisions based on the new knowledge. Management systems are accordingly crucial for decision making: Managers cannot decide whether or not to change previous decisions unless they know how well the organization is performing. Management systems give managerial decision makers that necessary information.

MARKET VS. NONMARKET ORGANIZATIONS

So far, almost everything said could apply equally well to private or public organizations. How are the ways that public managers use management systems different from the ways private managers operate? The differences are based on the differences between private, market organizations (in other words, organizations that sell their output, such as businesses) and public, nonmarket organizations (organizations, such as government agencies, that do not sell their output for a profit).[7] We will examine the differences between them in terms of the three steps of a management system: setting goals, tracking performance, and taking remedial action.

Differences That Affect Goal Setting

The first step of any management system is to set organizational goals, but there are three reasons why this is far more difficult for public than for business organizations.

1. *Public organizations generally have a larger number of competing potential goals.* The primary overall goal of the typical private sector organization is unambiguous: maintain or increase profit. Organizational efficiency and effectiveness are important because they usually lead to this goal. Public organizations, on the other hand, have legitimate primary goals that extend beyond narrowly defined efficiency and effectiveness, including responsiveness to the general public, responsiveness to the affected clientele, and political rewards for the legislature and executive. Often there is conflict among these potential goals. Thus a police department that is inefficient when viewed from a private sector perspective because it has too many officers may in fact be achieving a competing goal: decreasing unemployment.[8] Because potential goals are often in conflict, political leaders may sometimes prefer that goals not be made clear to avoid offending any group. Management systems can be used to help achieve *any* goal, but choosing a noncontradictory goal is more difficult in the public sector because there are far more possible choices.[9]

2. *Public organizations often operate under strong public pressure.* Public organizations often get the controversial, "hot" issues. How an engine bearing company turns out bearings is rarely controversial, but where public housing is located or whether the public school should offer sex education is.

3. *Public managers operate under fragmented authority structures.* In the private sector, a manager usually has only one boss. In a public organization, managers are likely to be contacted by many "bosses"— their direct superior in the organization, their supporting interest groups, the members of their supervising legislative committees, and the chief executive. All of these people have to be listened to. Roy Ash, who went from the private sector to federal government, explained the cross pressures of government administration to a group of private managers by saying, "Just imagine yourself as chief executive officer where your board of directors is made up of your employers, customers, suppliers and competitors."[10]

Goal setting in a public organization, then, is far more difficult than in a private market organization because of the value-charged subject matter, the publicity, the large number of competing potential goals, and the multiple power centers. When one is discussing goal setting in a public organization, accordingly, one must ask—*whose* goals?

Differences That Affect Performance Tracking

Once goals are set, organizational performance is tracked and measured against them. This stage is the hardest for government agencies, again because of the way they differ from market organizations. *Public organizations lack a profit measure, the most important feedback measure.* This is the single most important difference between public and private sector organizations. Profit serves a wonderful array of functions for a private organization. It allows the private managers to know whether they are doing well in terms of output quantity because if they are not selling enough, profit drops. It indicates how well they are doing in terms of quality. If output quality drops while the price remains the same, customers leave and the profit drops. It indicates whether the organization is keeping up with the latest innovations. If the company does not adopt the latest improvements, it will lose customers to the companies that do—and again, profits will drop. Therefore the single profit measure tells a private sector organization a great deal about both its efficiency and its effectiveness in terms of quality, quantity, innovations, and a series of other attributes.

Unfortunately, there is no such wide-ranging output measure for the public sector. Public management systems require a great deal of effort and information just to produce imperfect substitutes for the profit measures that come so naturally to the business organization. Thus, public sector organizations face a harder task because all the surrogates for output that public agencies monitor are usually not as useful as the single profit measure.

Differences That Affect Remedial Action

Once an organization has set goals and tracked performance, the final step of a management system is to use the information to take new actions. Again, public organizations face obstacles not encountered by business.

1. *Public organizations are less often managed by professional managers.* Many business executives chose their career because they enjoy management; they then devote their entire careers to it. In contrast, many public managers are not professional managers but were often trained in other professions. Thus lawyers run legal agencies, doctors run health agencies, and professional politicians run a large variety of other agencies. This lack of professional management training

means that often the top administrators of public agencies have more difficulty interpreting and using system-generated information.

2. *Public organizations have many more legal restrictions on their external actions, such as choices of missions and activities.* When the market for a company begins to diminish, the company has the flexibility to change its activities, and even sometimes its mission (by moving into a new field, for example). Public organizations can do only what they have been empowered to do. If health funds are being cut in favor of defense, the Department of Health and Human Services cannot begin turning out tanks. More realistically, it often by law cannot close inefficient district sites or terminate inefficient programs. Thus when the management system reveals a shortfall, public agencies find it far more difficult to respond creatively because of the legal constraints.

3. *Public organizations have far more restrictions on their internal actions; they cannot hire, fire, or promote as flexibly.* Public organizations are generally bound by "merit" systems that put severe restrictions on how managers utilize their personnel. It is easier to reward employees for good performances and sanction them for poor results in the private sector. So if the management system information seems to suggest that personnel should be utilized differently, many government agencies are unable to respond.[11]

Overview of Differences: Why Business Systems Cannot Be Directly Applied to Government

All of these differences are substantial and several more could be suggested, but it is more important to emphasize their direction. All of these differences—and probably any other major ones we may wish to add to the list—are ways in which the market (business) organization has an advantage in efficiency and effectiveness over the public organization. Private organizations have more freedom to set unambiguous goals; they have better information about how well they are achieving their goals; and in reacting to shortfalls, they have better control over their own direction and that of their employees. Moreover, these differences are intrinsic; they cannot be changed or corrected because they are built into the very nature of government institutions. These barriers make the generally fine performance of many government organizations all the more commendable. These barriers also suggest that management systems, which attempt to increase organizational information and control, are operating in a much more hostile environment in the public sector. A public manager, facing a very different environment than his or her private counterpart, must set different (and generally lower) goals and use different techniques in moving toward greater efficiency and effectiveness.

Every decade many governors and occasional presidents appoint committees and task forces drawn from the ranks of business executives. They are generally enjoined to make government more efficient. These appointed commissions often seem to believe that making government more efficient will be simple; it should just become "more businesslike." These beliefs—exemplified in the mid-1980s by the report of the Reagan-appointed Grace Commission—are clearly mistaken.[12] As indicated by the important differences discussed, government is not business; it has a unique set of tasks, concerns, and incentives. Accordingly, it is futile to attempt to transfer techniques, approaches, and systems from the private sector to the public sector without adaptation. They simply will not work.

INPUTS, PROCESSES, AND OUTPUTS

Input/Output Models

As noted, management systems are tools for increasing the efficiency and effectiveness of an organization. Any discussion of efficiency and effectiveness, however, must begin by defining organizational input and output. The functioning of any organization, public or private, can be expressed in terms of an input/output model (see Figure 1-1). A model is a simplification of reality in order to make analysis easier.

The input/output model is very simple. On the left side, going into an organization, are all its *inputs*—that is, anything that an organization uses to accomplish its purposes, including people, money, and equipment. For a school, for example, inputs would include teachers, chalkboards, buildings, and desks.

The second part of the model, shown in the middle of the diagram, is the organization's *processes* or *activities*. In the case of the school, its activities might include instructing the children in reading and arithmetic.

Organizational *output* is everything produced by an organization. Thus for a shoe factory, the output is shoes. For a public organization, output is more elusive. However, in the school example, output might be seen as the number of graduates. Or to take a more abstract view, the output of the school might be the increased academic skills of the students. Both alternatives are outputs. Obviously the second of these two possibilities comes closest to what the organization wishes to produce and

Figure 1-1. A simplified portrayal of an input/output model of an organization.

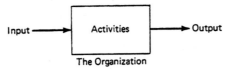

what managers want to measure. But the first is a lot easier to measure. This difficulty in defining and capturing output for public organizations will continually recur in our discussions.

For a clinic, the input would be the doctors, nurses, syringes, and medicines. The activities would include administering physical exams and giving inoculations. The outputs would include such effects as fewer sick days for the patients and a longer average life span in the community.

Most organizations have more than one output, and sometimes outputs are sequential, with one output creating another. For example, a health clinic can decrease the morbidity rate in an area (an output), and that output in turn can increase the area's tax base as more people are healthy enough to work—a longer-range output flowing from the first. Some management analysts give these different types of outputs different names. They reserve *outputs* for the immediate, short-term outputs; they call longer-range outputs *outcomes* and *impacts*. In this book, we will instead call all such results *outputs*—short-range, or *immediate,* outputs, leading to midrange, or *intermediate,* outputs, leading to longer-range, or *ultimate,* outputs. (This topic will be developed further in Chapter Five.) We will not worry about such refinements yet; in this chapter we will simply call all results affecting organizational outsiders *outputs*.

Sometimes it is difficult for managers to distinguish outputs from processes. A process is an activity that occurs within the organization and primarily affects people who work for the organization. An output, on the other hand, is an effect on outsiders. When school districts get these two concepts confused, they sometimes speak of their low student/ teacher ratios as an indicator of fine education. Yet student/teacher ratios are measures of processes—activities going on inside the school. They are truly valuable only if they lead to outputs—changes in students or in society. For a high school, outputs might include such changes in students as increased learning, better performance on standardized tests, and better ability to perform jobs or succeed in college.

The Importance of an Output Focus

Managers must be concerned with both the input and the output of their organization. Feedback systems set goals for and monitor both. In public organizations, input—particularly money—may be determined by outsiders (e.g., the legislature), and thus managers have little control over its total size. But even then the manager must monitor it and decide how much goes to each particular activity.

Output is even more important. It is the underlying reason for the very existence of the agency. Outputs also are often more directly controlled by managers. (The same organizational processes in Figure 1–1 are shown in slightly more complex form in Figure 1–2.)[13] Outputs are results; only

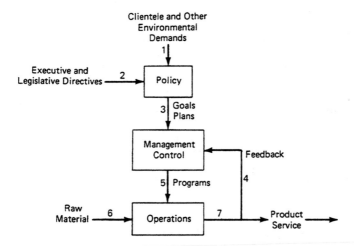

Figure 1-2. Abstract Model of Cybernetic System. A more detailed model of the same input/output process in Figure 1-1. The organization has been divided by the three functions that we have discussed: policy making, management, and operations. Arrows 1, 2, and 6 represent inputs. Arrow 7 represents outputs. Arrows, 3, 4, and 5 represent internal organizational activities such as those covered by management systems. *Source:* Adapted from Robert L. Swinth, *Organizational Systems Management* (1974), p. 23.

by tracking outputs can managers learn whether or not their organization is achieving what it was created to achieve. Moreover, a focus on outputs has other positive effects. When outputs are not regularly measured, employees must be monitored and appraised on the basis of processes— such matters as how hard they seem to work or the exact approaches they use. This monitoring of the details of processes is often called *micromanagement* and it is demoralizing to both supervisors and subordinates. However, if employers and employees can agree that certain outputs will be produced in the next week, month, or quarter, micromanagement is no longer necessary. The subordinate has the freedom to pursue those outputs in almost any reasonable way, as long as they are produced. This focus on outputs accordingly frees the subordinate and helps the supervisor and the organization as well.

For most public organizations, outputs are frustratingly difficult to define or measure. The most important, longer-range outputs of the organization and its programs are often particularly elusive. This difficulty in measurement sometimes causes managers to give up and to focus on processes (how many students are being taught?) instead of outputs (what are the students learning?).

Such a shift in focus misleads both managers and their organizations. Rather than give up, managers can turn to some of the approaches now available for overcoming difficulties in measuring and managing outputs. (We will begin discussing such output-oriented management techniques in Chapter Three and analyze them in greater depth in Chapters Five and Six.) But these details of technique must not be allowed to obscure the basic principle that government programs are created and funded to produce results. To be useful guides to managers, and to be truly useful to society, management systems accordingly must look beyond inputs and processes to focus primarily on outputs.

EFFICIENCY AND EFFECTIVENESS

Effectiveness and Efficiency Defined

Any manager wishes to make his or her organization both more effective and more efficient. These terms overlap, but they nonetheless can be distinguished. *Effectiveness* involves producing the desired outcomes (i.e., longer-range outputs). Thus a fire department that puts out a fire is considered effective. *Efficiency* is a measure of how well resources were used in producing the outputs. Thus if the fire department used five trucks and one hundred fire fighters to put out the fire, and only one truck and ten people were necessary, the fire department was effective but not efficient.

Thus effectiveness emphasizes the final outcome of an effort, whereas efficiency emphasizes the process leading to that outcome, asking whether it was carried out as well as it could be. For example, a health clinic with the goal of eliminating measles in the county is effective if measles are, in fact, eliminated. However, if it used three times more staff people than really needed to eliminate measles, it has not been efficient. A second example: If a group is using a hand-to-hand bucket brigade to put out a large fire and everyone is aligned just right for handing the buckets down the line with no wasted movement, the bucket brigade is clearly operating efficiently. But if the fire is spreading rapidly despite these efforts, the group is not effective.[14]

Management systems help managers make their organizations both more efficient and more effective. As we have noted a number of times, efficiency and effectiveness overlap, as does policy making and managerial decision making, and thus we can speak only of general tendencies. Nonetheless management systems are often used by the middle and upper levels of the organization to increase efficiency; in other words, they are often used after the broad policy goals have been set in order to decide how best to achieve those goals without wasting resources. Surprisingly, this particular use of systems is sometimes controversial.

The Argument That Efficiency Is Unimportant

Everyone would agree that effectiveness is more important than efficiency, but this book assumes that they are not in conflict and that efficiency is very important, too. Some critics would disagree, maintaining that efficiency is just not very important. They cite two primary arguments. First, they assert that even the largest imaginable savings will probably amount to only a small percentage of the total budget. Second, they draw a distinction between efficiency's focus on the *process* and effectiveness's focus on the *substance* of government programs. Most of the real waste in government, says this argument, is not inefficiency in the traditional "process" sense of lazy bureaucrats or $100 bolts and $700 door handles from a defense contractor or too much red tape. These process problems are what the person on the street thinks of, and what muckrakers like Jack Anderson make a career exposing, but they are too insignificant to matter.

These critics say that the important waste in government spending lies in the substance of the programs—their effectiveness. This waste would remain no matter how well the organizations were administered. For example, agricultural subsidy programs for years paid millions of dollars to already-rich farmers while crop surpluses continued to increase. No matter how efficiently the checks were sent to these farmers, the government in this view is still wasting the money it spends on the entire program. Similarly, the government annually spends billions of dollars on programs of dubious economic merit, including lumbering $400 million bombers, aid to "impacted" areas, and maritime subsidies. Compared to such waste, the argument goes, any savings resulting from "process" improvements (increased efficiency) in government programs pall into insignificance.

In Defense of Efficiency as an Important Goal

The basic points of the preceding argument are correct, but they do not add up to a compelling case. There are two strong counterarguments for the importance of efficiency. One is simply that the amounts of money to be saved are indeed important. Sophisticated political observers, used to dealing with programs costing billions of dollars, tend to look with some amusement at muckrakers who worry over the waste of a few million. But the fact that billions are being spent is essentially irrelevant. If a million dollars is important to a private firm, it retains its importance even when the federal government is spending it. It is true that saving thousands or millions should not siphon off the time and effort that might be spent on saving billions, but the two are rarely in conflict. A billion dollars saved in the huge federal budget may not seem like much, but as the late Senator Everett Dirksen once said, "A billion dollars here, a billion dollars there—pretty soon it adds up to real money."[15]

However, the main reason for the renewed interest in efficiency is the realization that it has an importance to the general public in signifying competence and legitimacy that outweighs the monetary aspects. The perception of inefficiency is widespread: The percentage of the public that believes that government "wastes a lot" of their money has increased dramatically (to 71 percent) in the past thirty years.[16] A majority of the public believes that of each dollar the government spends on helping the poor, only a dime actually gets to the people who need help.[17] When the public was asked to rank ten groups—such as banking, airlines, and local government—on "quality of services," local government was ranked dead last. It even trailed auto repairs.[18]

Tax reduction movements and balanced budget amendments across the country attest to the same intense public dissatisfaction with current government service delivery. When combined with polls showing almost no public support for curtailing current service levels,[19] it seems clear that the demand is for greater efficiency—the same or better services for less (tax) money. These demands are important to public managers whether or not the public's perceptions are accurate; the perceptions affect them and their jobs no matter how accurate they are.

During the same time that the public's belief in government waste soared, its belief in government competence and honesty plummeted. Although causality cannot be established, it seems likely that a perception of waste is one of the factors that leads to mistrust.[20] Public cynicism about government and its officials is widespread. A survey ranked twenty-five groups on "honesty, and ethical standards." Senators, members of Congress, local political officeholders, and state officeholders all ranked in the bottom half.[21] Questions about "competence" found similar cynicism. Again, it is important to note that these perceptions of incompetence may well be half-truths or less. Many studies that attempt to determine empirically whether the government is delivering services efficiently have found high levels of competence.[22] But the contrary perception remains strong, and management systems can counter it in two ways: by actually increasing efficiency, and by documenting organizational performance so that efficiency can be clearly shown.

This is crucial because efficiency is more important than the dollars saved or used more wisely—although these matter more than some jaded observers might admit. The problem of efficiency goes to the heart of the public's trust in government, its belief that government is controllable and not a careening juggernaut eating their tax dollars and giving little in return.[23]

A government that is widely viewed as both wasteful and heedless of widespread, intense demands for eliminating that waste is likely to lose much of the public's trust and respect, which are necessary for future program initiatives. Thus efficiency is not a conservative issue; the need for maintaining public confidence in the government's competence makes efficiency an important concern to those who view government as a positive tool for social action.

Budget Caps: An Alternative Path to Efficiency?

Developing, installing, and maintaining management systems require a great deal of continuing time and effort. Before starting on such an arduous path, it is important to consider whether there might be an easier way of achieving efficiency: budget caps. A large number of groups, including some who call for balanced budget amendments at the state and federal levels, have advocated budget caps as a shortcut to increasing efficiency. A budget cap would set organizational budget ceilings lower than current expenditure levels and put extremely strict restrictions on the rate of budget growth.

The idea behind such caps is that they alleviate the need for elaborate management systems. Top managers no longer need to set goals and monitor the agencies under them because the subunits, faced with the inevitability of having less money, will automatically become more efficient to get the most out of what they do have. In other words, "a hungry organization is an efficient organization."

Unfortunately, although such an alternative, with its "natural, internal incentives for efficiency," sounds alluring, it has been tried and it has failed. The hidden assumption is that the subagency's goals are the same as the top manager's and the public's, and thus the agency will find ways, with its lesser funds, to continue the desired service level. In fact, the budget cap is an abdication of responsibility. The experience of the Defense Department under President Eisenhower, when funds were allocated under a budget cap, is instructive. The services looked after their internal goals—prestige through shiny equipment—rather than the goals of the Defense Department. They cut less noticeable but more important outputs to finance their prestige outputs. The result was an emphasis on bombers when missiles were needed, an emphasis on new tanks when ammunition was needed, planes ill-suited for interservice missions and so on.[24] This result is typical. Instead of maintaining existing effectiveness while improving efficiency, budget caps have caused a loss of both as organizational subunits have gone off on their own. Thus public managers seeking greater efficiency will find that there is no substitute for the day-to-day struggle to set goals and monitor performance through management systems.

IMPROVING PUBLIC MANAGEMENT: MAJOR STAGES

Modern public management systems are only the latest manifestation of a long-standing quest to improve government service delivery. Changes in public administration during the past decades have been driven by changes in ideology. Based on the categories of a number of analysts, particularly Allen Schick, we can very roughly divide the past century of public management improvement into four broad stages, each marked by a change in public ideology.[25]

Stage 1: Economy (1880–1932)

This period was marked by various state and federal economy drives as well as the municipal reform movement in the cities, which proclaimed a determination to drive out waste by "professionalizing" (and "depolitizing") urban government. Throughout this stage, which could be said to include almost all of the preceding years as well, the U.S. ideology extolled limited government, and government's activities were defined by what it "had" to do. Reformers then attempted to perform these minimal necessary services for the least possible cost. Most of the techniques of this period were designed to eliminate waste and cut the costs of a given amount of government output. Innovations in administrative techniques during this phase include various cost-cutting consolidations and improvements in cost-monitoring and accounting procedures.[26]

Stage 2: Improved Efficiency Through Management (1933–1960)

The public's demand shifted from economy to efficiency by the early 1930s, and management techniques responded accordingly. The shift from economy to efficiency as the prime goal of management was accompanied by a similar shift in the accepted conception of the role of government. Influenced in part by the popularity of the New Deal, the post-1933 electorate no longer viewed the widening of government program scope and impact as being bad per se. No longer was the goal to perform the necessary minimum of activities for the least amount of money; the new goal was to do the most possible with a given amount of money. Thus under this broader concept of government's role, money, not the task, became the constraint. Tools of this period included efficiency drives and performance (i.e., activity-oriented) budgets.

Stage 3: Effectiveness Through Improved Policy Making and Planning (1961–1971)

This stage was marked by two major shifts. First, although the previous stages had emphasized improving government programs through improving management, this stage subordinated management. The key to improving government, said the proponents of the major changes of this period, was better planning and policy making. Second, the emphasis shifted from efficiency to effectiveness. Any consensus about the "proper" limits of government had disintegrated, and many citizens and public managers alike believed that government's role should be defined only on the basis of what would provide the most important impacts. Thus government no longer had the relatively simple task of carrying out well-defined activities as efficiently as possible. Instead, it now needed tools for discovering which activities it should undertake.

The changing public administration tools of this period reflected the new emphasis on planning over management, policy making over implementation, and effectiveness over efficiency. These tools included systems analysis and microeconomic analysis, often embodied in budgeting systems such as program budgeting (PPB). These tools were initially sold as a way of dramatically improving all forms of government decision making, leading to the triumph of "rationality" over "politics" in government. Of course the tools did not produce such changes. When they had only a modest impact, the resulting disappointment was heightened by the unreasonable initial expectations.

Stage 4: Effectiveness and Efficiency Through Improved Management (1971–present)

Not only is it difficult to perceive the outlines of a stage in which we are all participants, but also the current stage of public administration development seems a synthesis, thus blurring analytic lines further. The runaway prosperity of the 1960s was not repeated in the 1970s and 1980s; the economy grew at a much slower rate. Moreover, the ambitious domestic programs of the 1960s were widely seen as having fallen short.[27] Analysts seeking to learn why programs that seemed sound in principle faltered in practice fastened on implementation problems as the answer. The public and public managers responded with a new ideology that looked to improved program implementation (and thus management) for answers. Combined with a more conservative political mood and tight budgets, the government task once again was focused more on making old programs more efficient and effective than on the creative design of wide-ranging new programs. Analysts are too sophisticated to emphasize efficiency without effectiveness, but attention has shifted to improved management as a way of gaining both. The tools of this period reflect this emphasis, with a renewed interest in management systems on all types.

Overview

Obviously, the four stages are an analytic convenience. They overlap and they differ in time and duration from one level of government to another, but they do capture the broad shifts of public and managerial concern during the past century. Because conditions that created the fourth stage (tight budgets, leading to a more incremental approach to new program development) seem likely to continue for a long period, the emphasis on management systems seems likely to continue as well.

SUMMARY

A management system is a procedure for tracking the performance of an organization, usually on a month-to-month or quarter-to-quarter basis. It monitors performance by comparing actual organizational output to preset goals or objectives. As indicated by their name, management systems facilitate *management:* the coordination of people and resources in order to achieve policy objectives. Management turns broad, strategic (policy) decisions into operational realities. This process is facilitated by management systems; most large, well-run organizations have a number of management systems operating simultaneously.

Management systems are tools to improve the efficiency and effectiveness of an organization. Efficiency is a measure of the inputs used to produce outputs; effectiveness is a measure of whether the organization's outputs actually produce the desired effect. Management systems improve efficiency and effectiveness by providing information to aid in managerial decision making and by encouraging the constructive behavior of agency workers.

Most public management systems were originally developed in the private sector, but they have been substantially modified for use in government organizations. In almost all fundamental ways, government agencies are radically different from business organizations. The most important difference between the two is that government organizations lack the easily accessible, highly informative feedback provided by profit measures. In fact, perhaps the central quest of all public sector management systems is to derive reliable and useful surrogates for the missing profit measure. But there are other substantial differences between business and governmental organizations in terms of multiplicity of goals, power fragmentation, publicity, incentives, and roles. The task of managers (and management systems) is therefore far different in the public sector than in business.

Management systems often place a strong emphasis on efficiency. Government efficiency is important for the money saved, but it is more important because it correlates with the public's trust in the honesty, competency, and responsiveness of government. Such trust is the basis for citizens' support for their government and for needed new programs.

Efforts to improve the efficiency and effectiveness of government have a long history. In the 1960s and 1970s, many governments implemented extremely ambitious, policy-oriented approaches such as program budgeting and zero-base budgeting. Results often did not match expectations. Management systems are less policy oriented and less wide-ranging than these earlier approaches; they are also well suited to the current widespread interest in improving program delivery.

REVIEW QUESTIONS*

1. How does management relate to operations? How does it relate to strategic planning? Provide examples of each function for a public university and for a state department of human resources.
2. How do efficiency and effectiveness differ in evaluating
   a. an environmental protection agency?
   b. a hospital?
   c. a job-placement bureau?
3. Name several inputs, several processes (activities), and several outputs for
   a. a sanitation department.
   b. a recreation department.
   c. the Defense Department.
4. What is the effect of the absence of a profit measure on public management systems?
5. Are public organizations that sell their services, such as public hospitals, more like a public organization or a private organization in terms of the differences discussed in this chapter? Why?
6. To what extent does a public organization's feedback system approximate the feedback that the profit measure provides to a private organization? What are the most important differences?
7. Many authorities believe that a middle manager's job is more complicated than that of policy makers at the top of an organization or those actually carrying out the orders. Give an example of the duties of each level for a public organization in the following fields:
   a. education.
   b. transportation.
8. What arguments are made by those who believe that budget caps will lead to increased government efficiency? What are the counterarguments?

* The review questions in this and succeeding chapters are a means of self-testing comprehension. In conjunction with the chapter outline, they can also be used as a review guide. They are accordingly very straightforward. More conceptual, discussion-oriented applications of the reading are tapped through the short cases at the end of each chapter.

9. If a management system for a public health agency measured the number of inspections of restaurants, in what ways might it affect the agency workers' behavior? Affect managerial decision making?

10. What caused the most recent shifts in the ideology behind the changing tools of public administration? What might cause a new shift?

SUGGESTED FURTHER READING

ROBERT N. ANTHONY. *Planning and Control Systems*. Boston: Harvard Graduate School of Business Administration, 1965. The classic discussion of how management control systems should be defined and how they differ from operational control systems and strategic planning.

CHARLES T. GOODSELL. *The Case for Bureaucracy*, 2nd ed. Chatham, NJ: Chatham House Publishers, 1985. A spirited defense of the importance, efficiency, and effectiveness of public organizations and public managers.

JAMES L. PERRY and KENNETH L. KRAEMER, eds. *Public Management: Public and Private Perspectives*. Palo Alto, CA: Mayfield Publishing, 1983. A collection of essays, many of them written by executives who have served in both the public and private sectors, about the differences between government and business management.

ENDNOTES

1. As has been noted, the business world calls these same systems *management control systems*, but we will not use the term because it has misleading connotations. It suggests a primarily financial focus (because output can be measured monetarily in the private sector), and *control* suggests coerciveness and reactiveness. Unfortunately, the alternative term that we will use, *management systems*, also has drawbacks. It has widely varying definitions within both academia and government practice. In particular, it is sometimes used to include operating systems such as inventory and other systems such as personnel and budgeting. We will adopt a much narrower definition: The term applies only to performance measurement and monitoring systems.

2. The terms *management control, strategic planning,* and *operational control* are taken from Robert N. Anthony, *Planning and Control Systems* (Boston: Harvard Graduate School of Business, 1965). Although my discussion relies heavily on Anthony, I have purposely blurred some of his distinctions in order to avoid the term *management control.*

3. Since managers are of course managing *operations*, a summary of operational information is tracked through management systems. But smaller details about operations, although important, are not of interest to middle-level managers. The more specific operational details are usually tracked through their own system, usually called *operations control systems*. Such systems would include inventory reorder systems, bus scheduling systems, and schedules for paper flow.

Just as management and operations are distinctions that blend along the edges, so do management systems and operational systems. But as a general principle, operational control systems deal with more detailed, individualized, daily matters that are of interest to people directly involved in operations and their immediate, first-line supervisors. For example, they need to know how many days' supply of each type of inventory remains or (in a public transit company) whether a particular bus was on schedule this morning. Such information is too unaggregated to help middle-level and upper managers; they usually need to know only what percentage of all buses were on schedule this week or month. Operations control systems are beyond the scope of this book, but for a very good overview, see Stephen R. Rosenthal, *Managing Government Operations* (Glenview, IL: Scott, Foresman, 1982).

4. Woodrow Wilson, "The Study of Administration," *Political Science Quarterly*, 2 (June 1887). Wilson was too astute a political observer to believe fully his own distinctions, and there are even qualifications within the essay. But they influenced several generations of public administration analysts who did seem to take them literally.

5. An interesting attempt to deal with the elusive dividing lines between politics and administration is James H. Svara, "Dichotomy and Duality: Reconceptualizing the Relationship Between Policy and Administration in Council-Manager Cities," *Public Administration Review*, 45, no. 1 (January/February 1985), 221–32.

6. Analyses of feedback systems have a long academic history; an appendix in Anthony, *Planning and Control Systems*, catalogs and excerpts some of these. An excellent overview is contained in Edward Lawler and John Grant Rhode, *Information and Control in Organizations* (Pacific Palisades, CA: Goodyear Publishing Co., 1976).

Lawler notes that the thermostat analogy is discussed at some length in W. W. McKelvey, *Toward an Holistic Morphology of Organizations* (Santa Monica, CA: Rand Corporation, 1970); and the three steps are contained in Harold Koontz, "A Preliminary Statement of Principles of Planning and Control," *Journal of the Academy of Management*, 1 (April 1958), 48.

7. Of course, some "public" and "private sector" organizations overlap in some characteristics. A government organization that sells its output, for example, is both "public" and "market oriented," and accordingly falls between the classic distinctions discussed here.

The discussion of public vs. private differences may rank with the discussion of policy vs. administration as the two most discussed issues in the long history of academic public administration.

A good analysis and summary of public vs. private organizations is Graham T. Allison's "Public and Private Management: Are They Fundamentally Alike in All Unimportant Aspects?" in Frederick S. Lane, ed., *Current Issues in Public Administration* (New York: St. Martin's Press, 1982). For an interesting (but, to me, unconvincing) counterargument that these differences are not major, see Martha Wagner Weinberg, "Public Management and Private Management: A Diminishing Gap?" *Journal of Policy Analysis and Management*, 3, no. 1 (1983), 107–25.

There is a long tradition of lists of differences; they are summarized in Hal G. Rainey, Robert W. Backoff, and Charles H. Levine, "Comparing Public and Private Organizations," *Public Administration Review*, 36, no. 2 (March/April 1976), 233ff. See also Hal G. Rainey, "Public Agencies and Private Firms" in *Administration and Society*, 15, no. 2 (1983), 207–42.

Much of the empirical research on public/private differences is summarized in chapter 2 of Barry Bozeman, *All Organizations Are Public* (San Francisco: Jossey-Bass, 1987). Bozeman's own opinion, which emphasizes the increasing convergence of the two sectors, elicited a scholarly exchange: Barry Bozeman, "Exploring the Limits of Public and Private Sectors: Sector Boundaries as a Maginot Line," and Ronald C. Moe, "Law vs. Performance as Objective Standard," *Public Administration Review*, 48, no. 2 (March/April 1988), 672–74.

8. The newspapers provide almost weekly illustrations of times when the legislature and executive clearly direct a public organization to maximize some value other than economic efficiency and effectiveness. For example, Pennsylvania pays $492,000 in annual subsidies to a railroad used by 250 commuters per day. At this rate, the state could afford to buy each rider a new car every three years. George W. Downs and Patrick D. Larkey, *The Search for Government Efficiency* (Philadelphia: Temple University Press, 1986), p. 1.

Congress requires the Defense Department to heat American bases in West Germany with American coal, which must be shipped 3,000 miles (at the cost of millions) to a country rich in much cheaper natural gas. *New York Times News Service,* "Disputes Arise Over Shipping Coal to U.S. Bases in Germany," June 8, 1986.

In both cases, the government is choosing to maximize distribution or other political values over efficiency; this choice is certainly legitimate in a democracy (although these particular cases may be questionable). Management systems can aid in suboptimizing—doing these tasks as efficiently as possible, even if the tasks themselves are not societally efficient.

9. The difficulty of defining "waste" in light of vague or conflicting legislative directives and the like is discussed in William Hamm, "What Do We Mean by Waste in Government," in Jerome B. McKinney and Michael Johnston, eds., *Fraud, Waste and Abuse in Government* (Philadelphia: ISHI Publications, 1986), pp. 8–14.

10. Ash is quoted in Gordon Chase, "Managing, Compared," *New York Times,* March 14, 1978, p. 35.

11. The difficulty of personnel management in government as opposed to private sector organizations is lamented by a manager who has served in both: W. Michael Blumenthal, "Candid Reflections of a Businessman in Washington," *Fortune,* January 1979, p. 38.

12. The Grace Commission is more formally known as the President's Private Sector Survey on Cost Control, and its report is available from the U.S. Government Printing Office (Washington, DC, 1983). The Grace Commission has precipitated a huge number of works in reaction to its recommendations. Among the most useful are these:

U.S. Congress, Congressional Budget Office and General Accounting Office, *Analysis of the Grace Commission's Major Proposals for Cost Control* (Washington, DC: U.S. Government Printing Office, 1984).

Steven Kelman, "The Grace Commission: How Much Waste in Government?" *Public Interest,* no. 78 (Winter 1985).

Charles T. Goodsell, "The Grace Commission: Seeking Efficiency for the Whole People?" *Public Administration Review,* 44, no. 3 (May/June 1984).

Although all these works are critical of the Grace Commission, the most stinging blast may have come from Downs and Larkey, *Search for Government Efficiency,* p. 187: ". . . The Grace Commission Report sets a new standard for insensitivity to the politics and complexities of government organization."

13. Schematic feedback systems are analyzed at much greater length in Goran Arvidsson, "Performance Evaluation," in F. X. Kaufmann et al., eds., *Guidance, Control and Evaluation in the Public Sector* (New York: Walter de Gruyter, 1985), pp. 625–44. See also Dieter Grunow, "Internal Control In Public Administration," pp. 645–62 in the same volume.

14. This example is used in George Berkley, *The Craft of Public Administration* (Boston: Allyn & Bacon, 1981).

15. Dirksen is quoted in Donald Haider, "Presidential Management Initiatives," *Public Administration Review,* 39, no. 3 (May/June 1979), 259. The following section is a revision of sections of my article "Holding Agencies Accountable for Efficiency" in *Administration and Society* 15, no. 1 (1983), pp. 76-86. Reprinted by permission of Sage Publications, Inc.

16. The 71 percent figure comes from a November 1988 poll. (*Public Opinion,* March/April 1989, p. 22). Only 3 percent chose the response that the government does not waste much money. In 1958, only 45 percent responded that the government wasted "a lot" of money, and in 1964, only 48 percent said so (*Public Opinion,* March/April 1987, p. 27).

17. Richard J. Cattani, "Despite Reagan Revolution, Public Looks to Washington," *Christian Science Monitor,* December 11, 1981, p. 4.

18. *Gallup Report,* July 1986, p. 2.

19. This tension between a desire for lower taxes but the same (or increased) government service is a consistent finding of polls of the 1970s and 1980s. For example, see the *Los Angeles Times*'s national poll reported under the headline "High Demand for Government Services," *Public Opinion,* February/March 1985, p. 19. See also the poll results reported in *National Journal,* April 29, 1989, p. 1076; and *Public Opinion,* March/April 1989, p. 25.

20. A 1973 study provides partial support for the commonsense belief that the attitudes toward government competence will affect support for the general system. In the study the two attitudes were positively correlated, although causality is of course difficult to establish. Daniel Katz et al., *Bureaucratic Encounters* (Ann Arbor, MI: Survey Research Center, 1973), pp. 177–78.

21. The honesty rankings are reported in *Gallup Report,* August 1985, p. 3. State political officeholders, who ranked twenty-first, were only three places above car salesmen, the lowest group. The decline in the belief in the honesty and competence of U.S. institutions is reported and analyzed at great length in Seymour Martin Lipset and William Schneider, *The Confidence Gap: Business, Labor and Government in the Public Mind,* 2nd ed. (New York: Free Press, 1987). The authors conclude that although confidence in government institutions increased in the 1980s, confidence ratings remain far below the levels of the 1960s.

22. Empirical evidence for the efficiency of government vs. the efficiency of business is reviewed in Downs and Larkey, *Search for Government*

Efficiency, chapters 1 and 2. See also Charles T. Goodsell, *The Case for Bureaucracy*, 2nd ed. (Chatham, NJ: Chatham House Publishers, 1985). Both studies find what most people in the field of public administration have recognized—that government agencies are usually much more efficient and effective than the general public believes.

23. In other words, efficiency can be used by the public as a marker or surrogate indicator of effectiveness. If the government seems efficient—which for many programs is relatively easy to determine—it is given the benefit of the doubt that it is also effective. Thus a rapidly processed Medicare claim is a sign that the Medicare program is working satisfactorily. This is similar to a congressional committee that—as discussed by Aaron Wildavsky—uses small items and organizational efficiency to gauge whether the government agencies they oversee are using effectively the money they have been budgeted.

24. Alan C. Enthoven and K. W. Smith, *How Much Is Enough* (New York: Harper & Row, 1971). Similar findings abound. For example, a 1982 Rand study of the tax-limiting state laws (such as California's Proposition 13) found that they did not necessarily cut the fat; rather, the quantity and quality of key services such as police and fire deteriorated in most cities. Mark David Menchik et al., *Fiscal Restraint in Local Government* (Santa Monica, CA: Rand Corporation, 1982).

25. Different authors have attached different labels to the historical changes in government management. Mosher looked at it in terms of personnel and singled out the cult of efficiency (1906–1937), of management (1937–1955), and of professionalism (1955 on): Frederick C. Mosher, *Democracy and the Public Service*, 2nd ed. (New York: Oxford University Press, 1982), chapters 3 and 4.

Kaufman looked at the changes in terms of public ideologies and distinguished representativeness (until 1888), neutral competence (1888–1937), and executive leadership (1937 on): Herbert Kaufman, "Emerging Conflicts in the Doctrine of Public Administration," in Alan Altshuler, ed., *The Politics of Federal Bureaucracy* (New York: Dodd, Mead, 1968).

This chapter's categories (which are based on the political and career administrators' changing ideological and practical emphases on implementation) are most clearly related to those of Schick (which are based on these same actors' changing ideological and practical emphases on budgeting): Allen Schick, "The Road to PPB," in Fremont J. Lyden and Ernest C. Miller, *Public Budgeting*, 4th ed. (Englewood Cliffs, NJ: Prentice-Hall, 1982). Schick looks at the changes in terms of the budget and isolates control (1920–1935), management (1935–1960), and planning (1960 on). Like Schick's categories, those given in this chapter are decidedly not exclusive; some participants in the current process (such as some conservative members of Congress) undoubtably still view it in terms of economy; the categories are meant to suggest systemic emphasis.

26. Most studies of changes in government management approaches emphasize the federal government. This is somewhat defensible on the grounds that more managerial changes start with the federal government and move to state and local governments than vice versa. The following papers and books all provide a good account of the different facets of past changes in the methods of federal program execution: U.S. General Accounting Office, *Selected Government-wide Management Improvement Efforts—1970 to 1980* (Washington, DC: GAO, 1983); Marver H. Bernstein, "The Presidency and Management Improvement," in Norman C. Thomas, ed., *The Institutionalized Presidency* (Dobbs Ferry, NY: Oceana Publications, 1972), pp. 79–92; David S. Brown, ed., *Federal Contributions to Management* (New York: Praeger Publishers, 1971); James G. Benze, Jr., *Presidential Power and Management Techniques* (New York: Greenwood Press, 1987), especially chapters 1–3.

27. Whether the Great Society programs did in fact fall far short is not important to the point here. The public perception of shortfalls was sufficient to deprive these programs of much of their public legitimacy. For a defense of the at least partial success of many of these programs (a point of view closer to my own), see John E. Schwarz, *America's Hidden Success: A Reassessment of Public Policy from Kennedy to Reagan*, rev. ed. (New York: W. W. Norton and Co., 1988). For an extreme indictment of such programs, see Charles A. Murray, *Losing Ground: American Social Policy, 1950–80* (New York: Basic Books, 1984).

chapter two

Tracking Inputs:
Financial Management Systems

INTRODUCTION

The most important function of a management system is to track outputs or results. However, it is necessary to track inputs as well in order to determine how much the outputs cost. All inputs—whether people or desks or computers—can be expressed in monetary terms. The costs of desks and computers can be measured by their price, the cost of people by their salaries. Thus any system that is designed to track inputs will use money as its main measure. In other words, it will be a financial management system.

Financial management systems are more important in the private sector than in government. In business, outputs as well as inputs can be expressed as money. Such measures as revenue and profit are accurate reflections of business output. In business, accordingly, the financial management system is the most important ongoing system, and accountants are the most important system designers and operators.

In the public sector, outputs usually cannot be expressed in monetary terms. Therefore financial systems do not provide the most important data for government decision making, and accountants and accounting are correspondingly less important as well. Except for the very few public organizations that sell their output, financial management systems are used only to measure agency inputs, and other, non-money-based systems are used to track outputs.

Financial management systems are useful at each of the three levels of organizational decision making. At the top, or strategic planning level, such systems can be used to generate reports for the agency as a whole and for outside monitoring bodies such as legislative committees. These records of overall financial performance include such reports as balance sheets and statements of changes in fund balances, which are useful in providing strategic decision makers with an overall year-end picture. Similarly, financial systems can also generate information that is useful for the lowest, or operations, level of an organization. For example, they can help with internal control mechanisms to determine whether a bill has been paid on time or to detect embezzlement. In keeping with the focus of this book, however, we will not be concerned with either of these two uses of financial systems. Instead we will focus on how financial management systems can be used for the month-to-month decision making necessary at the middle, or management, level. The major techniques used for this purpose are primarily derived from private sector cost accounting.

Cost accounting is a method for determining (1) the total costs, direct and indirect, of a program, project, or activity and (2) the cost-per-unit output of the goods or services provided.[1] Such information helps managers determine the efficiency of their operations, and it guides their planning and budgeting. (When it is used as the basis of a financial management system, cost accounting is also often called managerial accounting.)

The Components of a Financial Report

A system for measuring costs is in many ways different from a system for measuring outputs. Yet, like all feedback systems, they share the same three steps: setting performance targets, tracking actual performance, and reacting to any differences between the two.

A financial report clearly shows the first two steps. First, standards are set (the expected costs, sometimes called the budgeted costs), and second, actual performance is measured (the actual costs). Thus the third step—taking action if there is a gap between the standard and the actual performance—is easier for the manager because the financial management system clearly shows any such gaps, indicating their origin and magnitude. (Table 2-1 is an example of a small part of a financial report for a program at the end of the second quarter.)

The difference between what is expected (or projected) to happen and what actually happens in any given period is called a variance. In

TABLE 2–1 Financial Report: Agency X (End of Second Quarter)

(All figures in thousands)

Cost Center	First Quarter			Second Quarter			Year-to-Date		
	budgeted	actual	variance	budgeted	actual	variance	budgeted	actual	variance
A	28	26.5	1.5	31	29	2	59	55.5	3.5
B	4	5	(1)	3	5	(2)	7	10	(3)
C	114	114	—	109	110	(1)	223	224	(1)
D	36	35.5	.5	38	46	(8)	74	81.5	(7.5)
E	19.5	17	2.5	21	20	1	40.5	37	4.5
TOTAL	201.5	198	3.5	202	210	(8)	403.5	408	(4.5)

The table indicates that Agency X kept costs well under control in the first quarter, and is running ahead of budget for the year. It further indicates that the worst cost overruns were incurred by cost center D, although all costs ran high in the second quarter. Remedial action (e.g., budget reductions) may well be necessary in the final two quarters to remain within the yearly budget.

other words, a variance is simply the difference between the target and the actual results. Variances act as red flags for the manager, indicating that things are not going as expected. Managers should always investigate the causes of any substantial variances, whether in a favorable direction (lower costs or greater output) or negative direction. If the variance is negative, the manager investigates the cause in hopes of avoiding it in the future. If the variance is positive, the manager needs to know how to repeat it in the future.

For most government agencies that are medium sized or smaller, summary financial data—such as Table 2–1—are easily kept and displayed on a spreadsheet program. Spreadsheets are easy to use and will automatically calculate variance and year-to-date figures.

All the managerially useful financial information that we have been discussing is usually based on data provided by the organizational accounting system. We will begin by examining the components of the accounting system that are most important for managerial information; afterward we will examine a few of the most important ways that financial information can help the manager both in making decisions and in affecting behavior.

THE FINANCIAL MANAGEMENT SYSTEM STRUCTURE

Processing the Figures: The Accounting Structure

Accounts Defined. Information must constantly be gathered for each category of a financial management system; this is done by means of accounts. Public organizations generally keep four types of accounts: (1) assets, (2) liabilities, (3) revenues, and (4) expenditures or expenses. But the most important for middle managers are the expenditure/expense accounts, and our discussion will focus exclusively on this one type.

An *account* is the smallest unit of an organization or program for which information is kept.[2] Thus if the smallest units into which an organization breaks its information are categories for its five subagencies, the organization has five accounts. If it breaks information into categories for all forty of its programs, it has forty accounts.

For each account (category) the system tracks all the money flows associated with that category. Twenty years ago this task was done by hand and was very laborious. Now almost all public agencies use computers to keep track of their money. Each time an expense is incurred, it is entered into the computer with a code number that assigns it to a particular category, or account. At the end of the reporting period, the computer automatically totals all of the expenses that have been entered for that account, and the manager can see how the actual results compare with what was projected.

Combining two or more accounts is a simple matter of addition.

Thus if a system has accounts for each program, and one agency administers three programs, we can easily determine the agency's total expenses by adding the three program accounts together. The computer software will do this task with just a simple instruction.

How Many Accounts?   How many accounts (i.e., separate money categories) should a financial management system track? Should there be a large number of small accounts or only a few, much larger accounts? The advantage of having only a few large accounts is that it minimizes the amount of bookwork for the organization. But there are substantial disadvantages.

For example, two counties are exactly alike in every way. The social services department in County X keeps only five accounts, one for each of its five programs. The social services department of County Y keeps forty accounts. It divides each of its five programs by the two branch offices administering them and by the four population groups served. When County Y wants to know the total amount spent in each of the program categories used by County X, all it has to do is add its smaller accounts together. But it also has a great deal of information that County X does not, such as how much was spent by each branch office or how much was spent on each population group.[3]

As illustrated by this example, information that is part of a larger account is irretrievable. It is very easy to add together several smaller accounts to get the perspective of a larger category; it is impossible to divide an account to get more detailed information because an account is the smallest unit for which information is gathered. In designing a financial management system, the designers must keep the number of accounts reasonable so that record keeping does not become burdensome. But today, with the excellent accounting software available, this "reasonable" number of accounts can still be much larger than in the past. Because each account can bring valuable new information, the system designers should decide close calls in favor of more accounts rather than fewer.

Combining Accounts: Cost Centers and Funds

Cost Centers.   Each account is a separate category of information, but when an executive asks, "What did X cost?" he or she is rarely interested in accounts per se. X needs to be something of importance to the organization, such as an activity (e.g., street paving) or a subunit (e.g., the engineering unit). Such distinguishable activities or organizational units are called *cost centers.*

A cost center is an organizational activity or unit for which there is a separate account or group of accounts. When we wish to know the costs of a particular cost center, we add together related accounts; we can then say that "installation and maintenance of street lights cost $90,000 this year" or "the engineering unit cost $470,000." Because a cost center is an activity or unit, such items as "salaries" or "equipment" could not be cost centers. They could, however, easily be items *within* a cost center.

Cost centers can be either direct service centers, which actually deliver the organization's output, or support centers, which provide supporting services to the direct service centers. A public university might have cost centers that are direct service centers, such as the departments (English, physics, etc.) that actually perform the university's main missions of teaching and research. The university would also have cost centers that are support centers, such as the accounting department. Similarly, a city sanitation department would have cost centers that are direct service centers, such as trash pickup, and cost centers that are support centers, such as the garage that maintains the trucks.

Additional examples of cost centers that are support centers for most agencies are (1) a copy center, (2) a legal staff, and (3) a motor pool. These are all self-contained units or processes. Of course, all organizations would have at least one cost center that is a direct service center. Such direct service centers reflect the "core" of the organization, such as teaching for schools and health care in a clinic. Often this core can be broken down further, and a number of the processes carried out by the organization can be separated out as cost centers. Thus a clinic could have separate direct service cost centers for its maternity program, its emergency room, and its routine care.

As suggested by their definition, cost centers do not always correspond to the divisions on an organizational chart. Individual processes or activities may be cost centers, even if they are not separate organizational subdivisions. In setting up cost centers, the only requirements are that the arrangement generates information that is useful for managerial decision making and that the cost centers be mutually exclusive (i.e., a single cost cannot be assigned to two different cost centers—that would be double counting). Of course, some employees[4] may well spend part of the day working on an activity covered by one cost center, then move on to an activity covered by another cost center. To which cost center should their salary be charged? Such employees must keep an activity log book, showing how much time was spent on each activity. This enables the accountants to assign a fair proportion of their salary to each cost center.[5]

In large organizations, cost centers contain other cost centers. Thus for the mayor of a city, one cost center is the public safety department. But the public safety department itself contains three major cost centers: the police department, the fire department, and the emergency rescue service. Finally, each of these will itself be divided into cost centers. The police department, for example, will be keeping separate figures for such units or activities as an investigative unit, a patrol unit, and traffic enforcement.

Once managers know how much of their organization's resources is consumed by each cost center, they can combine this input information with the output information that we will discuss in later chapters.[6] Using this information—about how much input each center consumed and how much output it produced—managers can determine which organizational units or processes are efficient and which are not. Only then can they make informed decisions about improving their agency's performance. Many cities, as well as states such as Oregon, Rhode Island, and Texas, have already instituted such systems. Others are moving in this direction.[7]

Let us recap this discussion by using a final example: a local streets department. The department might break itself into five cost centers: (1) engineering studies and planning, (2) street paving, (3) installation and maintenance of traffic lights and signs, (4) street cleaning, and (5) administration. The engineering and planning section and the administration section are support cost centers because they *help* the direct mission of the streets department. The other three centers—paving, traffic light installation, and cleaning—are direct service cost centers because they directly deliver the core services to the clients. By dividing its financial information this way, the streets department is able to determine where its money is going, that is, how much each function costs. For example, the street cleaning cost center may have had $320,000 in expenses last year. Just by itself, this is a useful figure to know.

Moreover, as we will discuss later, cost analysis can make these cost center figures even more useful by combining them with process or output figures to determine efficiency. Thus if 2,000 miles of city streets were cleaned ten times last year, we know that it cost $320,000 divided by 2000 times 10, or $16 per mile in direct costs to clean city streets. We can use such figures for a variety of uses (in decisions on contracting out, budgeting, etc.) that we will discuss later in this chapter. But it is important to note that we would never know this information if we had not divided the streets department's overall budget into cost centers.

Funds.   Virtually all state and local government organizations group their accounts (and in a broader sense, their cost centers) into larger financial classifications called *funds*. (The federal government also uses funds, but they are less important there.[8]) A *fund* is simply a separate category of money with its own self-balancing set of accounts, that is, a separate entity. Funds are perhaps best viewed as legal requirements; they have relatively little managerial use. Funds and cost centers are both groupings of accounts but are not related otherwise. A few cost centers draw from two or more funds; more often, an important fund (such as the general fund) will contain a large number of cost centers. Although the private sector has no equivalent to funds, they are widely used in the public sector. Box 2-1 is a list of funds used at the state and local level, with brief definitions of each.

The *general fund* is usually the most important and largest government fund, and it finances most of the government's day-to-day activities. Local governments also have separate funds for some legally restricted federal or state grants or for earmarked revenue sources; these are called *special revenue funds.* Bond-supported major acquisitions or construction projects are covered in capital projects funds. Most cities should also maintain a separate fund for their enterprises that charge fees, such as golf courses and water departments. All money going to or from these activities would be recorded in a separate enterprise fund.[9]

Box 2–1. Types of Funds

The seven types of funds employed by public organizations fall into three broad categories: *government funds, proprietary funds* (which handle most businesslike activities), and *fiduciary funds* (which hold money in trust for pensions). There are four government funds:

1. *General fund*—to account for all unrestricted resources except those required to be accounted for in another fund.

2. *Special revenue funds*—to account for revenues restricted to specified purposes—except expendable trusts and revenues reserved for major capital projects. (E.g., this fund would be used for highway construction that is financed by a gasoline tax.)

3. *Capital projects funds*—to account for resources segregated for the acquisition of major capital facilities—other than those financed by enterprise funds. (E.g., this fund would segregate bond proceeds and grants that were earmarked for a public arena.)

4. *Debt service funds*—to account for the accumulation of resources for the payment of interest and principal on long-term debt (generally, payments for bonds).

There are two proprietary funds:

5. *Enterprise funds*—to account for operations financed and operated in a manner similar to private business enterprises, usually involving the provision of goods and services financed primarily from user charges (e.g., water and sewer services, public power utilities, golf courses).

6. *Internal service funds*—to account for the financing of goods or services provided by one government agency to another on a cost-reimbursement basis (e.g., motor pools and copy centers).

There is one fiduciary fund:

7. *Trust and agency funds*—to account for assets held by a government unit as trustee or agent for individuals, private organizations, and/or other government units (e.g., pension funds).

(*Source:* Adapted from NCGA Statement 1: *Governmental Accounting and Financial Reporting Principles,* National Council on Governmental Accounting, 1979. Adapted to reflect the 1987 elimination of an eighth type of fund, a special assessment fund.)

Funds are used because governments must keep money that has been legally raised for one purpose separate from money for other purposes. For example, local governments often raise money through bonds for very specific, legally restricted purposes. It is important that this money be kept separate from general funds and spent only for the purposes specified; city governments generally do this by treating such money as a separate capital projects fund—in other words, a separate pot of money. Businesses rarely have such problems of legal accountability, and thus all their money is treated as a single "pot." Businesses accordingly have somewhat more flexibility in using their money and somewhat less onerous reporting requirements than do many state and local governments.[10]

Fund accounting began almost a century ago. In light of today's more sophisticated accounting systems, there is some debate over whether funds are still necessary for keeping track of government monies.[11] Nonetheless funds are well established in government accounting and are not likely to be eliminated. Moreover, they do not really help or hurt the more important areas of managerial information. In the discussion of financial management systems later in this chapter, the use of fund accounting at the state and local level will generally be assumed. However the funds will rarely be explicitly discussed because, although they increase the accounting chores somewhat, they should have no other major effect.

THREE BASES OF ACCOUNTING SYSTEMS

We have discussed accounts, the smallest units of information gathered about the organization's expenses. They are the building blocks; when combined, they provide information about all facets of the organization. But before we can build with them, we must fill them with the appropriate information. This is the role of the accounting system. There are three main bases of accounting systems; they differ primarily in their treatment of time—the point at which they register a transaction.

Cash Accounting

Cash accounting is the simplest way to keep accounts. As its name suggests, it is concerned only with the ebb and flow of cash. Cash accounting can be compared to maintaining a large cigar box on top of the administrator's desk. When a bill is paid, it is deducted from the cash account, and when money comes in, it is added to the account. At any given time the administrator can say how much money is on hand (in other words, in the cigar box) but that is all. The administrator cannot say if more money—or a huge bill—will arrive tomorrow.

For example, a clinic places a $1 million order for syringes in June, and the order is delivered and paid for in December. Cash accounting deducts the $1 million from its cash account in December when the bill is paid. Now the clinic proceeds to use the syringes over the next two years; however, there is no record of when the clinic actually uses them because, again, the total sum was deducted in December.

Because a cash accounting system provides such a meager amount of information, virtually no private company larger than a mom-and-pop store uses it. However, a number of public agencies do: As late as the mid-1980s, the New York State legislature continued to use cash accounting to track hundreds of millions of dollars.[12]

Accrual Accounting

Under an accrual accounting system a resource is not charged to the organization until it is actually consumed. An accrual system pays no attention to when a bill is paid; it may be before the agency uses the item or after. What is important in accrual accounting is that the item is expensed (deducted) when it is used. In the previous example, an accrual accounting system would register the expense for the syringes when it actually used them. If the clinic took syringes worth $120,000 out of inventory and used them in the third quarter, that is when the transaction would be registered, even if the syringes had been ordered and paid for a year earlier.

Accrual accounting focuses on expenses; cash accounting focuses on expenditures. In everyday language these terms are sometimes treated as synonyms, but they are not. An *expense* is a measure of consumption. Thus an agency can be charged with a $100,000 expense if it uses up all of its $100,000 shipment of paper in the third quarter. An *expenditure* is a payment. Thus the paper that the agency uses up in the third quarter may well have been paid for in the second quarter. It was in the second quarter that the agency made an expenditure of $100,000 for the paper; it is in the third quarter that it registered a $100,000 expense.

Sometimes an agency purchases an object that returns benefits over a long period of time. Such objects as large computers, automobiles, or even buildings return many of their benefits long after they have been purchased. Such large tangible objects that return benefits over a number of years are called *fixed assets*. It is obviously misleading to treat these objects as being completely "consumed" during the first quarter or even the first year that they are used. Accrual accounting avoids this through the use of depreciation. *Depreciation* is a means of charging a fixed asset to the agency using the asset, during the time it is being used. That is, depreciation treats assets as being used up or consumed over a period of time. If a car that costs $15,000 with a lifetime of five years (and no salvage value) is depreciated over five years, $3,000 of the cost of the car is treated as an expense each year.

In using depreciation, a manager must decide the number of years over which an asset should be depreciated and the monetary figure that should be used for the asset's value. Generally, the length of time over which an asset should be depreciated is a conservative estimate of the shortest time an asset will be used. The initial cost of the asset is the figure most often used in depreciation, although a number of prominent accountants have called for using replacement costs (which are usually higher) instead. In private businesses, both of these decisions are often made on the basis of Internal Revenue rulings. But when designing internal systems, public managers are able to base decisions on the values that return the best information for decision making.

So far, we have discussed expenses and expenditures but not revenues. Because most government agencies pay for their inputs but do not charge for their outputs (services), they are usually far more interested in tracking expenditures or expenses than they are in tracking revenues. Nonetheless it is worth noting that accrual accounting also treats revenues differently than does cash accounting. Cash accounting registers a revenue only when it is received (again, like an addition to the cigar box). Accrual accounting, on the other hand, registers a revenue when it is earned. Thus if the agency provides a for-fee service to a client, it registers the revenue when the service is completed, even if the bill is not paid until the following month or quarter.

An agency needs a system that will register the amount of resources it is using up during the time it is using them; only accrual accounting does so. In contrast, an accounting system kept on a cash basis can mislead the manager in several ways. For example, a local road maintenance agency could purchase a great deal of gravel in the third quarter, save it in inventory, and then use it the following year. A cash system indicates only the agency's expenditure in the third quarter; it shows nothing during the next fiscal year when the gravel is actually being used as inventories are drawn down. Thus the road paving agency looks less efficient in the third quarter than it actually is because it is charged with more inputs—gravel in this case—than it is actually using. Similarly, the same agency looks more efficient in the next fiscal year than it actually is because it repaves more miles of road without being charged with the inputs it is using from inventory. An accrual system properly registers the gravel as an expense throughout the next fiscal year as it is actually being used up; this prevents distortion of efficiency measures.

A cash basis accounting system can also mislead by registering the entire cost for a fixed asset at the time it is purchased. For example, if the same agency purchased three expensive road graders in 1993 and used them through 1998, the cash system registers a huge expenditure in 1993 (which appears a "wasteful" year) and then nothing for the following years. An accrual system would instead depreciate part of the cost of the graders over each of the next five years. This more accurately represents the agency's actual consumption of resources.

Thus for almost all purposes of managerial decision making, an accrual system is very useful and cash accounting is not. Nonetheless the overall organization does also need the information provided by a cash system because it needs to know when it pays its bills in order to monitor its cash flow. So even organizations that have accrual systems also track the type of information provided by a cash system. The reverse is not true, however; agencies that have cash accounting systems do not keep accrual information. Accrual systems, then, can be viewed as incorporating the information in cash systems but then going well beyond them.

Modified Accrual Accounting

In the public sector, a number of organizations use a form of accounting called *modified accrual*. As the name suggests, modified accrual falls between cash and accrual accounting (which is sometimes termed *full accrual* or *straight accrual* to distinguish it from modified accrual). In general, modified accrual differs from straight accrual because it accrues expenditures rather than expenses.

Modified accrual is more difficult to describe than either cash or accrual accounting because it is a hybrid and so does not have the "pure" rules that characterize the other two forms of accounting. In addition, as will be discussed, it is in the process of changing, of moving somewhat closer to straight accrual. Finally, modified accrual has a fair amount of flexibility. Accountants are allowed to follow several different paths (in the treatment of inventory, for example) and still be within accepted guidelines.[13]

In general, modified accrual differs from accrual in several important ways. First, encumbrances are an integral part of the system (discussed in the next section). Second, modified accrual has no room for depreciation. The absence of depreciation has major effects because fixed assets make up a large part of many organizations' expenses. This means that the total cost of major equipment, for example, is usually registered immediately. This presents a misleading picture of the actual use of resources by an agency. The treatment of depreciation, then, is the way that modified accrual accounting most distorts managerial information.

When treating revenues, however, modified accrual is increasingly similar to accrual in that it generally registers revenues when earned.[14] This treatment of revenue represents a recent change, and it illustrates the fact that modified accrual accounting is currently undergoing a great deal of modification. In the late 1980s the Government Accounting Standards Board (GASB), which sets accounting standards for government, began a decade-long process of reviewing and changing the standards for modified accrual accounting. In general, the adopted and proposed changes move modified accrual somewhat closer, step by step, to straight accrual accounting. The treatment of revenue was the first step; treatment of pension obligations and other thornier issues lie ahead. However, there seems little likelihood that modified accrual accounting will ever incorporate depreciation.[15]

In sum, modified accrual accounting has some of the attributes of both cash accounting and straight accrual. Straight accrual accounting is best for cost analysis, but modified accrual is better than cash accounting. Modified accrual will be particularly useful if its treatment of depreciation (and, sometimes, inventory) is at least roughly recalculated by the manager performing the cost analysis.

Encumbrances

One important piece of information seems to be missed by cash and accrual accounting systems: commitments or obligations created by orders that have not yet been paid for. For example, an agency orders $1 million of heating oil in October; it is delivered and paid for in December, and half of it is consumed in February and half in March. Cash accounting will deduct the $1 million from its cash account in December when the bill is paid. The accrual system will not register any expenses until February, when it will show an expense of $500,000; it will show an additional expense of $500,000 in March, when the last of the heating oil is consumed. Either approach could potentially cause the agency substantial problems. Because its accounting system did not indicate that a $1 million bill was coming, the agency may have spent all of its money on other things and not have enough left to pay the bill when it arrives in December.

All systems need to earmark money that has been committed so that it is not spent in the time between the order and the payment or consumption. Any system can do this easily by moving obligated money into a separate category; this earmarking is termed *encumbering* the money, and the money so marked is termed *encumbered*. Because encumbered money is no longer available, encumbering keeps managers from accidentally spending money that has already been committed. Thus an encumbrance system is a simple control device to prevent an agency from overspending its budget. Encumbrances are generally an integral part of modified accrual systems, but they can be added to cash and straight accrual systems as well. (In the federal government, encumbrances are often called *obligations*, although the principle is the same.) Encumbrances are used in forty-four states and in most localities.[16] (This discussion of the three bases of accounting is summarized in Box 2–2.)

Box 2-2. Three Bases of Accounting

WHEN A PURCHASED GOOD OR SERVICE IS REGISTERED

. Cash accounting—when paid

Modified accrual accounting—encumbered when an obligation is incurred (then, later, the encumbence is removed and an expenditure is registered when payment is due)

Accrual accounting—when consumed

WHEN A REVENUE IS RECORDED

Cash accounting—when received

Modified accrual accounting—when earned (if at all possible; some tax revenues are difficult to estimate)

Accrual accounting—when earned

TREATMENT OF FIXED ASSETS

Cash accounting—the entire sum is deducted when paid

Modified accrual accounting—the entire sum is deducted when the legal obligation is incurred

Accrual accounting—through depreciation, part of the initial cost is deducted each year as the asset is used up

WHERE THE SYSTEMS ARE USED

Cash accounting—by a few very small private businesses; a few local governments

Modified accrual accounting—by most state and local governments, except for their enterprise and internal service funds

Accrual accounting—by most major private businesses; by state and local governments in their funds most like private business (e.g., enterprise funds and internal service funds)

EVALUATION OF SYSTEMS

Cash accounting—not useful for management control purposes

Modified accrual accounting—better than cash accounting, but can provide misleading managerial information because it lacks depreciation

Accrual accounting—allows managers to determine which organizations or projects are earning or consuming resources during each period; key to useful management control information

---

Patterns of Usage

The federal government is slowly moving toward full accrual accounting, but most cities and states keep their general fund on a modified accrual basis.[17] Because the bulk of day-to-day expenditures comes from the general fund, most cities' transactions are therefore recorded on a modified accrual basis.

However, straight accrual accounting is used in some sectors of local government, because cities use an accrual basis for their enterprise funds. This is understandable. Enterprise funds, which cover for-fee items like water and municipal golf courses, are businesslike public activities. They thus use the same accounting system as businesses—accrual. Later in this chapter we will discuss how agencies can use internal service funds to set up cost centers that function somewhat like businesses. These centers would also employ straight accrual accounting (and thus depreciation); this helps to keep the agency's cost information more accurate.

MIDCHAPTER SUMMARY

Before moving on to the uses of the financial information, let us summarize the four major points of the preceding discussion of structure:

1. Financial information is best gathered by a relatively large number of accounts.
2. The information for these accounts is best gathered by accrual rather than cash accounting systems. In accrual systems, an expense is registered when a good or service is used up. This allows managers to track, week by week or month by month, what resources their organization is actually consuming. Many government organizations use a modified accrual accounting system, which differs from a pure accrual system in a number of ways, most notably in its lack of depreciation. Although better than cash accounting, a modified accrual system is not as useful for cost analysis as a straight accrual system because the absence of depreciation distorts cost figures for any agencies with fixed assets.
3. Single accounts, or combinations of accounts, are called *cost centers* if they represent a distinguishable unit or activity within the organization. These cost centers are often the most useful unit of analysis for managerial decision making.
4. In most state and local governments, accounts are also combined into funds, which are simply separate pots of money. They are used to ensure legal accountability for money that has been raised for particular purposes. They have no equivalent in the private sector and generally are not important for middle-level managerial decision making.

DETERMINING COSTS

After the accounting system gathers information about the expenses of an organization and its activities, how can this information be used by managers? The most important way is to assign costs to various organizational processes or units. These costs then guide the manager in judging the efficiency of the units, in avoiding overspending, and in making budget projections. Because these costs provide a clear efficiency measure, they can also be used to spur employees toward greater cost cutting and cost saving.

Thus this information can enable the manager to determine that each driver's license issued costs the motor vehicle department $25, or that the state department of transportation spends $900,000 to repave each mile of a four-lane highway. More sophisticated analysis sometimes allows the manager to say that it costs the motor vehicle department $30 to issue each of the first 10,000 licenses and $21 for each license thereafter, or that in-city roads cost $1.1 million per mile to repave and out-of-town roads cost $800,000 per mile. Such information is obviously very useful in looking at the efficiency of the units involved, in drawing up budget requests, or in evaluating the efficiency of proposed new methods.

In private enterprise, the process of assigning costs to units of service or output, termed *cost accounting,* is based on a very rigorous, highly developed methodology. This precision is more important in business than in government because business uses the cost accounting information to set prices and determine profits, often calculating unit costs down to the fraction of a cent. In the public sector, this general process is sometimes called *cost analysis* rather than cost accounting.[18] The use of the term *cost analysis* denotes a somewhat less rigorous process than most private sector cost accounting. This is in keeping with the different needs of most public managers and the more modest sophistication of most government accounting systems.

All cost analysis begins by breaking costs into types. The two major dichotomies are direct and indirect costs, and fixed and variable costs.

Direct and Indirect Costs

Direct Costs.   The most common and the most universally useful way of categorizing costs is direct vs. indirect. Direct costs can be charged directly to work; they are the costs that are most easy to notice and isolate. As the term suggests, *direct costs* are costs that are directly and separately incurred by a program or agency. For example, the salaries of all of the people involved in a program are part of the direct cost of that program. If the program is the sole user of a rented building, the rent is part of the direct cost.

Determining Indirect Costs.   *Indirect costs* are a program or agency's fair share of a cost that it jointly incurs with other programs or agencies. If five programs share a building, each program's indirect costs include part of the cost of heating, air-conditioning, and cleaning that building.

If six agencies use a computer, and one agency uses it about one-sixth of the time, about one-sixth of the overall cost of that computer is an indirect cost to the agency. (Although the terms are distinguishable, all *indirect costs* are often called *overhead* in the public sector.[19])

It is sometimes difficult to determine the fair share that should be allocated to a program or agency of a cost that is jointly incurred. (*Allocation* means taking a piece of the shared cost and attributing it to one agency or program.) For example, consider a program that shares a building with eleven other programs. It has a budget that is as large as the other programs combined; it has one-quarter of all the employees, and it uses one-third of the floor space. What is its fair share of the rental on that building? It might be one-twelfth because there are twelve agencies, one-half because that is its budget share, or one-third because it uses one-third of the floor space.

For internal management systems, most agencies write a "cost allocation plan" that guides the managers in determining the fair share of costs for recurring situations.[20] Usually the cost allocation plan simply uses common sense in determining a fair share of a joint cost. In the preceding case, probably one-third of the cost of the building should be allocated to the program as an indirect cost because it is using one-third of the floor space, and that is the most relevant factor.

Several other examples:

1. Computer expenses for a shared mainframe computer should probably be allocated by the amount of computer time used by each program or agency.
2. An asset shared by 200 programs should probably be allocated equally just because it is not worth the effort to figure out each program's exact share.

Often indirect costs are not immediately obvious, but they can be as high as the easily visible direct costs and thus cannot be ignored. If we add an agency's direct costs to its indirect costs, we derive total costs, usually called *full costs*. Full costs come close to what we mean when we talk about "real" costs—all the resources that a program or unit is actually consuming. To determine whether a program or agency is efficient, we need to compare its total output to its *total* input, and that means full costs.

Although most public agency financial systems are not set up to capture and allocate indirect costs, they should be. Lower-level managers often can get by with information on only direct costs because that is what they control. They usually have little say over building rentals, computer purchases, and other indirect costs. But middle and upper managers do make decisions about such costs, and they need to know full costs to make these decisions rationally. They are working with only half the necessary information when they know only direct costs. In recent years, federal grants to state and local agencies often allow agencies to recover indirect costs, and this change has encouraged the growth of accounting systems to document such costs. This is an encouraging development because the same information is then available for the agency's managers.

Internal Service Funds

There is a way to turn some indirect costs into direct costs: internal service funds. Most large organizations have subunits that provide services to other subunits. These would include copy centers, computer centers, inventory stocks, motor pools, legal staffs, and the like. Normally the costs of such subunits are simply treated as organizational overhead, and thus an indirect cost for other parts of the organization that use their services. But these costs can be turned into direct costs by setting up these units as cost centers that charge the other parts of the organization for their services.

Let us take a motor pool as an example. First, we must set it up as a separate cost center, with its accounts kept separate from other cost centers. Because it offers services to other internal units, we can call the motor pool cost center an "internal service unit." As noted earlier in this chapter, most state and local governments legally use "funds" as separate pots of money. So, second, we break out the motor pool's finances as a separate fund—an internal service fund. Unlike most government funds, which use modified accrual accounting, internal service funds use straight accrual, allowing the managers of these cost centers to use depreciation and thus reliably establish the true costs of each of their services.

Finally, based on these determined costs, the motor pool charges the other units of the organization that wish to use its services. Each car that is taken out, or each overhaul that is performed, is charged to the subunit that is using the car, usually on a per-mile or a per-hour basis. The charges are termed *transfer prices* to distinguish them from regular prices. A *transfer price* is a price charged internally—one unit of an organization charging another unit. Although it may seem strange at first for an organization, in effect, to charge itself, transfer prices provide very important information. Charging other units for the use of the copy center, the motor pool, or the legal staff helps the organization to determine who is using what resource. Moreover, these charges are also important in influencing managerial behavior. When managers are not charged for a service or object because it is an indirect cost, they may think of these things as "free" and overuse them.[21]

For example, the detective's bureau of the Midville police department has one copy machine on its own floor. When faced with a major copying job, the bureau chief must decide whether to do the copying in-house or send it out to the municipal copy center. Even if the bureau can do it in-house more cheaply, it is likely to choose to use the municipal copy center. If the bureau does it itself, the chief will be using personnel costs that are charged to the bureau. But because the municipal copy center does not charge, it seems "free." If the city turns the municipal copy center into a cost center with an internal service fund, and it begins charging, the detective bureau's behavior will change. The bureau chief will be more careful in deciding whether to do the copying in-house, or whether in fact to do the copying at all. The city's resources will be used more thoughtfully and efficiently. The city will also have an accurate record of all of the detective bureau's expenses—those of its own unit and those it "buys" from the central staff.

Fixed Vs. Variable Costs

We have already discussed dividing total costs into the categories of direct and indirect costs. Total costs can also be split a second way, into fixed and variable costs. It is important to emphasize that the fixed and variable costs for any program are not in addition to any direct and indirect costs. They are simply another way of looking at the same costs. Thus if the total costs for a program are $10 million, the sum of the direct and indirect costs will be $10 million; or if we decide to slice the same total cost pie another way, the sum of the fixed and variable costs will be $10 million.

Fixed costs are costs that remain the same even when the organization's volume changes considerably, whereas *variable costs* change as the volume changes. For example, an agency that has to serve 20 percent more clients this year than last would probably have to increase the amount spent on salaries, desks, and overtime because new people would have to be hired and given desks and current employees would have to work longer. But the same agency would probably not have to increase the amount spent on rent because a 20 percent increase in client load is unlikely to require larger offices. Thus rent is a fixed cost; salaries, desks, and overtime are variable costs.

The term *variable* does not indicate that the cost *per item* changes as the volume changes. Rather, variable costs are so called because their *total* changes as volume changes. For example, a copy center has fixed costs of $50,000 (for the purchase of the copy machine and for building rental). These fixed costs remain set at $50,000 whether the center handles 5 copies or 500,000 copies for the year. The center also incurs variable costs of 2 cents per page (for ink and paper). The variable cost *per item* does not change whether the center handles 5 copies or 500,000; it is still 2 cents per copy. But 2 cents is nonetheless a variable cost because the *total* for the variable cost changes: It is 10 cents for 5 copies and $10,000 (500,000 × 2 cents) for 500,000 copies.

The distinction between fixed and variable costs is somewhat arbitrary because if the volume change is large enough, almost all costs become variable costs. If the client load triples, for example, a new building would probably have to be rented, turning rent into a variable cost. Such extreme shifts in volume are very rare for public organizations, however. We can thus comfortably define fixed costs as those that remain the same within *normal* volume changes.

Separating fixed from variable costs is useful primarily in projecting future budgets. If the West Colorado health agency currently has a budget of $10 million and next year expects to double its volume, seeing twice as many clients, what should its new budget be? Probably not $20 million, but we don't have enough information to answer the question. We need to know the percentage of the current $10 million budget that goes to fixed or variable costs. As illustrated in Box 2-3, if the agency has $8

Box 2–3.

Three agencies—A, B, and C—have identical budgets of $10 million this year. Each agency will double its client load next year. How much money will each need?

The key is the mix between fixed and variable costs. (We will make the usually plausible assumption of a linear relationship between variable costs and workload.)

THIS YEAR

	AGENCY A	AGENCY B	AGENCY C
Fixed costs	$8 million	$5 million	$1 million
Variable costs	$2 million	$5 million	$9 million
Total costs	$10 million	$10 million	$10 million

NEXT YEAR

	AGENCY A	AGENCY B	AGENCY C
Fixed costs	$8 million	$5 million	$1 million
Variable costs	$4 million	$10 million	$18 million
(last year's variable costs × 2 because the workload has doubled)			
Total costs	$12 million	$15 million	$19 million

million in fixed and $2 million in variable costs this year, next year's budget should be $12 million. If, on the other hand, it has $9 million in variable costs and only $1 million in fixed costs, next year's budget should be $19 million.

Such projections of future costs when we expect agency volume to vary is the primary use of the fixed/variable distinction. A public agency that has the same volume and same internal needs over many years would be wasting its energy in separating fixed from variable costs, but for the minority of agencies that experience substantial swings in volume, the distinction can be a key to efficient management.

USING THE INFORMATION

The Value of Cost Analysis:
Generating Unexpected Data for Decisions

A number of agencies that claim to know the full costs of their programs do not; they merely estimate them. The accounts for a public agency must be kept on the basis of actual revenues and expenses and must be tracked by an accounting system that enters the expenses at the appropriate time in the appropriate account. The cash portion must similarly be kept on a bill-by-bill and receipt-by-receipt basis. Some agencies simply estimate their costs and revenues for the year for different program categories. Robert Anthony and Regina Herzlinger use the example of a school district that keeps only a few accounts, so it knows that it has spent $12.4 million at the end of the year.[22] When a state agency wishes to know how much the school district spent on "athletics" or on "basic academic instruction" the administrator simply estimates the amounts for these categories and returns the forms.

If the school district is not itself interested in this information, this system is acceptable. It is better not to allow outside reporting requirements to distort the information structure any more than necessary; insider decision-making needs are very important. However, the problem arises when the school district wants this information, too, and begins to treat the estimates as if they were real information. Approaches built on estimates are useful for keeping outside agencies satisfied; they are worthless for decision making.

As Anthony and Herzlinger point out, the reason estimates should never be used for decisions is that they never surprise. A school district may believe that it is allocating 70 percent of its budget to "basic academic instruction." If it sets up a separate cost center for this category and then keeps its accounts on a day-to-day basis, it may be surprised at the end of the year to find that it is spending only 50 percent of its budget on basic instruction. This unexpected piece of information can help the school district's managers decide if they wish to change programs or directions to move closer to 70 percent. However, under an estimate system, if the district managers think they are spending 70 percent, that is what they will enter on the books, even if it is a mistaken belief. The system cannot provide any surprises or any real information. It simply feeds back the assumptions with which the managers began. If the administrators begin to treat such information as real, these estimate-based systems are far worse than nothing because they lull administrators into believing they know the figures when in fact they do not.

Types of Decisions Aided by Cost Analysis

The preceding section suggests that cost analysis is valuable because it often generates unexpected information that can be used in decision making. But what types of decisions, specifically, can this information help illuminate? A few possibilities have been suggested throughout this chapter and will be explored in greater detail later, especially in the chapters on productivity measurement, monetary measures of output, and budgeting. It is useful here, however, to highlight some of the uses before discussing them in greater detail later in this book.[23]

One of the most important advantages of information about input is that it helps managers interpret information about output. Even by themselves, of course, output measures are useful; for example, it is helpful to know that a housing agency housed 400 people last year and 500 this year. But it is even more useful to combine such output figures with input information so that we can tell whether the agency's expenses per person housed increased or decreased as its output went up. If the agency housed 100 more people, but at the cost of doubling its expenses, the output figures are causes for alarm, not congratulations.

This combination of input and output information enables the manager to make more rational decisions in a number of areas, including:[24]

1. *Decisions about setting prices.* A financial system indicates how much a unit or output or project costs; this information can then be used to set prices. Occasionally these prices are for outsiders because a few government organizations—such as swimming pools, golf courses, license bureaus, and public hospitals—charge for their outputs. Usually such organizations wish to charge consumers their fair share of the costs, but they are often unable to do so without a financial management system that accurately captures these costs.

   Most government organizations, of course, do not charge outside clients for their outputs. But as discussed, agencies often have internal "customers" whom they can charge through transfer pricing. Again, a financial management system makes setting fair transfer prices possible, and transfer prices, in turn, encourage efficiency throughout the organization.

2. *Decisions about budgetary planning.* Every public organization, every year, must draw up and then defend a budget request. This requires the ability to forecast accurately the costs of different programs and changing levels of output. Both the planning and the defense are far easier with a financial management system that captures the costs of activities and programs.

3. *Decisions about contracting out.* More and more states and localities are contracting out some of their duties. They hire private firms to perform such activities as paving roads, collecting garbage, cutting trees, and even fighting fires. However, only a small minority of all governments do contract out, and a number of analysts have suggested that one reason is that most governments lack full cost accounting, and therefore they underestimate their own costs in delivering such services.[25] This inaccurate information makes the private alternative seem overpriced. Whether or not this supposition is true, a reliable financial management system would allow unbiased comparison of the costs of private delivery vs. government delivery, enabling elected officials to make better decisions about contracting out. Even when the decision is made to continue delivering the service through government, just the possibility of private delivery should encourage the public agencies to become more efficient.[26]

Of course, a financial management system does more than just illuminate decisions such as the three just noted. Like all management systems, it also has an effect on employees' motivation. It helps motivate employees to become more efficient by eliminating "free" overhead services that encourage overuse of the items. Second, it provides a clear record of resource consumption, and this provides fair, easily understood targets for employees to consider in cutting expenses.

MISUSES OF FINANCIAL MANAGEMENT SYSTEMS: MANIPULATING DATA FOR POLITICAL GAIN

Any system as important to government as a financial management system is bound to be affected by the temptation to misuse it for political gain. The information carried in financial systems can make political office-holders look good or inept; accordingly there is a great deal of temptation to manipulate the system.

One ploy is to carry debts on the books that in fact will never be repaid. However, as long as they are still listed on the books, they can be cited as future income and used to secure loans or to make an agency's net worth appear better than it is. Top administrators must force lower-level organizations to write off bad debts when they are clearly no longer receivable.

An Extreme Example: New York City

Agencies (or cities such as New York) that run into severe financial straits are likely to be even more inventive. For example, New York City creatively manipulated accounting techniques:

> Traditionally the city had maintained its books on a cash basis—that is, revenue was recognized when it was received, and an expenditure was recognized when it was paid. It is equally acceptable to keep the books on an accrual basis. . . . The requirement is only that an accounting system be employed consistently. But the city increasingly began to accrue only revenues, recognizing them at the earliest possible time, while the recognition of expenses was delayed until the actual cash outlay was made. The effect was to roll back to the current year revenues actually received in subsequent years and to roll forward expenses. As the budget pressures increased, rules were sometimes changed in the middle of the year in the relentless drive to squeeze the last dollar of spending authority from the seemingly inexhaustibly resilient city accounts.[27]

New York City's near bankruptcy, which continued to hamper the city's finances into the 1990s, was partly the result of political manipulation of the system and partly the result of the sheer inadequacy of the system. As such, it provides a useful if dramatic example of the importance of financial management systems. Although its failings began at the operational and management levels, its ultimate effects shook the strategic and policy foundations of all city agencies:

> The dreadful inadequacy of the city accounting systems was an important contributor to the problem. The comptroller's accounts and the city budget did not tie to each other, so it was almost impossible to track specific agency deficits. Revenue information was extremely poor. Federal and state aid payments, when they finally arrived, were usually not designated to an agency activity, so there was no practicable way of knowing how collections were faring against individual aid estimates. Agency record keeping compounded the problem: With all their accounting resources devoted to the process requirements of line-item budgeting, agency records of aid earned, drawdowns claimed, disallowances charged and payments received were disorderly and inconsistent at best and nonexistent at worst. Budget officials would phone around the agencies each quarter to try to discover how revenues were holding up; not surprisingly, the estimates were often wildly misleading. . . . Although inattention to line-item budget processing would bring

the city to a halt, there seemed to be no comparable penalty for letting the accounting problems slip.[28]

Political Emphasis on External Financial Information

New York City is a dramatic case, where neglect of financial management systems first led to management inefficiencies and from there to near bankruptcy. Of course, most failings of the financial reporting system are not so extreme, and therefore they do not have such dramatic effects. But at the same time it is important to note that political pressures rarely work in favor of the accrual-based cost analysis systems that public managers need because the political pressures are all for *outside,* expenditure-oriented reporting needs. Management systems of all types may be used to produce information needed by outside observers, but this is particularly true of financial systems. Both public and legislative interest focuses on money. To the legislature, controlling expenditures means controlling taxes and preventing politically damaging fraud. Thus outside reporting requirements produce systems that track the obligation of money, rather than its consumption, and that track objects bought (to prevent fraud) rather than the results achieved. This leads to modified accrual accounting and to line-item budgets. But the needs of outside observers, however valid, are not necessarily the needs of internal managers. These dual needs are an obstacle to clear, useful management systems for internal use—but not an insurmountable obstacle. Dual systems that produce both types of information are often very practical.

As has been emphasized throughout this chapter, it is not sufficient for a government body or organization simply to adhere to the basics of generally accepted accounting principles (GAAP)[29] in a yearly financial report. In a highly critical article,[30] Robert Anthony catalogs the large number of options open to government accountants who wish to show a small surplus (the politically optimal outcome) in the general fund. All of these options are within GAAP, but they nonetheless lead to highly misleading results. Moving beyond the bare minimum of GAAP to the use of accrual accounting, cost centers, and cost analysis is necessary to generate the information needed for better decision making and management.

In the next chapter we will look at another component of efficiency analysis: output measures to complement the input measures considered here.

SUMMARY

Although the situation is changing, public agencies lag far behind their business counterparts in tracking finances. For example, some public agencies still use cash accounting, which provides very little information that is useful for managerial decision making. Even those that have moved to accrual (or modified accrual) accounting systems rarely have a sufficient number of accounts and also rarely utilize internal cost centers, which allow managers to determine real costs for particular activities and subunits.

The account is the smallest unit of financial information. It usually covers only one small part of an organization or program; a broader, more complete picture can be gained by adding accounts together.

The same total costs of an organization can be divided in a number of different ways. The most universally useful division is between direct costs (those easily attributable to a particular program or unit) and indirect costs (costs that a program or unit shares with others). Full costs are the sum of direct and indirect costs; they are the best representation of the "real" costs of a program or unit.

A second categorization is fixed and variable costs. This distinction is useful primarily for organizations that experience substantial shifts in workload.

One principle used in financial management underlies *all* management systems: Actual performance is compared to projected performance, and any differences (called *variances*) need to be carefully studied by the manager.

REVIEW QUESTIONS

1. Why do financial management systems play a more comprehensive role in the business sector than in public management?
2. What is a direct cost? An indirect cost? A full cost? Provide examples of each for the obstetrics department of a hospital.
3. What is the distinction between a fixed and variable cost? Provide examples of each for a school district. When is the fixed/variable distinction most useful for the school?
4. What is an account? A cost center? A fund?
5. Why do governments employ funds, whereas the private sector does not?
6. Why are variances the key to any management system?
7. What is the difference in the information provided by cash, modified accrual, and accrual accounting? What are several transactions that would be recorded differently under each system?
8. What is the difference between an expenditure and an expense? Give examples.
9. What is a fixed asset? How is it treated under depreciation? What is the advantage of an accounting system that uses depreciation?

10. What is an enterprise fund? How is it used?
11. What is an internal service fund? How is it used?
12. In what specific ways can the information from a financial management system be used? Give examples.

SUGGESTED FURTHER READING

ROBERT N. ANTHONY and DAVID W. YOUNG. *Management Control in Nonprofit Organizations,* 3rd ed. Homewood, IL: Richard D. Irwin, 1984. A greatly extended examination of this chapter's topic. Presumes some prior knowledge of accounting.

CHARLES K. COE. *Public Financial Management* (Englewood Cliffs, NJ: Prentice-Hall, 1989). Chapters 2 and 8 are particularly relevant to this chapter's topic.

THE GOVERNMENT ACCOUNTING RESEARCH FOUNDATION and THE GOVERNMENTAL ACCOUNTING STANDARDS BOARD. *The Codification of Governmental Accounting and Financial Reporting Standards* (Stamford, Conn., updated regularly). Contains the text of the National Council on Governmental Accounting, American Institute of Certified Accountants, and Governmental Accounting Standards Board pronouncements.

LEO HERBERT, LARRY N. KILLOUGH, and ALAN WALTER STEISS. *Governmental Accounting and Control.* Monterey, CA: Brooks/Cole, 1984. Very clear and complete.

JOSEPH T. KELLEY. *Costing Government Services: A Guide for Decision Making.* Washington, DC: U.S. Government Finance Research Center, 1984. Well written and useful.

Case 2–1

Her school district gives Principal Roberta Patterson wide discretion in how she structures her internal financial reporting system. Lately Patterson has read an article on the advantage of cost centers and she wonders if the principle is applicable to her 3,000-student high school and its $10.6 million annual budget.

There are a number of activities under the school's direction that could be separated out, she realizes. A few of these—driver's education and some extracurricular activities—even charge fees. But they are not separated out in the budget or the financial reporting system now.

Patterson sees no advantage in changing this system. "Almost all of the school's activities are necessary, and there are few decisions to be made about them," she says. "So why make them cost centers? And those few activities that charge fees—bringing in about $80,000 per year—are relatively unimportant. Besides, they are not meant to turn a profit, and it's not even essential that they break even. So why bother with breaking out a lot of cost centers?"

1. What type of cost centers are possible for a typical high school of 3,000 students? What advantage is there in separate cost centers? Disadvantages? What is your recommendation?
2. Should those activities that charge fees be treated differently than other school activities when considering cost centers?

Case 2–2

The new head librarian for the town's public library wishes to issue a monthly report about the library's finances that can be understood and followed by all the library's employees. He finds the following actions have been completed in March and April:

a. On March 2 received $120 in patron fees; this represents a prepayment of the $40/month fee for April, May, and June.
b. On March 5 billed the book discussion club a $20 monthly rental fee for the April use of the library's conference room.
c. On March 8 ordered binding material for $5,000 (used at the rate of $500 per month, beginning on April 1).
d. On April 6 paid $5,000 for binding material.
e. On April 15 received $20 from the book discussion club.
f. Three years ago paid $24,000 for computer system; life of system is estimated at ten years (assume monthly depreciation).
1. Use the following format to show how the listed transactions would be entered if the original data were based on cash accounting, accrual accounting, and modified accrual accounting. (This format has no counterpart in accounting—it is simply a report to employees.) Enter data for March, April, and May. For each type of system, assume the beginning balance on March 1 is $15,000. Produce three tables, and identify the type of accounting represented by each.

Type of Accounting:

Date	Nature of Transaction	Amount of Transaction	Balance
3/1			$15,000

2. The library is studying contracting out for binding services. It uses modified accrual accounting, and charges only direct costs to its cost centers. What changes would the library have to make to these

components of its financial management system to decide if contracting is cost effective? Why would it have to make these changes?

3. If the library continues to do its own binding, explain the advantages and disadvantages of converting binding services into an internal service unit.

Case 2–3

As the newly hired management analyst for the county government, Eva Rullins found the first week of work demanding. Among the requests for help she found on her desk were two pleas for aid in allocating costs.

The Motor Pool

The largest county agency owns a fleet of twelve cars, which is operated as a motor pool serving the agency's four divisions. Each division is roughly equal in size. The head of the agency wishes to charge the costs of running the motor pool to the four divisions. The accounting system indicates that the motor pool has incurred the following total costs in the just-finished fiscal year:

Labor	$17,000
Depreciation of cars	16,000
Depreciation of maintenance equip.	5,000
Insurance	4,000
Gas	13,000

1. The records, based on odometer readings, show that division A used the cars for 80,000 miles, division B for 50,000 miles, division C for 40,000 miles, and division D for 30,000 miles. How much should each division have been charged for the use of the cars this past fiscal year?

2. The head of the agency wants to set a per-mile charge for next year, and he wishes to cover his full costs through the charge. He expects the total mileage to increase by 30 percent next year. If depreciation and insurance represent fixed costs, what should be the per-mile charge next year?

Department of Social Services

The county's department of social services, unlike the motor pool, does not have many records. Because it keeps its records on a department-wide, line-item basis, it is able to track only total costs for the entire department. However the department's top managers wish Rullins to come by for several days and teach them how to begin allocating costs to the four different primary functions that the department performs for its clients: income maintenance, health maintenance, job and training placement, and child welfare. The managers find the task daunting because each of the seven branch offices handles each of these four functions; in fact the same social worker may handle two or more of these tasks with each client.

1. What does Rullins need to know to help this department?
2. How could costs be allocated to these functions?
3. Under what circumstances would this information be worth the cost of gathering it?

Case 2-4

The municipal copy center offers free copying to all city departments. Last year its fixed costs were $45,000 and its variable costs were $30,000; it produced 1.5 million copies. Next year it expects to produce 2 million copies. In two years, it expects to produce 3 million copies.

1. What will be the copy center's total costs next year? What will be its cost per copy?
2. What will be the copy center's total costs in two years? What will be its cost per copy?

ENDNOTES

1. This definition is taken, with a few changes, from Frederick O'R. Hayes et al. *Linkages: Improving Financial Management in Local Government* (Washington, DC: Urban Institute, 1982), p. 90.
2. This definition and the following few paragraphs rely heavily on Robert N. Anthony and David W. Young, *Management Control in Nonprofit Organizations,* 3rd ed. (Homewood, IL: Richard D. Irwin, 1984), pp. 244–49.
3. This is similar to the example used by Robert Anthony and Regina Herzlinger, *Management Control in Nonprofit Organizations,* rev. ed. (Homewood, IL: Dorsey Press, 1980).
4. Unfortunately, English lacks a word for "paid organizational members" that does not carry some extraneous connotations. This book will refer to *employees* and *workers* and *organizational members* interchangably; as will be clear by the context, these terms will usually include managers.

5. A good overview of the use of logs and other forms of work measurement is Douglas M. Fox, *Managing the Public's Interest: A Results-Oriented Approach* (New York: Holt, Rinehart and Winston, 1979), pp. 208–14.

6. The need to design cost centers so that they clearly and directly relate to the output measures in a program is discussed in Thomas V. Greer and Joanne G. Greer, "Problems of Evaluating Costs and Benefits of Social Programs," *Public Administration Review*, 42, no. 2 (March/April 1982), 153–54.

7. Although it is now dated, a 1980 survey seems the latest attempt to examine the spread of cost accounting; it found these three states with cost information collected in relation to work or task performed. Other states have moved in this direction in the 1980s. Robert D. Lee, Jr., "Centralization/Decentralization in State Government Budgeting," *Public Budgeting and Finance*, Winter 1981, p. 77.

8. A list of federal funds is in Khi V. Thai, "Governmental Accounting," *Handbook on Public Budgeting and Financial Management* (New York: Marcell Dekker, 1983), pp. 332–34. Terminology differs between government levels. For example, businesslike activities that are covered at the state and local level in *enterprise* and *internal service* funds are in *revolving* funds at the federal level.

9. A useful empirical examination of the use of enterprise funds is Irene S. Rubin, "Municipal Enterprises: Exploring Budgetary and Political Implications," *Public Administration Review*, 48, no. 1 (January/February 1988), 542–50.

10. The fund requirements are more onerous for some governments than for others. Among the states, the number of funds varies from 2 in Delaware to 4,000 in Hawaii. In the middle, Massachusetts has 46, California 254, Illinois 700, and New York 900. Relmond P. van Daniker and Kay T. Pohlman, *Inventory of Current State Government Accounting and Reporting Practices* (Lexington, MA: Council of State Governments, 1980), pp. 4–5. Cited in Donald Axelrod, *Budgeting for Modern Government* (New York: St. Martin's Press, 1988), p. 233.

11. The debate over whether funds are useful is captured in two articles. One calls for the abolition of fund accounting: Robert N. Anthony, "Making Sense of Nonbusiness Accounting." The other defends funds: Regina E. Herzlinger and H. David Sherman, "Advantages of Fund Accounting in 'Nonprofits.' " Both articles appear in *Harvard Business Review*, May/June 1980, pp. 83–105.

12. Robert N. Anthony, "Games Government Accountants Play," *Harvard Business Review*, September/October 1985, pp. 161–70.

13. Besides the sources listed in footnote 14, a good treatment of modified accrual accounting is Robert Berne and Richard Schramm, *The Financial Analysis of Government* (Englewood Cliffs, NJ: Prentice-Hall, 1986), pp. 18–26.
    Because it does not seem basic to the managerial overview attempted here, this section does not emphasize the distinction between encumbering a sum at the time an order is placed and registering an accrued expenditure at the time of a legal obligation (often upon receipt of the good and an invoice).

14. Traditionally, modified accrual has recognized revenues during the period that they are "available and measurable." A good source on ongoing changes in modified accrual accounting is Barbara Chaney, "The Governmental Accounting Standards Board: How It Affects Local Government," *The Municipal Yearbook: 1989* (Washington, DC: International City Management Association, 1989), pp. 12–24. See also James R. Fountain, "Governmental Accounting: Where Is It Heading," *Public Budgeting and Finance,* Winter 1987, pp. 95–103, especially p. 100.

15. I infer this from the users' comments to the GASB reported in Chaney, "Governmental Accounting Standards Board," p. 17.

16. Axelrod, *Budgeting for Modern Government,* p. 235.

17. More cities than states seem to have modernized their accounting systems. By the early 1980s, virtually all cities had moved away from cash accounting, but a large number of state governments had not. Ibid., p. 255.

18. I have taken this distinction from Robert D. Vinter and Rhea K. Kish, *Budgeting for Not-for-Profit Organizations* (New York: Free Press, 1984), pp. 225ff. A synonym often used is *managerial accounting.* A good description of managerial accounting is given in Richard E. Brown and Hans-Dieter Sprohge, "Governmental Managerial Accounting: What and Where Is It?" *Public Budgeting and Finance,* Autumn 1987, p. 36:

    > Management accounting . . . differs from financial accounting in several key respects: it is for internal rather than external users and uses; it tends to be future-oriented, as well as historical in nature; its extent and form are determined by management rather than by external forces (the Financial Accounting Standards Board, Internal Revenue Service, etc.); and it is based in good measure on estimated procedures and is, therefore, far less precise.

19. Indirect costs and overhead are often used interchangeably in the public sector: Alan Walter Steiss, *Management Control in Government* (Lexington, MA: Lexington Books, 1982), p. 55. There are two

types of overhead: department-wide (e.g., the salary of the department head) and within agency (support functions such as the agency's accounting section). These distinctions are not central to our discussion, however.

20. Of course, the more money involved, the more sophisticated the techniques of cost allocation that are likely to be employed. Stepdown cost allocation approaches, for example, can run from very simple to very complex. This entire topic is covered in much greater detail in Joseph T. Kelley, *Costing Government Services: A Guide for Decision Making* (Washington, DC: U.S. Government Finance Research Center, 1984).

21. An interesting private sector application of the concept of cost centers is discussed in Frances Gaither Tucker and Seymour M. Zivan, "A Xerox Cost Center Imitates a Profit Center," *Harvard Business Review*, May/June, 1985, pp. 168–74. The use of profit centers is further developed in Chapter Nine.

22. This example is based on one in Anthony and Herzlinger, *Management Control*, pp. 95ff., but most of the details have been changed.

23. The call for greater use of accrual accounting and cost analysis linked to output measures in an integrated financial system is common at both the state and federal levels. For a federal example, see an article by the comptroller general: Charles A. Bowsher, "Sound Financial Management: A Federal Manager's Perspective," *Public Administration Review*, 45, no. 1 (January/February 1985), 176–84.

24. Again, these three areas are meant simply as examples of the large number of decisions clarified by knowing the true costs of all options. For another example, see Lawrence Southwick, Jr., and Pravesh Mehra, "The Probable Cost Impact of Creating a Metropolitan Police Force: An Accounting Variance Study Using Erie County, New York," *Urban Analysis*, 8 (1984), 55–84. The authors utilize sophisticated cost analysis to examine the costs of consolidating police forces within a region. They find that consolidation, a measure usually advocated for cost-savings reasons, often actually increases costs.

25. For example, E. S. Savas, "How Much Do Government Services Really Cost?" in *Urban Affairs Quarterly*, September 1979.

The role of accountants in structuring their information to elucidate such contracting out decisions is discussed in W. Bartley Hildreth, "Applying Professional Disclosure Standards to Productivity Financial Analyses," *Public Productivity Review*, 7, no. 3 (September 1983), 269ff. See also Toni Marzotto, "Cost Accountability for Public Managers," *The Bureaucrat*, Fall 1985; and Ted Kolderie, "The Two Different Concepts of Privatization," *Public Administra-*

tion Review, 46, no. 4 (July/August 1986), 285–91. Other works on privatization are cited in the notes to Chapter Six.

26. This is of course a very controversial area. For a report on the federal battle front, see Judith Havemann, "Contracting Out Called Wasteful, Demoralizing, *"Washington Post,* March 31, 1988, p. A21. An important analysis involved in the same controversy is U.S. General Accounting Office, *Revised Factors to Compare Government and Contractor Costs Are Appropriate* (Washington, DC: GAO; January 1986).

27. Charles R. Morris, *The Cost of Good Intentions* (New York: W. W. Norton & Co., 1980), p. 133.

28. Ibid., p. 238.

29. These standards are developed and interpreted for public sector organizations by the Government Accounting Standards Board. Its history and mission are described in James F. Antonio, "Role and Future of the Government Standards Accounting Board," *Public Budgeting and Finance,* Summer 1985, pp. 30ff.

30. Anthony, "Games Government Accountants Play."

chapter three

Management by Objectives

INTRODUCTION

Chapter One considered management systems in general; Chapter Two considered input-oriented management systems. These two chapters lay the groundwork for Chapters Three through Six, which cover the heart of this book: output-oriented management systems.

Because there are so many output-oriented management systems, we must break them into groups in order to consider them. These systems could be categorized in a large number of ways. For example, they might be divided by the type of organization in which they are used—systems in large organizations certainly look far different than those in small organizations. Or we might divide them by their degree of quantitativeness or by their degree of automation (whether or not they are primarily tracked by computer) or by numerous other distinctions.

This book will divide systems primarily on the basis of how their goals are set and tracked. Some systems set goals rather impersonally, using last year's figures or quotas. Some set them personally, in face-to-face bargaining. Similarly, some systems track goals impersonally, with a written report that periodically shows progress. Other systems track in a more personal way, with face-to-face meetings between subordinate and supervisor to discuss progress. (We will use the terms *supervisor, boss,* and *superior* interchangeably.)

Systems that set and track goals face to face are often termed *management by objectives,* or MBO. Such systems are most often used by managers whose outputs change from year to year. In other words, such systems are most often used with a project-oriented agency. A public research organization, for example, would commonly use an MBO system. Higher-level executives, whose "output" constantly changes, would commonly use an MBO system with their bosses.

Most output-oriented systems set and track goals through some means other than face-to-face bargaining. Because such "impersonal" systems lack a clearly agreed-on name, we will adopt their most common title: *performance monitoring systems.* Performance monitoring systems are used when the organizational output is relatively routine and unchanging, so it is less necessary to meet face to face to set and track goals. Clerical workers, sanitation workers, transportation workers, and others are likely to be covered by performance monitoring systems.

We now have the two main groups of output-oriented management systems: MBO systems, which set and track goals personally, and performance monitoring systems, which do not. Of course, it is possible to have systems that fall between these two extremes. For example, we could set goals face to face, but track them impersonally. We will briefly discuss these hybrid systems, but in fact once we have examined the two extremes of MBO and performance monitoring systems, hybrids naturally will fall into place.

Although it would be possible to discuss the functioning of output systems in the abstract, they are far easier to understand when examined in action. Thus the next two chapters will examine MBO, looking at its components, its advantages, and (in Chapter Four) its political effects. Much of these two chapters will apply as well to performance monitoring systems, so Chapters Five and Six will be able to build on the MBO discussion to examine their unique strengths.

Impact of MBO

The best known and most firmly established of all public sector output-oriented management systems is management by objectives (MBO). MBO has had a widespread influence. It is used in the most important federal departments (such as the Department of Health and Human Services and the Department of Defense), many state agencies, and over 60 percent of U.S. cities. For all its influence, though, MBO is a surprisingly simple feedback system. It is based on the concept of a contract between a manager and his or her subordinate. Both sides agree to certain objectives and to certain levels of personnel and money as reasonable support for those objectives. Then both supervisor and subordinate meet periodically to monitor progress on the objectives.

One might expect that such a simple system would have little impact on public organizations but that it would at least be easy to install and use. Both assumptions are wrong. When working, MBO systems can dramatically affect the efficiency, effectiveness, and even power alignments of a public agency. But at the same time, MBO is a deceptively difficult system to use; it fails more often than not when it is installed in public organizations.

History of MBO

MBO originated as a business method. Its basic concept has been used since at least the 1920s, but it was popularized by Peter Drucker in his 1954 book *The Practice of Management,* and it has been developed by both Drucker and other authors since then.[1] MBO was widely implemented in the business world throughout the 1950s and 1960s.

When the Republican Nixon administration assumed power in 1969, it brought large numbers of businesspeople to Washington as administrators. Not surprisingly, many began employing the MBO-type systems that they had used in the private sector. The Department of Health, Education and Welfare (HEW) led the way, under the guidance of Assistant Secretary Frederic Malek. When Malek moved to the Office of Management and Budget, he began a government-wide MBO system, termed *presidential MBO.* Presidential MBO died by 1976, partially because of Watergate but primarily for structural reasons to be discussed later. However, it left behind independent, internal MBO systems in many federal agencies. Moreover state and local organizations, in part inspired by the federal example, began to adopt MBO.

Today MBO systems are more widespread in government than ever. For example, the number of cities using MBO increased from 41 percent to 62 percent from the mid-1970s to the late 1980s.[2] This widespread influence may be hidden from the casual observer, however, because most government users give new names to their MBO-type systems, such as "goals planning systems," "performance tracking systems," and the like. Because MBO is the original and generic name, we will use it here.

THE STRUCTURE OF MBO

MBO's Components

The heart of an MBO system is the contract negotiated between a top manager and a subordinate manager. This contract has five components:

1. A major goal or objective with a completion date. (Although some MBO systems distinguish between broad *goals* and specific *objectives*, we will use both terms as synonyms.) An example of an objective for a public health agency is "Inoculate 75,000 people against flu during the next year."
2. A resource statement, for example, "$700,000 and four full-time positions are allocated to this objective."
3. A series of steps leading to that objective with completion dates for each. These steps with dates are termed *milestones*. An example of one milestone: "Deliver 10,000 doses of vaccine to each region by March 1."
4. Periodic meetings between the manager and the subordinate to monitor and discuss progress. These meetings might be monthly or quarterly.
5. A year-end assessment. The two managers review the past year's progress and use that information to begin the cycle for a new year.

What Objectives Should Be Tracked?

If one is managing by objectives, the choice of objectives becomes extremely important. Although objectives will differ widely from agency to agency, a number of guidelines can be suggested for all objectives. First, objectives should concern areas that are important to the organization. Second, they should be "stretch" goals, which often ask for more than in the past but are still achievable.

Finally, they should be linked to clear, output-oriented *achievement points*. Thus a poor objective would be "Enhance productivity of the clerical staff this year," whereas a good objective would specify a clear achievement point: "Increase clerical output by 7 percent this fiscal year while maintaining the current error rate."

The need for specifying clear achievement points is more often ignored than would be expected. Thus in the mid-1980s, one state agency's MBO objectives included such goals as "Reduce stress on employees"; the two major milestones for this goal (in their entirety) were "Assess the sources of stress within the workplace" and "Reduce stress levels where possible."[3] Of course it is impossible *not* to claim completion of this goal, no matter how little is accomplished, and that makes it a very bad (but unfortunately, not uncommon) goal.

Although the clear achievement point is usually quantified, occasionally it is not. For example, a good objective for a planning department might be "Finish plan for new subdivision and receive approval of all involved administrators by August 10." This objective could not be quantified, but it has a clear achievement point (approval by August 10).

When an achievement point is quantified, it is often called a *performance indicator,* or simply an *indicator.*[4] To sum up the terminology, then, an achievement point is any clear measure of performance; all objectives *must* have unambiguous achievement points. There are two kinds of achievement points: (1) nonquantifiable, such as "signature by January 5" and (2) quantifiable, such as "a 6 percent increase in the number of people trained." In most systems, the quantifiable achievement points, called indicators, are in the vast majority. Alternative ways in which indicators can be chosen and used will be a central concern of Chapter Five.

As mentioned, the achievement points should emphasize results rather than processes. Occasionally an internal organizational process may be having trouble and some MBO objectives may focus on it —which is fine. However, such internally oriented goals and objectives should never be the major focus of the system. The system's primary focus should be on outputs—results—not inputs and processes, because the organization's prime focus should be on outputs. For example, for a job-placement agency, and objective that said, "Increase the number of clients interviewed by 13 percent"would be too process-oriented unless it were accompanied by and output objective, such as "Increase by 15 percent the number of clients placed in jobs offering at least $16,000/year." The MBO goals should focus attention on the agency's mission: placing clients, rather than just interviewing them.

The five steps of the MBO process can be seen in Box 3-1, which illustrates how one MBO objective is tracked.

THE BENEFITS OF MBO

As can be seen, MBO is an extremely simple system. A top manager and subordinate negotiate an objective or several objectives and then track them together through the year. But despite its simplicity, an MBO system can produce dramatic management improvement. There are a number of gains from a well-working MBO system:[5]

The Fundamental Advantage: MBO Shifts Attention from Processes to Results. MBO emphasizes outputs or results instead of processes. This advantage underlies all of the other advantages that we will cite. Information flows, planning, and evaluations are all focused on organizational outputs.

The typical public manager is the prisoner of his or her in-box. Deadlines have to be met, people seen, letters answered. Thus there is very little time to focus on what is actually being accomplished. A cliché of administration is that "the urgent is the enemy of the important."

Often the "urgent" activities with the tightest deadlines have the least importance to the mission of the organization, yet they tend to monopolize a manager's time. MBO can help change all this. It can force top managers and their subordinates to determine the most important results (i.e., outputs) that they want to achieve in the coming year and periodically to review whether they are in fact progressing toward them. No longer is a clean in-box at the end of the day the best available indicator of performance. MBO emphasizes results, not activities. The urgent no longer drives out the important because MBO helps make the most important activities urgent, too, by coupling them with deadlines and with regular meetings to discuss progress.

MBO Improves the Downward Flow of Information. Most top government administrators would be stunned to learn how little their priorities are understood by middle-rank subordinates. The high-priority goals of top administrators are obscured by the large number of directives and other messages they must send out just to handle routine organizational problems. MBO helps solve this problem. Rather than searching through speeches and enigmatic memos for policy directions, managers need only look to their own MBO goals for a clear statement of the top

---

Box 3–1. Tracking One MBO Objective for One Year

The following six tables illustrate the documentation generated by one MBO objective as it is tracked over a year. Usually the documentation would be preceded by one or two pages explaining the project (in this case, a blood pressure screening and follow-up program), indicating why the objective was chosen and listing the resources (both money and personnel) required. We have not reproduced these first two pages, so the first table shows the milestones as they have been agreed to by the county manager and the director of the county health department. (The line preceeding the symbol for milestone 7 indicates that the step begins in January but is completed in February.)

Once they have agreed on objectives and milestones, the two managers will then meet at the end of each two-month period to discuss progress. The first such meeting (or management conference) is held at the very end of August and is based on the progress shown in the second table. When a milestone is completed it is filled in, and the second table indicates that all the milestone deadlines have been met. This is also reflected in the "satisfactory" rating shown in the overall evaluation box on the top right of the page.

But the third and fourth tables record a problem that arises in the September/October reporting period. Two milestones (5 and 6) have been missed. We skip the documentation for the November/December management conference, but the final fifth and sixth tables indicate a major problem during the January/February reporting period. As can be seen in the last table, remedial actions were being considered and taken.

Marshall County
Management Objectives for FY 1992

Department: *Health*
Objective *1*
Objective: To conduct free screenings for high blood pressure in all four major areas of the county, reaching at least 10,000 residents, and to follow up with those determined to have high blood pressure, with the goal of having at least 65 percent of this high-risk group taking remedial actions by year end.

STATUS REPORT FOR MONTHS OF:

OVERALL EVALUATION: [   ]

COMPLETION DATE

Milestones	July	Aug.	Sept.	Oct.	Nov.	Dec.	Jan.	Feb.	Mar.	Apr.	May	June
1. Develop plan for screenings and follow-ups; receive final approvals.	O											
2. Conduct first two screenings.		OO										
3. Screen 5,500 people.												
4. Conduct third and fourth screenings.			OO									
5. Screen a total of 10,000 people.												
6. Contact the following percentages of those found to be at high risk during screenings; check current behavior and send information on disease.				O 50%	O 80%	O 100%						
7. Recontact those not in compliance; make home visits to those who need help.								O				
8. Determine that the following percentages of those originally contacted are now following health guidelines.								O 40%	O 50%	O 60%	O 65%	

Marshall County
Management Objectives for FY 1992

Department: *Health*
Objective *1*
Objective: To conduct free screenings for high blood pressure in all four major areas of the county, reaching at least 10,000 residents, and to follow up with those determined to have high blood pressure, with the goal of having at least 65 percent of this high-risk group taking remedial actions by year end.

STATUS REPORT FOR MONTHS OF: July/August

OVERALL EVALUATION: | Satisfactory |

COMPLETION DATE

Milestones	July	Aug.	Sept.	Oct.	Nov.	Dec.	Jan.	Feb.	Mar.	Apr.	May	June
1. Develop plan for screenings and follow-ups; receive final approvals.	●											
2. Conduct first two screenings.		●●										
3. Screen 5,500 people.			○○									
4. Conduct third and fourth screenings.												
5. Screen a total of 10,000 people.												
6. Contact the following percentages of those found to be at high risk during screenings; check current behavior and send information on disease.				○ 50%	○ 80%	○ 100%						
7. Recontact those not in compliance; make home visits to those who need help.								○				
8. Determine that the following percentages of those originally contacted are now following health guidelines.								○ 40%	○ 50%	○ 60%	○ 65%	

Marshall County
Management Objectives for FY 1992

Department: *Health*
Objective *1*
Objective: To conduct free screenings for high blood pressure in all four major areas of the county, reaching at least 10,000 residents, and to follow up with those determined to have high blood pressure, with the goal of having at least 65 percent of this high-risk group taking remedial actions by year end.

STATUS REPORT FOR MONTHS OF: Sept./Oct.

OVERALL EVALUATION: | Minor problem |

COMPLETION DATE

Milestones	July	Aug.	Sept.	Oct.	Nov.	Dec.	Jan.	Feb.	Mar.	Apr.	May	June
1. Develop plan for screenings and follow-ups; receive final approvals.	●											
2. Conduct first two screenings.		●●										
3. Screen 5,500 people.		●	○									
4. Conduct third and fourth screenings.			●	○								
5. Screen a total of 10,000 people.				○ 50%	○ 80%	○ 100%						
6. Contact the following percentages of those found to be at high risk during screenings; check current behavior and send information on disease.					○							
7. Recontact those not in compliance; make home visits to those who need help.								○				
8. Determine that the following percentages of those originally contacted are now following health guidelines.								○ 40%	○ 50%	○ 60%	○ 65%	

Problem and Variance Analysis

Organization: *Health Dept.*
Objective 1: *Blood pressure screening*
For months of: September/October
Overall evaluation: Minor problem

Milestone(s)	Problem Description (Including Effect on Objectives)	Action Underway or Recommended
5	A total of 10,000 people have not been screened; delayed publicity for our last screening caused an unusually small turnout.	A new free screening session is currently being publicized, and we expect to reach 10,000 by November. Accordingly we request that milestone be moved to November.
6	A total of 50% of those in the high-risk group have not yet been contacted; we have currently reached 39%. Much of the shortfall is due to our efforts to begin a new screening (milestone 5 above). We believe we can reach 80% by next month, so no action is currently necessary.	

Marshall County
Management Objectives for FY 1992

Department: *Health*
Objective *1*
Objective: To conduct free screenings for high blood pressure in all four major areas of the county, reaching at least 10,000 residents, and to follow up with those determined to have high blood pressure, with the goal of having at least 65 percent of this high-risk group taking remedial actions by year end.

STATUS REPORT FOR MONTHS OF: Jan./Feb.

OVERALL EVALUATION: | Major problem |

COMPLETION DATE

Milestones	July	Aug.	Sept.	Oct.	Nov.	Dec.	Jan.	Feb.	Mar.	Apr.	May	June
1. Develop plan for screenings and follow-ups; receive final approvals.	●											
2. Conduct first two screenings.		● ●										
3. Screen 5,500 people.			● ○									
4. Conduct third and fourth screenings.				●	●							
5. Screen a total of 10,000 people.				50% ●	80% ○	100% ○						
6. Contact the following percentages of those found to be at high risk during screenings; check current behavior and send information on disease.						100% ○			100% ○			
7. Recontact those not in compliance; make home visits to those who need help.								○	○			
8. Determine that the following percentages of those originally contacted are now following health guidelines.								40% ○	50% ○	60% ○	65% ○	60% ○

71

Problem and Variance Analysis

Organization: *Health Dept.*
Objective 1: *Blood pressure screening*
For months of: January/February
Overall evaluation: Major problem

Milestone(s)	Problem Description (Including Effect on Objectives)	Action Underway or Recommended
6	Despite our earlier optimism, we have completed follow-ups with only 75% of the high-risk group. A key staff person quit over the Christmas holidays and her presence has been missed.	We request that another temporary staff person be hired. We also request that the milestone be moved to March.
7	Home visits have been lagging because follow-ups are not complete. The unusually bad weather has also made travel more difficult.	We are in the process of purchasing a four-wheel drive vehicle for travel in bad weather.
8	Because we are behind schedule, we find that only 27% of those originally contacted are following health guidelines. This number will remain low until we can follow up with all members of this group. Follow-ups will include mailings and home visits, both of which are behind schedule.	We now must acknowledge that we will not reach our year-end goal, although we expect to gain momentum in the coming months. We accordingly request that this milestone be changed to 60% by June. If accomplished, even the revised milestone will represent one of the most successful such screening programs in the state.

priorities. Year-long goals and monthly subgoals have been set, often with quantitative indicators. The level of ambiguity of downward communication is thus reduced.

MBO Improves the Upward Flow of Information. Often the information that reaches a top manager is incomplete or incorrect. There are two reasons for these distortions. One is simply random noise in the system. Organizational communication often resembles the child's game of telephone, where a message is begun at one end of the room and whispered from ear to ear, with the final message usually bearing little resemblance to the original one. This distortion arises even if each communication link tries very conscientiously to pass the information accurately.

Often different organizational levels do not in fact strive for accuracy, however, and that is the second cause of distortion. When a project runs into difficulties, the first impulse of any manager is not to tell superiors. Even if the manager is not directly responsible for the problem, he or she realizes that bearing bad news is not a good way to build popularity with the higher levels. And if the manager is responsible, all the more reason to put off telling one's superiors—perhaps the difficulties will work themselves out, perhaps a new boss will be appointed who can be snowed, or perhaps nobody will remember to ask about the project. By the time the subordinate reluctantly concludes that none of these miraculous events is imminent and the superior is finally informed of the problem, it is often too late to take timely, effective action. This problem has been termed the Bureaucratic Law of Gravity: Bad news never flows up.

However, each milestone in the MBO system acts as a trip wire, sending out early warnings. Incipient project difficulties are revealed as soon as the monthly meeting indicates that a milestone has not been met. And when problems are recognized early, it is simpler to take remedial action before they snowball.

MBO Brings Line Managers into Agency Planning. Public and private organizations both often find that their planning functions, run by the staff, and their operations, run by line managers, rarely connect. The planning office spins off studies and analyses, but the managers often take action without considering long-range factors.

Perhaps the most extreme examples of this separation of planning and action involves the planning offices of many municipalities. The planners work very hard and produce volumes of plans with color overlays and computer printouts. But when a zoning decision comes before the city council, it often takes action without even a glance at the long-range plans.

MBO attempts to connect operations to planning by bringing line managers into planning. In the hectic world of government administration, even a year is a long planning horizon. MBO's goal-setting process forces managers to think a year ahead and set priorities, and its monitoring process forces managers to compare their actions throughout the year to the original plans. Moreover, because they have a role in setting the goals and objectives, subordinate managers are far more committed to the objectives. They feel a sense of ownership because the people who will actually carry out the task have been asked to set priorities and plan it.

MBO Makes Personnel Evaluation Fairer.   Personnel textbooks and consultants have long urged managers to move away from trait-based evaluations, which have rating scales for such personality traits as "leadership," "honesty," "cooperativeness," and "originality." As we will discuss further in Chapter Eight, trait-based systems are extremely subjective. Almost all observers agree that it is much fairer to base evaluations on concrete performance rather than traits. Not only are such evaluations less subjective, but also they are much more directly related to what an evaluation is supposed to emphasize: job performance. Yet movement away from trait-based appraisals has been slow, in part because specifying concrete performance goals is so difficult in government.

MBO is a step toward setting objective performance indicators. It makes the evaluations fairer for those rated, while at the same time increasing managerial accountability, because it provides a means of evaluating and holding responsible specific managers. Accountability is elusive when dealing with the complex organizations and programs that often characterize government administration. This is particularly noticeable when dealing with intergovernmental programs, for example, local programs such as education that are funded by both state and federal agencies. A diagram of responsibilities in such program areas often looks like the wiring diagram for a complex machine: dozens of boxes, arrows flying in all directions, and dotted lines (indicating advisory responsibility) cutting through the arrows. In such welters of shared responsibility, accountability can get lost. Is it any wonder that performance evaluations emphasize traits like "promptness," given the difficulty of determining who has done what?

Because MBO establishes specific goals for each subunit, it becomes easier for a department head to determine where the difficulties originate when an important departmental goal is not attained within the assigned time period. MBO attempts to impose standards of accountability, and if this goal were even partially achieved it would produce a dramatic change in government administration. After three years as head of a large federal department, John Gardner said, "When you figure out how to hold a middle level bureaucrat accountable, it'll be comparable to landing on the moon."[6] MBO shifts the emphasis to measurable standards that both boss and subordinate agree are fair.

CHOICES IN STRUCTURING MBO SYSTEMS

Management systems are tools, and like all tools they are *contingent approaches*. In other words, no one tool (or no one management system) is correct for every problem or situation. Managers do not study system structures to learn about one "best" system; rather, they wish to learn about trade-offs—what can be gained and what can be lost by adjusting the system in any particular way. This idea of contingent solutions— different choices for different situations—is of course also important for structuring MBO.

MBO systems can be adapted to the particular needs of a manager or organization: The types of milestones can be adjusted, the time frame for reporting can be shortened or stretched, and the linkages to other levels can be implicit or formal. Let us consider each of these ways in which managers can tailor MBO to their specific needs.

Milestone Specificity

MBO devolves the choice of method to the people who are closest to the scene and thus most knowledgeable, thereby providing greater flexibility, higher morale, and more incentives for innovation. For all these reasons, MBO objectives and milestones should usually be stated in terms of outputs or results rather than processes. For example, if the overall objective is "Inoculate 70,000 people against flu by the end of the year," an initial milestone such as "Inoculate 25,000 people by March 1" provides the most discretion to subordinates. It specifies a destination (and gives the top boss a yardstick for judging results) but allows the subordinates to determine how to get to the destination. An initial milestone that read, "Inoculate 6,250 people in each of the four regions" would limit the freedom of subordinates by greater specificity. An initial milestone that read, "Hire three nurses and four doctors by February 1; deliver the vaccine by February 10" would remove even more discretion from subordinates.

In determining whether milestones should specify processes, top managers must consider the past record of the subordinate managers and the political sensitivity of the task. Generally, it is better to allow wide discretion about processes by focusing only on results.

Time Frame

Top managers can also manipulate the discretion of lower managers by shortening or stretching the time between management conferences. It is important to emphasize that this should be done at the beginning of the year; once set, the MBO schedule should be followed. However, in setting the yearly timetable, the manager can schedule management conferences at extremely close intervals—every two weeks perhaps—to maintain closer control over subordinates, or the manager can allow subordinates more discretion by scheduling monthly or even quarterly meetings. Management conferences that are more infrequent than quarterly probably do not provide the timely feedback integral to MBO.

Linkages

A full-fledged MBO system is linked from level to level by formally connected objectives. Thus the objectives from the top of the department have milestones, and each milestone becomes an objective for a lower level, which supports it with milestones. These milestones in turn are used as objectives by the next level and so on. This structure is sometimes termed a *linking pin* structure and is illustrated for four levels in Figures 3-1 and 3-2.[7]

Of course in all MBO systems the policy goals of one level should be considered in setting the objectives for the next lower level, so that all MBO systems have an *implicit* link from level to level. The question

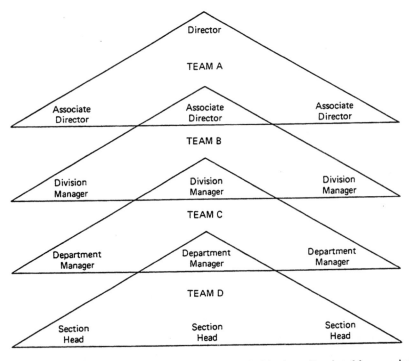

Figure 3-1. Link-pin approach to setting multiple-level objectives. Reprinted by permission of publisher, from. *MBO for Nonprofit Organizations,* by Dale D. McConkey, page 49. © 1975 AMACOM, a division of American Management Association, New York 10020. All rights reserved.

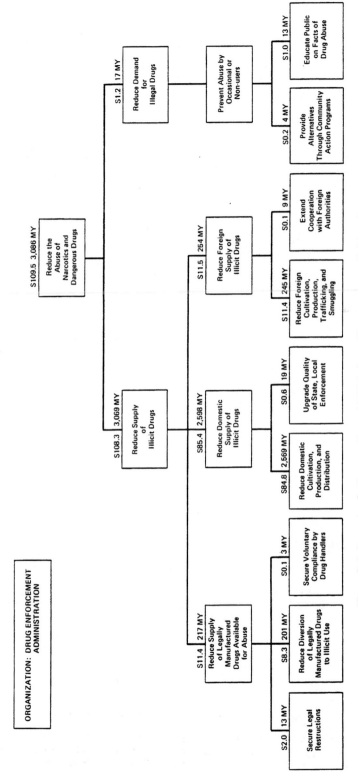

Figure 3–2. Example of a Program Pyramid. This figure illustrates how a linking pin structure can be applied to a law enforcement program. *Source:* U.S. Department of Justice, *Handbook for the U.S. Department of Justice Management-by-Objectives System,* Office of Management and Finance, p. 11.

is whether to make this link *formal* and to have the exact same areas tracked by each level, using the same terminology, so that the milestones of one level become the goals of the next.

There are advantages to the formal linking-pin structure. It ensures uniform pursuit of the top manager's goals, and it makes coordination clearer because the same terms and same goals are being pursued by each branch. Certainly such a structure is an excellent approach for organizations that have successfully used MBO for an extensive period of time or that have very concrete outputs.

However, a formal linking-pin structure from top to bottom for an organization with many levels requires a great deal of work and coordination, and the lead time can mount exponentially. Because the third level does not know what its broad objectives are until the second level has negotiated and firmed up its milestones, and the fourth level must in turn wait for the third, there is sometimes an extremely long period between the beginning of the process and the establishment of MBO objectives for the bottom levels. Paperwork increases as well.

Thus a formal linking-pin strategy is only for advanced MBO users, and not even for all of them. For organizations just beginning MBO, or those with a large number of levels or nonquantitative outputs, it is probably better to avoid a formal linking-pin structure. The coordination costs of a linked system can turn a useful MBO system into a paper-gorging, time-consuming nightmare.

Overview: Maintaining Flexibility of MBO Goals

Both business firms and government agencies are sometimes beset by events outside their control, but government agencies are particularly vulnerable to such environmental forces. Expected appropriations may be delayed, court suits may produce injunctions or changes in procedures, and cooperating agencies at other government levels may be rendered ineffective by internal problems or changes in leadership.

Under such circumstances, an unchanging MBO objective would become irrelevant. It is futile to continue to track an objective that is no longer even remotely attainable. Instead, as shown in the sample project at the beginning of this chapter, objectives and milestones should be adjusted when necessary. Like the original goal setting, this is done through bargaining between superior and subordinate. The MBO process is not meant to produce unchanging commandments; instead it should produce dynamic goals that respond to shifting conditions. Of course, when evaluating agency performance, a distinction will be made between objectives that have to be adjusted because of unavoidable environmental problems and those that are adjusted because of poor internal performance.

WHY MBO FAILS: RECURRING PROBLEMS
(AND POSSIBLE SOLUTIONS)

MBO fails more often than it succeeds. However, its benefits are so substantial that most agencies that are unsuccessful in their first attempt to institute an MBO system simply pick themselves up and start again. But this pattern is unnecessary because almost all system failures can be avoided. The designers and installers of MBO systems simply need to anticipate the most common serious problems and move against them early. Accordingly, this section looks at the six most common pitfalls and their solutions.

Problems Caused by Lack of Top Support

Support from the top of an organization is absolutely necessary for the success of any management system. It is best to have the strong support of the very top administrator, but if not, support from at least the second-in-command is required. The top of the agency controls the incentives—budget shares, promotions, even attention—that motivate behavior. If top support is lacking, installing MBO or other management systems is futile.

New management systems require organizational members to change comfortable patterns, learn new approaches, and take new risks. Unless these members see that the top of the agency is really committed to the system, they will be unwilling to undergo the discomforts of a changeover. (In the next chapter we will discuss ways of enlisting the support of the top administrator.)

Let us look at an illustration of the need for top support: presidential MBO. MBO first came to the federal government in 1973, when the Office of Management and Budget (OMB) directed all federal departments to develop MBO systems. President Nixon, in concert with OMB, was going to act as the top manager, with the departmental secretaries as subordinates. In turn, the departmental secretaries were to develop internal systems for their own departments as well. OMB then met quarterly with departmental officials to track some departmental progress toward the goals and discuss any problems that may have arisen. However, these quarterly meetings were not consistently held even during the height of presidential MBO, fiscal year 1974, and soon they fell to zero.[8]

There were a number of reasons for this failure, but the primary problem was the lack of top support from the President and OMB. Neither had the time, commitment, or ability to monitor the large number of goals for each of the eleven departments and ten agencies that were asked to submit them.

When President Bush attempted to institute a government-wide MBO system more than a decade later, he tried to avoid some of the most egregious problems of Nixon's government-wide system.[9] Bush emphasized that departments should choose only a few important goals to report to OMB and that departments should primarily view MBO as a device for themselves. Of course, many federal departments by Bush's era had already been using MBO for many years. For all his attempts to avoid the previous problems, however, Bush nonetheless faced the continuing problem of finding sufficient time to provide support for such a huge, government-wide system. It seems much better managerially to let federal departments run their own systems rather than treat them as units within an all-encompassing system, with the president as a super manager.

In sum, then, the Nixon experiment failed because it made the president the top of a government-wide system, and the president could not find the time nor the political capital to give MBO the consistent, engaged top support that all management systems need. Although Watergate (which removed the president and the OMB people behind MBO) was the death blow, presidential MBO's demise was preordained.

The internal federal systems begun under Nixon often fared little better because the fact that MBO began with an OMB directive badly damaged its acceptance by most managers. Its role as guardian of the budget makes OMB one of the least loved government agencies, and because MBO was viewed as simply its creature, the system received a generally chilly reception.

For example, the Department of the Interior had ironically begun an MBO system of its own before OMB required all federal agencies to install systems. But their head start was so short that most workers in the Department of the Interior wrongly saw the system as OMB's project. Thus, despite the excellent technical system for goal setting and monitoring, the system ran into trouble the minute that the top support—from OMB and the president—seemed to weaken. This result left the staff and managers backing the Interior MBO system feeling ambivalent. They felt they were getting the worst of both worlds—the severe disadvantages of being seen as OMB's puppet but not the leverage that real OMB backing would bring. Said one MBO staff person, "I wish OMB were a lot more interested. Then I wouldn't have so much trouble selling the system. I could just say 'send me this report on project progress' and I would get it. Now I have to plead for it, and even then I often don't get it."[10] Yet at the same time he was capable of decrying the OMB link:

We try to avoid referring to our system as MBO. People around this department think of MBO completely as [OMB director] Ash's baby, and so when we ask some bureau people for a document or something, they'll tell us they don't have to cooperate because "them guys are gone." People refuse to give us documents of information to feed the system. They think the system went out with Ash, that it's dead, so they say "Why should we feed a corpse?" We're going to need a lot of support from the new Secretary to overcome this attitude.

What was true with MBO in its very first government tryouts is still true today: No major management system can survive without top support. In later chapters we will examine some ways in which this support can be generated. But although such support is absolutely necessary for a system's success, it is not by itself sufficient. Even with top-level backing, MBO systems can soon falter and die. Let us consider some of the other common causes of failure.

Goal-Setting Problems

Objectives in the MBO system must be set through a process of negotiation between the top manager and subordinates. If either party dominates the goal setting, the system fails.

Managers who are used simply to giving orders sometimes find it easy to continue this pattern under MBO. Often without realizing it, they can turn goal-setting sessions into lectures, without listening to or incorporating suggestions. Such an autocratic approach loses most of the advantages of MBO; the objectives are now quotas. The subordinate managers are not psychologically committed to the objectives because they had no real part in determining them. That is, they do not feel a sense of ownership.[11] For the same reasons, the MBO standards are not perceived as fair and objective when they are used for personnel evaluations.

The top managers also lose a great deal when they determine quotas rather than negotiate because negotiation gives them new information about their organization. Said one participant in the MBO process of the U.S. Forest Service,

> Last year the top of the Forest Service—the Chief and his men—wanted to make reforestation a top priority. But when the regions sent back their proposals for objectives, they all added up to only two-thirds of the acreage that the Chief had in mind. This led to negotiations, and the region people said, "Sure, we can give you that much acreage, if you're willing to give up this and that." And the Chief realized their problems more, and that he had to give something up if he really wanted that reforestation. Under the old system he might have gotten his reforestation, if he had just given an order. But he never would have realized what he was losing through lower-level tradeoffs; this way *he* made the tradeoff decisions.

If many of the advantages are lost when the top manager unilaterally sets the MBO objectives, the same problem arises when the subordinate unilaterally determines them. This problem is less likely to arise naturally;

it is more often the product of various consultants and texts that counsel top managers to allow subordinates to set their own objectives. Doing so, they advise, will cause the lower managers to assume responsibility for their own performance, and they will set standards for themselves even higher than those the top manager would have suggested.

Certainly this result sometimes occurs, particularly in organizations that have a completely nonadversarial relationship between supervisors and subordinates and that deal with highly professional matters. But for the vast majority of public organizations that do not fit these two criteria, total abdication of standard setting to the subordinate is a recipe for disaster. Subordinates may not know what the top of the organization's main objectives for the year are. In that case, no matter how sincerely chosen, their objectives may not be the ones most useful to the organization. In addition, the tendency of employees who feel threatened by the system (as most will) is to choose goals that are very easily achieved.

This balance between subordinate and superior is a precarious one. North Carolina used a statewide management system with many MBO features throughout the 1970s and 1980s. Its manual for supervisors seemed to hop back and forth in attempting to convey the balance necessary in running a management conference. First it seems to emphasize the employee's participation: "Listen. Get the employee to voice his needs, express his opinions before you state yours. Otherwise you may squelch some constructive thinking." But one sentence later, "At the same time, be sure you stay in control at all times." One paragraph later it skips back again: "Be sure that the plan which you are developing includes the ideas of both of you." But finally it comes down on the side of the superior: "Try to resolve any differences and reach a mutual agreement, but remember that the final decisions and approval of the plan are yours."[12]

Although undoubtedly confusing to the managers who read the manual, such ambiguity is understandable. It is difficult to strike a comfortable balance between the objective-setting powers of the supervisor and of the subordinate.

However, if an exact balance is elusive, it is clear that the extremes of quotas on one hand or total employee power on the other hand are disastrous for the objective-setting process. The desired end result is "stretch" objectives—ones that are reachable, but only with an added effort. If too tough, objectives merely demoralize workers. If too easy, they serve no purpose. One city, Phoenix, Arizona, has recognized this difficult balance by having subordinates and superiors set three MBO targets for each objective: one requiring a minimal stretch, one a larger stretch, and one that can be accomplished only by an outstanding employee. Although this system seems to work well in Phoenix, which has had an extensive MBO system for almost twenty years, such an approach is usually too cumbersome for most organizations.

Instead, managers and subordinates must settle on a goal that entails some stretch but not too much; true negotiation is required to provide MBO objectives that both encourage the efforts of the subordinate and give the superior information about potential obstacles. Only genuine negotiation produces a feeling of participation, and thus psychological commitment to the objectives.

Problems Caused by Staff Takeovers

Management texts have long distinguished between *line* and *staff* positions in an organization. The distinction blurs badly at the edges, but the two terms are useful, and we will use them here. *Line managers* are *directly* responsible for the output of an organization; in addition, they have a number of subordinates reporting directly to them. *Staff* personnel have more indirect roles, usually in an advisory or adjunct position. Thus for a social services agency, line managers would oversee the casework. Staff people might be aides to the line managers, holding such positions as legal counsel, data processor, or accountant. (The distinction blurs if an accountant oversees ten other accountants; such a manager is simultaneously both line and staff.)

One of MBO's strengths is that it is a manager-to-manager system, so that those who must accomplish the task have a hand in setting the goals. This advantage dissipates if staff personnel begin to run the system. Because the staff often has more time than the line managers, reporting requirements often slowly increase. In response, managers begin to delegate more and more details of the system to their staff, finally becoming mere onlookers. When this development began in a major federal department, one observer described the process:

> The Secretary would ask [the division head] about a problem, and the division head would turn to the appropriate bureau head who could only answer because he would have one of his MBO staffmen whispering in his ear. Since the Secretary's question was prompted by *his* MBO staff in the first place, it became a pure staff-to-staff system with the managers merely shuffling through their parts, like uninvolved actors under the direction of their staffs. They might as well have been puppets.

Such MBO systems begin to feed on themselves, with MBO staff at one level dealing with MBO staff at the next level. The line managers themselves, the supposed cornerstone of the system, take no real part in it. This process can be reversed, as illustrated by the organization described in the previous quotation.[13] The managers saved their MBO system by a few simple steps.

First, they eliminated almost all staff positions that were exclusively concerned with MBO. For most medium-sized organizations, all MBO-generated work can usually be handled as a small side issue by regular staff. Even for extremely large public organizations, MBO staff should be kept to a minimum: Two or three people whose exclusive duties are MBO should be more than enough for even the largest state agencies; the remainder of the MBO tasks should be handled as part of the ongoing process of management.

Second, the organization battled staff takeover by restricting attendance at the management conferences to supervisor and subordinate. If few (or better, no) staff personnel are allowed at these conferences, line management is strengthened in two ways. First, the conferences are more exclusive, increasing the prestige of both those attending and the system itself. Second, the exclusion of staff from the management conferences forces the line managers to be briefed on the various problems in achieving objectives *ahead of time*. No longer can managers wait until the agency head raises a question during the conference and then turn to their ever-present staff to learn the answer for the first time. They now must be briefed by their staff before they go alone into the conference, so they will not be caught unaware by the questions of the agency director. Thus the managers are forced to become more aware of far more problems within their organizations than previously, and often this knowledge proves useful even when the agency director asks no questions about it.

Problems Caused by "Paper Crushes"

MBO systems can drown in their own paperwork. Sometimes such paper crushes are symptoms of a staff takeover. Certainly the staff is the most likely producer of paper because staff people are used to generating analyses. But line managers are also potential paper generators. When a manager has missed a milestone, his or her natural tendency is to precede the management conference by attaching page after page to the record, illustrating how outside events, or other managers, are to blame.

Supporting documentation can produce an endless paper spiral, with each new page requiring comment or rebuttal, which generates new comments, and so on. MBO is a face-to-face system. A draconian limit on supporting documentation may be necessary to ensure that the system stays off the paper. The New York City Transit Authority strictly enforces a rule that no MBO report can be more than a single sheet of paper.[14] Although some organizations may wish to allow a few more pages, such limits are very useful.

WHY MBO FAILS: MISREPORTING

The Problem of Misreporting

Misreporting is a widespread problem, but one of the easiest to correct. Misreporting (or more colloquially, "cheating") includes subordinates who report work that has not been done and administrators who manipulate data about organizational performance.[15]

Raising the topic of cheating seems to suggest a "Theory X" view of employees as individuals who are looking only for ways to cut corners, for the easy way out. However, once the first manager begins to cheat, other managers have only two choices. They can inform on the cheater, which most are not willing to do, or they can pad their own figures simply to keep up. Thus widespread cheating in management systems is less a reflection on managers (who may be forced to cheat very much against their personal inclination) than it is on the system designers. Moreover the widespread knowledge of uncorrected misreporting breeds cynicism among all managers, destroying much of the aura of legitimacy that any management system needs to function.

Cheating is a symptom of a system that was designed or installed without proper concern for systemic incentives. The problems of the U.S. Postal Service are an excellent example. The Postal Service prided itself on its output-oriented management systems, installed when it became a quasi-private corporation in the 1970s. These systems measured a large number of inputs and outputs and ranked the performance of various units and administrators on the basis of these measurements. These rankings were important for the managers' job tenure and promotion chances. However, headquarters had only a very small unit to check a large number of readings from numerous, highly decentralized regional units. In the third year of the system's operation the inevitable occurred, and a scandal of major proportions arose when top executives of the postal system discovered that many lower-level managers had been falsifying output data: "Sources believe that pressure from postal headquarters has prompted many managers around the country to do the same thing. 'Apparently when it comes to telling a lie or [losing] one's job, many managers have taken to protecting their skins,' said one postal official."[16]

The Postal Service case is not uncommon. In 1985, employees of the Philadelphia office of the Internal Revenue Service responded to high performance objectives for processing tax returns by hiding or destroying returns. They ran at least 7,000 returns through the paper shredder. Other returns were abandoned in the women's rest room, stuffed into drawers, and carted out the door.[17]

Similar problems struck one state when it initiated an MBO system. During the goal-setting stage, some employees would suggest annual performance goals for themselves that had, in fact, been completed even before they were suggested. Few of these cases were ever discovered.[18]

One Solution to Misreporting: Increasing the Sanctions

The Postal Service system provides a clear example of unbalanced incentives. It seems commonsensical to say that if a system (like that of the Postal Service) increases the benefits for cheating on output data, disincentives toward such cheating must simultaneously be installed. Yet this precept is often ignored. There are two primary disincentives for cheating. One is increasing the penalties for misreporting; this is the path eventually taken by the Postal Service. After the cheating had finally been discovered, the postmaster general reacted by increasing the severity of the sanctions (the disincentives):

> I have repeatedly stressed that I expect all managers to strive for productivity improvements. However, I do not in any sense countenance unrealistic productivity goals, supported by little more than exhortations, or artificial data designed to reflect their alleged accomplishments. . . .
>
> But I want to be clearly understood. Nothing less than completely factual reports are acceptable. Henceforth, a manager or employee who intentionally falsifies, attempts to falsify, directs or induces others to falsify WLRS or other management data will be subject to dismissal from the postal service.[19]

Another Solution: Developing Alternative Information Sources

The second approach to increasing the disincentives for cheating is to increase the probability that any misreporting will be discovered.

One of the most important attributes of MBO and most output-based management systems is that the operating unit or the managers report on their own progress toward the goals. Said one author,

> In reporting at every level, hierarchy is conducive to concealment and misrepresentation. Subordinates are asked to transmit information that can be used to evaluate their performance. Their motive for "making it look good," for "playing it safe" is obvious. A study of 52 middle managers (mean age 37) found a correlation of $+.41$ ($p < .01$) between upward work-life mobility and holding back "problem" information from the boss; the men on their way up were prone to restrict information about such issues as lack of authority to meet responsibilities, fights with other units, unforeseen costs, rapid changes in production, scheduling or work flow, fruitless progress reports, constant interruptions, insufficient time or budget to train subor-

dinates, insufficient equipment or supplies, and so on. Restriction of such problem information is motivated by the desire not only to please but also to preserve comfortable routines of work: if the subordinate alerts the boss to pending trouble, the former is apt to find himself on a committee to solve the problem. The aphorism "Never volunteer for anything" is not confined to the Army; it is part of folk wisdom.[20]

Thus subordinate managers are not likely to wish to report bad news, and most upper-level management staffs are too small to monitor the operating units closely. This difficulty appears at every level of government. In business, such difficulties are much less important: Tangible outputs are generally involved, falsification of output records generally involves cheating the company, and there are overlapping systems of inspection. But there are few such systemic safeguards in government agencies, which are often self-contained and which often produce slippery social outputs.

Formal Techniques for Securing Alternative Information Sources. Sometimes this problem can be surmounted through a formal, parallel reporting system that taps different sources and thus serves as a double check. This can be done in many ways. Some agencies use "internal audits," which are unannounced checks conducted by a person or unit that is independent of the reporting unit. A variation—used for record-keeping agencies such as the Social Security Administration or the Internal Revenue Service—is an audit system that randomly selects a set percentage of transactions (perhaps 3 percent) for a double check each day. Another formal technique is to require parallel reporting sources. For example, some social agencies require both the client and the agency employee to submit a report on services rendered; if the reports do not match, a check is instigated.

Informal Techniques for Securing Alternative Information Sources. In dealing with MBO, which is project oriented and therefore changes its output focus from year to year, it is sometimes more difficult to set up formal double-check techniques than it is for other management systems that track the same data year after year. Accordingly, *informal* mechanisms of double-checking can be used to check the MBO project data—phone calls to involved sites, asking for copies of field reports, and so on. Usually these informal mechanisms are done with the full knowledge of both superior and subordinate.

A less common approach was employed by the staff overseeing the MBO system in a large federal department. The seven-person MBO staff attached to the secretary's office sometimes used spot checks on particular details to check the overall accuracy of the MBO reports. However, they primarily utilized contacts "down in the ranks" who would blow the whistle on any attempt to cover up difficulties that particular programs encountered. Finding and cultivating these contacts was considered at least as important as the technical aspects of their job. Said one member of the secretarial MBO staff,

> Cultivating these sources is extremely important. It's the most vulnerable part of the system because without this information the whole MBO system wouldn't work. It's a personality thing; I'd say 50 to 60% of this job is interpersonal skills.
>
> We have to have independent information so that the bureau head can't get in there and snow us.

Often the informants are untraceable, but sometimes the use of these sources poses the espionage-type problem of "blowing their cover."

> We have to be careful in using what we get from the ranks, because once the bureau head realizes what's going on he'll reach down and silence that guy. Sometimes that leaves us with a very difficult problem—whether to bring up a matter which we know will expose a guy, or let it go and save that source for next month or next year.

Despite such dangers, sources would inform fairly regularly. Part of the reason was that they were talking to young, friendly staff aides, not to intimidating older officials. Another more compelling reason was suggested by a staff person: The informants responded to a chance to get their problems heard at the top. "Sometimes people in the ranks know how to get something done but just can't get through to their bosses. So they give it to us and the Secretary can bring it up with him."

It is important to note that this "secret" double-checking (which may sometimes raise ethical questions) can be useful, but it is not the usual approach. Most parallel reporting systems are formal and institutionalized.

Maintaining the Incentive Balance: Other Options

Of course no management system can be completely free of misreporting, but public management systems are particularly susceptible to cheating because they often lack the systemic balances necessary to discourage it. In maintaining these balances, it is not necessary to follow the Postal Service example by having strong penalties (such as dismissal) or a high likelihood of discovery (as with the MBO system just discussed). Instead, the system builders can choose to keep both the rewards and the punishments very modest. This has been the path taken by the federal productivity measurement effort, an ongoing effort for the past twenty years to track the overall efficiency of the federal government. The team directing the effort has little clout and no means of punishing those who file false data reports. The only way to keep the data accurate, then, is to make the rewards for intentional falsification approach zero. Thus the federal effort stresses keeping all productivity data unattributed so no agency's poor record will become publicly known; it also emphasizes that OMB will not use the data in budget decisions. This balance is so important to the system that even important legislators could not break it. Said one productivity reporting official,

> A number of agencies fear that the data will be used in making budgetary decisions. They also fear that the rate of productivity improvement could be cited on the Hill to justify manpower cuts.
>
> A while back we had a request from [a powerful senator] for our figures. We put him off, suggesting he could get it from the particular agencies. And so far as we know, he did.

Of course a system that keeps its sanctions low to ensure accuracy is not a very strong management system. Positive and negative sanctions—especially rewards for performance—are an important way to affect workers' behavior, one of the major goals of a management system. Moreover, making decisions based on system data—the other use of management systems—will also probably shift budget shares and other rewards. Thus keeping uses of the data low to ensure their accuracy may sometimes be necessary, but it leaves the system as only a curiousity, a source of subsidiary data that is not directly employed. This relationship between the use of a management information system and the sanctions for cheating is graphically summarized in Figure 3-3. As indicated, robust systems with real impact will of course register "high" in the use of data, which will require "high" safeguards against cheating.

Incentives are most likely to get out of balance when a system is new, or even more likely, when an existing system changes functions. Thus a system can work without substantial problems for many years as an auxiliary information source, with both use and quality-assurance systems putting it in the low/low cell of Figure 3-3. When a new management team takes office and tries to increase organizational performance, it will often begin to rely heavily on the existing system for important decisions. Yet the new team often neglects to increase the system's double-checking arrangements and its sanctions for misreporting to bring them into balance with the new, higher rewards. Such an adjustment must be made in order to be fair to the overwhelming majority of employees who are honest and do not want to be forced into misreporting by an unbalanced system.

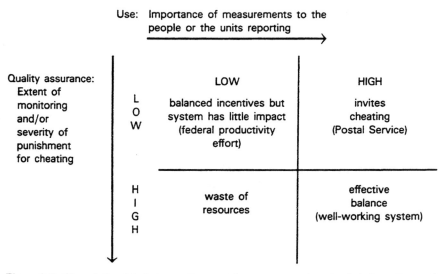

Figure 3–3. The relationship between the use of a management system's information and the system's sanctions and/or safeguards for misreporting.

WHY MBO FAILS: GOAL DISPLACEMENT

Goal Displacement Caused by the Absence of Management Systems

As the name suggests, *goal displacement* occurs when an organization or its members begin to pursue goals other than the "proper" organizational ones. The problem of goal displacement is not confined to management systems; in fact it afflicts organizations without such systems in a far worse form. For example, a small town's public library may be open only during the day because its employees prefer these hours, despite the fact that this schedule makes it far more difficult for the public to use the library. This is a clear example of goal displacement; the organization is being run as if the goal were the comfort of the employees rather than the benefit of the public.

Public administration literature is rife with stories of workers who are the most productive members of their organization but are punished or fired because they broke some minor procedural rule. Again, this is goal displacement: The top administrators have lost sight of what the organization was designed to do. In the public sector, the most common and pernicious form of goal displacement takes place when processes become the new goal. Thus an organization prides itself on staying within its budget, the promptness of its employees, or the neatness of its reports, when the real work of the organization is neglected.[21]

MBO and all other forms of output-oriented management systems can make a major contribution toward preventing this form of goal displacement. As we have considered at some length, MBO focuses attention on outputs and away from processes; it forces organizational members to ask what they are really accomplishing. Like all output-oriented management systems, MBO is designed to increase what sociologists call *goal congruence,* that is, more closely aligning the personal goals of the organizational members with the goals of the organization as a whole. If there is goal congruence, an individual who is pursuing his or her own personal goals in the workplace advances the organization's goals at the same time. Thus these systems are some of the most important and most effective ways of fighting displacement.

All the more ironic, then, that output-oriented management systems cause their own forms of goal displacement. This result is very similar to developments in medicine, where each improvement in health care carries its own bad side effects. We do not reject the improvements for these reasons, however; the test is whether the result of the new treatment, including its bad side effects, is better than the previous state of affairs. In fact, some theorists have suggested that this process is how we progress; we never solve problems completely, but we solve old problems by techniques that bring new, smaller problems as side effects; we then work on solving those problems, which begins the process again.

Goal Displacement Caused by Management Systems

Many output-oriented management systems create goal displacement because they provide incentives for the workers in an organization to deliver the *measured* output or output attributes while neglecting the unmeasured ones that are also important.

If a government agency's mission is job placement, for example, and success is measured by the number of applicants *interviewed,* the incentive is for the agency's workers to interview the applicants rapidly, with little follow-up effort. If the management system instead measures success by the number of applicants *placed,* the incentive is to concentrate on applicants who have the most training or experience (and thus are the most easily placed) even though these may need the help least.[22] In both cases, goal displacement has occurred.

The problem is difficult to escape. In a clerical operation, if the management system measures only the number of forms processed, the incentive is to process forms rapidly, with little regard for accuracy. If instead accuracy is the only attribute measured, speed may fall to extremely low levels as each form is checked over and over. Even if both speed and accuracy are measured, other output attributes—outreach or politeness to clients—are likely to be sacrificed so that all efforts can be concentrated on the measured attributes.

A newspaper dispatch from the Midlands of England reports on an unusual form of the same problem:

> Complaints from passengers wishing to use the Bagnall to Greenfields bus service that "the drivers were speeding past queues of up to 30 people with a smile and a wave of a hand" have been met by a statement pointing out that "it is impossible for the drivers to keep their timetable if they have to stop for passengers."[23]

If a system measures "routes on schedule" rather than "passenger miles," such a result is inevitable. The problem of goal displacement is summed up in the aphorism "you get what you measure."

It is important to note again, however, that this is in some ways a more welcome problem than the type of goal displacement that afflicts organizations without output-oriented management systems. At least the organization's attention and efforts are directed to outputs, not processes, and the measurements that accompany such systems aid in discovering and combating displacement when it does occur.

The previous examples illustrate the fact that there are real differences between *goal displacement* and *misreporting,* even though the two terms are sometimes confused. In misreporting, the reported performance does not occur—someone does not tell the truth. In goal displacement, the reported performance is true—it is just too narrow to be what is really needed.

Unchecked goal displacement can destroy a management system. It provides perverse incentives to neglect important outputs and distorts managerial information. Consequently the system loses all credibility with both workers and managers.

Three Solutions to Goal Displacement

There are three partial solutions to the problem of goal displacement: multiple measures, supplementary information, and "intermediate" measures.

Using Multiple Measures.   One partial solution is the use of multiple output measures.[24] Because monitoring a single type of organizational output or attribute will lead employees to neglect others, it is generally helpful to monitor two or more related attributes to avoid imbalance. These related attributes, each creating incentives that balance the incentives of the other, are "paired attributes." At the broadest level, for example, quantity/quality are paired attributes; an output-based system that did not structure its incentives for both would find that emphasis on one creates a dysfunctional neglect of the other.

Determining the paired attribute for any given goal category is both an intuitive and an analytic exercise, the correct choice varying with the item produced. The "twin" to any one output category is the attribute or output that is most likely to be neglected by workers who pursue that category. For example, an objective that called for cutting application process time by one-third would seemingly provide incentives for hastiness and sloppiness. Therefore it could be balanced by an objective that called for lowering (or maintaining) the existing error rate in application processing. Many possible second objectives would not provide such a balance. The first objective, concerning time, would not be balanced, for example, by a second objective calling for an outreach program to attract more applications.

Choosing the categories of measurement in order to provide the correct incentives is situation specific, and more often art than science. But it nonetheless seems true that management systems whose designers have at least recognized (and attempted to meet) the problems of unbalanced goal incentives are more likely to succeed than those whose designers have not.

Basing Rewards on Nonsystem Information. One of the reasons employees pursue measured outputs while neglecting all other outputs is that often rewards—for example, salary increases or budget increases—are tied only to the measured outputs. Thus a second way of avoiding system-produced goal displacement is to avoid using the system as the *only* source of information for budgets, promotions, or personnel evaluations. Being the only source clearly overloads the system because it increases the incentives for workers to focus only on those outputs that are measured; it possibly increases the incentives to misreport as well.

Not every bit of routine work can (or should) be covered by an objective, and yet there must be an incentive for not totally neglecting such routine tasks. There should be other sources of information that are considered for all decisions, and the information from the MBO system should be considered in light of these sources. In other words, achievements in the MBO system should be subject to a "reasonable person" approach.

Under a "reasonable man" approach (a term borrowed from law),[25] both the subordinate and superior agree that not everything can be specified in the "contract" that an MBO goal represents. Therefore they agree that the contract implies responsibility for *all* output that a "reasonable person" would assume a given goal to entail. Thus if an MBO objective called for "cutting the error rate for medical benefit applications by 50 percent," the objective would not be considered to have been achieved if the rate were indeed cut in half but the processing time for each application tripled.

This reasonable person approach, then, removes the incentive for employees to neglect all unmeasured goal categories just to achieve the measured ones. If slippage in routine, unmeasured categories is unreasonable, and if it becomes known to the monitoring officials, employees will gain no credit for achieving the narrow measured goal. However slippage in unmeasured categories is harder for monitoring officials to detect than slippage in measured categories, where the monitoring system automatically registers it. Thus there are two steps to the reasonable person approach. The monitoring official must seek out information that is not covered in the output system to supplement information that is. Second, he or she then holds the subordinates responsible for maintaining previous levels of performance in these nonmeasured areas, if a reasonable person would expect such maintenance to be implicit in the objectives.[26]

To do these two things, the monitoring official must have a flexible attitude toward the system, not depending on it to the exclusion of all other information; moreover, the official must be physically proximate to the organization in order to gain some of the supplementary information needed through direct observation and the rest through informal contacts. (This topic will recur in later chapters, which discuss ways of tying management systems to budgets and to merit pay and bonuses.)

Using "Intermediate" Measures.   A third approach to lessening goal displacement caused by management systems is to use "intermediate" output measures that come closer to the "ultimate" goals of the organization. However this approach is more applicable to other output-oriented systems, and so we will consider it in greater detail in Chapter Five, which concerns performance monitoring systems.

BUSINESS AND MBO

As are all management systems, MBO is rooted in the business world. It began there, and its principles were developed there. It is useful, then, to review the ways it must change in moving to the public sector.

The lack of a profit motive and other concrete output measures greatly handicaps the public sector MBO system. Without the advantages of a profit motive based on pricing, the business world would have the same problems of choosing output measures and the resulting displacement that plague government. This problem is exemplified by the Soviet Union. Because prices in the USSR are not set by a market, it has traditionally run its whole economy the way the United States runs its government agencies. (This certainly gives a clue to the USSR's economic problems.) Thus a Soviet factory that produces window glass had a typical experience:

When windowglass output was measured in tons, it was advantageous for the enterprise to make glass extra-thick—which meant saving on processing and handling. But from the point of view of the national economy, of course, this meant a reduction in the area that could be covered with a given tonnage of glass. When the measure of output was redefined in areal terms, i.e., square meters of glass produced, the enterprise found it advantageous to make glass extra-thin. The enterprise's effort to do what seemed advantageous to itself meant a waste of resources for the economy as a whole—a Soviet discussion of the problem reported that one-fourth of all glass arriving at construction sites was broken, which the author blamed on the excessive thinness of the glass.[27]

One way the USSR could mitigate, if not solve, such problems is by moving to a straight market system. If the glass factory were operating in a market, its poor products—whatever the reason for their inferiority—would not be bought. Thus just one figure, indicating profit or loss, would represent the public's assessment of a far larger number of output standards—including thickness, esthetic appeal, and quality—than any quota system could hope to match.

The business world also has other advantages. It is easier to link objectives from level to level in a business organization because of shared, often very concrete measures. It is easier to prevent misreporting because, as discussed, in business the measures are more tangible, the penalties higher (embezzlement is often involved), and alternative information sources more accessible. Little wonder that businesspeople who try to transplant MBO without adaptation to government are rarely successful.

In the next chapter we will examine some of the political effects of MBO and their impact on the success of the system.

SUMMARY

Management by objectives (MBO) is the most influential and widespread public management system. It is also extremely simple: A top manager and his or her subordinate agree on annual objectives as well as substeps (termed *milestones*) leading to these objectives; they then meet regularly to monitor and discuss progress toward these goals.

Despite its simplicity, a well-working MBO system can greatly improve managerial efficiency. Most importantly, it focuses attention on outputs. In addition, it clarifies communication in both directions, makes planning an integral part of management, establishes accountability, and makes personnel evaluations less subjective.

Many MBO systems fail in their first incarnations. Despite their simplicity, they are vulnerable to goal-setting difficulties, staff takeovers, and stifling paperwork. Top managers who are alert in anticipating these problems can usually overcome them, however. In addition, all management systems—including MBO—must battle goal displacement and misreporting.

Goal displacement is the process by which agency workers pursue goals other than the desired organizational ones. In agencies that have no output-oriented management system, goal displacement often takes the form of pursuing personal goals or pursuing procedural rules as ends in themselves. Because an output-oriented management system shifts the workers' focus (and the incentives) to outputs, it greatly diminishes these forms of goal displacement. But ironically, it creates its own form of displacement: Workers often pursue the measured attributes or outputs to the neglect of the overall picture. In other words, the system can encourage a type of tunnel vision, in which the workers seem to focus only on measured outputs and ignore all others. There are several ways to combat this problem. Multiple measures, chosen to balance incentives, should always be used. It is also useful to base rewards only *partially* on the system's information. Such approaches can at least alleviate the (never quite curable) problem of system-induced goal displacement.

Like goal displacement, misreporting plagues all output-oriented management systems. Top managers who carefully balance any incentives to cheat with counterincentives, such as verification procedures and publicized sanctions for misreporting, can virtually eliminate this problem.

REVIEW QUESTIONS

1. What are the five components of an MBO system?
2. What types of goal displacement does MBO help? What type does it cause? Give examples for two types of programs.
3. What approaches can be taken to fight MBO-produced goal displacement? Why are they effective?
4. Discuss this statement: A manager who cheats in reporting output data is more often a victim than a culprit.
5. What considerations should determine whether a manager formally links the goals at each level of an organization?
6. Why is it usually preferable for MBO milestones to be stated in terms of results rather than processes? When is this not true?
7. What considerations should determine how often management conferences are held?
8. Staff people often have more discretion over their time than line managers; why, therefore, should they not handle most of the MBO procedural matters?

9. Is establishing accountability more important in government than in private management?
10. In what ways can MBO improve a personnel evaluation system?
11. What are the common problems in the MBO goal-setting stage? How are they solved?
12. What are the advantages of a well-working MBO system?
13. Choose a public program or organization with which you are familiar, and set up an MBO plan with eight or ten milestones. Does the plan have clear achievement points? Is it primarily focused on outputs rather than processes? What difficulties arise in setting up such a plan?

SUGGESTED FURTHER READING

PETER DRUCKER. *Managing for Results.* New York: Harper & Row, 1964. An early and very influential book on MBO.

DALE D. McCONKEY. *Management by Results.* Reading, MA: Addison-Wesley, 1983. A guide to MBO and its installation in both public and private sectors.

PAUL MALI. *MBO Updated.* New York: John Wiley, 1986. At over 800 pages, more useful as a reference manual than an introduction, but still helpful. Chapter 18 has a number of useful case studies, including ones from government.

JOSEPH C. SANTORA. *Management by Objectives: A Selected Periodical Guide* Monticello, IL: Vance Bibliographies, 1982.

Case 3–1

Robert Marshall has just been tapped by the governor to head the state department of Children's Services. The department has three major divisions: health care, human services, and education.

Marshall was previously chief executive officer of Tabby Shoes, a firm that grosses $100 million annually. He used an MBO system successfully at Tabby's and expects to do the same now.

His first goal-setting conference, however, was not a success. He met with the head of the human services division, Steve Little. Little is a career manager in his mid-fifties, admired by his co-workers for his fierce dedication to his division. Even his admirers admitted, however, that his management style was a little weak.

Little came to the conference clearly unhappy. "I received your memo asking me to think about quantitative objectives for the coming year," he said, "and I was at the management retreat two weeks ago when you explained how this was not an attempt to regiment us or tell us what to do. But it's still nonsense. Maybe quantitative goals make sense for a shoe company. But we're dealing with people—children—here, not numbers. And myself and the people in our division are experts. We've dealt with this area all our lives. With all due respect, I think you should emphasize the role that you have expertise in—budgeting and all—and let us do our work without political interference."

Marshall tried to reassure Little. "I have no intention of interfering with your people, Steve. But I think it helps clarify your thoughts as well as mine to know where we'd like to go for the coming year."

Marshall met with Little for one-half hour and suggested that they could work together on setting objectives. However, Little arrived at the next management conference with a long face and no suggestions of his own. He found fault with any suggestions made by Marshall, and the session broke up without progress.

During the next few weeks Marshall got several calls from influential legislators. All followed the same pattern of noting that they had heard "reports of political interference" in the children's agency, and although they were sure that the reports were unfounded, they were also sure Marshall would want to know.

Little is a civil service employee and would be difficult to fire or demote. Marshall has the strong backing of the governor, but doesn't want to hurt him politically. On the other hand, Marshall doesn't want to serve four years as a figurehead in the department. He ponders his next move.

1. Has Marshall done anything wrong until now?
2. What additional information should Marshall gather?
3. What should be his next course of action?

Case 3–2

Marsha Krukow is a career civil servant and head of the county social services department, which serves the area's low-income citizens. The department has eight branches scattered over a large county, with a total of 217 employees.

In her seven years as head of the department, Krukow has prided herself on her management system. The system gathers information for each branch office on the number of applications evaluated, the number of clients served, error rates, and several other measures. Krukow has used these figures in rating the performances of her managers, for promotion and merit money, as well as for decision making about staffing levels and office locations.

Lately Krukow has begun to hear disturbing rumors. Kathy Tennello, who is office manager of the largest county social services office, has had an outstanding record in her three years as director. Her office has consistently processed more forms with fewer employees than the others, and the error rate has been excellent. Accordingly Tennello had received several large merit raises. It had seemed strange to Krukow that Tennello's office had so many more applications than other offices, but she had not followed up.

Tennello, says the rumors, has been padding her figures by adding fictional "ineligible" applications, which (because they are listed as rejected) are not caught or double-checked elsewhere in the system.

Krukow has sent out two memos in her seven years, warning that "serious measures will be taken" if the management reports are falsified. But now that she is faced with her first real case of cheating, she is inclined not to pursue it further. "If I investigate and find the rumors are right," she thinks, "I'll undoubtedly look bad in the newspapers, I'll bring a scandal on the department, and I may have a long court fight on my hands if Tennello fights a suspension or dismissal. Besides, I don't want to lose Tennello, who in all other ways is a model manager."

Krukow decides to reissue a new, stronger memo about punishment for cheating and to call Tennello and drop hints about "unusual" data discrepancies. Krukow feels virtually certain that after these measures Tennello will no longer falsify data.

Two weeks later she hears rumors that a second office manager has been falsifying data for the last six months. The manager is probably the weakest one in the system.

1. Did Krukow handle the Tennello situation correctly?
2. What should she do about the new rumors?
3. What should she do to avoid future similar problems in this area?

ENDNOTES

1. *The Practice of Management* (New York: Harper & Row, 1954); Drucker further developed the concepts in *Managing for Results* (New York: Harper & Row, 1964).

There is a sizable handful of works that consider government MBO empirically. The first group was written in the excitement of the first introduction of MBO. Among them are Rodney H. Brady, "MBO Goes to Work in the Public Sector," *Harvard Business Review*, 51-2 (March/April 1973), 65–74; Frederic V. Malek, *Washington's Hidden Tragedy: The Failure to Make Government Work* (New York: Free Press, 1978); Richard Rose, *Managing Presidential Objectives* (New York: Free Press, 1976).

In the 1980s, there were good descriptions of Charlotte's MBO program (pp. 111–17) and Dayton's hybrid MBO system (pp. 44–51) in Paul D. Epstein, *Using Performance Measurement in Local Government* (New York: Van Nostrand Reinhold, 1984). An MBO system within the federal Department of Health and Human Services is described and analyzed in Michael E. Fishman, "Implementing Results-Oriented Management in a Large Federal Agency," in Joseph S. Wholey, ed., *Organizational Excellence* (Lexington, MA: Lexington Books, 1987); several local government MBO systems are portrayed in Paul Mali, *MBO Updated* (New York: John Wiley, 1986), pp. 762–87.

Two more prescriptive treatments of governmental MBO are George L. Morrisey, *Management by Objectives and Results in the Public Sector* (Reading, MA: Addison-Wesley, 1976); and Dale D. McConkey, *Management by Results* (New York: Amacom, 1983), which covers both sectors.

2. The 41 percent figure is from a 1976 national survey. The figure then rose to 59 percent in 1984 and finally 62 percent in 1988. Gregory Streib and Theodore H. Poister, "Established and Emerging Management Tools: A 12-Year Perspective," *The Municipal Yearbook 1989* (Washington, DC: International City Managers Association, 1989), pp. 45–54. In all surveys, most of those using MBO were pleased with it.

3. North Carolina Department of Corrections, 1985, internal memo.

4. Some works, such as that by Elkin and Molitor, go a step further and indicate that performance indicators must always be ratios. See Robert Elkin and Mark Molitor, *Management Indicators in Nonprofit Organizations* (Baltimore: Peat Marwick, 1984), p. 1.

5. These advantages are noted in most of the works cited in note 1. It seems noncontroversial to say that well-working MBO systems produce these benefits, but an empirical question would be: How often do they work well? The most complete review of empirical studies focusing on MBO alone was published in 1981: Jack N. Kondrasuk, "Studies in MBO Effectiveness," *Academy of Management Review,* 6, no. 3 (July 1981) 419–30. His review of 185 studies concluded that MBO was more likely to succeed in the private sector than in the public sector and in the short term rather than in the long term. (The later part of this chapter discusses the likely causes of these findings.) He concludes that the evidence supports a "contingency" approach to MBO: It works in some situations, but not all, and the determinants of success are unclear. See note 11 for other empirical evidence.

6. Quoted in Robert Sherrill, "The Hatchetman and the Hatchetmyth,"

Potomac (Sunday supplement to the *Washington Post*), February 6, 1972, pp. 13, 26. Cited in Brady, "MBO Goes to Work."

7. For example, it is discussed in Morrisey, *Management by Objectives.* The discussion does not draw the same conclusion as I do, however. The linking-pin concept of management (without regard to MBO) was initially developed in Rensis Likert, *New Patterns of Management* (New York: McGraw-Hill, 1961), pp. 113–15, 181–87.

   A good illustration of a linking-pin approach to goal setting in the Commerce Department is Katherine M. Bulow, "Agency Administration: Cleaning Up the Government Attic," *The Bureaucrat,* Winter 1985–86, pp. 47–51.

8. Presidential MBO is profiled in Rose, *Managing Presidential Objectives.*

9. Paul Blustein, "Administration by Bush: Management by Objective," *Washington Post,* April 14, 1989, p. A25.

10. Interview with manager, U.S. Forest Service, 1975. I interviewed more than forty people involved in federal management systems, particularly MBO. The interviews ranged in duration from fifteen minutes to five hours. Most took place in 1975–76, although follow-up interviews were conducted in 1978 and late 1983. Unless noted, all future quotes in this chapter are from these interviews; respondents were promised anonymity.

11. The question of the effect of participation on goal acceptance and later on employee production is a controversial one. Probably the most complete survey of all existing empirical studies is John L. Cotton et al. "Employee Participation: Diverse Forms and Different Outcomes," *Academy of Management Review,* January 1988, pp. 8–22. The authors find that particular types of participation—long term and concerning important issues—do increase employee production as well as (less controversially) satisfaction.

   Experimentation on the subject has shown fewer positive results for participation, although such experiments are problematic because they have two substantial flaws. First, they are often done with very simple tasks (assembling a model, for example) that do not clearly relate to the generally much more diffuse tasks of government. Second, they focus almost entirely on whether the management approaches raise employee production. But higher employee production is not the main reason for using MBO. Perhaps for a simple assembly task on a factory floor, increased production is most important. But for most government tasks, and especially those of middle managers (where MBO is used most), it is more important to direct effort toward one direction rather than another and to speed up communication of important new information between employees and subordinates. MBO does these things.

However, because it is interesting, let us briefly review the experimental findings on two major issues: First, compared to non-goal-setting approaches, do MBO-type approaches raise employee production? Yes, generally by a very substantial amount. Second, what particular aspects of MBO cause this increase in production? More specifically, which of these three components cause it: the setting of goals, the participation, or the feedback?

Generally, the experimenters have found that production is definitely enhanced by two of the three things: goal setting and feedback. Setting goals, preferably setting relatively difficult goals, is very important. No matter how goals are set, as long as they are accepted as legitimate, they enlist increased effort. Moreover, experimenters have found that frequent feedback is very important. People do better when they know that they will be talking to others about their progress in the future.

The most controversial issue is whether the third component, participation, adds anything to the goal setting and feedback. The tentative answer is sometimes, in some ways. Generally, if the employer "sells" the goal to the employee, and the employee accepts the goal as legitimate, employees will reach the same level of production whether or not the employee participates. But these are two important conditions. Often the best way for the employer to "sell" the goal and for the employee to accept it as legitimate is participation.

Gary P. Latham wrote many articles in the 1980s about experiments that indicated that participation was not important to increased production. See, for example, Gary P. Latham and T. P. Steele, "The Motivational Effect of Participation Vs. Goal Setting on Performance," *Academy of Management Journal,* (September 1983), pp. 406–17. Miriam Erez wrote many articles indicating that it was important. See, for example, Miriam Erez and R. Arad, "Participative Goal Setting: Social, Motivational and Cognitive Factors," *Journal of Applied Psychology,* 71 (1986), 591–97. Latham and Erez resolved their differences and reached the consensus reported above by a series of joint experiments, summarized in Edwin A. Locke, Gary P. Latham, and Miriam Erez, "The Determinants of Goal Commitment," *Academy of Management Journal,* January 1988, pp. 23–39.

It is important at this point to repeat the point made earlier: Experiments indicate that MBO-type approaches (especially goal setting and feedback) clearly increase employee production, although increasing production is just one small part of the gains. Moreover,

MBO's emphasis on participation is an important means to some of the other MBO gains, such as increased communication and greater flexibility.

12. Department of Administration, State of North Carolina, *Work Planning Performance Review: Supervisor's Manual* (Raleigh: North Carolina Department of Administration, 1978), p. 11.

13. The organization was the Public Health Service (PHS).

14. Mali, *MBO Updated,* p. 767.

15. This subsection on misreporting draws heavily from my article "Unbalanced Incentives in Government Productivity Systems: Misreporting as a Case in Point," *Public Productivity Review,* March 1983.

16. Bob Williams, "Cheaters Facing Firing," *Federal Times,* December 11, 1974, p. 3.

17. L. A. Times News Service, "Backlog Plagues IRS Center Using New Computer," in (Raleigh) *News and Observer,* April 7, 1985, p. 30A.

18. Personal interviews with managers, North Carolina Department of Human Resources.

19. Williams, "Cheaters Facing Firing."

20. Harold L. Wilensky, *Organizational Intelligence* (New York: Basic Books, 1967), p. 43. The quoted study is from W. Read, "Factors Affecting Upward Communication at Middle Management Levels in Industrial Organizations," unpublished dissertation, University of Michigan, 1959.

21. Goal displacement was first analyzed extensively by Robert K. Merton, for example, Robert K. Merton, *Social Theory and Social Structure,* rev. ed. (Glencoe, IL: Free Press, 1957), pp. 199ff.

A typical example of goal displacement: The Labor Department of one state refused to grant an operating permit to a McDonald's restaurant because it had no ramp to aid handicapped people trying to enter the basement. The permit was withheld over the manager's protest that there was no reason for customers—whether handicapped or not—to enter the basement. George W. Downs and Patrick D. Larkey, *The Search for Government Efficiency* (New York: Random House, 1986), p. 1. Designers of management systems would hope to focus organizational employees' attention away from pure process ("a ramp is always needed") toward actual outputs ("how many handicapped people have been aided this month"), but as will be noted, systems do not always solve displacement problems.

22. This example is adapted from one of the earliest and most influential studies of government goal displacement: Peter M. Blau, *The Dynamics of Bureaucracy* (Chicago: University of Chicago, 1955; rev. ed. 1963).

23. Quoted in Patrick Ryan, "Get Rid of the People, and the System Runs Fine," *Smithsonian Magazine,* September 1977, p. 140.

24. Multiple measures are a common prescription for goal displacement. They are among the solutions discussed in John G. Tabor, "The Role of the Accountant in Detecting Information Abuse in Social Program Evaluation," in Thomas D. Cook, ed., *Evaluation Studies Review Annual 3* (Beverly Hills, CA: Sage Publications, 1978).

25. The term is used as an aid to interpretation in contract law, among other legal uses.

26. The adoption of reasonable person approaches is an attempt to avoid the "rigidity cycle" first identified by Anthony Downs: An organization makes a series of rules (or measures); employees find loopholes and uncovered areas of which they take advantage; the organization in response makes yet more detailed rules or measures, in the impossible hope of covering everything. The result is a rule-bound, rigidified organization with understandably alienated employees. Anthony Downs, *Inside Bureaucracy* (Boston: Little, Brown, 1967), p. 160.

27. Robert W. Campbell, *The Soviet-type Economies* (Boston: Houghton Mifflin, 1974), pp. 48–49.

Similarly, because the measure for Soviet construction agencies is "major projects begun," the Soviet Union is dotted with large construction projects that were underway but not finished for twenty years or more. Daniel Ford, "Rebirth of a Nation," *The New Yorker,* March 28, 1988, p. 64.

chapter four

Political Effects of MBO

INTRODUCTION

Politics is defined as "who gets what."[1] Thus any conflict over limited resources is a political conflict. Management systems affect "who gets what" both internally and externally.

Internally, management systems move power *within* the bureaucracy. (We will use the term *bureaucracy* throughout this book as it is usually used in public administration—as denoting any large organization. Although in everyday speech the term carries a pejorative connotation, it does not do so in public administration or in the social sciences. Thus we can speak without irony of "an extremely efficient bureaucracy.")

Externally, management systems can aid some outside groups or clients at the expense of others. For example, sometimes systems generate information about which programs are more efficient and effective, and public release of this information can decrease the political strength of the weaker programs—and their client groups.

All management systems have such political effects. This chapter focuses on those of MBO, particularly internal political effects. The political impact of MBO is a matter of some controversy. Landau and Stout, for example, strongly condemn such systems for centralizing the organization through "rigid control modes."[2] Jun, on the other hand, sees well-working MBO systems as devices for decentralization and the implementation of Theory Y.[3] However, much of this seeming disagreement about whether MBO centralizes or decentralizes power stems from not specifying what types of organizations are being discussed. MBO often has very different internal political effects on small agencies than it does on large, civil-service-oriented ones.

This chapter begins by focusing on internal politics—how does the implementation of MBO change the power configurations within an agency? After looking at smaller organizations, we will use a case study of a large federal department to illustrate the discussion of larger organizations. But the theses of this chapter are not specific to the cases used as illustrations. MBO will cause similar power shifts in all large, civil-service-oriented government organizations, whether they are local, state, or federal. We then discuss whether such common power shifts are good. Finally, the case study is used to illustrate some important points about the implementation of management systems in all government bureaucracies.

MBO'S INTERNAL POLITICAL EFFECTS IN SMALL AGENCIES

Of the numerous agency characteristics that can affect the internal political impact of MBO, probably the two most important are the agency's size and its civil service patterns.

At the local government level, most agencies are relatively small, and the civil service systems are weak or at least flexible. Because of these characteristics, top officials can usually control their agencies if they really want to.[4] In such cases, the political effects of MBO's installation will depend entirely on the management style of the agency heads. MBO involves a partial sharing of power between subordinate and superior in the goal-setting and goal-tracking stages. Thus if the agency heads are already participative managers, MBO will produce few internal power changes. If the local agency heads are autocratic, a well-working MBO system will often move power down; subordinates can use MBO's goal-setting and goal-tracking negotiations to have a say in the agency's plans and operations for the first time.

Looking at these types of agencies, then, we can say that MBO is often a decentralizing device. But its impact is often much more dramatic in large departments or agencies such as those in the federal government or in the largest states; we will examine them next.

MBO'S INTERNAL POLITICAL EFFECTS
IN LARGE GOVERNMENT AGENCIES

The Independence of Bureaus

The largest federal and state departments are often so large that the department heads cannot control their organization without management systems. Moreover, such agencies are often characterized by extremely strong civil service systems, which all but preclude elected officials (presidents or governors) from installing many of their own people. Thus the politically appointed department head does not have direct control over most of his or her subordinates because it is very difficult to hire, fire, or promote them.[5] It is in such cases that the internal political effects of MBO are most dramatic and important.

The subunits of these large departments are often called *bureaus*, and are often controlled by career civil servants. Although the bureaus should be responsive to their superior, the politically appointed department secretary, frequently they are not.[6] One reason for this is that in many large federal and state departments, top bureau and agency administrators have far more power than the departmental secretaries to whom they are nominally subordinate. Herbert Kaufman has assembled a number of testimonies to this relative independence:

> Francis E. Rourke, a leading student of bureaucratic power in America, said in 1969, "It is possible for an administrative agency to establish a position of virtually complete autonomy within the executive branch." Another authority, when studying the U.S. Forest Service, in 1975 took it for granted that "to some degree, of course, all large bureaus, particularly those with highly specialized missions, enjoy considerable autonomy from the departments of which they are part." Harold Seidman, long a high officer in the old Bureau of the Budget, noted in his 1980 analysis of the government, "Without the loyalty, or at least neutrality of their principal bureau chiefs, [secretaries] can be little more than highly ornamental figureheads." Or as one commentator on the transition to Ronald Reagan put it, "Watch the bureaus, not the cabinet. . . . The new administration's real tone will be determined less by those at the top than by the second line."[7]

This pattern holds for most large federal departments. In the Defense Department, for example, the individual service components—Army, Navy, and Air Force—have long had more power than the head of the department. When in the latter part of the Carter administration a new under-secretary was appointed to gain some control, he failed and resigned within nine months. One news account indicated,

> It is generally agreed that competing power clusters have defied rational civilian control. . . . Mr. Resor, a former Secretary of the Army, had been expected to change that. How, exactly, was not clear. Although he was the third ranking Defense official, his aides numbered a handful versus about 20,000 Pentagon employees. Some observers called Mr. Resor a "straight arrow" public servant who simply got "frozen out" by a bureaucracy whose power games he had no taste for.[8]

One of the most important reasons for this bureau autonomy is that the long tenure of career civil servants, who often occupy top bureau spots, allows them to build supporting alliances with legislative committees and powerful interest groups that cannot be matched by the newly arrived secretaries. A second reason is that the top managers within a bureau can credibly claim greater expertise than the politically appointed departmental secretaries; this aura of expertise is a very useful weapon in the political battles over power.

Experience suggests that for large bureaucracies, MBO centralizes by substantially shifting power away from the line agencies up to the department head. It does this in basically four ways.

First: Shifting Power Up by Clarifying Downward Communication

Part of the reason that orders of the top level of a large organization are not carried out is that lower-level managers do not understand the desires of the top, or if they understand, they hide in the ambiguity in order to resist. There is less possibility of this problem under MBO. As discussed in the last chapter, the milestones and frequent face-to-face meetings greatly clarify the wishes of the top of the organization. Thus lower-level managers are less likely to misunderstand the priorities of the department's leaders, or to be able to claim a misunderstanding in order to resist.

Second: Shifting Power Up by Clarifying Upward Communication

We have discussed how missing a milestone acts as a trip wire, bringing up information about problems that lower managers would prefer to keep hidden. Information is power. Because the department head—

the secretary—now has early knowledge of problems and other developments, the initiative lies with him or her, rather than with lower levels.[9]

Third: Shifting Power Up by Creating and Documenting a "Cycle of Failure"

These two impacts have centralizing implications, but they are primarily directed at making communication clearer and the organization more efficient. However, MBO also has effects that are more unambiguously political.

One of the results of the autonomy of bureaus is that many well-entrenched bureaus and agencies have "sacred" or untouchable functions that secretaries can rarely if ever invade. Usually this area is both politically and ideologically important to the agency. As we will see, the Social Security Administration (SSA) for years resisted almost any direction from the Secretary of Health, Education, and Welfare (HEW) regarding the basic Social Security program. This area was untouchable because it was one in which SSA was widely perceived to be highly efficient; therefore SSA could credibly claim that any intervention by the HEW secretary was "political interference."

Such resistance to secretarial control cannot be overcome simply by the secretary setting MBO goals or objectives for the untouchable area; such an attempt would probably be successfully resisted. But if the bureau or agency fails to meet agreed-on MBO objectives in less sacred but related areas, the secretary gains credibility in claiming bureau ineptitude. Because MBO forces an organization to commit itself in advance to very specific output levels, poor organizational performance that might have been plausibly explained away post hoc as "expected" is now clearly labeled as a failure. The shortfall is unambiguous because the organization indicated earlier, in agreeing to the objective, that it believed itself capable of reaching the goal. This agreement gives the secretary an advantage in setting goals that impinge somewhat more directly on the sacred area the following year. With each new failure the secretary gains in power vis-à-vis the subunit. He or she can say, in effect, "I allowed you to do it your way, and yet you didn't attain the level of achievement that you yourself agreed to as reasonable a year ago. Now try it my way."

MBO thus generates its own momentum. Given an initial failure, stricter goals and higher standards can be set, making it yet more probable that the bureau will be seen as failing the next year. Under this continuing documented "cycle of failure," each year's failures pave the way for tougher goals the following year, and the process begins again. This process allows an assertive department head progressive to gain control over previously untouchable areas.

Fourth: Shifting Power Up by Decreasing External Departmental Influences

All of the preceding three effects of MBO systems are ways in which power is moved up *within* the department to the department head. MBO also centralizes, however, by moving power from outside the department to the department head.

The government implementation process is a highly permeable one, in which large numbers of outside interests can reach into the unfolding process and influence it. Much of the group's ability to influence policy and programs, however, depends on ambiguity. When there is no "correct" way to interpret various departmental policies and no unambiguous direction from the top on how various programs are to be implemented, middle and lower managers often take their cues from affected outside interest groups. Managers in the field are particularly vulnerable to strong local pressures.

Because an MBO system specifies in substantial detail the desired policy directions and implementation steps that the secretary wants, it removes much of the ambiguity in which interest group direction flourishes. Lower-level managers feel less need to look to the outside interest groups for direction, and they are less able to claim ambiguity if their decisions are questioned by their superiors. Moreover, MBO objectives speed up the policy-making and implementation processes, allowing less time for interest groups to lobby and influence policy.

These ways that MBO can move power up are illustrated by a brief look at one of the MBO pioneers, the federal department of Health, Education, and Welfare (HEW), which was later renamed the department of Health and Human Services (HHS).

AN ILLUSTRATIVE CASE OF INTERNAL POWER SHIFTS: HEW'S SUCCESSFUL MBO SYSTEM

Moving Power Up Through the Cycle of Failure: A Case Study

The first MBO system in the federal government was that of HEW, begun by Frederick Malek, who later moved to OMB and oversaw the government-wide presidential MBO. HEW's pioneering role gave it the longest-lived MBO system by the late 1980s, as the system—in HHS, the reincarnation of HEW—approached twenty continuous years of operation. This longevity makes it a particularly good focus of study because a major question about all management systems is: How can they be institutionalized so that they continue even when leadership changes? The choices made in the early years of HEW's MBO system were clearly ones that gave it the strength to succeed and endure.[10]

As noted, the Social Security Administration (SSA), one component of HEW, long resisted any direction by the HEW secretary. By the mid-1970s this battle was coming to a head. SSA resistance to secretarial control stemmed both from unusual organizational characteristics and a long history of virtual autonomy. SSA was a strikingly "nonpolitical" organization, with career people serving in all but a handful of top positions. Moreover SSA's highest administrators had been with the organization from almost its beginnings, when it was seen as the cutting edge of social reform. They were very able, but also fiercely dedicated to the organization and its autonomy in an idealistic way lacking in other organizations. When SSA's efficiency began to slip from its strikingly high previous levels, SSA administrators were reluctant to admit problems and vehemently opposed to allowing the department head a voice in the solutions.

SSA was thus widely cited as the component of HEW most resistant to the secretarial MBO system. Said one person on the secretary's MBO staff after several years of such battles, "SSA has never had an objective which deals with the way they spend most of their money—sending out checks, etc. We on the staff have been trying for years to get them to put one down, but they always squirm out of it. They argue 'It's not worth the Secretary's attention; it's purely routine.' "[11]

But the first five years of MBO's existence in HEW is a graphic indication of the way such battles are slowly won by the secretary. In any MBO system a subordinate "wins" (i.e., maintains autonomy) by having MBO objectives that are

1. Policy oriented rather than operation oriented. Policy goals (e.g., "devise a policy for problem X") are preferred by subordinates because they can be used as an endorsement of "wish list" items and because they deal with future programs, and thus by definition do not affect ongoing untouchable areas.

2. Lacking in concrete indicators. Objectives that call simply for "increasing" or "improving" are ambiguous and thus leave ample room for discretion, unlike objectives calling for a "5 percent increase by March 1."

3. Easy to achieve. If an objective must concern operational matters and use concrete indicators, it is at least desirable that it can be achieved with little additional effort.

The First Five Years: Results. Of course there is no objective way to prove that power has shifted in a large organization, but these three

MBO characteristics are useful indicators for judging power shifts in HEW. In each case, the indicators moved in a direction that showed the secretary to be gaining more power over the units under him, in this case SSA.

For example, the number of policy-oriented goals steadily fell from 44 percent of all goals in year 1 to 7 percent of all goals in year 5.[12] The secretary was moving SSA toward his concerns of program operations. Similarly, the number of objectives specifying concrete indicators (the only objectives that are truly meaningful) progressively moved from 17 percent of all goals in year 1 to 71 percent in year 5. Even the percentage of goal achievement moved in the direction of the secretary's wishes—it fell. (The percentage moved from 90 percent success in year 1 to roughly 60 percent in years 4 and 5.[13])

It might seem strange that increased goal failure is a victory for top management, but virtually all observers viewed it as signaling the increased success of the system. The failure rate rose principally because increasingly important and challenging objectives were chosen under secretarial pressure (aided by the "cycle of failure"). Each year SSA was less able to claim competence and ability to handle its own affairs because the previous year's goals indicated that it was in fact not performing at a high level. The secretary could then use that documented failure to push for tougher goals the next year, rather than the easily achievable objectives that SSA might prefer. Thus the cycle continued year after year. In the third year, for example, for the first time several of the objectives were initially suggested not by SSA but by the secretary's office—again an indication that the department head was gaining at least some power over a previously independent subunit.

Moving Power Up by Decreasing External Influences: An Example

It was earlier suggested that a fourth way that MBO shifts power up for large civil-service-oriented organizations is by tightening the implementation process, lessening the power of outside groups. An agency within HEW/HHS, the Public Health Service (PHS),[14] provides a good example of this process. PHS operates in an arena of extremely intense interest group activity, involving dozens of important actors, including medical groups, insurance companies, various state and local bodies, as well as congressional and PHS factions.

One way these groups influence PHS activities is by acting early, often using leaks as a cue and weapon. Said one PHS member, "That's one thing about this agency. Each faction of it—and there's a lot of factions—has allies on the outside in interest groups and in Congress, and they feed them all the documents. So these groups are often protesting proposals to the Assistant Secretary before we've even sent him the memo making the proposal."

However this process was greatly modified when an aggressive assistant secretary for Health,[15] using MBO, speeded up the PHS implementation process, leaving these groups with much less time to comment on (and bargain about) tentative PHS decisions. Although PHS had a long-standing prohibition against distributing internal draft documents to outsiders, these groups began pressuring officials in PHS for formal access to drafts as one way of gaining more bargaining time. For example, the head of the PHS unit working on utilization review responded by asking the assistant secretary for permission to share these early drafts: "As you know, I am concerned that the unfavorable reaction we have received regarding our policy of not sharing draft regulations with outside groups is not helping us much."[16]

The request was not granted, but it reflected the frustration of interest groups who now found their time for influence suddenly shortened by MBO. At all levels of government, speeded-up implementation processes are usually less easily influenced by large numbers of interest groups, and MBO is a decision-forcing device that is often used to speed up implementation. Thus MBO moves power from outside to the secretary because it gives lower-level or field officials less discretion to satisfy interest groups (because departmental policy is clearer) and also because it speeds up the implementation process, shortening the time that groups have to influence policy.[17]

RECAP: WHEN MBO IS NOT A CENTRALIZING DEVICE

Particularly in business texts, MBO is often referred to as a decentralizing system. The preceding argument is that MBO often increases the power of the heads of the large departments. Why the contradiction?

Part of the difficulty is semantic. MBO centralizes the decisions over goals, while simultaneously allowing managers the freedom to choose the means for reaching those goals. Thus this removal of controls over means or procedures can be viewed as a type of decentralization. MBO thus clearly increases the day-to-day autonomy of most subordinate managers, who are free to achieve the agreed-on results in any reasonable way they choose.

Probably the main cause of the seeming contradiction, however, is that centralization and decentralization are relative terms—directions rather than categories. Thus in the highly structured, centralized approaches that characterize many private corporations, any sharing of power with subordinates is a move to decentralization. For many businesses, just the fact that objectives are set through negotiations between superior and subordinate represents a substantial devolution of power.

Nor are all government agencies of one type. The Forest Service has long been a very tightly structured, almost quasi-military organization. Thus when it implemented an extensive MBO-based system, it represented a step toward decentralization. As discussed in the first section of this chapter, many small- and medium-sized government agencies are run tightly from the top, and there, too, MBO is a decentralizing device. But in the pluralistic world of most large state and federal bureaucracies, where most of the power generally lies below the department head's level, sharing power is usually a move to centralization.

POWER SHIFTS: WIDER IMPLICATIONS

The question suggests itself: Is the final result of MBO in large government organizations merely that one group of individuals prevails over another group? In other words, is MBO just another weapon in the personal power struggles that seemingly go on continuously within government bureaucracies?

On the whole, it seems that MBO's impact is more important. Unlike many bureaucratic power struggles, the one that MBO affects is not primarily personal; the two sides represent significantly different values and approaches—on the one hand, the career civil service, and on the other, the top-level, politically determined department head and his or her staff.

Why Moving Power Up Is Good: The Argument for Accountability

Of course an MBO system does not close the government policy-making or implementation process. These processes remain extremely open and porous, with a great deal of power being exerted from lower organizational levels and from outside interests. But MBO does move *some* power up to the secretarial level that was not there before. There are at least two normative or "democratic theory" arguments for such centralization, and they can be stated in terms of the two roles of department heads.

If department heads are viewed as *political appointees,* the democratic theory advantages of moving control from alternative power centers lower in the ranks up to the top are obvious. The department heads are more visible to the public at large, and they can be (and are) removed when voters choose to change administrations. Between elections, they can be removed simply by displeasing those (such as the governor or president) who are most attuned to the voters, and under all conditions they keep in fairly close touch with prevailing public opinion.

If department heads are instead viewed simply as the *highest managers* (ignoring the *direct* political influences on them), there are still substantial advantages in moving power to them from the lower ranks because they are subject to a wider degree of cross pressures than any lower manager. These more inclusive pressures and the wider array of tasks under their jurisdiction make it likely that the decisions of the secretaries will be informed by a more "democratic" (widely inclusive) view of the various trade-offs involved than would the decisions of lower-level managers.

The Importance of Accountability to Democracy

All of these elements, then, seemingly promote the greater accountability of government institutions to the wider public. Moving power up the hierarchy and tightening the implementation process make the organization's leader more clearly responsible for the organization's actions; and he or she is generally a political appointee who is responsive to those who are in the public eye and subject to votes—the executive or the legislature. Power moves from the interest groups and lower-level managers to the top of the departments; the nominal, "political" leaders gain actual control. This is vital to accountability, for as Kaufman has noted,

> If leaders exert but little influence on the actions of subordinates then one of the axioms of democratic government ceases to apply. In general terms, democracy in the modern state presupposes that changing a handful of officials in high places will ultimately change the actions of thousands of employees throughout the system. Subordinate compliance is thus a pillar of democratic government.[18]

Another Reason Why MBO's Move of Power Upward Is Good: Incentives for Installing Systems

Well-working MBO systems generally increase the efficiency and effectiveness of public organizations by concentrating organizational effort on top-priority items and by decreasing the time lag for delivery of various programs. Thus we wish to encourage the installation and use of such systems. But to install and use them, the support of the top of the agency is absolutely necessary. Nixon's presidential MBO is just one example of many systems that failed because they lacked consistent top support. This support is a prerequisite for success at every level of government. In New York City, Arthur Spiegel headed an effort to turn around the "welfare mess" by instituting management systems that completely changed the way workers proceeded, the types of information gathered, and the amount of accountability. His efforts were widely seen as a dramatic success. But as he notes, "The operational tautness began disintegrating the day that [the mayor] announced his decision to leave office."[19]

Why should a department head or other top official take the great amount of time and energy necessary to establish or continue such a system? In circumstances such as we have been discussing, MBO can improve program implementation; however, this may not be highly valued by some department heads. Certainly all of the structural incentives point toward other activities. For example, the average tenure of federal department heads is roughly two years; if they wish to make a name for themselves in that time, the most obvious path is to get important new programs through Congress as permanent monuments. Other potential high-visibility, high-reward activities include giving speeches and advising presidents. Program administration, no matter how good or bad, usually receives no notice from either the public or the press. All of the incentives reward those externally oriented activities that most cabinet officers (who are usually politicians, not administrators) are inclined to pursue anyway. The structural incentives for the organization are similarly unfavorable: Agency "savings" are rarely returned to the agency, and the public rarely believes or rewards claims of increased efficiency.[20]

Thus society benefits when such systems are used, yet there are few incentives for department heads to adopt these systems. In fact, most of the personal incentives pull in other directions. Thus for society to gain the increased efficiency and effectiveness imparted by most management systems, it is necessary to provide the implementors (agency personnel and top administrators) with reasons other than efficiency and effectiveness for using the system—that is, side benefits.

One of the most important side benefits of MBO—probably the most important one—is the increased power it gives department heads. They adopt the system in order to secure additional control; society gains because there is also increased efficiency and democratic accountability. There would be no such gains if the top managers did not adopt MBO in the first place, and the upward shift of power is a major incentive to adopt it.[21]

MBO's Side Benefits for Other Organizational Members

If MBO provides the top of very large departments with increased power, it also affects other members of the same large organizations. The primary benefit that MBO provides middle managers seems to be access. Said one participant in a subdepartmental, internal system, [the agency head . . .] is out of town more than two weeks per month, giving speeches and meeting with groups. So an administrator can't just pick up a phone and get a decision from him. But administrators all know they have regular meetings with him to work out any problems. And in between these MBO meetings, the deadlines give the higher administrators leverage to get actions and decisions out of the lower ones. They can say "I have to report all this is completed to [the agency head] by our meeting next week."

In the frenetic world at the top of large government departments, access is difficult, yet it is the prerequisite for influence. MBO guarantees regular, frequent access to the top decision makers, and this side benefit enlists the support of many administrators who are ostensibly "controlled" by the system. When a new secretary was named during the first few years of the HEW MBO system, the managers of all the directly subordinate units petitioned him to continue the system—a clear indication that it was meeting their needs.

Such side benefits are the key to implementing management systems. Because efficiency and effectiveness are rarely rewarded, designers of management systems must very self-consciously structure in side benefits for all whose acquiescence is necessary for the system's success. (Chapter Eleven will discuss such side benefits in greater detail.) But the most important determinant of success is the support of the head of the system. Thus the key to MBO's success in large, civil-service-oriented organizations (and the primary reason that the rest of society gains increased program efficiency and effectiveness) is the power that the system shifts to the department head.

THE EFFECT OF THE DEPARTMENT HEAD'S PERSONALITY ON MBO

The personality of the department head greatly affects the success of departmental MBO systems in two ways. Personality affects whether the secretary supports the system at all; it also affects his or her skill in using the system once it is instituted. Let us look first at the way personality affects the decision to adopt or support the system.

Deciding Whether to Adopt MBO: Personality and the Need for Control

Department heads gain an incentive to install MBO because, at least in some very large organizations, it gives them power. However, this incentive has no meaning for department heads who do not wish to have some influence over their department's activities. Certainly there are some department heads who by reason of personality prefer to reign, not to rule. They glory in the ceremonies and prestige that accompany their rank, and they have no desire to muddy their pleasures with the problems of decision making.

Luckily, most department heads do not seem to be of this personality type. Although they are usually politicians, not managers, they rankle at the pattern suggested by one former assistant secretary: "There are three levels of administration in Washington: "routine" which is handled by the lowest level; "decision-making," which is handled by people at the intermediate level; and "trivialities" which are the business of the person at the top."[22]

A proactive, take-charge orientation is the major personality factor affecting the choice of whether to adopt MBO, but a number of other personality factors affect how well it is run once adopted.

Personality Traits That Aid in Running an MBO System

MBO is a tool, and although it works serviceably for most managers, it responds best to the most skillful tool wielder. There are at least two personality-based attributes that help a secretary use an MBO system: assertiveness and skill in handling errant subordinates.

Assertiveness. A department head with minimal interest in MBO is unlikely to assert himself or herself during the various MBO steps, allowing line subordinates to slide over many matters. To do so, however, is to lose most of the benefits of the system. One staff person said about Secretary Caspar Weinberger,

> [A top subordinate official . . .] was in our MBO meeting, and he went down our list of problems—A, B, C, and then G. Secretary Weinberger stopped him and went back to D and the guy said "mumble, mumble" and moved back to G. The Secretary had to bring him back to the point again. These guys will try to gloss over difficulties, but if the Secretary's sharp he won't let them do it.[23]

Handling Line Subordinates. The most successful agency heads usually have a feel for politics and for people, and they bring this strength to their management of the MBO system. Elliot Richardson, who was secretary of several federal departments and installed MBO systems in each one, was cited by many as having an unusually fine political touch. Said one member of the MBO staff,

Elliot Richardson had a tremendous feel for people, for picking the right time when to push somebody and when to lay off. Often we in the staff were disappointed when he wouldn't push something we thought needed it—a manager fouling up, for example. But Richardson wouldn't want to embarrass the guy in front of his subordinates, or he'd want the manager's support for another project; and he was generally right.

But sometimes he did follow the staff advice. Once one manager was particularly recalcitrant and a staff member marked a line in Richardson's briefing book, noting "this might be a good place to start pounding the table." And sure enough, just like on cue, when he reached that line Richardson began pounding the table and giving every appearance of a great burst of spontaneous anger.

Because MBO can shift power, it may create some antagonism. The ability to "push sometimes, lay off sometimes" is invaluable in holding the antagonism to the minimum necessary to get the job done. Thus a department head's desire to have at least some control over the department's ongoing activities must stem from personality rather than from any external rewards. Once the decision to use the system is made, personality will again be important in affecting the skill with which the system is directed and utilized. Public managers seeking clear-cut, concrete solutions may find it disillusioning that twenty years of government experience with MBO indicate that its success often depends on such intangible factors as personality and internal incentives. But this is not a fatal flaw; it is in fact unavoidable because no management system works automatically, and personal input will always be an important factor in the loosely structured world of government. MBO is a flexible system that will work serviceably for virtually any department head who (for whatever reasons of personality) wants to have a major influence in the department and is willing to accept the occasional friction that MBO may cause in order to receive the benefits that it imparts.

SUMMARY

Support from the very top of a government agency is a prerequisite for the success of a management system. Without the active backing of the top person (or perhaps one of the top two people), the system will be neglected and die, because only the top officials have the power over the budgetary and promotion incentives that can overcome the inevitable resistance to change.

Unfortunately, these top officials have very few incentives to focus on efficiency. However, management systems do more than increase organizational efficiency; they also often shift organizational power toward the top—which is sometimes enough of an incentive for top officials to support management systems.

Management systems are not centralizing devices in the classical sense; they entail *sharing* power between top administrators and subordinate line managers. Accordingly, in smaller, hierarchical government agencies, where most of the power is at the top, MBO can often lead to a greater share of power by subordinates. But for some very large government bureaucracies, where most of the power is held by subordinate managers (the bureau heads), MBO's power sharing means a substantial shift in power up to top departmental officials. Power moves up because MBO clarifies accountability, documents failures, and reduces interest group influence by speeding up implementation. Such a shift means that the officials whom citizens can most easily see and influence become the ones who can actually guide agency actions; this is a gain for democratic control. Of course these power shifts do not lead to total executive control; that would be very undesirable. The premise here is much more modest: Top political executives should have a major voice (along with the legislature, its committees, and affected interest groups) in public policy. In some sectors of the state and federal governments, these top executives have lost virtually all their power to an alliance of interest groups, career civil servants, and legislative committees. In such cases, MBO can help put the executives back into the game from which they have been excluded.

Only top officials who value increased influence, however, will install MBO to gain the advantages of the power shifts. Thus a proactive personality is a major advantage for top MBO officials, but other personality factors, including assertiveness and a sense of timing, will also help executives oversee an MBO system.

REVIEW QUESTIONS

1. Why does MBO's success usually depend on support from the top?
2. How does MBO affect internal power alignments in small government agencies?
3. How do large civil-service-oriented government agencies at the federal or state level usually differ from small agencies in power alignments?
4. In what four ways does MBO move power up in large bureaucracies?
5. What types of MBO goals predominate when most of the power lies with the subordinates? Why?
6. It would seem more democratic if power is completely dispersed throughout the organization so that many officials control small parts of it. What are some counter arguments?
7. What incentives act on subordinate managers to support MBO?

8. Why is MBO likely to be unsuccessful if the top official has no personal interest in increasing his or her control over the organization? What other incentives are important?

SUGGESTED FURTHER READING

JACK H. KNOTT and GARY J. MILLER. *Reforming Bureaucracy: The Politics of Institutional Choice.* Englewood Cliffs, NJ: Prentice-Hall, 1987. Well-written and enjoyable overview of the politics of public management. Particular emphasis on the political implications of many "reform" proposals.

THEODORE LOWI. *The End of Liberalism,* 2nd ed. New York: W. W. Norton & Co., 1978. The most influential argument for curtailing the power of interest groups in government policy making and implementation.

RICHARD P. NATHAN. *The Plot that Failed: Nixon and the Administrative Presidency.* New York: John Wiley, 1975. Despite the sensational title, a straightforward account of the Nixon administration's changing strategies for assuming greater control over the executive branch.

Case 4–1

Anne Cooper was recently named city manager of Glenburg, a middle-class city of 95,000. The mayor and city council that hired her were unanimous in describing her main mission as "tightening up" city services, which they perceived to have grown inefficient and haphazard. They promised a free hand in accomplishing this task.

Cooper promptly began an MBO system, calling in each departmental administrator to negotiate goals for his or her organization. The primary goal for the sanitation department, for example, was to maintain the same level of service with a labor reduction (through attrition) of 8 percent. The primary goal for the police department was to put more officers per shift on the street by hiring (cheaper) civilian workers to take over many clerical tasks.

Cooper found the goal-setting conferences difficult and prolonged. Although the department heads finally grudgingly agreed to the goals, they showed little enthusiasm.

Cooper decided that her leverage would be improved by some public pressure. Accordingly she gave a presentation at the city council and put out a press release that gave the specific numerical goals for each department. "We will accomplish them," she said. "I pledge it without reservation to the people of this city. If we don't we are wasting their tax money."

The papers and TV newscasts played up her goals, and public attention was intense and favorable. The mayor and city council, on the other hand, seemed distinctly uncomfortable. "If you fall short it's going to make us look bad, too," one city council member told her off the record.

In the first few weeks after her announcement the department heads seemed only slightly more responsive to her efforts, though they were clearly somewhat uneasy and confused by the public attention.

A city manager of a neighboring city cornered her at a regional meeting; "I'm not sure that under your circumstances that was a good move," he said. "Aren't there substantial risks?"

1. Was Cooper's strategy a good one? What can she gain by this approach? Lose?
2. What alternate strategies were open to her? Evaluate their advantages and disadvantages in comparison to her decision to "go public."
3. Are there any circumstances in which her action would be more defensible? Less?

ENDNOTES

1. The definition originally was longer: "Who gets what, when and how." Harold Lasswell, *Politics: Who Gets What, When and How* (New York: McGraw-Hill, 1938).
2. Martin Landau and Russell Stout, Jr., "To Manage Is Not to Control: Or the Folly of Type II Errors," *Public Administration Review*, 39, no. 2 (March/April 1979), 148–56.
3. Theory Y, of course, is Douglas McGregor's term for a management style that trusts and empowers the employees. Jong S. Jun, "Introduction" (to MBO symposium), *Public Administration Review*, 36, no. 1 (January/February 1976), 2.
4. A study of executive power over line agencies indicates that city executives often have a great deal of power, including more power than the city legislature (i.e., the city council), whereas in state government the legislature often has more power. See Glenn Abney and Thomas P. Lauth, "Influence of the Chief Executive on Line Agencies," *Public Administration Review*, 42, no. 2 (March/April 1982). Nonetheless there is a wide disparity in the governor's control over administration; see Glenn Abney and Thomas P. Lauth, "The Governor as Chief Administrator," *Public Administration Review*, 43, no. 1 (January/February 1983), 40–49. Abney and Lauth also find a strong gubernatorial interest in management, especially in terms of efficiency.

5. Many examples of how executive control is greatly attenuated by "merit" civil service systems are given in Jack H. Knott and Gary J. Miller, *Reforming Bureaucracy: The Politics of Institutional Choice* (Englewood Cliffs, NJ: Prentice-Hall, 1987), chapter 12. A comprehensive survey of how strong the civil service system is in each state is provided in Deborah D. Roberts, "A New Breed of Public Executive: Top Level Exempt Managers in State Government," *Review of Public Personnel Administration*, 8, no. 2 (Spring 1988), 20–36.

6. The following sections are a substantially revised adaptation of my article "Establishing a Management System: The Interaction of Power Shifts and Personality Under Federal MBO," *Public Administration Review*, 43, no. 3 (May/June 1983), 238–45. Reprinted with permission from *Public Administration Review* by the American Society for Public Administration (ASPA), 1120 G St., N.W., Washington, D.C., 20005. All rights reserved.

7. Herbert Kaufman also notes that a task force of the first Hoover Commission commented that "the bureau chief is in a formidable position to disregard a department head if he chooses to do so." From U.S. Commission on Organization of the Executive Branch of the Government, Task Force on Departmental Management, *Departmental Management in Federal Administration*, prepared for the commission (Washington, DC: U.S. Government Printing Office, 1949), pp. 33–34. Leonard D. White, a pioneer in the study of public administration, reserved an entire section of the fourth edition of his long-lived textbook for the "tradition of bureau autonomy." From *Introduction to the Study of Public Administration*, 4th ed. (New York: Macmillan, 1955), p. 78.

The Rourke quotation is from *Bureaucracy, Politics, and Public Policy*, 2nd ed. (Boston: Little, Brown, 1976), p. 65.

The U.S. Forest Service quotation is from Glen O. Robinson, *The Forest Service: A Study in Public Land Management* (Baltimore: Johns Hopkins University Press, 1975), p. 22. The Seidman quotation is from *Politics, Position, and Power: The Dynamics of Federal Organization*, 3rd ed. (New York: Oxford University Press, 1980), pp. 135–36. The transition to Ronald Reagan quotation is from Philip M. Boffey, "The Editorial Notebook," *New York Times*, December 9, 1980. All these quotations appear in Herbert Kaufman, *The Administrative Behavior of Federal Bureau Chiefs* (Washington, DC: The Brookings Institution, 1981).

Two cases commonly cited as extreme examples of this situation are Hoover's FBI, which virtually ignored a series of attorney generals, and the Army Corps of Engineers throughout the 1950s and 1960s.

The fragmented nature of federal executive power is nicely captured in Harold Seidman's text, *Politics, Position, and Power.*

8. "A Straight Arrow Quits the Pentagon," *New York Times*, March 11, 1979.

9. Halperin divides the noncompliance of subordinates into three categories: "(1) the subordinates don't know what their superiors want; (2) they are unable to do what their superiors want; (3) they refuse to do what their superiors want." Morton H. Halperin, *Bureaucratic Politics and Foreign Policy* (Washington, DC: The Brookings Institution, 1974), p. 238.

    MBO meets each of these three problems: It makes the superior's priorities clear; it also establishes short-range milestones, and any failure to meet them quickly pinpoints areas of either difficulty or resistance; the system provides for face-to-face meetings to work out the problems or differences. In addition, as indicated later, the documentation of past shortfalls can strengthen the superior's hand in combatting resistance.

10. The HHS MBO system has been devolved to the bureaus under some of the department heads, then reinstituted in the secretary's office under others. However in a number of HHS bureaus, it has been in continuous operation for the entire period. For an interesting in-depth case study of how the system operated in one agency of HHS in the 1980s, see Michael E. Fishman, "Implementing Results-Oriented Management in a Large Federal Agency," in Joseph S. Wholey, ed., *Organizational Excellence* (Lexington, MA: Lexington Books, 1987).

11. Quotations are from the interviews cited in Chapter 3, note 10.

12. The numbers from which the percentages are derived are as follows:

	SSA Objectives: Total Number	Policy Oriented*	Operations Oriented	Objectives Specifying Concrete Achievement Standards**
Year 1	9	4	5	1.5
Year 2	5	3	2	2
Year 3	5	—	5	4
Year 4	7	—	7	6
Year 5	7	.5	6.5	5

*Policy-oriented objectives concern matters that have yet to receive congressional approval; operational objectives deal with postcongressional action matters—that is, true implementation.

**This category eliminates all objectives, whether policy oriented or operations oriented, which are expressed in essentially ambiguous terms, such as *enhance, improve,* or *refine.*

13. There are several different ways in which the goal achievement can be measured. One possibility is to express the number of completed milestones as a percentage of all scheduled milestones. However a goal or objective's final milestone is often the one that makes all the other ones meaningful. Thus it can be misleading to say that an objective with ten steps is 90 percent successful if nine of the steps have been implemented.

The approach taken here has been to use the year-end evaluations prepared by the HEW secretary's office, in consultation with the subordinate agency. In the first three years a three-point scale was used ("achieved," "partly achieved," and "not achieved"); later a four-point scale was instituted ("achieved," "substantially achieved," "partially achieved," "not achieved"). The percentage of total goal completion is expressed by the number of awarded points as a percentage of all possible points. For the first five years, the success figures were (in order) 90, 80, 75, 55, and 65 percent.

14. PHS had historically been the title of only one part of HEW's health division—an elite corps of health providers. However, beginning in the period covered here, the title was given to all components of HEW's health division. This new, expanded PHS was headed by the assistant secretary of health.

15. Dr. Richard Cooper.

16. Internal HEW memo, October 19, 1975.

17. Of course, this statement assumes that the agency views its mission as more than simply carrying out every wish of its clientele. Perhaps the most extreme example of a department that gave the impression of being without such a sense of mission was the Department of Housing and Urban Development. In the early 1980s, HUD established three criteria for determining whether its managers deserved a bonus. Two of those three criteria were (1) "Decisions rarely, if ever, questioned by client groups." (2) "Decisions consistently praised by affected groups." Leonard Reed, "Bureaucrats 2, Presidents O," *Harper's Magazine,* November 1982.

Although it is of course important to maintain the support of interest groups, HUD's approach of basing two-thirds of its job evaluations on whether clients are perfectly happy seemingly would leave little room for any actions that *ever* overrode some interest groups for any reason. In hindsight, these goals seem to reflect the skewed priorities that led to the massive HUD scandals.

18. Herbert Kaufman, *Administrative Feedback* (Washington, DC: The Brookings Institution, 1973), p. 4.

The most famous argument along these lines, advocating a "tightening up" (reduction in permeability) of the federal implementation process, is Theodore Lowi, *The End of Liberalism*, 2nd ed. (New York: W. W. Norton & Co., 1978). Of course Lowi looks principally to Congress for the direction, not to departmental secretaries. This approach is termed a "public interest" approach to democratic control (and contrasted to other approaches) in Judith Gruber, *Controlling Bureaucracies* (Berkeley, CA: Berkeley University Press, 1987), pp. 22ff. It is discussed and extended in Terry Moe, "The Politicized Presidency," in John Chubb and Paul Peterson, eds., *New Direction in American Politics* (Washington, DC: The Brookings Institution, 1985), pp. 235–72. Many of the assumptions underlying Moe's arguments about presidential control of the bureaucracy are attacked in Joel D. Aberbach and Bert A. Rockman, "Mandates or Mandarins? Control and Discretion in the Modern Administrative State," *Public Administration Review*, 48, no. 2 (March/April 1988), 606–12. Another sophisticated development of the argument is that of Joseph Cooper and William F. West, "Presidential Power and Republican Government: The Theory and Practice of OMB Review of Agency Rules," *Journal of Politics*, 50, no. 4 (November 1988), especially 884–92. My argument in this chapter is compatible with that discussion.

19. Arthur H. Spiegel, III, "How Outsiders Overhauled a Public Agency," *Harvard Business Review*, January/February 1975.

20. Chapters 8 and 11 explore this problem of incentives at much greater length.

21. There are numerous case studies that illustrate how a management system can be used to redirect the efforts of employees. One example is Richard C. Sonnichsen, "Communicating Excellence in the FBI," in Joseph S. Wholey, ed., *Organizational Excellence* (Lexington, MA: Lexington Books, 1987). When the new FBI leaders wished to move its focus from smaller crimes to white-collar crimes and organized crime, they changed their management system to reflect the new priorities. They de-emphasized the old measures of arrests and convictions to emphasize the quality of the arrests and convictions. (In the terminology of the next chapter, they moved to measures further down the chain of outputs.) The results, said Sonnichsen, were very positive.

Perhaps the state-level case study that most closely parallels this chapter's federal one is Theodore H. Poister and Thomas D. Larson, "The Revitalization of PennDOT," *Public Productivity Review*, 11, no. 3 (Spring 1988), 85–104. The authors note how the Pennsylvania Department of Transportation, an agency that was basically out of the control of top managers, was revitalized by an MBO system. By 1987, the department's productivity had increased dramatically, and the department had accordingly gained in political support as well. The authors note that the system soon began to encourage participation once its initial (control) mission was achieved:

> Established to gain control over what was perceived to be an unresponsive organization and to hold the bureaucracy accountable to top management, MBO remains the single most important management system in PennDOT. Although it has always been appropriately subordinated to the overall agenda of top management, in the latter years there has been much less emphasis on the control aspects and greater concern with soliciting participation from managers in developing objectives that will further the overall missions of the department (97–98).

22. I've done a minor bit of updating by changing "man" in the last line to "person." The quotation is from Charles Frankel, *High on Foggy Bottom* (New York: Harper & Row, 1968), p. 148.

23. Quotations are again from the interviews cited in Chapter 3, note 10.

chapter five

Performance Monitoring Systems

INTRODUCTION

There are many possible systems for monitoring the output of public organizations, but as noted in Chapter 3 we will somewhat arbitrarily divide all output-oriented systems into two broad groups: MBO systems and non-MBO systems that do not involve negotiated objectives and regular face-to-face management meetings. We will give the name of *performance monitoring systems* to this latter category, which includes all non-MBO output systems.

Many agencies use a performance monitoring system to track a number of important organizational outputs on a continuing basis, year after year. Reports on these output measures are circulated to top managers each month or quarter, often with a comparison to last year's figures. (Box 5-1 is an example of several such reports.) Performance monitoring systems are widely used in government. For example, one national survey of city governments found that 67 percent employed such systems.[1]

Performance Monitoring Systems Vs. MBO

As might be expected, pure MBO systems and pure performance monitoring systems are often combined to create various hybrids. But in their pure form, performance monitoring systems differ from MBO in five ways. We have already discussed two of these differences: Performance monitoring systems do not have negotiated goal setting, nor do they have follow-up face-to-face meetings. They also differ in three other ways.

Performance Monitoring Systems Usually Focus on Relatively Routine Tasks. Performance monitoring systems often cover the routine tasks performed by the operating level of an organization, such as processing forms, paving streets, reading meters, and collecting garbage. MBO, in contrast, is often used for one-time-only projects such as those handled by middle and upper managers.

Performance Monitoring Systems Usually Focus on Organizations, Not Individuals. Performance monitoring systems can track the outputs of individuals (i.e., How many clients did Employee X place in jobs this month?), but much more often, they track agency-wide processes (How many clients did Division Y place in jobs this month?). Thus most of these systems lack the individual measures of MBO, which emphasize both the individual manager and the unit that he or she directs.

We often build the measures for each organizational unit by combining measures that have already been gathered for each individual worker. (This task can be done by hand or by computer if each similar job is given a code—an activity number—that allows the computer to

---

Box 5–1.

The following tables provide three examples of performance monitoring system reports, each from a different city. The first table is taken from a New York City report on an agency that deals with children's services.[2]

The second table represents output measures and standards (no actual performance has yet been entered) for the police department in Dayton, Ohio. It is particularly good in showing how broader objectives (given in the first column) can be measured through several indicators (given in the second column).

The last table represents a series of performance indicators for a recreation centers program for the city of Winston-Salem, North Carolina. The report is notable for the way it divides its indicators into measures of effectiveness, efficiency, and workload.

As noted, the Dayton objectives come from a report published before actual data had been gathered. But both the New York City and the Winston-Salem reports clearly show the standard for the time period covered, then show how well the city performed in meeting the standard. Such comparisons are the heart of all management systems; any variances between standards and actual performance can then be acted on by management.

New York City Human Resources Administration

Missions and Indicators	FY 1987 Annual Actual	Annual Plan	Fiscal Year 1988 Four-Month Plan	Four-Month Actual	FY 19. Prelimir Plan
	AGENCY-WIDE INDICATORS				
Financial resources:					
Expenses (millions)	$ 4,801	$ 4,877	$ 695	$ 733	$ 5,152
Full-time employees	26,254	28,525	26,720	26,658	27,989
City-funded	24,360	26,534	24,785	24,801	26,166
Other	1,894	1,991	1,935	1,857	1,823
Full-time equivalent of					
part-time employees	41.0	41.0	DNA	12.5	DNA
Per diem employees	1,473	2,200	1,493	979	2,200
Total paid absence rate	4.52%	4.00%	4.00%	4.20%	4
Sick leave	4.11%	3.63%	3.63%	3.75%	3
Workers' compensation	0.41%	0.37%	0.37%	0.45%	0
Cost of paid overtime (000)	$ 9,186	$ 8,354	$ 2,464	$ 2,561	$ 8,045
	MAJOR MISSION INDICATORS				
Special Services for Children					
Full-time employees	4,205	4,618	4,284	4,148	4,582
Service complaints received	27	*	*	9	
Complaints resolved	12	*	*	5	
Resolved within 10 Days (%)	0	100%	100%	0	100
Abuse or neglect allegations:					
Cases	46,713	52,786	16,752	14,820	58,906
Children	76,536	86,486	27,863	24,865	96,617
Cases unfounded (%)	65%	60%	63%	64%	65
Cases acted on within one day following report to central register (%) (SCR)	94.0%	100.0%	100.0%	93.1%	100.
Cases acted on within one day following report to central register (%) (SSC Internal)	99.3%	100.0%	100.0%	99.2%	100
New protective service cases opened (a)	16,817	21,114	6,366	5,335	20,617
Protective cases for which (recidivistic) reports of abuse and neglect are received	DNA	*	*	DNA	
Percent for which reports are founded	DNA	*	*	DNA	
New cases per worker per month	6.7	7.0	7.0	6.8	7
Article X petitions filed in family court	13,809	21,203	5,187	5,221	30,43.
Average protective worker caseload	28.1	22.0	26.0	28.9	22

ew York City Human Resources Administration *(continued)*

Missions and Indicators	FY 1987 Annual Actual	Annual Plan	Fiscal Year 1988 Four-Month Plan	Four-Month Actual	FY 1989 Preliminary Plan
	MAJOR MISSION INDICATORS *(continued)*				
C field office preventive services cases (cumulative)	5,470	6,022	4,592	5,312	7,226
ntract preventive services cases (cumulative)	12,983	13,909	9,120	8,264	14,850
ntract preventive services cases referred by SSC (%)	29%	40%	32%	34%	40%
ildren placed in foster care while receiving:					
Field office preventive services	329	*	*	36	*
Contract preventive services	572	*	*	40	*
Percent of preventive services caseload	4.9%	5.0%	*	0.4%	5.0%
VRA requirements:					
Uniform case records completed on time (30-day, 90-day, and 5-month case reviews)	87%	100%	100%	76%	100%
Legal actions completed on time (%)	85%	100%	100%	88%	100%
ster care:					
Children in foster care	18,245	21,130	18,918	18,998	by 3/88
Children discharged from foster care	DNA	DNA	DNA	DNA	DNA
ster care bed gain (net)	1,942	5,280	1,629	1,210	by 3/88
gth of time to complete doptions (years)	2.10	2.00	DNA	2.85	2.00
ildren with goal of adoption dopted (%)	29.7%	31.1%	10.4%	6.8%	30.0%
luntary agency services:					
doptions	842	940	376	248	1,176
doptive placements completed within 27 months (%)	51%	65%	DNA	DNA	65%
ect care services (by SSC):					
doptions	56	60	20	13	63
doptive placements completed within 27 months (%)	59%	65%	DNA	DNA	65%
gram assessment:					
gency assessments completed	55	55	0	0	59
gencies requiring administrative ction	21	*	*	0	*
ontracts cancelled as a result f agency assessment	0	*	*	0	*

e: DNA = Data Not Available

1985 Departmental Objectives, Dayton, Ohio
Group: Community Services

Responsible Agency: Department of Police

Objectives	Performance Criteria	Community Objectives	Units 84 Act.	85 Est.
* 1. To assist with overseeing the implementation phase of the communication dispatch system (CAD/MIS) for police and fire departments	1a. Date contract awarded	DH13		3/85
	b. Date renovation of signal building completed to house CAD system	DH14		12/85
	c. Date CADS is fully operational			6/86
* 2. To assist with the rewrite of CJIS	2a. Date specifications developed for CJIS rewrite	DH13		6/85
	b. Date CJIS system fully implemented			9/86
* 3. To develop a coordinated property matching system for the MIS that will result in increased recovery of stolen property in future years	3a. Date system designed	DH13		5/85
	b. Date records are entered into computer			7/86
	c. Date system fully implemented			9/86
4. To limit average response for priority 1 calls to 5–6 minutes and for all other calls to 11–12 minutes	4a. Average priority 1 call response time (minutes)	NV5		5 min.
	b. Average overall response time (minutes)			11 min.
* 5. To increase public awareness throughout the City of Dayton of the Abandoned Vehicle Program	5a. Date comprehensive news media release in 1985 explaining the Abandoned Vehicle Program	NV5		3/85
	b. Number of presentations made to neighborhoods on Abandoned Vehicle Program			14
* 6. To develop and implement a procedure policy with regard to pawn shops, junk yards, and second-hand dealers	6a. Date input solicited from pawn shops, junk yards, and second-hand dealers	NV5		3/85
	b. Date draft for preliminary approval submitted to department director			6/85
	c. Date new procedure fully implemented			10/85

Objective	Measure		
* 7. To implement a review model for criminal cases that are denied filing by the prosecutor's office	7a. Date review panel established to determine if further investigation is needed	DH13	3/85
	b. Dates quarterly reports of panel findings and recommendations submitted to department director		6/85 10/85 12/85
* 8. To insure personal contact by investigation detectives on 90% of the complaints from Dayton citizens within 72 hours	8a. Number of complaints received	NV5	0%
	b. Percentage of complainants personally contacted within 72 hours		
	c. Percentage of complainants personally contacted within 5 days.		10%
9. To limit the number of residential burglaries to 1982 levels while decreasing the occurrence of residential burglaries by 4% in the highest residential burglary sector in each police district	9a. Number of residential burglaries for 1982	NV5	5,759
	b. Number of residential burglaries in 1985		
	c. Percentage of reduction in each of the highest sectors		4%
10. To limit the number of commercial burglaries to 1980 levels while decreasing the occurrence of commercial burglaries by 4% in the highest commercial burglary sector in each police district	10a. Number of commercial burglaries for 1982	NV5	
	b. Number of commercial burglaries in 1985		
	c. Percentage of reduction in each of the highest sectors		4%

Note: *High-priority objectives.

133

Program Management Report, Winston-Salem, North Carolina

Program: Recreation Centers

	Expected for Year	Actual 1986–1987			Prior Year		
		3rd Qtr.	4th Qtr.	Year-End Total	3rd Qtr.	4th Qtr.	Year-End Total
Effectiveness Measures							
Percent of time cleanliness standards are maintained at all facilities	95%	96%	95%	96%	95%	95%	95%
Percent of program participants rating the cleanliness, safety, attractiveness, crowdedness, and accessibility as "satisfactory"	95%	92%	95%	94%	93%	94%	93%
Number of serious injuries (requiring medical attention) per 1,000 participants	.05	.02	.01	.03	.04	.01	.02
Percent of total attendance enrolled in supervised programs	65%	53%	47%	52%	50%	51%	49%
Percent of time service calls for minor maintenance of recreation centers are answered within 48 hours	95%	99%	96%	96%	91%	92%	91%
Attendance at structured programs	275,430	132,542	64,273	362,433			

Efficiency Measure

Cost per service call	$37.50	$39.50	$34.72	$35.08	$44.13	$36.48	$38.73

Workload Indicators

Number of service calls received	625	228	174	795	234	168	718

Highlights

- The program exceeded its goals for the percent of time all facilities meet cleanliness standards and the percent of time service calls are answered within 48 hours.
- Although the objective for the percent of total attendance enrolled in supervised programs was not achieved, there was a 3% increase over prior year, and actual attendance at structured programs exceeded expectation.
- The recreation centers program received a higher number of service calls during FY86–87. Many of the service calls were for minor maintenance-related tasks; therefore, the costs per service call was lower than expected.

135

add the individual job readings together.) If we simply track what Bob Smith, a hard-working city street paver, does each day, we have useful *operational-level* information that will help first-level supervisors. But such information does not fit comfortably into a management system because the information is too detailed to be of any use to middle and higher managers; they have no need to know what a specific worker did on a specific day. It is only when we aggregate (combine) the information on the performance of the ten or twelve people working with Bob Smith, and total it for the month, that we now have information useful to middle management: "Unit C has paved two more miles than expected this month."

Performance Monitoring Systems Use the Same Output Categories Year After Year. Because they concentrate on continuing, routine, agency-wide processes, performance monitoring systems use the same measures year after year. This continuity is valuable because it allows year-to-year comparisons. MBO systems, on the other hand, often deal with the project-oriented tasks of middle and upper managers. Because a manager's priorities often shift, the outputs measured by MBO are likely to shift each year as well. For example, the director of a clinic may emphasize outreach measures in the first year's MBO goals that she negotiates with her subordinates. In the second year, after enough patients have been secured, she may emphasize cost control. And in the third year, under new pressures, she may emphasize measures of quality control. Meanwhile the performance monitoring system may continue, year after year, to measure routine items such as number of visits, number of return visits, and number of complaints.

MBO and performance monitoring systems are complementary, not competitive. Thus a transportation department may use a performance monitoring system to track the performance of its paving division. Each year the division's outputs will be tracked by the same continuous output measures, such as "miles paved" and "potholes filled." The same department may track the performance of an upper-level manager by a changing series of MBO output measures. One year these measures may emphasize repairing relations with the legislature, while the next year they may emphasize increasing organizational efficiency. Both systems measure organizational output; both are useful for their differing roles. In sum, the distinctions between the two types of systems are useful for analysis, but it is not uncommon for these distinctions to blur in practical application. (The basic differences between the two systems are summarized in Table 5-1).

TABLE 5–1 Differences Between "Pure" MBO and Performance Monitoring Systems

	MBO Systems	Performance Monitoring Systems
Changes in outputs measured	Outputs measured usually project-specific, with annual changes as projects change	Usually continuing output categories, with only rare changes
Scope of data collected	Covers individual manager and his or her unit	Covers entire division or agency
Types of tasks covered	Usually projects	Usually continuing operations
Goal setting	Through face-to-face negotiation	Often unilateral or based on past performances or engineered standards
Data collection and monitoring	Done by managers; discussed in face-to-face conferences	Done by staff; information distributed to managers in regular memos or reports

"Pure" forms of either MBO or performance monitoring systems are rarely used alone. Many agencies use both or combine them in a hybrid system.

CHOOSING OUTPUT INDICATORS: GUIDELINES

Any complex government organization produces literally dozens of outputs. Out of all of these outputs, which should be tracked? This choice is more important for a performance monitoring system than for MBO. MBO is a project-oriented system, and therefore the objectives tend to be temporary; each year new projects or outputs are chosen as priorities shift. But a performance monitoring system's measures are used year after year to provide a long-range record of organizational performance, and so the initial choice of outputs to be measured commits the system for a number of years. Once the procedures for gathering, collating, and analyzing data are in place, any change in output indicators may involve great organizational disruption. Thus the choice must be made carefully.

When we speak of choosing outputs to track and measure, we are speaking of choosing particular performance indicators. As discussed in Chapter 3, a performance indicator is a numerical measure of some aspect of organizational performance. For a high school, "number of graduates" would be one possible performance indicator, as would "number of college scholarships earned." There are of course many others. Performance indicators are usually just called *indicators;* another synonym is *measures.*

Some of the more important guidelines for choosing output measures were considered in Chapter 3. In particular, any system's indicators should be *multiple,* chosen with an eye to offsetting the tendency to displacement. Moreover, the overall management system should be based on a "reasonable person" approach. That is, not all organizational rewards should be tied to a single system of indicators; other, nonsystem information should also be considered in making many of the most important reward decisions. Not every aspect of performance can be covered by an indicator. So this reasonable person approach is meant to reduce the incentives for misreporting and for displacement that would arise if the system determined every facet of each individual's career.

Beyond these suggestions are two other principles worth noting: Data needs should be determined without regard to data availability, and systems should avoid too many measures.

Determining Data Needs before Determining Data Availability

One of the most common mistakes made in designing an output monitoring system is to begin by surveying the data available and then using availability as the primary consideration in choosing which outputs to measure. This is the wrong order. Such a procedure is reminiscent of the anecdote about the pedestrian who late one night came across a very drunk man on his hands and knees, frantically searching for something under a lightpost. The pedestrian asked him what he was looking for. "My keys," replied the drunk, pointing. "I lost them over there in the bushes."

"If you lost them over there," asked the puzzled pedestrian, "then why are you looking for them way over here?"

"Because," said the drunk, "this is where the light is."

Data can be very illuminating, but an organization must make sure that they are in fact illuminating the area that the organization is most concerned about. An agency that tracks particular data primarily because they are available puts itself in the same position as the drunk. Agency decision makers should first sit down and determine what particular indicators would best measure what the organization accomplishes. In other words, what information would be most useful in making decisions? Only after deciding what data would be most useful should they consider whether such data are available. If the data on hand do not serve the purpose, new sources of data can be chosen by carefully balancing usefulness against the convenience of gathering. Beginning the choice of output indicators by surveying the available data subconsciously biases the process—designers begin to think that the available data are the best, after all.

Avoiding Too Many (or Too Few) Output Measures

The more output measures that are used, the more likely the organization will be tracking a reasonable composite of its real activities, and the less tendency there will be for misreporting and goal displacement. But at the same time, the more measures that are tracked, the more unwieldy the management system becomes. Large numbers of indicators—some programs gather over 100—can obscure the handful of indicators that are really important for decision making and guiding behavior. Moreover, there are usually costs involved in gathering each new measure—costs in time, effort, and money. Therefore managers need to consider whether the value of an additional measure outweighs the costs of gathering and monitoring it.[3]

In general, it is easier to track a large number of outputs for organizations whose work is highly routinized, highly unchanging, and very tangible. Thus far more outputs can be tracked for a sanitation department or a transportation department than for a police SWAT team or a planning department. For most programs, three indicators would be too few, twenty too many. But a more exact balance must be worked out for each agency on a case-by-case basis. During the last decade, administrators working in most types of government programs have helped develop a large and growing literature that suggests specific output indicators for each type of function.[4]

WHICH OUTPUTS TO MONITOR?
ANALYZING THROUGH CHAINS OF OUTPUTS

Developing Chains of Output

The question of which outputs should be monitored can be analyzed through the concept of "chains" of organizational outputs. "Chains of outputs" is a simple concept.[5] All programs have a number of effects—some immediate and produced directly, others delayed and produced by ripple effects. A *chain of outputs* is simply a diagram of the expected outputs for one program; it begins with the most immediate, localized effects and proceeds, step by step, to the broader societal impacts.

The easiest way to develop an output chain is to begin with the most immediate and obvious output and to ask, "Why do we want this output?", then to take the resulting answer, and ask the question again. This process can be repeated until a natural stopping point is reached.

For example, for an antiflu program administered by a public clinic, the most immediate and obvious output may be "number of patients treated." Depending on the definition of "treatment" this indicator falls right on the edge between an output and a process measure. As we have discussed and will further discuss, it is always better to focus on outputs—effects on people outside the organization—rather than internal processes or activities. However sometimes the two blend along the edges. One of the advantages of the chain is that it is unaffected by these close calls between "activities" and "immediate outputs." If we accidentally begin with a process measure, building a chain will shortly bring us to true outputs.

The next link of the chain is produced by asking, "Why did we wish to treat a large number of patients?" and taking the most immediate answer: "To inoculate them." This reply establishes the next link, "number of patients inoculated."

But why inoculate them? "To produce fewer cases of flu." But why do we wish fewer cases of flu? "Fewer flu cases" is not a free-standing good; for example, it would be a useless measure if the treatment cured flu but caused a worse disease. The answer is "to improve life expectancy and reduce sick days." Why? The chain may go a bit longer, but eventually a final "ultimate" output such as "greater happiness for all" is likely to be the ending point. Such final outputs can be left for philosophers, not managers;[6] but the immediate and intermediate outputs that lead to them are very useful. Different observers will produce slightly different chains for the same programs—somewhat shorter or longer, a few different links—but the basic pattern will remain very similar. The chain for the health clinic is shown in Figure 5-1, with chains for other programs. Some plausible links have been omitted to shorten the chains for reasons of space.

A note here about terminology: As first discussed in Chapter 1, we will use the terms *immediate outputs,* which produce *intermediate outputs,* which produce *ultimate outputs.* According to some dictionary definitions, the word *ultimate* indicates one single final point, but the term can also be used to mean "fundamental" (or sometimes loosely, "near the end"). We'll employ the latter, broader definitions, so that we can have more than one "ultimate output." That is, the term will designate the last few outputs in the chain.

Some authors prefer different terminology. They define *outputs* much more narrowly, as only the immediate effect of a program. In their terminology, *outputs* lead to *impacts* (similar to our *intermediate outputs*). Impacts, in turn, lead to *outcomes* (our *ultimate outputs*). Either set of terms is serviceable, but of course *outputs, impacts,* and *outcomes* blend into each other, and therefore it is often impossible to be certain whether a particular effect is an impact or an outcome. One advantage of this book's terminology is that its terms *(immediate, intermediate,* and *ultimate)* emphasize the blend, indicating that there is no clear, sharp dividing lines between the categories.

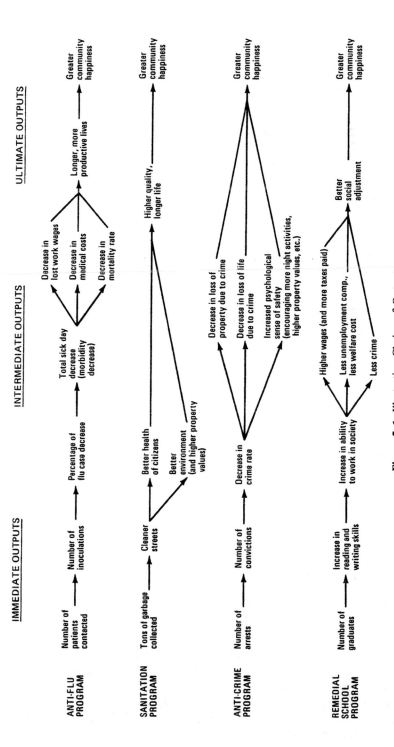

Figure 5-1. Illustrative Chains of Output.

141

Moving Down the Chain: Advantages and Disadvantages

There are two truisms about the chain of outputs for any program. First, the initial outputs, the ones listed to the left of any chain, are the easiest to measure because they are the most tangible and most immediate results. Management systems require frequent, often month-to-month, measurements; accordingly, such systems often focus on the easy-to-measure outputs to the left. This is particularly true of performance monitoring systems, which have very frequent reporting periods.

Unfortunately, the second truism about chains is: The initial links are also the ones most susceptible to goal displacement. For example, it is relatively easy for workers in a school program to increase the "number of students graduated" if that is the output measured. However, this increase may not affect a link further down the chain, such as "increased student skills in reading and writing."

As we move further down the chain, to the right, we come closer to our "real" desired outputs. But these intermediate and ultimate outputs are harder to measure (especially routinely), and they are often affected by factors outside our program. Thus "higher wages" is further down the chain for the remedial school program in Figure 5-1, but it is difficult to measure and many nonprogram factors (such as an improving economy) may have affected it.

Proxy (Surrogate) Measures

Where does this discussion leave us? Of course, it is impossible to stop every month to determine increases in intermediate and ultimate outputs such as a school program's increase in reading and writing skills. However it is important for top managers to realize that their immediate output measures such as "number of patients inoculated" or "number of students graduated" are meaningless in themselves. They are simply *proxies* or *surrogates* for the desired intermediate and ultimate outputs. A proxy is a measure that acts as a stand-in for the actual output that we wish to measure. When we use such surrogate indicators, we are making the assumption that the links in the chain will not break and that increases in early measures will lead to increases in the desired ultimate outputs.

Most indicators used in management systems are to some extent surrogates or proxies because it is often so difficult to measure the desired ultimate outputs. In fact, because many ultimate outputs are long-range effects, they may not be clear for a decade or more. Often, then, we use measures of immediate and intermediate outputs as proxies for the ultimate outputs that we cannot currently measure. In and of themselves, proxies are necessary and useful; but the manager must always remember that they are in fact stand-ins.

Recap: Processes Vs. Outputs

As discussed in Chapter 1, process (also called activity) measures are sometimes confused with output measures, but they are quite different. A process measure registers what goes on *inside* an organization. Thus they might include such categories as number of students taught, forms processed, or miles traveled.

An output measure, on the other hand, reflects the *product* of an organization. In other words, an output measure registers an effect or change on people who do not work for the organization. Diseases prevented, lives saved, skills learned, fires extinguished, and criminals arrested are all output categories. Because outputs represent the reason the organization exists, they are far more important than process measures.

As with all distinctions, there are some grey areas in real life. At the very edge, some process measures begin to blend into the measures of very immediate outputs. But most often, the distinction between the two is easy to make. We simply need to ask of any indicator, "Is this an indicator of something going on inside the organization (a process measure); or is it an indicator of effects on outsiders (an output measure)?"

An Extreme Example of Proxy Indicators: Workload Indicators

Most managers would like to emphasize measures of ultimate output, but they often employ measures of immediate and intermediate outputs as surrogates. Sometimes, however, managers push the use of proxy measurements one step further. They abandon outputs altogether and begin using indicators of internal organizational processes as proxy measures. These process-based proxies are often called *workload indicators.*[7] For a police department, for example, process indicators might include measures of witnesses interviewed, miles patrolled, and forms completed. None of these items shows the department's effect on outsiders; therefore none of them clearly indicates whether the department is doing a good job. For that, we need output indicators such as arrests made, convictions secured, and crime rates.

Workload indicators are an extreme example of proxies because process indicators are very far removed from the desired output—so far removed that we should be suspicious of whether they have much to do with increasing the output at all. For example, this year an agricultural extension agent may travel more miles in visiting farmers and process more forms, and thus his workload indicators have risen. Yet the agent may well not have helped the farmers one bit more. It is often necessary to keep track of processes for reasons of internal management, but treating such workload indicators as output surrogates is generally risky and undesirable.

One final example: As we briefly noted in Chapter 1, some school programs claim excellence because of a low student-teacher ratio. However, this is simply a workload indicator. School officials are assuming a chain of outputs that leads from a low ratio to more individual attention to pupils, which in turn leads to better learning. But do the links of this chain actually hold? Some educational research indicates that student-teacher ratios, contrary to common assumptions, do not seem to lead directly to these other outputs. Therefore school officials would do well to keep looking further down the chain to find what the low student-teacher ratio is actually producing as an output.

Managers usually can find measures that are both accessible and yet well down the chain of outputs simply on a commonsense basis. But one way to strengthen and reinforce this process is to tie the management system to program evaluation; we will discuss this approach in Chapter 6.

Output Chains, Efficiency, and Effectiveness

The concepts of efficiency and effectiveness are easily related to chains of output. As discussed in Chapter 1, efficiency asks, "Did we perform the job without wasting resources?"; effectiveness asks, "Did the job achieve the desired result?"

Let us begin by considering the chain of outputs for a fire-fighting unit. With some links omitted, the chain might look roughly like this: number of alarms answered—number of fires fought—number of fires extinguished within a certain time—amount of property saved and number of lives saved—greater community peace of mind about fire—happier lives overall.

Because efficiency focuses on waste, it is usually measured by dividing immediate outputs by input (cost). For a fire-fighting unit, an efficiency measure would probably be based on an immediate output indicator like "number of fires fought"; this indicator would produce the efficiency measure "cost per fire fought." Thus efficiency focuses on outputs that are in the early part of the chain. (Sometimes efficiency measures are even less ambitious. They are occasionally based on dividing a process measure by cost, which, of course, makes them a type of workload indicator.)

Effectiveness focuses on the last part of the chain because it is a measure of whether a program has achieved its desired results (i.e., intermediate and ultimate outputs). One effectiveness measure for the same fire-fighting unit might be "reduction in number of lives lost in fires."

Attempting to Measure Final Outputs: The Use of Surveys

As we have discussed at length, it is very difficult to measure the long-range (effectiveness) outputs that lie near the end of the output chain. Program analysts have recently begun to use citizen surveys experimentally to measure such long-range outputs. The analysts have recognized that near the end of almost all output chains for public organizations, there could be a link entitled "increased public satisfaction with this program." Therefore program evaluators have attempted to survey citizens' or clients' opinions on program effectiveness and then to see how well the opinions reflected more objective indicators of effectiveness.

The results are mixed.[8] Sometimes the survey results seem to mirror actual agency performance; at other times they do not seem to correlate with other, more "objective" indicators. Surveys are particularly untrust worthy if the public rarely has direct dealings with the agency. For example, most citizens who have not recently been victims of crime are unlikely to be able to make precise judgements about how well the police are performing. Yet asking only those who have recently been vicitmized is likely to produce a biased sample, too. Understandable, the victims may feel that police protection is inadequate, even though the number of crimes is actually down. Surveys also can be distorted by low public awareness of an agency or an overreaction to a single isolated incident that may have received publicity.

It is just because surveys are such an attractive feedback device that their shortcomings have been emphasized here. But these pitfalls should not obscure the many advantages of using surveys: If we wish to know how well an organization is working, why not ask its "customers"? The analogy to private sector feedback is strong and inviting. Surveys can be especially useful when they question people who *directly* and *frequently* interact with the government program. Thus people leaving a post office can be polled on how long they had to wait and how courteously they were treated. Similarly, patrons of a public golf course, patients treated in a public clinic, and home owners who receive municipal garbage pickup are all likely candidates for a meaningful survey.

In sum, then, surveys can sometimes be very useful as *one* measure of organizational output. Although their use in the public sector has been increasing rapidly,[9] they should still be used much more than they are. Nonetheless survey results are often flawed or incomplete and so they cannot stand alone as a total, all-encompassing measure of agency performance.

The Importance of Chains

The entire concept of chains of outputs suggests a rather abstract, other-worldly approach to the nitty-gritty problems of measuring organizational performance. However this impression is misleading; the concept has some very real and practical uses in designing and analyzing management systems. Before taking any action on their management systems, managers should develop a chain for each of their programs. (Thus an agency with four programs would have at least four separate chains.)

Such an exercise has a number of beneficial results. For example, it forces managers to think through what they really want to measure and how measurable it is; this moves them away from the temptation of choosing indicators on the basis of availability. Developing a chain before designing a management system also alerts managers to likely displacement problems (the further left an indicator is, the more prone to displacement) and to measurability problems (the further right, the more difficulty in measurement). It alerts them to difficulties with environmental impacts on the indicator (the further right, the more outsiders can affect it) and helps them balance the system (the measurements should include at least some indicators toward the right). (These considerations are summarized in Box 5-2.) Managers wishing to tie their management systems to budget systems—particularly program budgets—will find that these systems are based on an implicit chain of outputs, as we will discuss in Chapter 7. Finally a chain of outputs helps managers and program evaluators meet on common ground, as we will discuss in Chapter 6. In sum, it is almost impossible to understand clearly what the output indicators for a program are telling the manager without displaying them as a chain.

INDICATOR CHOICE AND MEASUREMENT THEORY

Reliability, Validity, and Output Measures

Our discussion of measures can be connected to the concepts of measurement theory. No measurement is totally error free, whether it is a measurement we make in the physical sciences, in management, or in everyday life. For example, even if our weight did not change, we would probably get some small variations in the result if we weighed ourselves many days in a row. But if error is inevitable, we nonetheless wish to recognize and minimize it to the extent possible. The two most important ways of categorizing and analyzing the errors associated with our measures are *reliability* and *validity*.[10]

Reliability reflects replicability—whether the same results will be secured on repeated observations. If our scale in the preceding example

Box 5–2.

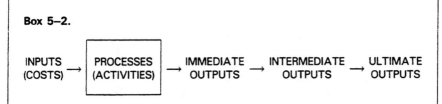

PROCESSES

Advantages in tracking: Extremely easy to measure (called workload
measures)
Disadvantages in tracking: Little relationship to desired outputs

IMMEDIATE OUTPUTS

Advantages in tracking: Relatively easy to measure
                                    Little affected by nonprogram forces and events
Disadvantages in tracking: Only moderate relationship to desired outputs so
prone to displacement

INTERMEDIATE OUTPUTS

Advantages and disadvantages in tracking: Midway between immediate and
ultimate outputs

ULTIMATE OUTPUTS

Advantages: Represent desired outputs, so little displacement
Disadvantages: Because they are long-range and diffuse: difficult to measure,
especially on a frequent basis; often affected by nonprogram forces and
events

continually showed the same weight, we would call the measure reliable.
Reliability indicates that the differences shown by a measurement are
actual differences and not illusory differences due to the measurement
itself.

Validity, as the name suggests, is a determination of whether an
indicator truly measures the concept it is intended to measure. A measure
can be reliable but not valid. If our scales are consistently registering our
weight as 20 pounds too heavy, we may constantly get the same number
for our weight (reliability); but the measure is not valid (it does not reflect
our true weight).

Thus useful measures must first of all be reasonably reliable; they
are useless if they move around wildly because of random error in the
measurement process itself. Once we have reliable measures, we next need
to assure ourselves of their validity—are they truly reflecting what we
really wish to measure? Only measures that are both reasonably reliable
and reasonably valid will provide useful information.

We say "reasonably" reliable and valid because, as already noted, some error is unavoidable. The objective is to minimize the error, not eliminate it. Toward this end, it is often useful to employ multiple measurements, a process sometimes termed *triangulation*. As one measurement text notes, "Underlying the need for triangulation is the premise that any single measure carries with it its own characteristic sources of error. . . . [Accordingly] errors of reliability and validity are reduced through using multiple and overlapping measurement strategies."[11]

Managerial measurement—measurement of outputs—fits comfortably within this framework. We have throughout past chapters emphasized the importance of multiple measures in order to avoid measurement errors. Moreover, our discussion of the chain of outputs can be recast in terms of reliability and validity. We can look at the validity of immediate output indicators (proxies) by judging whether they accurately reflect our primary organizational goals—the intermediate and ultimate outputs further down the chain. When we speak of the links in the chain holding, we are speaking of validity—that the immediate measures are accurately informing us about the intermediate and ultimate measures. Thus for a police department management system, the immediate output measure "number of arrests" is a valid measure of the ultimate output measure "public safety increase," if an increase in arrests leads to an increase in public safety. We want each of our proxies to be a reliable and valid measure of the intermediate and ultimate outputs that lie further down the chain.

Are the *immediate* output measures used by most public management systems likely to be both reliable and valid proxies? They are likely to be reliable because categories early in the chain of output are usually quite concrete—number of fires fought, number of students graduated, number of people arrested. Because they are so concrete, they raise few problems of reliability; most fair-minded observers would probably count the same number of fires fought or students graduated. The results can be easily replicated. But items early in the chain have greater problems with validity. As long as we assume that what we "really" want is the ultimate output—safer lives from the police system, more productive citizens from the school system—the early items may sometimes be weak in validity.

Further down the chain, validity is less of a concern. However, because the desired outputs are so global—safer streets, greater productivity—operationalization problems and thus potential measurement error become much greater. Also, these outputs are often long range and thus often difficult to measure on a month-to-month basis. To the extent that we trust our measurements, intermediate and ultimate output indicators have greater face validity. The measurement problems are daunting, however, which again reinforces the point: Management systems need some measures drawn from the early part of the output chain and some drawn from later parts of the chain.

Employing a Broad Perspective on Indicator Choice

Any indicators chosen for a management system must be reliable and valid measures of what they purport to measure. But at the same time, managers need to take a very broad perspective because the choice of indicators often also carries additional *psychological* and *political* ramifications for the organization.

We have already discussed some of the psychological aspects of indicators. Indicators in management systems are not chosen simply to measure current performance; they are also carefully chosen to affect behavior. They thus serve a dual role of (current) measurement and (future) incentive. Tracking (and thus emphasizing) a particular indicator that carries symbolic import to organizational members may well change employee behavior and morale.

For most forms of scientific and social scientific measurement, the analyst is unhappy if the measurement process itself changes what it is supposed to measure. In contrast, such effects are deliberately sought when performance indicators are chosen. Thus managers must at least intuitively consider psychological effects when deciding the number and type of measures to be employed.

A second reason for employing a broad perspective is that some indicators also carry political implications. For example, many studies have indicated that an increase in the indicator "hours patrolled" by the police does not usually lead to an increase in the ultimate output of a "safer community." (Patrol presence has surprisingly little effect on crime.) Nonetheless citizens may demand frequent, visible police patrols in their neighborhoods. Thus the indicator "hours patrolled," although not a valid measure of "increased safety," should probably still be kept for political reasons.

The vast majority of proxy indicators do not have such political overtones, of course, and thus agencies should drop them if they do not lead to ultimate outputs. But public sector managers must remain aware that, occasionally, an indicator that does not validly measure the organization's professed ultimate output may nonetheless be useful because of its political importance.[12] In sum, managers must utilize performance indicators that are reliable and valid. However, the fact that people's psychological and political values play such a central role in public management means that the manager must also be sensitive to these concerns in choosing particular indicators.

MIDCHAPTER SUMMARY

Before moving on to ways of setting standards for outputs, let us summarize the discussion of how outputs are chosen for monitoring. Most programs have dozens of potential output measures (i.e., indicators), yet we rarely have the time or resources to track all of them. There are a number of guidelines for choosing which indicators to monitor:

1. Drawing a chain of outputs for each program is an important first step. A chain begins with the most immediate output, then proceeds step by step toward outputs representing broader or longer-lasting social impacts. The chain is important because it suggests new potential indicators, but especially because it shows the relationship of indicators to each other.

2. Unless politics dictates that a particular indicator be tracked, indicators should always be chosen on the basis of how well they inform decision making or affect behavior. They should of course never be chosen just because the data are already being gathered.

3. Multiple indicators are crucial, but they should also be *balanced.* Some outputs should be drawn from the beginning of the chain because they are the easiest to measure short term and because the organization clearly controls their production. Unfortunately, they are also the most prone to displacement. Other indicators should be drawn from further down the chain because they are usually the most valid measure of the desired ultimate output. They have the disadvantage, however, of being difficult to gather on a month-to-month basis and of often being affected by nonorganizational forces.

4. Surveys of clients' or citizens' satisfaction with the program can provide very useful intermediate measures. Surveys have some limitations, and always need to be used with other indicators, but they nonetheless should be used more often.

5. Because they are so remote from the organization's primary purpose, workload indicators—measures of the organization's internal processes—should be accorded much less importance than output measures.

SETTING OBJECTIVES FOR PERFORMANCE MONITORING SYSTEMS

We have considered some ways of choosing which indicators the performance monitoring system will track. But once particular indicators (e.g., reduction in number of flu cases) are chosen, we are not done. We still need objectives or standards for those indicators (e.g., how much of a reduction in the number of flue cases do we want?) Performance monitoring systems, by definition, do not use MBO-type negotiations to set standards for each output category. However, as with all management systems, standards are necessary because output data are meaningless without a yardstick (standard) for comparison.

There are four ways to set objectives or standards in *any* management system. We will begin by briefly recapping the use of MBO-type negotiations; we will then examine the other three means of standard setting employed by most performance monitoring systems.

Standard Setting by Negotiation

Negotiations between subordinates and superiors are the best way of setting objectives, for all the reasons discussed in Chapter 3, including greater commitment to goals and greater exchange of information. Even many hybrid performance monitoring systems use this approach. Of course, if a performance monitoring system is tracking twenty-five outputs, it would be too time-consuming to negotiate standards for each one. Many of these standards can be derived by past performance or engineered standards, as will be discussed later. But if twenty-five outputs are being monitored, only a handful are really important in evaluating units and making management decisions, and these important objectives should preferably be set through a joint superior-subordinate effort. Both sides in this negotiation will want to consider the past performance data and standard time data in setting goals, but other intangible aspects will also be reflected in their final agreement.

Standard Setting Based on Past Performance

Many organizations report current output data side by side with last year's or last quarter's output figures. In such cases, past performance is implicitly used as the standard. Sometimes, in a slight variation, an organization may set as its objective "last year's output plus 5 percent." Productivity systems, which will be discussed in the next chapter, use base years for comparison. Thus productivity systems implicitly use past performance as the output standard.

Past performance information is useful, but it should not be used by itself as a valid standard for current output. Some organizations may have performed so badly in the past that even if this year's performance is 20 percent better, it is still poor. Other organizations may have performed so well in previous years that simply equalling the previous year's output is a high achievement. As these examples indicate, past performance figures do not really indicate how efficiently the organization is performing.

They should be considered in setting standards, but they should not stand alone.

Standard Setting Based on Superior-Assigned Quotas

Sometimes the top manager simply assigns a performance target to each unit. Chapter 3 discussed the problems with this approach: Agency workers do not feel committed to standards that they took no part in setting and valuable information is lost without the give and take of negotiation. Nonetheless quotas are listed here because they are (unfortunately) often used in standard setting for performance monitoring systems.

Standard Setting Based on Engineered Standards (Standard Times)

Especially for routinized tasks such as street cleaning or garbage collection, many governments turn to traditional industrial engineering to help them set reasonable output standards. Standards set by any of this large group of techniques are sometimes termed *engineered standards.*

The basis of engineered standards is the concept of standard times. A *standard time* is the amount of time it should take to complete a particular task. Time standards can be set in a number of ways. Let us begin with the most famous: time and motion studies, which have most often been used with factory workers. Each action of the workers is broken into smaller motions, assigned a time (say, .5 seconds) and then added together to get a standard time for the whole procedure. Although they are famous (or infamous), time and motion studies are essentially irrelevant to public sector needs.

However, there are ways of deriving standard times that do have some application in the public sector; the most common is called *currently derived standard times.* Under this approach, a number of experienced workers are gathered and timed while they work through one unit of output, such as one client interviewed, one stoplight installed, or one application completed. The average time of these experienced, well-trained workers becomes the standard time for that output or procedure.[13]

Uses of Standard Times. Standard times are generally used to compare our performance in the current year to what it "should" be. For example, if we know that we "should" pick up 1 ton of garbage every two hours, because our standard time has established that level, and we instead average 1 ton every three hours, the variance between the standard and actual performance suggests that we first investigate and then take remedial steps.

An organization can use individualized standard times to set objectives for larger organizational processes. If the standard times indicate that six clients can be processed by one worker in an hour, an agency with ten workers can easily set its agency-wide output standard for clients processed per hour (10 × 6). The resulting output goals—sixty clients processed per hour or one hundred tax forms reviewed per week—are sometimes called *work standards*. It is simply a matter of arithmetic to use standard times to establish monthly or quarterly standards for all sorts of agency-wide processes and outputs. The manager then knows that if output falls far below these standards, the organization is not performing at peak efficiency. As the name suggests, standard times set up a goal or yardstick by which performance can be evaluated.

Distortions of Standard Times. Many public agencies say they use standard times when in fact their standard times have been established in a distorted manner. The most common error is the use of *average* times for the whole organization. For example, if a form-processing organization wished to determine a standard time for completing its forms, it would take the number of forms that had been completed for the week, divide by the number of employee hours that had been worked that week, and call the result a "standard" time. The problem is that an average time is not an accurate standard time. If, for example, most of the work force had been recently hired when the measurement was made, the average-based "standard time" would embody all that inexperience. The same is true if the work force is less educated or less motivated than that of years past.[14]

Standard times are accurate only if they are based on the measurement of well-trained, experienced workers. Simply taking an average of all workers means that standard times will shift as employee characteristics shift. This will result in a rubber yardstick—an unreliable measure that stretches and shrinks depending on how well the work force is doing instead of how difficult the work is. Managers can never be sure what they are measuring when they use average times.

Objections to Standard Times. Many public employee labor unions have long opposed standard times that are not based on average times. Clearly if average times are the only available standards, public managers must use them. Although they are better than no standards at all, they are a very poor second indeed. Standard times are controversial with other actors as well; in fact they comprise one of the touchiest areas of public administration. Even the advocates of standard times are made uneasy by their occasional misuse and misinterpretation.

The concept of standard times connotes the image of Taylorism. Working at the beginning of this century, Frederick Taylor helped establish the study of administration.[15] He has the not totally deserved popular reputation as someone who viewed workers as machines and who cared only about their efficiency without being interested in their psychological or sociological well-being. Today managerial theorists understand that nontangible psychological and sociological factors are the most important determinants of workers' performances. Yet for many people the entire concept of work measurement carries at least the faint scent of Taylorism— of standing over workers with a stopwatch.[16]

Even those most committed to standard time measurements must not overemphasize their importance. Such measurements are only one component of a performance monitoring system, which in turn is only one measure of employee and organizational performance. However, if used correctly, standard times provide managers with information that is available in no other way.

Combining Standard-Setting Techniques

We have considered the four major ways of setting standards for all management systems: negotiations, quotas, past performance, and engineered standards.[17] As noted, the use of quotas (goals set unilaterally by the superior, based simply on personal estimation) is undesirable, though common. Each of the other three techniques is useful in its own sphere. More important, however, the three techniques also complement each other. For example, a manager who wishes to use past performance as the standard will feel far more comfortable if he or she knows that a unit's past performance ranked high when measured by standard times. Similarly, when standards are set by negotiation, both superior and subordinate must come to the standard-setting meeting with some idea of their preferred goal or standard. Their knowledge of past performance and (if available) of engineered standards will help both sides of the negotiation to decide what is "reasonable."

CURRENT PATTERNS OF PERFORMANCE MONITORING SYSTEM USE

Some performance data are gathered by all federal agencies because they are required to report year-end output data for government-wide productivity surveys (briefly discussed in the next chapter). However even though all federal organizations gather some output data, they do not all have true performance monitoring systems. Only perhaps half the agencies use the data as an aid to decision making, and it is only these agencies that can be said to have working performance monitoring systems.[18]

Nonetheless even 50 percent usage in the massive federal government represents a very substantial employment of such systems. Many state governments also have solid performance monitoring systems, with New Jersey, Pennsylvania, Wisconsin, and California among the national leaders in terms of sophistication.

As previously noted, 67 percent of all American cities use such systems, a substantial increase over the past decade. A recent survey[19] indicates that the municipal functions most often covered by such systems are police, fire, solid waste, public transit, health and hospitals, and social services. More than 90 percent of the respondents felt that such systems were either "very" or "somewhat" effective. Surveys have also indicated that most of the cities using performance monitoring systems use MBO as well, and it is to a final comparison of these two systems that we now turn.

RECAP: COMPARING MBO AND PERFORMANCE MONITORING SYSTEMS

Although performance monitoring systems operate somewhat differently than MBO systems, it is important to emphasize that their similarities far outweigh their differences. Both are output-oriented management systems that enable managers to guide organizational performance by setting standards, tracking progress, and taking remedial action if necessary. Like two versions of a single tool, neither system is universally preferable to the other; each system is best directed at different levels of the organization and different types of programs.

Both MBO and performance monitoring systems have most of the same advantages in aiding managers, including early information for decision making and clearer communication of goals to employees. Both types of systems are plagued by the same types of problems. Both require the manager to make difficult choices about which particular outputs to track, and for both the choice is aided by the chain of outputs. The systems share the need for top support to succeed, and they share problems of misreporting and goal displacement. The solutions to these problems, discussed in Chapter 3, are also the same for each. Finally, both systems have external and internal political effects, and the external effects—the result of choosing to emphasize some outputs rather than others—are very similar. Such effects are the topic of the next section.

THE POLITICAL USES OF PERFORMANCE MONITORING SYSTEMS

Politics is "who gets what." Therefore management systems have "political" effects because some groups win and others lose with each new system-based decision. Even seemingly neutral goals such as "efficiency" have political implications. For example, when efficiency is increased by replacing meter readers with computerized, automatic meter-reading machines, some societal groups (such as middle-class taxpayers) gain, while other groups (such as low-skilled workers who might have held the jobs or aspired to them) lose.[20]

Often the political thrust of a management system is more direct. Two short examples of the political understructure of performance monitoring system choices are provided by the Nixon AFDC drive and the North Carolina state trooper performance ratings.

The Nixon Management Systems and AFDC

The Nixon administration came to office on a pledge of cleaning up the waste in the Great Society programs that it inherited. One of the major programs targeted in the resulting efficiency drive was the main federal welfare program—Aid to Families with Dependent Children (AFDC). AFDC was financed in large part by the federal government but administered by the states. Its performance levels were tracked by a Nixon administration management system that followed two major categories: (1) overpayments and (2) ineligible recipients receiving aid. Standards for the two categories were set at 5 percent for overpayments and 3 percent for ineligible recipients, and states that exceeded these levels were threatened with a cutoff of funds.

Over a period of time the drive in fact lowered the error rates in these two categories considerably (although not, for most states, below the standards). This effort was applauded by a wide spectrum of the U.S. public, including many who were sympathetic to the poor, because "efficiency" is a much-respected, seemingly neutral goal.

In fact, however, the monitored categories were clear attempts to direct workers' behavior in specific political directions that had little to do with efficiency. Overpayments were sanctioned, but not underpayments. Moreover, the system focused on ineligible applicants who received payments, but it did not monitor the opposite problem, eligible applicants who were denied their rightful benefits. The management system therefore provided strong incentives for erring on these unmeasured categories. A local social services department worker with an ambiguous application now had an incentive to deny benefits. If the applicant was actually entitled to benefits, the mistake was nowhere tracked or sanctioned. On the other hand, if the applicant was admitted to the AFDC rolls and later proved ineligible, the mistake was recorded and punished. The choice of outputs monitored by the Nixon administration under the guise of neutral "efficiency" were in fact strong incentives to err on the side of underpayment and denial of benefits to the eligible.[21]

State Trooper Performance Ratings

Not long ago a North Carolina newspaper revealed that the new state trooper performance ratings contained thirteen monitored categories, one of which was "number of tickets written." Legislators and their constituents raised a large cry, protesting that such a category constituted a quota. Speeding drivers began to complain that the only reason they received a speeding ticket was because the trooper had to meet a quota. The head of the Department of Crime Control and Public Safety defended his new performance measurement system, emphasizing that the ticket category was only one of thirteen. Such information was valuable, he said, but it would not greatly affect workers' behavior.[22]

Nonetheless, the state legislature showed a rare interest in management systems. It passed a law that said that not only could there be no quota but also the state patrol could not even *consider* the volume of citations written when making decisions on promotions or granting merit pay increases. In response to the law, and over the objections of the department head, the category was discontinued. Months later, figures were released showing that at the time the new category of "tickets written" was added to the performance evaluation system, the number of tickets written increased by 45 percent.[23]

As illustrated by these two examples, management systems necessarily involve politics—who gets what. No matter what outputs are affected by a system, some people will gain while others lose. This result is both inevitable and, if handled correctly, desirable. But to handle it correctly, managers must realize these political effects; they should not be lulled into believing that management systems, by emphasizing efficiency, are therefore apolitical and "neutral." All government actions (whether based on systems or not) involve choices; designers and users of management systems need only recognize this, and proceed to make their choices on considered and defensible grounds.

SUMMARY

All output-oriented management systems that are not MBO systems can be called performance monitoring systems. Such systems generally focus on units rather than individual managers and on routine, continuing tasks rather than on one-time projects. Because of these characteristics, they are often most valuable for dealing with the lower levels of organization, whereas middle managers and staff people are more often covered by MBO.

Valid output measures are often difficult to establish for performance monitoring systems. As with MBO, goal displacement and misreporting are also troublesome. Output indicators are more likely to be valid if they are multiple, chosen on grounds other than data accessibility, and if they register both immediate and long-range impacts. This final balance is made easier by the concept of a chain of outputs, which indicates the expected links between immediate actions and outputs and desired long-range impacts. To maintain the focus on results, the manager must constantly strive to adopt some indicators that are well down the chain of outputs.

Once the outputs to be measured have been determined, the manager must also determine how much of the output he or she expects—in other words, a standard. There are four principal ways of setting standards: negotiations (the basis of MBO), past performance, unilateral quotas (undesirable but common), and engineered standards. Engineered standards are usually based on a "standard time," which is the amount of time it "should" take an employee to complete a task. Often more than one of these four techniques is used in determining a standard.

These and other system choices almost inevitably have political effects. That is, some people inside or outside the organization fare better or worse than they would without the system. Chapter Four discusses internal political effects, particularly power shifts; this chapter emphasizes some external effects. Users and designers of systems must acknowledge these effects, rather than hiding behind claims of neutrality, because no possible choice (including the choice of having no system) can be truly neutral.

Ultimately, a performance monitoring system can be judged by whether it provides the data that managers find most useful in deciding the hardest, most important, recurring questions, and also by whether it motivates employees to act in ways desired by managers and the public.

REVIEW QUESTIONS

1. Distinguish between MBO systems and performance monitoring systems.

2. Construct a chain of outputs for a county job-placement program. Suggest what outputs could be tracked most easily and which would be most meaningful for capturing real impact.

3. Construct a chain of outputs for a clinic-based health program that deals mainly with promoting birth control among low-income teenagers. Suggest which outputs would be easiest to track and which would be most meaningful. (In this and the following question, it will be necessary to more specifically define what the agency or program actually does before beginning the chain.)

4. Construct a chain of outputs for a state social services agency that locates and aids physically abused children. Suggest which outputs would be easiest to track and which would be most meaningful.

5. What criteria should guide managers in choosing how many indicators to track? What would be the difference in the type and number of indicators chosen between an agency that helps runaway teens and one that delivers mail?

6. What type of organization or program is most suited to standard setting based on past performance?

7. Name four organizations that are suited for standard setting based on engineered standards.

8. Is a management system more likely to have political effects when it is working well or when it is failing? Why? (Be sure to define both *political effects* and *failure*.)

9. Name three programs for which surveys would be most useful in judging organizational performance. Name three for which they would be least useful.

10. What determines whether a system's chosen indicators lead to results that are reliable? Valid?

Case 5–1

California's 300-employee bureau of rehabilitation has the sole duty of running a program that trains convicts in new skills. Through a work-release program, it puts them in part-time jobs while they are still in prison, then tries to place them in permanent jobs that utilize their new skills once they have been released.

The new head of the bureau wishes to institute a management system for the organization. Suggest

1. What measures should be tracked.
2. At what intervals these measures should be tracked.
3. How goals for each measure should be set.
4. Probable problems with each measure—that is, which are most prone to displacement, cheating, and so forth.
5. Ways such problems will be alleviated.
6. How the information generated by the system will be used.

The budget should be assumed to be given. The suggested system should balance short-term and long-term indicators; it should emphasize outputs over processes or inputs, and it should be practical.

Case 5–2

The city-financed free clinic of Middleton offers medical services to street people and other indigents. The clinic has nine employees, including three doctors and four nurses. Lately costs have been accelerating rapidly, and the clinic is under political attack. A new head has been appointed to make the clinic more "efficient." His first step is to begin an output-oriented management system.

Describe the management system that he should install, with particular attention to

1. What measures should be tracked (each type of disease treated may need a separate output chain, so pick just two or three major ones)
2. At what intervals these measures should be tracked
3. How goals for each measure should be set
4. Probable problems with each measure—that is, which are most prone to displacement, cheating, and so forth.
5. Ways such problems will be alleviated
6. How the information generated by the system will be used

The budget should be assumed to be given. The suggested system should balance short-term and long-term indicators; it should emphasize outputs over processes or inputs, and it should be practical.

ENDNOTES

1. Gregory Streib and Theodore H. Poister, "Established and Emerging Management Tools: A 12-Year Perspective," *The Municipal Yearbook 1989* (Washington, DC: International City Managers Association, 1989), pp. 45–54.
2. *The Mayor's Management Report* (New York: Citybooks, February 1988), pp. 411–12, City of Dayton, "Annual Objectives, 1985"; City of Winston-Salem, *Annual Budget Program, 1986-7, Year-End Report*, November 11, 1987.
3. A system that seemingly fell into the trap of too many measures is a small nursing agency with "103 finely grained output measures and 21 efficiency measures per nurse," which were weighted in various ways. Regina Herzlinger, "Why Data Systems in Nonprofit Organizations Fail," *Harvard Business Review*, January/February 1977, pp. 81–86.

   Because humans are inefficient data processors, it seems very likely that when more than a dozen or so indicators are reported a few assume de facto importance and the rest are ignored. Sometimes this tendency is even formalized by agencies that isolate and highlight a few "key indicators" out of their dozens of monitored indicators. But then one must explain why the time and cost is expended in gathering the non-key indicators.

4. Of course, it would be impossible to discuss here possible output measures for the hundreds of government functions. Because measures differ according to the needs of managers and the specifics of each jurisdiction, managerial judgment is usually the best guide.

For those uncertain of their needs and looking for initial suggestions of measures for local government, a good overview with useful checklists is Harry P. Hatry et al., *How Effective Are Your Services?* (Washington, DC: The Urban Institute and The International City Managers Association, 1977). By far the most extensive treatment of specific measures for each possible government area is George J. Washnis, ed., *Productivity Improvement Handbook for State and Local Government* (New York: John Wiley, 1980).

Even the 1,460 pages of the Washnis book, however, cannot capture all possible measures, and accordingly there are a number of periodical articles published each year on possible measures for different areas. To take just four areas for example:

Measures for criminal justice are treated in an entire issue of *Public Productivity Review,* 3, no. 3 (Fall 1984); see also Gloria Grizzle, "Adult Corrections Performance Measurement: A Conceptual Framework," *Policy Studies Review,* 6, no. 1 (August 1986).

Measures of nursing are treated very well in Richard Jelinek and Frank Pierce, "A Nursing Systems Approach: Productivity and Quality of Care," *Public Productivity Review,* 6, no. 3 (September 1982).

An empirical overview of some indicators used in higher education is "Nation Reports Found Spurring College Changes," *The Chronicle of Higher Education,* July 30, 1986, p. 1. A nationwide survey of colleges and universities finds that most (88 percent) track their graduation rates, and 29 percent survey their alumni five or ten years after graduation. "Value added" tests of student gains (i.e., testing at the beginning and end of college) was believed appropriate by 67 percent of the responding institutions but used by only 9 percent.

Measures for staff functions are explored in Gerald L. Barkdoll and Anne E. Greene, "The Staff Functions: Measuring the Performance of These Maligned Contributors," in Joseph S. Wholey, ed., *Organizational Excellence* (Lexington, MA: Lexington Books, 1987).

The best continuing guide to measures developed for each area is the journal *Public Productivity and Management Review.*

5. The concept is discussed in Edward A. Suchman, *Evaluative Research* (New York: Russell Sage Foundation, 1967), pp. 51–73. A very useful and practical exposition is Michael Quinn Patton, *Utilization-Focused Evaluation* (Beverly Hills, CA: Sage Publications, 1978), pp. 179–198.

   Such chains are sometimes termed hierarcies of objectives. Adopting the nomenclature of some authors in this area ("missions, goals, and objectives"), our *ultimate outputs* could be recast as *desired missions,* the *intermediate outputs* as *desired goals,* and the *immediate outputs* as *desired objectives.* However, our approach differs in emphasizing the need to operationalize measures for each level, not just for the objectives.

   If we were less concerned about the link to management systems, such a chain could be developed in the opposite direction, by beginning with the program's more far-reaching goals and working back by asking, "How could this be produced?" This is a classic form of business strategic planning, but it is rare in the public sector because it assumes a long lead time and a relatively small group of decision makers who can reach a consensus on overall goals. Both of these traits are very uncharacteristic (and generally undesirable) in a democracy (as discussed in Chapter One and developed extensively by such authors as Aaron Wildavsky and Charles E. Lindblom). Proceeding in the suggested direction gives a focus and practicality to a discussion of the agency's more far-reaching goals.

6. However, in the late 1960s a few social scientists became interested in measuring societal happiness. These ultimate "social indicators" of societal happiness are established by asking respondents to judge their personal happiness or well-being on a continuum such as a seven-point scale. Generally, Americans are a quite happy people. Not surprisingly, the correlation between self-rated well-being or happiness and public policy is relatively low. The quality of the personal environment—for example, family relationships—have a much stronger effect.

   A valiant attempt to link empirically government programs, social indicators, and citizen surveys about broad quality-of-life issues is Y. H. Cho and F. S. Redburn, "Public Policy and Community Life in American Cities: A Search for Linkage," *International Journal of Public Administration,* 5, no. 4 (1983).

7. Potential workload as well as output indicators are discussed for various government functions in Harry P. Hatry et al., *Efficiency Measurement for Local Government Services* (Washington, DC: The

Urban Institute, 1979). Workload indicators are also discussed in the sources in note 4.

8. Among the recent articles on the use of surveys to determine organizational effectiveness are Brian Stipak, "Citizen Satisfaction with Urban Services: Potential Misuse as a Performance Indicator," *Public Administration Review,* 39, no. 1 (January/February 1979). Stipak argues that the link between citizens' responses and actual agency performance is very weak. So do Karin Brown and Phillip B. Coulter, "Subjective and Objective Measures of Public Service Delivery," *Public Administration Review,* 43, no. 1 (January/February 1983), pp. 50–58. Also see Michael R. Fitzgerald and Robert F. Durant, "Citizen Evaluation and Urban Management: Service Delivery in an Era of Protest," *Public Administration Review,* 40, no. 6 (November/December 1980).

   In opposition is Roger B. Parks, "Linking Objective and Subjective Measures of Performance," *Public Administration Review,* 44, no. 2 (March/April 1984). Parks makes a case that objective and subjective measures are linked. Yet even his article does not support the idea that they should be a primary focus of monitoring because he links them only through an involved construct. See also the Stipak-Parks debate in "Communications," *Public Administration Review,* November/December 1984, pp. 551–52.

   An excellent model of a very strong ongoing consumer survey is provided by U.S. General Accounting Office, *Social Security: Quality of Services Generally Rated High by Clients Sampled* (Washington, DC: GAO, January 1986), and its successor, *Social Security: Clients Still Rate Quality of Service High* (July 1987).

   In the late 1980s, Michigan used an outside pollster—Lou Harris Associates—to poll recipients of state services: "Michigan Tries Survey of Customer Satisfaction," *Governing,* February 1988, p. 15.

   Surveys can be used to measure performance even when the clientele is internal. For example, in the Equal Employment Opportunity Commission (EEOC), external clients are surveyed, but so are internal ones, such as EEOC attorneys using products from investigative units. See Polly Mead, Elizabeth Rasmussen, and John Seal, "Quality Assurance in the EEOC," in Joseph S. Wholey, ed., *Organizational Excellence* (Lexington, MA: Lexington Books, 1987).

9. Client or citizen satisfaction measures—usually surveys—are a rapidly growing technique in municipalities. At least 69 percent report using them for some function. Streib and Poister, "Established and Emerging Management Tools," p. 50.

10. Good sources on this topic include Earl Babbie, *The Practice of Social Research,* 3rd ed. (Belmont, CA: Wadsworth, 1983), pp. 113ff;

Jon C. Nunnally, Jr., *Introduction to Psychological Measurement* (New York: McGraw-Hill, 1970); and Edward G. Carmines and Richard A. Zeller, *Reliability and Validity Assessment* (Beverly Hills, CA: Sage Publications, 1979).

11. Allen D. Putt and J. Fred Springer, *Policy Research: Concepts, Methods and Applications* (Englewood Cliffs, NJ: Prentice-Hall, 1989), p. 135. I have transposed two sentences here, but without changing the authors' meaning.

12. Of course, indicators that are not valid but are kept for political reasons can be viewed another way: as part of a parallel chain of outputs for the program in which the ultimate output is "gain political support." If so viewed, they are very valid measures—of the political goal. Although defensible conceptually, this way of viewing the chain of outputs usually does not prove practical for most managers. It would lead to the conclusion that managers should emphasize *only* the items with the highest political payoff, and it implicitly assumes that government agencies' overriding goal should always be maximizing political rewards. In designing a management system, it is usually more helpful for practicing managers to view political considerations as one more (major) item to consider *in addition* to the chain of outputs, rather than treating short-term political payoffs as the basic goal of their program (and thus the chain).

13. Establishing times is discussed in Maria P. Aristigueta, "Operations Review, Work Measurement, and Work Standards," and W. H. Weiss, "How to Work-Sample Your Employees," both in John Matzer, Jr., ed., *Productivity Improvement Techniques* (Washington, DC: International City Managers Association, 1986), pp. 37–63. A good book-length work that extensively covers variations on time standards is Marvin E. Mundel, *Improving Productivity and Effectiveness* (Englewood Cliffs, NJ: Prentice-Hall, 1983).

14. The Social Security Administration (SSA) uses average times rather than true standard times. It is criticized for doing so by the General Accounting Office, which calls the two categories "does take times" and "should take times." U.S. General Accounting Office, *Need to Improve Unit Times for Estimating Field Office Staff Budgets* (Washington, DC: GAO, August 1986).

15. Frederick W. Taylor, *The Principles of Scientific Management* (New York: Harper & Row, 1911).

16. The extremely tight employee control implied by time and motion studies is back in a new form—computerized monitoring. For example, in one SSA data processing center, about 1,000 workers "are expected to meet quotas as they punch their computer keyboards—for instance, 138 forms per hour for those entering annual wage

forms of SSA recipients. The computer keeps a running total on the screen of the forms completed, and it can compute the amount of time actually worked by the employee that day."

Similarly, computer monitoring of each worker's speed, efficiency, and accuracy is being widely used for telephone operators, supermarket cashiers, bank tellers, and hotel maids, among others. Peter Perl, "Monitoring by Computers Sparks Employee Concerns," *Washington Post*, September 2, 1984, pp. 1ff.

This seems an omniscient form of operations control in a pervasive, Tayloresque sense. Such systems greatly reduce autonomy to a much greater extent than simply having a weekly goal and allowing the employees to reach that goal any way they wish. Such systems must be implemented with the active involvement of employees or employee groups and then used very judiciously to avoid serious problems with both ethics and morale.

17. Some might suggest that borrowing standards from another jurisdiction—a similar neighboring city, for example—is a fifth way of deriving standards. But we can probably exclude it on two grounds, one definitional and one practical. Definitionally, such standards had to be developed by the neighboring city at some point, and when it developed its standards, it must have used one of the four techniques we have discussed. Thus "borrowing" is not a separate approach; it is based on one of the other four. More practically, there are usually so many differences between even "similar" jurisdictions—wider streets for garbage collection, more poor people for a social services agency, and so on—that output standards are difficult to borrow. The great variation in pay scales makes input standards similarly difficult to transfer.

For an attempt to overcome all these problems by picking very similar cities, then constructing a research design to compare performances by holding other factors constant, see David N. Ammons, *Municipal Productivity: A Comparison of Fourteen High Quality Service Cities* (New York: Praeger, 1984).

18. The estimate that half of all federal agencies use performance monitoring systems is entirely an educated guess; no government-wide survey seems to have been done. There are encouraging signs: Some of the very largest agencies such as SSA and virtually all components of Defense use such systems. But there are also discouraging signs: A GAO survey of nine federal agencies found few really using such systems and taking action on their results. The reason was unfortunately predictable: "The most serious and widespread problem with seven of the nine agency [productivity] programs was the lack of top level support for their activities." U.S. General Accounting

Office, *Increased Use of Productivity Management Can Help Control Government Costs* (Washington, DC: GAO, November 10, 1983), p. 16.

19. These and the following survey figures are drawn from Streib and Poister, "Established and Emerging Management Tools." The 67 percent of cities that report such systems undoubtedly include at least a few cities that claim systems (because they know they "should" have them) even though their systems are fragmentary or little used.

Still, there are a number of fine municipal systems. Another article cites notable performance monitoring systems in Charlotte, Cincinnati, Dayton, Dallas, San Diego, New York City, and Phoenix—and of course there are many more. "Cincinnati Measures Service Success," *Public Administration Times,* April 1, 1985, p. 4.

20. A discussion of the class bias and other political aspects underlying the "municipal efficiency" drives of eighty years ago is Martin J. Schiesl, *The Politics of Efficiency: Municipal Administration and Reform in America: 1880–1920* (Berkeley: University of California Press, 1977).

21. Ronald Randall, "Presidential Power Versus Bureaucratic Intransigence: The Influence of the Nixon Administration on Welfare Policy," *American Political Science Review,* 73 (1979), 798–800.

The process was paralleled by developments in California under Governor Reagan. It is discussed in John Mendeloff, "Welfare Procedures and Error Rates: An Alternative Perspective," *Policy Analysis,* (Summer 1977) 3, no. 3, 257–74.

22. William M. Welch, "Ban on Quotas Seen Creating Review Trouble," *Raleigh News and Observer,* May 24, 1981, p. 33.

23. Pat Stith, "Tickets Up 45% Under Evaluation Plan," *Raleigh News and Observer,* October 7, 1981, p. 1.

chapter six

Further Topics in Performance Monitoring Systems

INTRODUCTION

The basic aspects of performance monitoring systems were introduced in the previous chapter. This chapter builds on that introduction by considering three separate topics: combining output measures into a productivity measurement system, measuring outputs in terms of money, and tying performance monitoring systems to program evaluation. These three topics do not tightly connect with each other; they are all simply different, more advanced uses of performance monitoring systems, and each topic will be treated in a separate section of this chapter.

SECTION 1: PRODUCTIVITY MEASUREMENT SYSTEMS

Aggregating Output Measures: When Useful?

We briefly discussed the fact that management system indicators are sometimes built by aggregating (combining) measures that have been gathered about the performance of each operations-level employee. Employee-by-employee figures are rarely of any use to middle and upper managers, but we can produce something useful by combining them, generating seven or eight figures that indicate what an *entire unit* did, say, last month. We might then have figures that tell us something about the unit's quantity in several different areas and other figures that tell us about quality and speed of response. All of these would be useful management indicators. However, in this chapter we wish to consider another, more dramatic form of aggregating information.

Once we have combined the operations-level figures to establish perhaps a dozen management indicators for a program, we may be tempted to keep going and combine these dozen indicators even further, finally deriving just one "super indicator" that tells us how well the organization is doing overall. Is this a good idea? Should we track various program outputs separately and report them separately, or should we aggregate all the indicators into one number to indicate overall performance?

Some combining of similar indicators may be useful, particularly if dozens of indicators are monitored. Thus combining forty program indicators into six or seven is often wise because it puts the information in a form that is easier to comprehend and use.[1] But if combining forty indicators into seven is a defensible choice, combining them into one overall "index" is generally not very useful, and often harms the system. Almost nothing is gained by such a move—managers have no trouble understanding six or seven indicators, so compression is not necessary— but a great deal may be lost. For example, if the overall index indicator is down, top managers do not have the specific information to learn where the problem is located. Such information is contained in the separate indicators, and it is lost when they are all combined into a single super indicator. Moreover, single overall indicators encourage goal displacement because workers soon determine which aspects are most manipulable and heavily weighted, and concentrate on them.

Nonetheless, many agencies continue to attempt to use only one number. "Productivity systems" are the most important and influential systems that use a single number. In this section we will briefly examine how output indicators are weighted because weights are used in all forms of aggregation. We will then move on to the most extreme form of aggregation: productivity measurement systems. We will discuss these systems at some length, despite their pitfalls, because they are so often used in the public sector.

A Prerequisite to Aggregation: Weighting Indicators

When combining indicators into overall measures, it is generally necessary to weight the more important indicators. The basic premise behind weighting is straightforward: Not all outputs come in comparable units, and not all outputs or output measures are equally valuable. Weighting is a way of making the output measures comparable in units and importance.

As an extremely simplified example, let us imagine a small-town police department that tracks only three crime statistics: burglaries, rapes, and murders. The city manager wishes to combine these indicators as a crime index and then reward the police department if the index falls—a type of negative output measure. Last year the town had thirty burglaries, one rape, and one murder. This year the town had only ten burglaries, but there were five murders and five rapes.

The Unweighted Index. If the city manager does not weight the separate output indicators, he or she can simply add all crimes together to derive a total crime index. Thus for last year, the index would be 32 (30 burglaries + 1 murder + 1 rape). But this unweighted index is probably misleading. This year, when there were five murders and five rapes but only ten burglaries, most citizens would feel that the real amount of crime had gone up, but the combined index would say that it had fallen to 20 (5 + 5 + 10). The problem is that the index treats all crimes as equal, so a murder counts as much as a burglary. This defies common sense. The solution is to weight the types of crime.

A Weighted Index. One very simplified way of weighting the measures is to count each murder as fifty, and each rape as fifty; a burglary is counted as one. Under the new weighted system, the crime index for the first year totaled 130 (50 for the murder + 50 for the rape + 30 for the burglaries); this year the index would be 510 (250 for the five murders + 250 for the five rapes + 10 for the burglaries). The new index, by weighting outputs, indicates the obvious: This year was much worse for crime.

Any attempt to combine indicators—whether into seven or eight final indicators or into one overall super indicator—will require weighting some outputs. Although there is an unavoidable element of subjectivity in choosing how heavily to weight various outputs, it can be minimized by clearly informing all those affected by the system about the weights being used and why they were chosen. If at all possible, the weights assigned to each indicator should be determined in consultation with all involved workers; if the decision is made unilaterally by top managers, it will sometimes be seen as manipulating the system.

Productivity Measurement Systems: Basic Components

Because public sector management systems are new, the terminology is still unsettled. Nowhere is this terminological confusion more obvious than in the use of the term *productivity system*. Productivity is a measure of how much output is produced for a given measure of input. In other words, it is a ratio measure of efficiency. Thus any management system that attempts to improve an organization's efficiency—for example, MBO—*could* be called a productivity system. Some managers and authors follow this logic and use the term *productivity system* to refer to all public management systems. Others use the term in a slightly more restrictive way to refer to all performance monitoring systems. We are going to follow a yet more restrictive approach: *Productivity systems* are performance monitoring systems that express their measurements in a single productivity figure; that is, they use a single super indicator to register the organization's performance.[2] Thus productivity systems are just one type of a performance monitoring system.[3]

Measuring Productivity

Most productivity measures are expressed as a ratio of output to input. Output can be any product of an organization. Productivity systems often use activity measures as surrogates for real outputs, sometimes combining them with actual output indicators. Thus the productivity system for a sanitation department might measure such real outputs as tons of garbage collected or such process indicators as number of houses serviced. For a social services agency, the productivity system might register the number of forms processed or clients seen or dollars distributed. (Box 6–1 illustrates such indicators for a municipal water supply program.)

For most productivity systems, input is expressed as labor. Labor used to be expressed as *man years;* now the term is more often *labor years* or even *person years*. The concept is the same: The number of people working multiplied by the number of years they work equals labor years. If it takes twenty people six months apiece to produce a particular output, we would say that the input for that system was ten labor years (20 × ½).

"Raw" Productivity Figures. A productivity system establishes a "raw" productivity figure for a year by dividing the output for that year by the input (expressed as labor). If thirty people take one working year to turn out seventy-five automobiles, the raw productivity for that year is 75/30 = 2½.

Comparing Years. To any outside observer it would be unclear, however, what 2½ in this example really indicates. One way of anchoring the figure is to compare it to past years. Most productivity systems do so by deciding arbitrarily that one year will be their yardstick, or *base year,* and then comparing all other years to that year.

The base year is usually the first year for which there is input and

---

Box 6–1. Water Supply Units of Work or Output

ACTIVITY	UNIT OF WORK OR OUTPUT
Pumping Operations	Number of gallons pumped
Purification	Number of gallons purified
Water Quality Testing	Number of water samples tested (by test type)
Main Service	Feet of mains constructed (by size of main)
	Number of mains tapped (by size)
	Feet (or miles) of main inspected
	Feet (or miles) of main flushed and chlorinated
Repair Operations	Number of breaks repaired (by type)
	Number of leaks repaired (by type)
Meter Service	Number of meters installed
	—removed
	—serviced
	—adjusted
	—repaired
	—replaced
Fire Hydrant Service	Number installed
	—serviced
	—repaired
	—replaced
	—painted
	—inspected (operated)
	—flushed
Valve Service	Number serviced
	—adjusted
	—repaired
	—replaced
	—inspected (operated)
Customer Service	Number serviced
	—service connections
	—service connections discontinued
	—service connections repaired
	—meters read
	—complaints investigated
Miscellaneous Inspections	Number of inspections (by type)
Pressure and Flow Surveys	Number of surveys completed
Billing and Collections	Number of bills rendered
	Number of collection operations

Source: Harry P. Hatry, *Efficiency Measurement for Local Government Services* (Washington, DC: Urban Institute, 1979), p. 20.

---

output data. The base year is arbitrarily given the value of 100, and future years are expressed as a percentage of the base year. If an organization's output this year is 5 percent higher than the base year's output, and its input remains the same, it has a productivity rating of 105. If its output stayed the same but its input increased by 10 percent, its productivity rating falls to 100 divided by 110, or 91. Box 6–2 summarizes these procedures, and Figure 6–1 shows productivity figures for a number of years for the entire federal government, with 1977 as the base year.[4]

Measuring Inputs in a Productivity System

There are problems with traditional input measures used by productivity systems, however. Because they use "labor" as the measure of organizational input, they can easily be distorted. Labor does not capture all the real resources used by an organization or program.

Labor as the Sole Input: An Example of Distortion. A city agency operates with ten employees; its only expense is their salaries of $20,000 apiece. Therefore its total traditional measure of input is ten labor years, and it uses $200,000 (for the ten salaries) in resources per year.

The next year the city agency replaces nine of its ten employees with a computer that it *rents* for $580,000 per year. Its output remains the same. Now its traditional measure of input is one labor year (it has one employee left), and it uses $600,000 in resources (the computer rental plus one salary per year). Common sense suggests that the agency's productivity has plummeted. To produce the same output, it now uses three times as many resources ($600,000 to $200,000). But a traditional productivity system will register a huge *increase* in productivity, showing a 90 percent drop in input (from ten labor years to one), because it uses only labor as the input measure.

Total Factor Productivity. Because productivity systems based on the traditional input measure of labor are often incomplete or distorted, more complete measures are needed. For greatest accuracy, all of the

---

Box 6–2.

THE FOUR BASIC STEPS OF TRADITIONAL PRODUCTIVITY MEASUREMENT

1. Gather all data on input of the organization in terms of labor years (or labor months).
2. Gather all data on the output that is to be measured for the organization. How much did it accomplish this month or year?
3. Divide output by input to get a raw productivity figure for the year.
4. Divide this year's raw productivity figure by the base year's raw productivity figure. Multiply by 100 for the productivity rating.

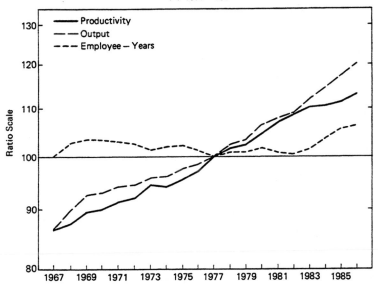

TOTAL FEDERAL SAMPLE
Productivity, Output, and Employee — Years, FY 1967 — 86
FY 1977 = 100

Figure 6–1. *Source:* Bureau of Labor Statistics, U.S. Department of Labor, February, 1989.

TABLE 6–1 Federal Government—Total Sample: Indexes of Output per Employee Year and Related Data, 1967–87 (1977 = 100)

Fiscal year	Output per employee year	Output	Employee years
Index: 1967	86.5	86.4	99.9
1968	87.5	89.6	102.5
1969	89.6	92.5	103.3
1970	90.0	92.8	103.1
1971	91.4	94.0	102.8
1972	92.0	94.2	102.4
1973	94.6	95.7	101.2
1974	94.1	95.9	101.9
1975	95.5	97.5	102.1
1976	97.1	98.3	101.1
1977	100.0	100.0	100.0
1978	101.7	102.3	100.6
1979	102.3	103.1	100.7
1980	104.5	106.1	101.5
1981	107.0	107.6	100.5
1982	108.6	108.9	100.3
1983	110.2	111.6	101.3
1984	110.2	114.1	103.5
1985	110.9	117.0	105.5
1986	112.7	119.8	106.2
1987	113.0	121.5	107.5
Average annual percent change:			
1967–87	1.4	1.6	.1
1982–87	.8	2.3	1.5

resources used by an agency or program should be measured; this is termed *total factor productivity.* As discussed in Chapter Two, money captures all forms of input, and therefore a total factor productivity system will use money as its input measure. In the preceding example, a total factor productivity system would have used $200,000 and $600,000 as the respective input measures. It would have registered the more accurate answer—that the productivity had fallen by two-thirds because the input tripled for the same output. Box 6–3 summarizes this example.

Total factor productivity systems, then, use monetary figures for all inputs. When tracking input over a number of years, such systems use "constant" dollars, that is, dollars that have been adjusted for inflation. If constant dollar figures were not used, an organization might use the same resources (inputs) this year as last but nonetheless appear to be using more because of inflation.

Distorted Incentives. Distortions of the traditional productivity measurement caused by inefficiently substituting capital for labor (like the previous computer example) would rarely occur if productivity measures

---

Box 6–3.

	YEAR 1	YEAR 2
Labor years	10	1
Total cost	$200,000	$600,000
Output	100 units	100 units

Traditional Approach

"RAW" PRODUCTIVITY FIGURES

Year 1: 100 units/10 labor years = 10
Year 2: 100 units/1 labor year = 100

If year 1 is the base year, its productivity rating is *100;* year 2's rating is *1,000.* Productivity is registered as increasing tenfold.

Total Factor Approach

"RAW" PRODUCTIVITY FIGURES

Year 1: 100 units/$200,000 = .0005
Year 2: 100 units/$600,000 = .00016

If year 1 is the base year, its productivity rating is again *100;* year 2's productivity rating is one-third of that, or *33.3.* Productivity is properly shown as falling by two-thirds.

were simply of academic interest. But productivity measures are often used to gauge the efficiency of an agency, and such important matters as the agency's budget or managerial salaries and promotions hinge on the ratings. Under these circumstances, government managers have an incentive to drive up their ratings any way they can. One way of doing so is to substitute machines or other unmeasured capital costs for personnel costs, no matter how inefficient such a substitution actually is. Thus the incomplete input measure of the traditional productivity system encourages public managers to make inefficient choices.

The use of labor as the sole input measure is common in productivity measurement throughout the economy, including the statistics on total U.S. productivity reported in the newspapers monthly. It is on this basis that we read constant stories that other countries, particularly Japan, are increasing their productivity faster than the United States. However, the distortion problem is much less bothersome when measuring private sector productivity. Private companies such as General Motors or IBM have no incentive to drive up their productivity rating. Profits and market shares are the basis for their rewards; productivity measures are just a minor piece of information. Thus, if private companies substitute capital for people, we can feel confident that they are acting for reasons of efficiency, and not to increase their productivity rating. Thus the ratings for the private sector remain relatively accurate.

Moving to Total Factor Productivity. The use of labor as the sole input measure is relatively acceptable for the private sector, but it can gravely distort managerial incentives in the public sector if the productivity measures are used for rewards. Why, then, has not more of the public sector moved to total factor productivity?

We discovered the answer in Chapter Two. Many government agencies have extremely primitive accounting systems and cannot determine how much money (in other words, what resources) their subagencies or programs are actually using. Among the most common problems are cost centers that are not compatible with the output data and the inability to include a share of capital costs (through depreciation) to get a total cost. But even agencies that lack useful accounting systems do have accurate personnel records, and so they are forced to use them as their surrogate measure of input. Moving to more accurate financial management systems, which would indicate total costs—direct plus indirect—for each program or subagency will allow government agencies to build total factor productivity systems. Combined with all of the other advantages cited in Chapter Two, total factor productivity provides yet another important reason for improving public agency financial information through the use of accrual systems and cost accounting.

Overcoming Problems with Longitudinal Output Measures

As we have seen, the heart of any productivity system is that it takes the measures of productivity for one agency for one year and compares it to the earlier years of that agency, using the base year as a yardstick. This procedure is simple enough when, year after year, the agency is doing the same tasks in the same ways that it did before. However, a problem arises when the output of the agency—its assigned task—changes.

For example, let us consider a state agency that handles unemployment compensation claims. The state legislature passes a measure that requires the agency to gather more information from each client. Because this law requires the agency to process a much longer, more complicated form for each applicant, it cannot possibly process the same number of clients per worker that it did before. Such changes in tasks raise the specter of junking the old productivity readings and beginning again from year one. If there is no way to compare this year to previous years, then every time the state legislature or internal changes affect the organizational procedures, a system would have to be restarted. Since changes often occur every year, there would be no way to compare and evaluate productivity or judge how well an agency is doing.

We need to find a way to equate this year's task with previous years so that we can say, for example, that this year's longer forms were "worth" (i.e., took as long as) one and one-half of last year's forms. We could then just multiply this year's output by 1.5 to see how well the agency is doing compared to the previous year. Such comparisons are possible through the use of standard times.

As discussed in the last chapter, currently derived standard times are established by timing a number of experienced workers as they work through one unit of output, such as one client interviewed, one stoplight installed, or one application completed. The average time of these experienced, well-trained workers becomes the standard time for that output or procedure. Thus, if these workers take twenty minutes for this year's form and ten minutes for last year's, we now have standard times for each form. If the same number of employees who turned out 10,000 forms last year turned out 5,000 this year, we feel confident in saying that productivity has remained steady because the standard time indicates that this year's form should be seen as being the same as two of last year's. We do not have to discard the productivity system, or begin again. Standard times provide a common measure that allows comparison of different outputs across the years.

In sum, productivity measurement systems turn all performance information into a single indicator that compares the current year's performance to a base year. Productivity measurement systems are usually not the most informative or useful performance monitoring systems for managers because they aggregate their information so highly. However they are widely used. Because city councils or state legislatures may request such a system, public managers should feel comfortable in designing and using them.

SECTION 2: VALUING OUTPUT IN MONETARY TERMS

As noted, private market organizations have a substantial advantage over public organizations because their outputs are measurable as revenues and profits. These monetary measures are almost always clearer and more comprehensive than any surrogate that can be established by public organizations because monetary measures capture so many things—output quality, quantity, consumer acceptance—all in one figure.

However a few public organizations *can* charge for their output. These organizations occupy a middle zone between private, market organizations and public, nonmarket ones. Among these middle-zone agencies are public hospitals, colleges, clinics, and license bureaus. What distinguishes these public agencies from those that cannot charge?

Agencies That Cannot Charge

Many government agencies cannot even consider tracking their output in monetary terms because they cannot charge. For example, organizations whose primary purpose is to transfer income, such as veterans' bureaus, social services departments, and unemployment compensation agencies, can hardly charge the very groups to which they are giving money.

A second group of agencies that cannot charge for output is those providing what economists term *public goods*. Public goods are outputs that cannot be provided to some members of an affected group without providing them to all. Defense is a public good. There is no way that the U.S. armed services can defend your neighbors from an enemy and not simultaneously defend you. Therefore if the generals came door to door in your neighborhood selling defense, you would be rational in refusing to pay; if your neighbors pay, you will be covered too. Yet if everyone thought the same, no military defense would be bought, even though everyone wanted it. Like defense, all public goods are indivisible outputs that cannot be denied to "free riders" who refuse to pay their fair share of the cost.

Again, *public goods* is a technical term that applies to only a minority of the goods produced by government programs. Accordingly, most outputs of public agencies are not public goods. For example, college educations and medical care are not. If it wished, the government could easily deny nonpayers access to colleges or hospitals. It could not deny access to such public goods as defense, space exploration, health regulation, flood control, mosquito abatement, and others. So society avoids the problems of free riders by taking defense and other public goods out of the marketplace and charging everyone for them through the compulsory tax system.

There is yet a third type of agency that should not charge for its outputs: an agency that produces a service whose consumption we wish to encourage. For example, it would be counterproductive for public high schools to charge because we do not wish to discourage potential consumers. We want to encourage consumption because a high school education produces what economists call *positive externalities*—that is, good side effects.[5] A high school education not only helps the direct consumer (the student); it also has the side effect of helping us all by raising the country's educational level and, ultimately, our standard of living. The stronger the positive externalities of a good or service, the less governments should charge because we want to encourage consumption. Thus government agencies do not usually charge for early education,[6] health screenings for contagious diseases, or drug rehabilitation programs because of their important positive externalities.

We have eliminated the possibility of charging for three huge categories of public agencies: those that transfer income, those that provide public goods, and those that deliver services with very large positive externalities.[7] However, there are a few important remaining public services that do not fit into any of these categories. Among them are public swimming pools, tennis courts, and other recreational facilities; public housing; public transportation; and some aspects of public hospitals. Should these agencies charge?

Advantages of Charging

If a public agency can plausibly charge for its services, it gains two important advantages by doing so.

1. *It encourages consumers to use the resource wisely.* If consumers are not charged for a government output, they will treat it as free and use it more than is economically efficient. Thus if an agency does not charge for a service that costs the agency one dollar per person, people will use the service even if its value to them is only twenty cents. Charging forces consumers to ask whether a service is really worth the cost.

2. *It provides managers with marketlike feedback.* Monetary revenues

(and the profit measure that results) give private businesses an excellent overall feedback measure. Public agencies that charge for their services can approximate this business-type feedback, which ensures that managers will have a clear, objective measure of the relationship between their inputs (costs) and outputs (revenues).[8]

Discrimination Against the Poor? Perhaps the most serious argument against public agencies charging for their output is that it discriminates against the poor, who will therefore be denied government services. If true, this would indeed be a compelling reason not to charge. However if public agency pricing is handled correctly, this problem can be overcome. Public agencies can gain many of the advantages of charging for their output without harming the poor if they establish fees based on income, providing the poor with reduced prices or free services while maintaining full charges for those able to pay. Thus a public swimming pool can issue means-based cards that set a price for each swimmer. Public universities can charge substantial amounts coupled with extremely generous scholarships based on financial need.[9]

How Much Should Be Charged?

In the private sector, managers need not worry about mispricing their output over a long period of time. If they charge too little, they will fail to cover their costs and go out of business. If they charge too much, their customers will go to competitors, and again they will go out of business. Market forces leave little discretion in the choice of a price level.

Most public agencies, on the other hand, do not have marketlike competition. In fact, most are monopolies, and therefore choosing a price is much more difficult. Robert Anthony and David Young suggest a few basic principles to use as guidelines in pricing the output of government agencies:[10]

1. For efficiency purposes, some pricing is often better than none. Doubts about the exact level should not deter price setting.
2. If a public agency has market competitors offering the same service, it should not charge more than they do. For example, a public college that is in the same town as a similar private college should not charge more than the private college. If it did it would discourage all customers who were able to pay the full price; they would go to the cheaper private school. Only students receiving financial aid would go to the public school, and this would hurt the public college over the long run.

3. If it does not violate principle 2., an agency should charge at a level equal to its expected full cost for the good or service.

4. An agency should charge prospectively, rather than waiting around to see if there are any cost overruns and then charging that amount. Knowing that the price is fixed provides managers with incentives to cut costs and be efficient. (For example, one of the most dramatic changes in health care was the federal requirement in the mid-1980s that health care fees reimbursed by Medicare and Medicaid be set *before* treating the patient. This change was based on this principle of prospective pricing.)[11]

Charges and Transfer Prices

As discussed, only a small minority of government agencies can or should charge their *clients* for their services. However many public agencies can and should charge for their services *internally* when transferring goods and services from one subagency to another. As discussed in Chapter Two, internal prices, which are called transfer prices, allow service-oriented subsections of an organization to become profit centers. Charging for such internal services provides the advantages of a profit center, such as accountability and competition, while providing advantages that have been noted for charging clients, such as motivating users and generating better managerial feedback. At the very least, the transfer price should be set at a level that recovers the direct cost; if the transfer price is to be compared to outside alternatives, it should be set to cover the expected full cost of the good or service.

Valuing Outputs in Monetary Terms Without Charging: Benefits Assessment

Occasionally even agencies that do not sell their output wish to know its monetary value. Of course, assigning a dollar value to an output does not produce all the benefits of actually charging for it. Because no one actually pays, it does not provide incentives for the consumer to avoid overuse. Nonetheless there are real advantages to assigning monetary value to output. Because it provides the common denominator of money, such a procedure allows a program's benefits to be compared to its costs (i.e., benefit-cost analysis), and it also allows the benefits of one program (e.g., education) to be compared to the benefits of another (e.g., health).

Assigning dollar values to items not normally bought or sold on the market is often termed *monetizing* or *benefit assessment*. Benefit assessment attempts to answer the question: "If this item were being sold on the market, what would consumers be willing to pay for it?" All techniques of benefit assessment are attempts to determine this hypothetical willingness to pay. The sum of all consumers' actual willingness to pay for a program is taken to be its true societal value.

Generally, benefit assessment is a relatively time-consuming process. Therefore it is much more likely to be used in once-per-year program evaluations rather than in the month-to-month monitoring of management systems. Nonetheless because it is occasionally used, we will briefly consider several of the main techniques used to turn a series of separate outputs into a single monetary figure. Julius Margolis suggests that there are two basic types of monetizing techniques: direct and indirect.[12]

Direct Monetizing Approaches: Surveys.   The direct approach in determining consumers' willingness to pay for an output usually involves surveying a random sample of potential consumers, asking them what they would be willing to pay for a particular level of an output. This is often called contingent valuation surveying because the questions are expressed contingently: "If you could decrease water pollution in a nearby river by 50 percent, what would you pay? What would you pay for 70 percent?"[13]

Such direct questioning certainly seems the most reliable way to determine willingness to pay. But it can have substantial distortions: Sometimes those surveyed will distort their answer, especially if they do not think they will have to bear whatever price they name. Thus they will overestimate the value to them of a particular item because they know the tax burden will be borne by the entire community. More often, the distortion in answers arises because most people simply have not thought about how much they would be willing to pay for decreased noise or better health. Even their most sincere answers often bear little resemblance to what, in fact, they really pay when actually putting their money on the line. There has been increased interest in survey techniques in recent years, however, as researchers have found new ways to minimize these problems.

Indirect Monetizing Approaches.   As the name suggests, indirect approaches attempt to examine the behavior of people and then to infer what they would be willing to pay from the way they act. For example, what is the value of a government program that decreases the noise and pollution around an airport? No one ever directly buys or sells the output "decreased airport noise." But acting as detectives—using indirect monetizing approaches—we can roughly determine what people are willing to pay. Consider two similar houses, one near the airport, the other one away from the airport's noise and pollution. If the houses are nearly identical in all other ways, then the difference in the selling prices of the two houses is an implicit price that buyers and sellers have put on avoiding the noise and pollution of the airport.

Another indirect approach uses the chain of outputs. Often it is difficult to monetize the immediate output of a government program, but by moving down the chain of outputs, we can find an intermediate output that is much easier to monetize. Thus if we are attempting to determine the value of 1 million gallons of irrigation water per day for a parched area, assigning a monetary value to the water is very difficult. It becomes much easier, however, if we look at what the water produces—in this case increased crops, which lead to increased profits—and use the added net value of that output as a benefit measure for the water. Thus if the irrigation makes it possible to increase profits by $1 million without raising prices, the value of the water is close to $1 million because the farmers should be willing to pay almost that amount to gain the profit.

Similarly, we can assign a monetary value to benefits of an injury prevention program by valuing the intermediate outputs of each avoided injury. Each injury averted will in turn lead to fewer doctor costs, fewer hospital costs, and fewer wages lost. These represent the monetary value of each averted injury because society should be willing to pay roughly this amount to avoid these monetary losses. Once we can estimate the number of injuries prevented, we can multiply that figure by these monetary values to determine the monetary benefits of the program.

Direct and indirect techniques of benefit assessment are not mutually exclusive. It is usually better to use both when attempting to assign a monetary value to program outputs. If the estimates from both approaches agree, the manager can be relatively confident that the estimate is roughly accurate. If not, the manager can use the differing answers to test high and low parameters, or the manager can attempt to refine the estimate further.[14]

Section Summary

One way of combining the measures for all of a program's outputs is to put a single monetary figure on them. If this figure is accurate, it can provide the public organization with many of the advantages of feedback in the private sector—including comprehensiveness and clear equivalence to the input (cost) figures.

The monetary figure can be established by charging for the output, and there are a number of programs for which charges could be instituted without hurting the poor. Much more infrequently, imputed monetary benefits can be assigned to the output, based on a calculation of what consumers would be willing to pay. These benefit assessment techniques are complex and often imprecise; they are more useful for once-a-year program evaluations than for the more frequent monitoring necessary for management systems.

SECTION 3: TYING PERFORMANCE MONITORING SYSTEMS TO PROGRAM EVALUATION

Differences between Program Evaluations and Management Systems

Many government agencies have regular program evaluation operations, which take a long look at the overall success of a program: Is it actually improving its clients' health, or allowing the elderly to live better, or reducing crime? *Program evaluation*[15] attempts to determine a program's real effect; it usually tries to move beyond immediate outputs, examining intermediate and even ultimate output measures.[16]

Most often, program evaluation proceeds by carefully comparing a wide range of output indicators before the program began and then examining the outputs after the program is underway. The evaluators are looking for changes that have been caused by the program; they accordingly attempt to minimize the possibility that any changes they find may have been caused by outside forces. One way of doing so is to compare the before and after indicators for the group receiving the program to indicators for a similar group that did not receive the program; this group is termed a control group. Of course, program evaluation is usually much more complex than suggested in the last few sentences.[17] Often an evaluation will take three months or longer to complete, and the final report generally runs to dozens of pages.

Very few program evaluation operations are linked to management systems, for many reasons. Management systems tend to be internally run, providing information for immediate managerial decisions. Often they are administered by personnel with business or computer backgrounds. Program evaluations, on the other hand, are often handled externally, with agency staff working in conjunction with academics or other consultants. They focus on long-term policy decisions, not managerial decisions, and are often administered by personnel with social science or statistical backgrounds. Given the great differences in implementors, focus, personnel, and jargon, the lack of linkage between the two types of systems is not surprising. However, this lack shortchanges both sides. A linkage can help management systems fight goal displacement, and it can help make evaluation studies more relevant. Let us turn to evaluation first.

The relevance of program evaluation has long been heralded as a means by which upper-level government managers can strengthen their programs. Yet studies of the direct effects of evaluations are discouraging. Some of these studies are summarized by Davis and Salasin:

> Weiss found evaluations' "most common complaint is that their findings are ignored." Wholey concluded that "the recent literature is unanimous in announcing the general failure of evaluation to affect decisionmaking in a significant way." Cohen states "There is little evidence to indicate that government planning offices have succeeded in linking social research and decisionmaking."[18]

Of course there are occasional success stories, but most other investigators also conclude that evaluations fail to change directly the inefficient and ineffective government programs. In fact, most supporters of program evaluation have shifted their defense to the more modest claim that the cumulative impact of evaluations, year after year, shapes government thinking and approaches in subtle but real ways.[19] This is a very important effect. However, most government managers, under pressure for tangible accomplishments, are likely to be less than enthusiastic supporters of program evaluations if their results are always so diffuse.

A major reason cited for the disappointing lack of direct impact is that in the past evaluations have often focused on nonmanipulable aspects of a program. Thus program managers receive no useful information from an evaluation that simply indicates that a program does not work. They need evaluations that are more narrowly and practically focused, ones that tell them what particular aspect of a program is not working and why. One way of focusing a program evaluation is to use a consistent set of output indicators, carefully linked to the day-to-day concerns of the managers. Integrating evaluations with management system categories provides such indicators.

Connecting Program Evaluation to Management Systems

Connection of a management system to program evaluation has three major characteristics, all of which require close cooperation between the designers and users of each element.

1. Program evaluations are regularly scheduled, usually one per year. The evaluators explicitly use the chain of output to structure their evaluation (as many now do) and—more importantly—draw the links to be explored from the ongoing management system. Thus if the management system records "patients contacted" and "inoculations given," the evaluators examine whether such categories lead to a "real" effect: Does an increase in the number of patients

contacted increase the number of inoculations given? Does that in turn lead to "fewer sick days"?[20] In other words, are the indicators early on the chain *valid* measures of the more important outputs further down the chain?

2. All workers who are covered by the management system are told of the results of the evaluation. At the end of the year, when units and individuals are evaluated, measures that have been shown to lead to desired outcomes are given greater weight than those shown to be sterile.

3. If necessary, output measures in next year's management system are modified on the basis of the evaluation results.

An Example.   These three steps can be illustrated by using an example loosely based on an actual system. A statewide extension program trains homemakers from poverty-level families, emphasizing topics such as nutrition; it also answers telephone inquiries about nutrition. The management system tracks four outputs: "training sessions held," "number of homemakers beginning training," "number completing training," and "answered inquiries to (telephoned or mailed) household questions." The hypothesized chain of outputs is shown in Figure 6-2.

The program evaluation focuses on the connections between the various output measures. It finds that most homemakers who do not finish the training receive little benefit (thus the category "number beginning training" has little use) and that individuals motivated enough to inquire about a practice are the ones most likely to put the advice into action. Acting on this information, top administrators use the categories of "completion" and "inquiries" as the primary basis of their evaluations; they also explore the possibility of dropping or at least deemphasizing the "number beginning training" category for next year.

In another actual case, evaluators in York, Pennsylvania, found very little relationship between response time of the police (an indicator early on the chain) and case clearance (solution) rates (an indicator much further down the chain). Even when the police responded more quickly, there was little or no increase in the solution of the cases. Accordingly they suggested deemphasizing response time and exploring other measures (care at the crime scene and enlisting of witnesses) that might be closely related to solving crimes and therefore more important to track and reward.[21]

The Advantages of Tying Management Systems to Program Evaluation

The Advantages for Management Systems.   The advantages of such an explicit connection to program evaluation for management systems is clear. Goal displacement is greatly diminished because agency workers,

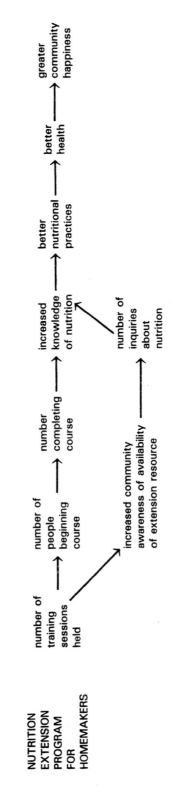

PROCESSES AND/OR IMMEDIATE OUTPUTS

INTERMEDIATE OUTPUTS

ULTIMATE OUTPUTS

NUTRITION
EXTENSION
PROGRAM
FOR
HOMEMAKERS

number of
training
sessions
held

number of
people
beginning
course

increased community
awareness of availability
of extension resource

number
completing
course

number of
inquiries
about
nutrition

increased
knowledge
of nutrition

better
nutritional
practices

better
health

greater
community
happiness

Figure 6-2. Chain of Outputs for Nutritional Training Program.

knowing that only the categories that have a strong relationship to desired intermediate outputs will be rewarded, are less inclined to neglect un-measured outputs. It makes little sense to neglect everything to build up measured outputs if a regularly scheduled evaluation may discredit these categories. With goal displacement lessened and real outputs linked to the management system categories, the system is more likely to be viewed as relevant by all concerned, again increasing its efficacy.

The manager also gains a fresh view of the monitoring system. In the unlikely event that the program evaluation shows absolutely no re-lationship between an immediate output monitored by the management system and the desired long-range outputs, the manager must consider why he or she is tracking that particular immediate output. Unless there are legal or political reasons, it is probably best to drop it and search for a better surrogate.

The Advantages for Evaluation.   Such a connection has a great advantage to evaluators as well. Evaluation texts stress producing "usable" evaluations, but determining what will be usable is often impossible. By using management system categories to investigate the causal chain, eval-uators assure themselves of studies that are focused. In addition, because the management systems will continue to gather data, such evaluations lend themselves to replication, and thus to producing longitudinal studies. Evaluation texts also emphasize that users and managers should be in-volved in the evaluation, and a connection to management systems requires their involvement. The connection forces both sides to ask, "What do we really want to know?" "What are our management system categories telling us?" Moreover, such periodic program evaluations do not just passively examine whether the measured immediate outputs lead to desired intermediate goals; they can also *cause* such a link because evaluations lessen goal displacement and force workers to look at and develop all aspects of a program.

To summarize, connecting the two elements is simple: The evaluators must use the categories developed and used by the management system to focus their evaluation; the management system designers must use the data of the evaluators in weighting and redesigning their systems. The link must be formal, ongoing, and publicized. The results are less dis-placement and thus more accuracy for the management system, and a more focused and usable program evaluation. Connecting the two ap-proaches helps both to achieve their full potential.

Management Systems and Unclear Production Functions

We have discussed using program evaluation to determine whether a given program's particular activities and immediate outputs do in fact lead to the intermediate and ultimate outputs that we expect. This topic leads into one of the primary criticisms of management systems: that the links on the organizational chain of most public programs—linking inputs to organizational processes and then to immediate, intermediate, and ultimate outputs—are much less clear than for the private sector, and that therefore management systems are much less useful.

Critics of management systems often emphasize that many areas of government activity lack a clear "production function." These critics are using the term much more broadly than economists would, but by formal economic definition, a *production function* is a mathematical statement of what outputs a particular group of inputs will produce. Thus a production function for corn will predict how much corn (output) can be produced by a certain amount of labor, land, water, and fertilizers (inputs). The relationship between the inputs and the outputs for growing corn are quite clear, and if we were to design a chain of outputs for corn growing, we could feel very confident that each link will lead to the expected next one.

Although no government program approaches corn in predictability, a number of programs, especially at the local level, are relatively predictable. Garbage pickup, street construction, and street maintenance are all areas where managers can often predict the likely output for a given amount of labor and materials, because they understand how the inputs and activities produce the outputs.

Of course, we can rarely be so confident when considering many other government programs, especially in the social services area. Critics accordingly charge that management systems are relatively useless in these situations because we lack a clear production function, or more accurately, we do not understand the means (usually called *technology*) necessary to produce many desired outputs (such as fewer drug addicts). According to this argument, it is relatively unimportant to measure outputs for many government programs because even when there is a clear shortfall, we do not know how to correct it. For example, George W. Downs and Patrick D. Larkey assert,

> Researchers and government officials alike have an excessive faith in the management value of productivity data. When dealing with an undeveloped and poorly understood technology (e.g., crime prevention, health planning) . . . the possession of accurate, quantitative indicators of goal accomplishment can still leave decision makers in the dark about how well government agencies are doing and what to do next.[22]

They later say, "What keeps the inflation rate high, health costs rising, inner cities deteriorating and reading scores of high school students dropping is not a lack of clarity about what the objectives should be. It is knowing what to do."[23]

Responses to the Production Function Argument

Although they state some of the criticisms well, Downs and Larkey ultimately (though guardedly) support management systems. But what can we say to those critics who see little use for management systems? There are a number of responses to the argument that government management systems often have little value because we are often so unclear about government production functions. Implicit in the arguments of many critics are several assumptions that are usually not true for well-working management systems.

One assumption seems to be that government management systems will track immediate outputs alone, on the assumption that they will lead to intermediate and ultimate outputs. The critics correctly point out that this assumption of tight links between immediate and intermediate outputs can easily be mistaken in the public sector. But as we have emphasized throughout this book, managers cannot and should not make such an assumption. They should be careful to use multiple indicators, and they should be careful to use at least some indicators further down the chain of outputs. In addition, we have suggested another way of battling the problem: using program evaluation to check the achievement of intermediate and ultimate outputs, and then using that information to suggest new measures for the management system if necessary.[24]

A second implicit assumption of the critics seems to be that many users of management systems believe that discovering a problem is the same as solving it. However, most system users recognize that this would be an indefensible belief, even in the private sector, where production functions are often much better understood. Moreover, even in the private sector, a clear link between problems and solutions is only true for the simplest programs, where shortfalls ("the french fries are too soggy") are easily and quickly remedied once discovered. For most private sector problems ("our market share is off") the solution is often obscure even when the problem is known. Thus government is similar to private industry in this regard.

Indeed, the critics' argument is exactly backwards. Critics charge that the fact that we do not fully understand the production function for many government programs makes management systems much less useful. In fact, the exact opposite is true. Management systems are often *more* valuable when we are not sure of the technology to produce the desired outputs. The search for the solution cannot even begin until the problem is recognized. Often government does not even know it is falling short on educating children or fighting poverty until its output measures show the shortfall. Management systems point out the problem, which is the first step toward a solution. And once a shortfall is recognized, management systems are again important. Even if the managers must fall back on trial-

and-error remedies, such approaches are only plausible if they can gain quick feedback on what is working and what is not. Again, only management systems can tell them.

Particularly when dealing with social programs, the process can become even more complex than suggested so far. Sometimes society is not even sure what the problem is. Is the underlying problem of cocaine addiction among teenagers insufficient entry-level jobs to provide hope and an outlet for their energy? Or is the problem that too much cocaine is crossing our borders? Or is the problem that the breakdown of family structure has given too few teens enough guidance and self-esteem to resist cocaine? Each of these formulations would suggest different goals and objectives for an anticocaine program.

When dealing with such complex areas, management systems encourage interactive social learning. In response to feedback from the management systems, the organization may over time change not just its means of reaching a goal but also the goal itself. Goals affect means, and means affect goals,[25] and this interactive process is much smoother when there is sufficient information about both. Management systems help provide that information, and they need make no assumptions about understanding the production function in order to perform these duties.

SUMMARY

Although there are drawbacks to attempting too much, some management system designers wish to aggregate outputs, combining a large number of outputs into one number—or at most, a few numbers. These more complex, aggregate systems take a number of forms. The most common is the productivity measurement system, which usually divides output by input and compares the result to a base year. The input component of a productivity system has traditionally been expressed as labor, but this leads to distortion. Total factor productivity measures, which are based on monetary measures of input, are more accurate.

A second way of aggregating outputs is to express all outputs as a single monetary figure. The technique for assigning monetary values to outputs not bought or sold on the market is termed *benefit assessment*. Benefit assessment is a time-consuming technique, more often associated with once-per-year program evaluation systems than with month-by-month management systems.

Charging for government goods and services (often through levying user fees) is another, more direct way of establishing a monetary figure for output. Most programs run by government are not in the private sector precisely because it is impossible to charge for their outputs. Such programs include income-transfer programs and programs, such as defense, that produce "public goods." Nonetheless, charging a fee does result in substantial efficiency gains for those few programs for which charges can be levied. Such programs generally must be careful to shelter the poor through sliding scales or rebates.

Many agencies have regular program evaluations as well as output-oriented management systems, but few agencies formally tie these two together. They should. The tie to management systems helps make the evaluations more focused and usable. There are also advantages for management systems because program evaluations look at outputs on the right of the chain of outputs—that is, intermediate outputs—that a monthly management system usually does not have the time or ability to monitor.

Program evaluations are one of the most important ways to ensure that the links assumed in a management system's chain of outputs are indeed remaining linked together. Determining whether immediate, intermediate, and ultimate outputs are being produced by a program gives the manager important information, whether or not the technology of producing the outputs is clearly understood. If the technology is clearly understood, managers can determine solutions for any problems that may be indicated by the system. If it is not well understood, managers can quickly learn if their current efforts are not succeeding and use the system in their trial-and-error attempts to find approaches that will produce better results.

REVIEW QUESTIONS

1. What criteria should guide managers in choosing how many indicators to track? Name a program for which there would probably be relatively few indicators necessary; name one that would need many.

2. Why does the traditional productivity measure encourage inefficient decisions about resource use?

3. What criteria should guide managers in aggregating separate output indicators into overall indicators? How should the weights assigned to separate indicators be determined?

4. What financial data are necessary to calculate total factor productivity? Why must they be in *constant* dollars?

5. What are the advantages of basing program evaluations on management system output categories?

6. What are the advantages of assigning dollar values to output? The disadvantages? If benefit assessment is viewed as a weighting of outputs, on what are the weights based?

7. What is the difference in benefits to the organization between charging for an output and assigning a price through benefit assessment?

8. Name four government services that are not usually charged for, but should be. Why? What are the arguments against charging?

9. Besides those mentioned in this chapter, what are three government programs for which the technology of producing the outputs is relatively clear? What are three programs for which it is relatively unclear?

10. How will the role of management systems change between the two groups of programs named in question 9?

PROBLEMS

1. The Youngville Employment Security Agency placed 365 people in jobs this year, using 105 labor years. Last year, it placed 350 people, and used 95 labor years. Treat last year as the base and calculate this year's productivity rating.

2. For the agency in problem 1, each labor year cost $16,000 last year and $17,000 this year. The agency had other expenses of $120,000 last year and $90,000 this year. Calculate the total factor productivity rating this year, using last year as the base. Compare its accuracy to the rating established in problem 1.

3. The Youngville City Clinic inoculates 3,500 people in year 1, 4,000 people in year 2, and 3,800 people in year 3. It sees 10,000 people in year 1, 11,000 people in year 2, and 12,000 people in year 3. It uses 40 labor years in year 1, 50 in year 2, and 50 in year 3. It has decided to weight its two output indicators and combine them into a single measure; it will weight each inoculation as being "worth" three visits, and year 1 is the base year. What is the agency's productivity rating for years 2 and 3?

4. The preceding agency has just established a new accounting system. Its direct costs in year 1 were $700,000; its indirect costs were $200,000. For year 2, direct costs were $800,000, indirect $250,000. For year 3, direct costs were $800,000, indirect $300,000. Calculate the total factor productivity rating for the clinic for the three years, using year 1 as a base.

5. In 1991, its base year, the community college taught the full time equivalent of 120 college credit students and 210 technical students; its total costs were $510,000. In 1992, it taught 105 college credit students and 220 technical students, with a total cost of $550,000. In 1993, it taught 130 college credit students and 190 technical

students, with a total cost of $600,000. The statewide community college board has determined that college credit students should be given a weight of 2; technical students, 1.5. What is the productivity rating for the community college for 1992 and 1993?

Case 6–1

When James Scott was named chief of the transit department of a large midwestern city, he was told by the mayor, "That place is a mess and its inefficiency and inflated payroll is hurting me politically. Clean it up, but don't hurt me even worse politically while you're doing it."

Scott came from a smaller transportation department in the South, and he was shocked by the conditions in his new department. Buses and subway trains were badly maintained and constantly out of order. Schedules were rarely met; all subunits were overstaffed; pay levels were very high, with a large number of senior drivers making over $50,000 annually with overtime.

The system has 480 bus routes and two subway lines; it serves 600,000 passengers per day. There are two central barns that handle all repair work. Drivers are paid for a full day although some of them are busy only during rush hour. Ridership fell off last year after a fare increase but has leveled off during the past few months. The system still loses $20 million per year, which is paid by the city.

As the first step toward improvement, Scott wants to start a performance monitoring system. Because he is not sure if the work force will cooperate, he believes that he needs measures that can be double-checked easily, that do not require too much paperwork, and that can be tied to productivity contracting. One of his staff people suggests that six or so output categories be tracked, the most important being "number of passengers per day." Scott believes that six is too large a number of categories to track. Moreover, he doubts that it is fair to place very much emphasis on the number of passengers because so many factors outside the control of the transit workers, such as the economy and the weather, can affect that reading.

1. Is Scott correct? Which outputs should be tracked for the trains? The buses? The barn?
2. Does a performance monitoring system for an organization that charges (such as this one) differ substantially from a system for more typical government agencies?
3. Are fare receipts the most important output measure? Why?
4. How should the information be gathered, by a separate unit or by managerial self-reporting?

5. For what specific decisions can Scott use the information once it is gathered?

Case 6–2

Like many older industrial cities, New Boylan (population 145,000) is slowly declining, and its tax base cannot keep pace with the demand for services. New Boylan has a relatively poor population, with 20 percent of its citizens below the poverty line (calculated before any transfer payments). The remainder of the city is divided between working class and middle class. The city ran a deficit of $6 million last year, which it handled primarily through loans from the state and through some creative accounting. This fiscal year is just beginning, but its deficit is likely to be about the same size.

Although the city has severe financial problems, the mayor and city council do not wish to raise any across-the-board taxes for fear of accelerating the exodus of the middle and working classes to the suburbs. Virtually all city services are stretched past the breaking point, among them

1. Swimming pools. The city runs three free swimming pools; there is also a private pool in town that charges $2.25 for admittance. The vast majority of patrons are between the ages of six and fifteen. The three city-run pools can each hold 180 swimmers, but they are greatly overcrowded. There is often a two-hour wait to get in, and many discouraged would-be swimmers no longer try. Each pool is open 155 days per year and each costs $60,000 per year to operate.

2. Public housing. There is a waiting list of over four years for a place in the city's five well-kept, low-rise public housing complexes. Each complex contains 120 two-bedroom apartments, and only families making under $11,200 per year are eligible. All renters pay $200 per month, about 40 percent of the cost for comparable housing in the private sector. (For complex historic reasons, the city has the ability to set its own rents, unlike many federally financed units that must follow federal rent guidelines.)

3. The city bridges. The city built, owns, and now maintains the three aging bridges over the river that separates it from its main suburbs. The only way of avoiding the bridges is to drive twenty-five minutes out of the way, to a narrow land connection. The bridges are now free, but the city is considering instituting a toll that would cover at least part of its annual maintenance costs of $215,000 per bridge. Each weekday, approximately 10,000 cars travel over each of the bridges (5,000 in each direction). Surveys indicate that about 40

percent of the users are suburbanites who work in the city, 20 percent are city dwellers who work in the suburbs, 20 percent are suburbanites who shop in the city, and 20 percent are miscellaneous.

4. Enriched education. After the federal government withdrew funds for supplementary education programs, the city has continued to fund them. All children who score at least one grade below standard on an achievement test are eligible for the voluntary, two-afternoon-a-week program; results have been quite encouraging. The program is free for all 4,000 children participating, but the city can ill afford its price of $1 million per year.

One of the mayor's new advisors recently received a degree in economics from the University of Chicago. The key to better service in all four areas, she tells the mayor, is to charge the clients enough for the service so that more (or all) of the costs are covered. For perhaps one or more of the services, she concedes, there could be sliding scales, rebates, or some other aid for the poor.

1. Adopting the advisor's logic, suggest changes for each area, defending your price. (When not enough information is available, assume the missing information and then proceed from that assumption.)
2. Evaluate the practicality of the new or increased prices for each service.
3. Which areas should have special pricing arrangements for the poor? Which should not? What should those arrangements be?

SUGGESTED FURTHER READING

THEODORE H. POISTER. *Performance Monitoring.* Lexington, MA: Lexington Books, 1983. Uses the Pennsylvania Department of Transportation as a case study and model of building and using performance monitoring systems. Excellent on details of assembling such a system; particularly strong on linking measures.

Public Productivity and Management Review. (San Francisco: Jossey-Bass, Inc., Publishers). A quarterly journal that focuses on public management systems and performance indicators. Before 1989, it was published under the title *Public Productivity Review.*

JOSEPH S. WHOLEY, ed. *Organizational Excellence.* Lexington, MA: Lexington Books, 1987. An edited collection of articles on management systems, especially performance monitoring systems. Most of the authors report on their analysis of a particular agency's system but then posit broader points about systems in general.

ENDNOTES

1. Of course, decentralized organizations with many quasi-independent components will need to have a very large number of indicators to cover each of the components. For example, the New York City public school system has a management system with over 1,577 performance indicators, although the real managerial work within each school would be based on relatively few indicators. See Joseph Viteritti and Daniel G. Carpancy, "Information, Organization and Control: A Study of System Application," *Public Administration Review,* 41, no. 2 (March/April 1981), 260.

2. Efficiency measures can be combined into a single indicator in other ways than the productivity measures considered here, but they are little used in government. For example, police and other agencies have been ranked by a very sophisticated measure that produces a production possibility frontier for the trade-off between two or more different outputs, then ranks different public agencies by an "efficiency percentage" based on how far inside the frontier their combined output falls. This approach is sometimes called *data envelope analysis,* or *DEA.*

   This has the potential to be an extremely powerful evaluation tool, but it is clearly more useful for one-shot analyses than for monthly or quarterly management system reports. For an application to police, see Roger B. Parks, "Metropolitan Structure and Systemic Performance: The Case of Police Service Delivery," in Kenneth Hanf and Theo A. J. Toonen, *Policy Implementation in Federal and Unitary Systems* (Boston: Martinus Nyhoff Publishers, 1985), especially pp. 180–91. For a good overview that points out remaining methodological difficulties with the technique, see Michael K. Epstein and John C. Henderson, "Data Envelope Analysis for Managerial Control and Diagnosis," *Decision Sciences,* 20, no. 1 (Winter 1989), 90–119.

3. Sometimes "productivity" measures are criticized for emphasizing only the quantity of output and ignoring quality. This bias was not uncommon twenty years ago, but it is very rare today. Quality measures are built into the system, sometimes by direct measure (number of items rejected, consumer complaints, etc.), sometimes by adjustment of the output numbers to reflect quality, as discussed in the section on longitudinal measures.

4. The federal effort is very comprehensive—covering almost the entire 3 million employees—and very long lived, having passed a quarter century. It is now directed by the Office of Personnel Management. Frequent publications discuss productivity trends and measurement

problems, for example, Carolyn Burstein and Donald M. Fisk, "The Federal Government Productivity Improvement Program: Status and Agenda," *Public Budgeting and Finance,* Winter 1987, pp. 36–47.

The table is from U.S. Bureau of Labor Statistics, *Federal Productivity Summary Data, Fiscal years 1967–1987,* Washington, DC, 1989, p. 7. For a comparison to private industry, see U.S. Bureau of Labor Statistics, *Productivity Measures for Selected Industries and Government Services,* Washington, DC, February 1988.

5. If they become extensive enough, the positive externalities of an output may be so great that the output begins to approach the category of a public good.

6. Some policy analysts have called for the use of vouchers in education as a way of gaining some of the advantages of the private market without actually charging students or their parents for the education. Each student's parents would be given a voucher that could be "spent" in the public or private school of their choice, thus introducing competition among service providers. Despite a great deal of theoretical discussion of vouchers, there have been few empirical tests of the concept. One exception is a study of vouchers for recreation (where of course the consumer information problems are much fewer than for schools): John L. Crompton, "Recreation Vouchers: A Case Study in Administrative Innovation and Citizen Participation," *Public Administration Review,* 43, no. 6 (November/December 1983), 537–46.

7. This is not to imply that efficiency is the only criterion for assigning a service to the public sector. For some important functions—police power perhaps—society may wish to keep the programs in the public sector for reasons of accountability and control. For other programs— perhaps running prisons and conducting elections—society may keep them in the public sector for reasons of state legitimacy. This point is developed in David R. Morgan and Robert E. England, "The Two Faces of Privatization," *Public Administration Review,* 48, no. 6 (November/December 1988), 979–87.

8. The idea of charging for an output begins to suggest the question: Why not gain yet more of the advantages of the market and let the private sector provide the service? This question leads into the topic of privatization, whereby services that were previously delivered by government organizations are turned over to the private sector, sometimes to competing units under government regulation, sometimes to a single private organization under a direct government contract. We consider many of the prerequisites to privatization in this book, including an accounting system that allows us to decide whether the private sector is indeed cheaper, and a series of output

measures that allow us to hold the private organization accountable. But a direct examination of privatization is a massive topic and outside the scope of this book.

For some popular but very readable overviews of privatization, see Jeremy Main, "When Public Services Go Private," *Fortune*, May 27, 1985, pp. 92ff; and Carolyn Lochhead, "Serving the Public Privately," *Insight* February 22, 1988, pp. 42–44. See also Martin Tolchin, "More Cities Paying Industry to Provide Public Services," *New York Times*, May 28, 1985, p. 1. Tolchin finds that 41 percent of cities and counties use private industry for commercial solid waste collection, 38 percent do so for street lighting operations, and 48 percent do so for legal services.

For a more scholarly overview of the topic, see Roger B. Parks, "Alternative Service Delivery: Some Questions," *Management Science and Policy Analysis*, 3, no. 4 (Spring 1986), 18–20. Parks suggests that we do not know when private is cheaper than public, and he suggests areas of future research.

For an article skeptical of privatization, see Ronald C. Moe, "Exploring the Limits of Privatization," *Public Administration Review*, November/December 1987, pp. 453–59.

See also the works cited in the notes to Chapter Two.

9. Good examples of how a series of cities have adapted user fees for poor citizens are given in Penelope Lemo, "User Fees, Once the Answer to City Budget Prayers, May Have Reached Their Peak," *Governing*, 2, no. 6 (March 1989), 24–30.

10. Robert N. Anthony and David W. Young, *Management Control in Nonprofit Organizations* (Homewood, IL: Richard D. Irwin, 1984), pp. 181–82.

11. As indicated, this approach of setting the reimbursement in advance and then letting the provider pay the remainder (or pocket the profit) underlies the biggest change in medical care delivery in several decades. In the 1980s the federal government's Medicare program began paying doctors and hospitals set fees for each type of service, instead of merely reimbursing all expenses at a later time. The set fees are based on DRGs (diagnosis-related groups), and are sometimes called DRG allowances. For an extended but clear discussion of these and other changes in the relationship between medicine and the market, see the special *Newsweek* issue edited by Gregg Easterbrook, "The Revolution in Medicine," January 26, 1987, pp. 40ff.

12. Julius Margolis's article was one of the earliest: "Shadow Prices for Incorrect or Nonexistent Market Values," in Robert Haveman and Julius Margolis, *Public Expenditures for Policy Analysis* (Chicago: Markham, 1970), pp. 314–29. As might be expected, both the ter-

minology and the economic consensus on allowable approaches has changed somewhat since then.

One of the very best current discussions of benefit assessment techniques is R. G. Cummings, D. S. Brookshire, and W. D. Schultze, *Valuing Environmental Goods: An Assessment of the Contingent Valuation Method* (New York: Rowman and Allanheld Publishers, 1986). Another good source on cost-benefit analysis, especially contingent valuation surveys, is John R. Stoll, Robert N. Shulstad, and Webb M. Smathers, Jr., eds., *Nonmarket Valuation: Current Status and Future Directions* (Southern Rural Development Center, 1984). Perhaps the most influential defense of cost-benefit analysis from the assaults of other economists is Robert D. Willig, "Consumer's Surplus Without Apology," *American Economic Review,* September 1976, pp. 589–97.

13. Costs and benefits that extend into the future would have to be discounted back to present value before being aggregated, but that is beyond the scope of this discussion.

14. There are other approaches for imputing monetary value beyond the ones discussed here. One frequently used approach values willingness to pay for public parks (such as Yellowstone) by calculations based on the travel costs required to get there. As with all cost-benefit analyses, the issue quickly gets tricky, however. The value must be adjusted downward to reflect any good times the consumer had on the way to the park. Moreover, just the existence of the park may have a value for nonusers (called the option value) that must be included to determine the park's total value.

15. The procedure of program evaluation goes under a number of names, including program analysis and performance auditing. The name changes generally reflect the fact that a different professional group is conducting the evaluation. A book with a number of interesting cases on performance auditing is Richard E. Brown, Meredith Williams, and Thomas P. Gallagher, *Auditing Performance in Government* (New York: John Wiley, 1982). A book that outlines the steps and procedures very well is Ronald M. Malan, James R. Fountain, Jr., Donald S. Arrowsmith, and Robert L. Lockridge II, *Performance Auditing in Local Government* (Chicago: Government Finance Officers Association, 1984).

16. Although program evaluations generally do focus on long-range results, the 1980s saw a trend, at least at the federal level, for evaluations to focus more on the beginning of the output chain, thus becoming more like performance monitoring systems. U.S. General Accounting Office, *Federal Evaluation: Fewer Units, Reduced Resources, Different*

Status from 1980 (Washington, DC: GAO, January, 1987), pp. 28, 42–43, 50–52.

This action seemed partly a response to Reagan-era cutbacks in evaluation funds; evaluators could get more evaluations for their dwindling dollars since it is easier and cheaper to examine short-range impacts. Although it may aid managers' short-term interests, it leaves no one looking at long-range impacts.

17. Generally, program evaluation is more difficult than performance monitoring for a number of reasons. One of the most straightforward differences is simply client availability. The client has generally left the environment of the organization (school, prison, etc.), and he or she becomes progressively more difficult to keep track of. Yet a sustained effort—for example, updating files every year or so—is a much easier way of keeping addresses current than trying to contact ex-clients five years later.

However, there are more important, intrinsic differences that also make program evaluation harder. It is more difficult even to get agreement about what intermediate and ultimate outputs should be monitored because they are more subject to competing political perspectives; many actors who agree on a program (e.g., Head Start) may not agree on its ultimate goals. As discussed in the notes for Chapter Five, this fact underlies our suggestion that the output chain is best built from the immediate out, rather than vice versa. Moreover, side effects that are not even the focus of the evaluation may prove to be the most important (if unexpected) result of the program. Finally, as we have discussed, intermediate and ultimate outputs are the ones most difficult to operationalize and measure and also the ones most subject to outside forces.

18. The quotation is from Howard Davis and Susan Salasin, "Evaluation and Change," in Lois-Ellen Datta and Robert Perloff, eds., *Improving Evaluations* (Beverly Hills, CA: Sage Publications, 1979), p. 257. Although there has been greater acceptance of the reduced role of evaluations since the quotation was written, the situation remains basically the same. For example, see Gerd-Michael Hellstern, "Assessing Evaluation Research," *Guidance, Control and Evaluation in the Public Sector* (Berlin and New York: Walter de Gruyter, 1986), esp. p. 282.

19. This is basically the position taken by Davis and Salasin, "Evaluation and Change," pp. 259–60.

20. Techniques that might be used in examining causal links are discussed in Charles M. Judd and David A. Kenny, "Process Analysis: Estimating Mediation in Treatment Evalations," *Evaluation Review*, 5, no. 5 (October 1981), 602–19.

21. John M. Stevens, Thomas C. Webster, and Brian Stipak, "Response Time: Role in Assessing Police Performance," *Public Productivity Review,* September 1980, pp. 210–30.

22. George W. Downs and Patrick D. Larkey, *The Search for Government Efficiency* (Philadelphia: Temple University, 1986), p. 4.

23. Ibid., p. 170. As noted, our later discussion of counterarguments addresses some mistaken assumptions that Downs and Larkey do *not* make.

24. As pointed out in Chapter One, management indicators can also be important (even when the technology is unclear) by registering and encouraging organizational efficiency. The public has a right to expect that an agency that is not positive about how to achieve ultimate outputs (effectiveness) will at least not unnecessarily waste resources on processes (efficiency). Management systems can help, and this in turn can maintain public support for the agency's search for better technologies.

25. The notable statement of this argument may be Charles E. Lindblom, "The Science of Muddling Through," *Public Administration Review,* 19 (1959). An interesting development of some managerial implications is Robert Behn, "Management by Groping Along," *Journal of Policy and Management,* 7, no. 4 (Fall 1988), 644–63.

chapter seven

Connecting Budgetary Systems to Management Systems

INTRODUCTION

Chapters Seven through Ten will all discuss ways that output-oriented management systems can be connected to other organizational systems and processes. Chapter Seven will examine how management systems can be tied to budgetary systems. Chapter Eight will look at ties to rewards and to personnel systems. Chapter Nine will look at connections between management systems and structural choices. Finally, Chapter Ten will explore the ways that management systems interact with different approaches to productivity improvement.

As noted a number of times, management systems must have a purpose: They must either inform decision making or affect behavior. If they do neither, they have no reason to continue. Connecting management systems to one of these other organizational facets (budgeting, personnel, structure, or changes) makes it much more likely that the systems will indeed have some impact.

THE ROLE OF BUDGETS

The relationship between output-oriented management systems and budgeting is confusing, in large part because the term *budgeting* has a wide range of meanings. In general, a *budget* is a specific plan for future spending. Thus each year the president draws up a proposed federal budget for the next year; the Congress considers the proposal and then passes a final budget, which approves specific levels of future spending by federal departments and agencies.

When viewed from this megalevel of annual budgets for the federal, state, or local government, budgeting has only a weak connection to management. Instead, the budget is a reflection of the policy (i.e., strategic planning) choices of the executive and legislature. It answers such questions as "What do we wish to emphasize more—health or recreation?" and "Do we prefer to cut taxes or increase government services?" Politicians can endorse a wide range of often contradictory policies when they are campaigning, but the budget process forces them to "put their money where their mouth is"; in other words, to make the hard policy choices inherent in a limited amount of money. Viewed in this way, budgeting is the core of the strategic planning or policy process rather than of the management process. In other words, it is primarily concerned with choosing the job to be done (policy) rather than with getting the job done once it has been chosen (management). Management systems kick in *after* the main budgetary decisions have been made.

However, there is a second meaning of budget that is less Olympian than the state or federal annual process. That is, a budget is also the spending plan for the year that is drawn up by an organization once the broad budgeting decisions have been made by the executive and legislature. Such a spending plan is usually broken into quarterly or even monthly components (unlike the annual megabudgets), and then current costs and revenues are checked against the projections (i.e., standards) in the plan.

This internal, short-term, manager-oriented process is not the budgeting process covered in the newspapers or discussed in most books on the politics of budgeting. This second budgeting process begins after the decisions of the first, megabudgeting process have been made. The two processes depend on each other, but they have very different purposes and procedures. Although the same term is used for both, we will try to be unambiguous in separating them for discussion when necessary.

There are some shared characteristics of both processes. For example, both involve the same types of documents (although the megalevel uses these documents for annual statements, whereas organizations use them for quarterly or monthly ones). Also, both processes involve some of the same political manipulations.

In this chapter we will briefly examine the four main budgeting formats that are used both at the strategic planning level and at the internal management level. We will then discuss how closely strategic planning budgeting systems should be tied to management systems. Finally, we will discuss some internal political effects of different budgeting procedures and systems.

BUDGET FORMATS

At both the policy and management levels, four principal budgeting formats are used. Each format is based on somewhat different budgetary information, and each displays its information in a somewhat different manner. As is true with all management systems, the way in which information is arranged or structured is important. Changing the format in which information is presented often changes the questions that are asked of the information, and ultimately changes the decisions made.[1] (Some organizations speak of different budgetary *systems* rather than *formats;* either term is appropriate.)[2]

Line-Item (Object-of-Expenditure) Budgeting

Line-item budgeting, also called object-of-expenditure budgeting, is the most common budgetary system. As the name suggests, an object-of-expenditure budget bases its categories on the items purchased, typically such items as supplies, personnel, and travel. Because each item category is listed on a separate line, it is also called a line-item budget. Line-item budgeting has a long history, dating back a century, and today it is still the most used approach. However even many agencies that continue to use it also supplement it with one of the other three approaches that will be discussed in this chapter.

Most of the categories used in a line-item budget recur in all types of organizations at all levels of government because most agencies use a uniform system of accounts, a standardized format for listing (and then tracking) government expenditures.[3] For a small city, a line-item budget would appear as in Table 7–1. Note that it categorizes expenditures by the items purchased, subdivided by the organizations using them. A top decision maker who wishes greater control over his or her agency's expenditures can easily generate greater detail by adding subdivisions of either the objects purchased (e.g., dividing supplies into typewriters, PCs, and desks) or by further subdividing the organizational structure (e.g., dividing the police department into its various sections). Figure 7–1 shows such a detailed line-item budget for the vice squad of Nashville's police department.

Allen Schick, in an influential essay about the different emphases of

TABLE 7–1. Appropriations by Department

DEPARTMENT	Personal Services	Supplies	Other Charges	Capital Outlay	Total
Mayor and Council	$ 35,789	$ 2,960	$ 16,489	$	$ 55,238
City manager	179,539	1,410	11,715	6,635	199,299
City clerk	55,063	5,625	16,727	3,950	81,365
Municipal courts	106,456	885	74,242	670	182,253
Library	385,853	11,920	96,496	5,843	500,112
Personnel—safety	149,181	1,720	31,509	5,854	188,264
City attorney	186,971	4,460	17,021	213	208,665
Management services	1,443,051	521,690	(871,984)	69,548	1,162,305
Community development	311,770	6,020	26,661	5,580	350,031
Building safety	395,540	11,815	26,599	17,500	451,454
Police	3,747,627	234,731	330,576	327,555	4,640,489
Fire	2,096,199	56,853	54,907	64,727	2,272,686
Parks and Recreation	1,671,445	213,415	544,628	242,693	2,672,181
Public works	3,146,192	616,320	3,469,423	871,773	8,103,708
Nondepartmental:					
Debt service			5,309,010		5,309,010
Capital improvements				1,445,263	1,445,263
Contributions	3,303		956,615		959,918
Contingencies			1,793,609		1,793,609
Annual budget	13,913,979	1,689,824	11,904,243	3,067,804	30,575,850
Bond funds, grants, etc.				8,338,466	8,338,466
Redevelopment, housing			956,000		956,000
Other grants	431,808				431,808
Total financial program	$14,345,787	$1,689,824	$12,860,243	$11,406,270	$40,302,124

Summary by Object (spanning header above Personal Services, Supplies, Other Charges, Capital Outlay, Total)

each type of budget system, pointed out that a line-item budget primarily emphasizes *expenditure control*.[4] Before such budgets became common, it was difficult to tell whether an organization was spending more money than it was given or less. It was also difficult to tell whether the organization was buying what it should or instead wasting or embezzling sums of money. A line-item budget answers such concerns. The legislature sets up highly detailed categories with clear inputs specified for each—so much money for supplies, for example, and so much money for travel. The accounting system is set up to track all expenditures by using these same object categories. Because a line-item budget is so concrete and so detailed, at the end of the year it is easy for auditors to determine whether the money appropriated was spent for the objects specified and for the amount specified. This tight control over the ways in which funds are expended is a real strength of line-item budgeting and not to be dismissed lightly. Nonetheless, it is not enough for the needs of today's complex government organizations.

A line-item budget focuses on inputs, emphasizing the objects bought and the money spent on them. It does not focus on how these objects

DB-23 BU268

METROPOLITAN GOVERNMENT OF NASHVILLE AND DAVIDSON COUNTY
BUDGET PREPARATION SYSTEM
DETAIL REPORT - 1988

PREPARED 08/20/87

101-452.321.001   GENERAL FND GSD -- POLICE DEPT   -- VICE CONTROL-PERSONAL SERVICES

OBJECT GROUP DESCRIPTION	OBJECT /CLASS	DESCRIPTION	FY 1987 YEAR-END	FY 1988 REQUEST	FY 1988 MAYOR'S	FY 1988 FINAL	FY 1988 ADJUSTED
100 PERSONAL SERVICES	0956	POLICE CAPTAIN	31,960 / 1.0	32,422 / 1.0	32,422 / 1.0	32,422 / 1.0	35,300 / 1.0
	2997	POLICE MAJOR	35,806 / 1.0	36,322 / 1.0	36,322 / 1.0	36,322 / 1.0	41,902 / 1.0
	3256	POLICE OFFICER - INVESTIG	602,328 / 26.2	639,169 / 27.0	639,169 / 27.0	644,873 / 27.0	595,254 / 22.0
	3770	CLERK III	17,895 / 1.0	18,203 / 1.0	18,203 / 1.0	18,203 / 1.0	19,823 / 1.0
	3840	STENO CLERK III	19,264 / 1.0	19,534 / 1.0	19,534 / 1.0	19,534 / 1.0	11,990 / 1.0
	4870	TYPIST CLERK III	21,898 / 1.2	17,953 / 1.0	17,953 / 1.0	36,156 / 2.0	39,396 / 2.0
	6148	POLICE LIEUTENANT-INVEST	72,118 / 2.4	60,692 / 2.0	60,692 / 2.0	90,988 / 3.0	105,892 / 3.0
	6149	POLICE SERGEANT-INVESTGAT	133,010 / 5.0	135,055 / 5.0	135,055 / 5.0	135,055 / 5.0	155,529 / 5.0
	9004	SHIFT DIFFERENTIAL	14,596 / .0	14,596 / .0	14,596 / .0	14,596 / .0	23,410 / .0
	9011	STATE IN-SERVICE TRAINING	22,200 / .0	.0	.0	.0	.0
	9014	OVERTIME	190,513 / .0	145,112 / .0	118,769 / .0	144,000 / .0	148,422 / .0
	9017	EDUCATIONAL INCENTIVE (SW	.0	11,868 / .0	.0	11,868 / .0	13,448 / .0
	9050	PAY PLAN IMPROVEMENTS	.0	.0	127,960 / .0	127,960 / .0	.0
OBJECT TOTALS			1,161,588 / 38.8	1,130,926 / 39.0	1,220,675 / 39.0	1,311,977 / 41.0	1,190,366 / 36.0
200 CONTRACTUAL SERVICES	235	MEMBERSHIPS,REGISTRATION	1,595	1,644	1,644	1,644	1,644
	244	TELEPHONE AND TELEGRAPH	2,322	2,322	2,322	2,322	2,322
	266	FURNITURE,OFFICE MACHINES	120	121	121	121	121
	281	MOTOR POOL	130,100	159,100	159,100	159,100	159,100
	283	OUT-OF-TOWN EXPENSE	979	1,024	1,024	1,024	1,024
	298	EQUIPMENT RENTAL	1,494	1,540	1,540	1,540	1,540
OBJECT TOTALS			136,610	165,751	165,751	165,751	165,751
300 SUPPLIES	311	OFFICE SUPPL.&STATIONERY	551	573	573	573	573
	331	SUPPL.FOR LAW ENFORC.OFFI	106	109	109	109	109
	346	REF.BOOKS,MANUALS,PAMPHLE	338	351	351	351	351
	355	BATTERIES (OTHER THAN AUT	214	220	220	220	220
OBJECT TOTALS			1,209	1,253	1,253	1,253	1,253
700 GRANTS,CONTRIBUTIONS,INDEM	746	PERFECT ATTENDANCE AWARDS	750	750	750	750	750
OBJECT TOTALS			750	750	750	750	750
SECT TOTALS			1,300,157	1,298,680	1,386,429	1,479,731	1,358,120
DIV TOTALS			1,300,157	1,298,680	1,386,429	1,479,731	1,358,120

Figure 7-1.

are used or what results they produce. Line-item budgets provide virtually no information that can help top policymakers plan their agency's future direction. Similarly, middle managers seeking to know how efficient the agency has been, or seeking ways to make it more efficient, will again get no useful information from a line-item budget. It is little help to know that $241,500 was spent for salaries if the question is "What do these salaried people accomplish?" Both for legislatures and for top executives, a budget is usually the principal document that reflects their major decisions; it is the primary record of "who gets what." For such a central document to focus *solely* on inputs is a distortion of emphasis. Government is not primarily constituted to buy things; government's central role is to accomplish tasks. Line-item budgeting does not address this central role.

Performance Budgeting

A performance budget (sometimes called an activity budget) focuses on processes rather than inputs. Its categories are expressed as activities, often with workload indicators. Sometimes, if information is available, a performance budget moves a little further right on the chain of outputs and also lists the most immediate outputs. The information in a performance budget is not useful for asking *whether* the agency should be carrying out a task. Performance budgeting simply accepts the job to be done. However, it is useful in examining how efficiently this task is being carried out.

For a streets department, for example, a performance budget will list the total amount spent on filling potholes, the number of potholes filled, and (easily derived from the other two figures) the cost per pothole filled. A performance or activity budget will similarly provide information on cost per child taught, or for a health clinic, cost per patient seen or per inoculation given. (As noted in Chapter Two, these are usually termed *unit costs.)*

In other words, performance budgets emphasize cost analysis, indicating in the budget the number of activities (and occasionally, the number of very immediate outputs) that each budgeted sum is expected to produce. Such cost analysis information about processes and immediate outputs is most valuable to the middle manager, whose job it is to get the most from available resources and who must usually take the organizational mission as given.

The following box illustrates part of a performance budget from Sunnyvale, California. The city calls its budget a "program performance" budget, and in fact it has some program budget components; however, it fits most comfortably into the performance category because of its strong emphasis on activities and unit costs.

Sunnyvale, CA—Performance Budget Cultural and Recreation Programs

Cultural Element Expenditures

	ACTUAL FY 1985/86	PROJECTED ACTUAL FY 1986/87	APPROVED BUDGET FY 1987/88
OPERATING:			
Parks & recreation management	$ 345,157	$ 365,000	$ 400,471
Aquatics pgm. & swim ctr. maintenance	261,777	250,000	287,750
Community center & recreation div.	378,894	460,000	514,796
Neighborhood recreation activities	667,942	675,000	750,546
Physical recreation services	481,605	515,000	573,925
Cultural arts services	411,099	413,000	471,293
Tennis activities	66,032	65,000	74,235
Special groups recreation	68,819	83,000	57,369
Assisted recreation	403,402	470,000	496,777
Library admin. & system development	220,541	239,000	295,119
Sunnyvale patent info. clearing house	172,897	170,000	181,806
Adult services	889,587	925,000	942,259
Circulation & extension services	611,747	557,000	826,505
Children's services	234,677	260,000	279,769
Library technical services	373,098	405,000	455,565
TOTAL OPERATING	5,587,274	5,852,000	6,608,185
CAPITAL PROJECTS	735,431	1,396,227	4,524,074
DEBT SERVICE	157,968	65,520	75,728
TOTAL	$6,480,673	$7,313,747	$11,207,987

SELECTED SERVICE-LEVEL OBJECTIVES

■ Provide aquatic programs at five locations and maintain four swimming pools in a superior condition at an operation and maintenance cost of $1.37 per participant hour, and with an annual subsidy level for this program not to exceed $192,651.

■ Provide neighborhood recreation services at a satisfactory level in the twelve city parks and at twenty school sites at $1.21 per participant hour and $123.04 per participant in Youth Sports Program, and with an annual subsidy level for this program not to exceed $550,612.

■ Acquire, catalog, process, and maintain the collection of library materials at a total of 232,307 units, with a cost of $1.96 per unit.

■ Provide patrons with current library holdings information, catalog book titles to OCLC Class I standards, process items acquired within forty-five days of receipt, and maintain automated online catalog 95 percent of the time.

■ Provide physical recreation services at a satisfactory level for $455.40 per adult athletic league team and for $2.59 per other participant hour, and with an annual subsidy level for this program not to exceed $276,266.

■ Provide unstructured organized open gym programs at one location year around as scheduled in the Parks and Recreation Quarterly Activities Guide, 85 percent of the time.

Sunnyvale, CA—Performance Budget Cultural and Recreation Programs *(continued)*

■ Provide classes, workshops, and programs in performing arts, visual arts, and special interest activities at a satisfactory level at $1.96 per participant hour, and with an annual subsidy level for this program not to exceed $326,717.

■ Provide professional theater experience through the implementation of a summer repertory program.

■ Provide thirteen tennis courts in superior condition at the Sunnyvale Municipal Tennis Center, with related tennis lessons and services, on a 100 percent fee-supported basis.

■ Provide special groups with direct funding for group activities at a satisfactory level for an overall cost of $3.09 per special group participant.

■ Provide recreation programs and other services for older adults at the Multi-Purpose Senior Center and for individuals with disabilities at a satisfactory level at $3.26 per participant hour for older adults, with $25.19 per participant hour for individuals with disabilities, and with an annual subsidy level for this program not to exceed $483,034.

■ Provide patrons with patent, trademark, and copyright information at $2.27 per request for service, and provide instructions in the accessing and use of these research materials.

■ Develop and maintain a quality adult book collection by providing 2.0 adult books per capita and by replacing 5 percent of the collection annually.

■ Provide circulation and extension services by circulating library materials of a total of 891,000 units at a cost of $0.93 per unit and by issuing patron cards and maintaining the physical organization of library resources.

■ Provide bookmobile services by maintaining twenty biweekly stops and two experimental stops 90 percent of the time.

■ Respond successfully to patron requests for children's reference assistance and reading guidance at the appropriate age level 95 percent of the time.

■ Develop and maintain a quality children's book collection by providing 3.0 books per child and by replacing 5 percent of the collection annually.

BUDGET AND PRODUCTIVITY NOTES

■ A budget supplement to upgrade the Quarterly Activities Guide published by Parks and Recreation for community information has been included in the Community Center program.

■ Additional part-time hours were added to the Assisted Recreation
program to reflect the termination of a vocational training program
at De Anza College, which used to provide meal preparation, serving,
and clean-up service at the Senior Center. Staff examined various
alternatives to provide replacement service and part-time hours proved
to be the least expensive option.

■ Parks was able to expand the use of preemergents for weed control
and growth regulators to lessen the need for pruning and edging this
last year.

SELECTED PERFORMANCE INDICATORS

■ Number of patrons entering the library and
percentage of previous year (turnstile count)   698,000   105.0%

■ Number and percent of participants who
receive any Red Cross certification   120   20.0%

■ Number and percent of all adult (16 years
or older) registrants for division special
class/workshop programs placed in
requested program   7,000   90.0%

■ Number and percent of all youth (under 16
years of age) registrants for division special
class/workshop programs placed in
requested program   10,000   75.0%

■ Number and percent of requests for park
buildings and picnic facility usage that
resulted in completed permits   2,000   95.0%

■ Number and percent of physical exercise
classes planned that were provided   76   95.0%

■ Number and percent of games conducted as
scheduled on official league schedules   720   100.0%

■ Number and percent of the eligible youths
(age 13–19) provided recreation activities   4,050   45.0%

■ Number and percent of the eligible (10,000)
youths (age 2–12) provided recreation
activities   7,500   75.0%

■ Number of performances conducted that
achieved 50% house capacity (100 seats)   380   97.0%

■ Number and percent of requests from older
adults to receive referrals of appropriate
community resources to address their

Sunnyvale, CA—Performance Budget Cultural and Recreation Programs *(continued)*

immediate needs fulfilled compared to
requests made   10,000   95.0%
■ Number of total volunteer hours that were
acquired and percentage relative to total
staff hours for all library programs   5,524   4.4%

Cultural Element Selected Performance Measurements for FY 87/88

Task Description	Type of Units	Units	Unit Cost	Hours	Cost
Supervise unstructured swimming	participant hours	95,960	$ .44	5,550	$ 42,388
Aid in planning & implementing co-sponsored club service	participant hours	180,000	.20	496	35,684
Provide an unstructured open gym program	participant hours	60,000	1.80	3,759	107,716
Provide creative arts special activities/ workshops/programs	participant hours	31,300	3.86	4,561	120,748
Conduct Sunnyvale Summer Repertory	participant hours	13,500	.51	390	6,823
Provide tennis program	participant hours	55,000	.93	100	50,992
Provide recreation service to individuals with disabilities	participant hours	6,500	13.30	3,774	86,480
Provide Senior Nutrition Program	number of participants	14,400	6.59	4,210	94,872
Provide recreation program/service for older adults	participant hours	106,000	1.12	4,897	119,009
Respond to request for information	patent services	80,000	.76	1,918	60,595
Select books	books selected	9,433	29.89	2,192	281,965
Provide reference assistance/reading guidance	patron services	311,950	.80	9,758	250,636
Provide periodicals material/assistance to patrons	patron services	185,400	1.07	8,656	199,203
Check out materials	Item checked out	847,000	.38	17,234	317,639
Register patrons/update & delete patron records	patron reg'd/ updated/ deleted	32,100	3.38	6,914	108,458
Bookmobile checkout	Item checked out	44,000	.74	1,785	32,549
Provide reference assistance/reading guidance	patron services	79,300	1.30	4,354	103,062

Sunnyvale, CA—Performance Budget Cultural and Recreation
Programs *(continued)*

- Number and percent of requested pages of U.S. patents mailed to deposit account holders within 24 hours of request — 88,200 — 98.0%
- Number and percent of deposit account orders received and processed within 24 hours of request — 17,150 — 90.0%
- Number and percent of U.S. patents, trademarks and copyright information processed and filed within two days of receipt — 118,750 — 95.0%
- Percent of requests for interlibrary loan material successfully responded to — 95.0%
- Number of periodicals received and processed and the percent available within 10 days — 19,720 — 100.0%
- Number of books processed and the percent available for circulation within 45 days — 14,120 — 80.0%
- Number of items ordered from the selection process and the percent received — 13,894 — 95.0%

Program Budgeting

Some authors use *program budgets* as a synonym for performance budgets.[5] We will adopt the more common approach, using *program budgeting* as the title of budget systems that are also called PPB or PPBS (Planning, Programming, Budgeting Systems). A program budget (or PPB) emphasizes organizational output, the actual impact that an organizational program has on outsiders. It is an integrated system that treats the budget as the central planning document and attempts to make it more "rational" by clarifying the means and ends involved in budgetary decisions. It was refined during the Eisenhower years in "think tanks" such as Rand, and it was first installed in the Kennedy administration's Department of Defense by Robert McNamara. Today it lives on in the Defense Department,[6] as well as in a large number of federal, state, and local agencies.

Program budgeting has four major components. First, it has a *structure* that is expressed in terms of programs rather than organizations. Sometimes these programs cut across agencies; more often one agency has a number of programs. Programs are then divided into subprograms, and these in turn are divided into elements (also called *activities*).[7] Table 7–2 shows the program budget structure for part of the state budget of Pennsylvania, which calls its programs and subprograms *categories* and *subcategories*.

Second, PPB has *projections*, which show the future costs of programs as an aid to planning. Third, it has *program memoranda,* which express the goals of the expenditures. Table 7–2 shows (shortened) versions of these as well. Finally, it has *analytic studies,* which examine whether the program is actually achieving its goals (and is worth continuing). These studies are usually based on such analytic tools as program evaluation, supplemented by benefit-cost analysis and cost-effectiveness analysis.

All of these components address the PPB emphasis on planning and long-range (intermediate or ultimate) outputs. The structure is based on shared output goals rather than on inputs or processes, and the program memoranda make these shared goals explicit. The five-year plans project far into the future, and the analytic studies use program evaluation to determine a program's long-range outputs and then apply cost-benefit analysis to see whether these outputs are worth the amount spent on them.

Ideally, the program budget aspires to evaluate programs in terms of their intermediate or ultimate outputs: deterrence gained, lives saved, jobs produced, and so on. But when these long-range indicators are missing, it falls back on immediate outputs.[8] Moreover, PPB recognizes that not every program can be analyzed each year, and so each year's analytic studies cover only the most important or changing programs.

Budget Formats and the Chain of Outputs

Each type of budget emphasizes a different section of the chain of outputs. Line-item budgeting starts at the far left of the chain, emphasizing how the money budgeted relates to inputs. Performance budgeting moves to the right, emphasizing how the money budgeted relates to organizational processes and to the most immediate outputs. Program budgeting (PPB) moves yet further to the right of the chain, emphasizing the effect of the budgeted money on intermediate and even ultimate outputs.

Accordingly, an ideal program budget appears far different from the line-item or performance budgets. For a streets department, for example, a line-item budget would display the gallons of asphalt and the number of tons of gravel purchased. The performance budget would display the cost per pothole filled or the cost per mile paved. The program budget would display the number of additional people that the new road brings downtown or the savings in commuting time that it produced.

To take another example, a line-item budget of a health clinic would be expressed in terms of the costs of syringes, doctors' salaries, and other inputs. A performance budget would use workload indicators such as cost per patient examined or cost per X-ray taken. At its best, a program budget would express its cost in terms of the number of limbs preserved, diseases prevented, lives saved, or years of life restored.

As indicated earlier, however, ideal program budgets are very difficult

TABLE 7-2. Sample Program Structure: Commonwealth Program IV Protection of Persons and Property

Category	Subcategory	Element
General administration and support		
Traffic safety and supervision		
Control and reduction of crime	Crime prevention	
Maintenance of public order	Criminal law enforcement	
Provision of public services to local governments	Reintegration of adult offenders	Maintenance of inmate security
Water damage control and prevention		Maintenance of inmates' physical-mental health
Protection of the forest resource		Counseling of inmates for personal and social problems
Occupational health and safety		Education of inmates
Consumer protection		Occupational and vocational training of inmates
Community and housing hygiene and safety		Inspection of county and municipal institutions
		Social investigation
		Supervision for social and personal change
		Financial and professional assistance to county probation departments
		Screening to determine risk

Sample Program Structure Statements and Program Plan Logic

Commonwealth program-protection of persons and property
Goal
 To provide an environment and social system in which the lives of individuals, and the property of individuals and organizations are protected from natural and man-made disasters, and from illegal and unfair action.

Program category-control and reduction of crime

Subgoal: To provide a high degree of protection against bodily injury, loss of life, and loss of property resulting from unlawful or unfair actions by individuals or organizations; to provide a sufficiently secure setting for offenders in order to safeguard the community and provide for their health and well-being; and to cure or alleviate the socially aberrent behavior of the offender and to assist the offender to function to the best of his potential upon release from an institution or while on probation.

Program subcategory-reintegration of offenders

Objective: To decrease the recurrence of crime by replacing criminal behavior with socially acceptable behavior

Impacts: Number and percent of persons released convicted for new crimes
Number and percent of evaluation of inmates reflecting gain in social skills and emotional controls
Number of releases under supervision of court parole or Pennsylvania Board of Parole
Number of admissions who are parole violators

Program element-counseling for personal and social problems

Outputs: Number of inmates receiving recommended individual counseling
Number of inmates receiving recommended group counseling
Number of inmates receiving recommended self-improvement group counseling
Number of inmates receiving recommended psychiatric treatment

Need and/or demand: Number of inmates recommended for individual counseling
Number of inmates recommended for group counseling
Number of inmates recommended for self-improvement group counseling
Number of inmates recommended for psychiatric treatment

Funds required: Direct state activities
Payments to jurisdictions

Manpower required: Man years
Funds required

Program statement

Financial statement

Manpower statement

SOURCE: Robert J. Mowitz, *The Design and Implementation of Pennsylvania's Planning, Programming, Budgeting System* (Harrisburg: Commonwealth of Pennsylvania, 1970) p. 53.

to construct because organizations often do not have all the necessary output data. Thus even many budgets that are called "program" are actually hybrids that combine many features of performance budgets. Box 7-1 shows part of a program budget for Charlotte, North Carolina; the budget also has some performance budget characteristics. Not shown are the multiyear projections and the in-depth analyses that must also accompany the document to make it a true program budget.

Zero-base Budgeting

Zero-base budgeting (ZBB) is the most recently developed budgetary system. It began in Georgia under Governor Jimmy Carter and moved to Washington in 1977 when Carter became president. At the peak of its popularity, in the late 1970s, ZBB was installed by a large number of state and local governments. In 1981 the federal ZBB system was discontinued by Ronald Reagan, and in the following years its popularity declined at the state and local levels as well. Nonetheless it continues to be used by a number of states and localities.

Under ZBB each program area (called a decision unit) is divided into different funding levels (called decision packages).[9] These funding levels for each program are then compared to the funding levels of other programs, and the choices ranked in order of preference. Box 7-2 displays three decision packages for a county lunch program. Note that each package tells how much it would cost individually, and how much additional output the package's cost would provide. Package 2 would provide 710 more meals for roughly $476,000; package 3 would provide an additional 500 meals for an additional $311,000.

Under ZBB, every program in the county would develop similar packages. Then the county administrators would rank the packages against each other. Thus the administrators might rank package 1 of the hot-lunch program very high—perhaps 30th on the county's list, behind only some basic packages for police, fire, and the like. But package 2 for the lunch program would probably be ranked lower—because the worst-off hungry people were taken care of by package 1—perhaps 390th, behind many other packages from health care, education, and other county programs. Package 3 would probably be ranked even lower. At some point, the county administrators would total the cumulative cost of all the packages up to a point (say, the 460th-ranked package) and draw a line. All the packages above the line are funded; all those below it are not because the county has run out of available funds.

Note that despite its title, ZBB does not actually evaluate each program from a zero base; each program's first package is not zero but some basic level of funding. (A more detailed example of the ZBB

Box 7–1.

This box and the following table represent part of a program budget for the Police Department of Charlotte, North Carolina.

COMMUNITY SERVICES: GENERAL GOVERNMENT—POLICE

Objectives and Achievements

■ Deploy patrol resources to achieve a response time of seven minutes or less for 90 percent of emergency calls for service and ten minutes or less for 90 percent of immediate calls for service: *Adam Patrol Division responded to 91 percent of emergency calls within seven minutes; 91 percent of immediate calls in ten minutes. Baker Patrol Division responded to 87 percent of emergency calls within seven minutes; 86 percent of immediate calls in ten minutes.*

■ Dispatch 95 percent of emergency calls within three minutes and 100 percent within five minutes: *91 percent of emergency calls were dispatched within three minutes and 98 percent were dispatched within five minutes.*

■ Dispatch 85 percent of immediate calls within three minutes and 95 percent within five minutes: *72 percent of immediate calls were dispatched within three minutes and 94 percent were dispatched within five minutes.*

■ Develop and implement patrol plans from crime analysis reports in order to decrease targeted crimes in specific areas; have 75 percent of the patrol plans achieve a reduction in the targeted crime: *Twenty-one patrol plans were prepared for Adam Patrol Division with sixteen resulting in decreased crime; twenty-three patrol plans were prepared for Baker Patrol Division with twenty-two resulting in decreased crime; thirteen aerial patrol plans were developed, all of which resulted in a decrease in the targeted crimes.*

■ Investigate and successfully close 90 percent of assault with a deadly weapon cases; 90 percent of homicide, suicide, and questionable death cases; 55 percent of rape and other sex offense cases; 35 percent of robbery cases; 29 percent of auto theft cases; 46 percent of fraud cases; and 30 percent of arson cases: *Through February 1987, 86 percent of assault with a deadly weapon cases, 52 percent of rape cases, 41 percent of robbery cases, 30 percent of auto theft cases, 47 percent of fraud cases, and 38 percent of arson cases had been closed.*

■ Develop and implement eight apartment Identification Watches, geared to mark personal valuables and observe and report suspicious activity: *Ten apartment Identification Watches have been implemented.*

■ Conduct two Basic Recruit Schools of approximately 500 hours of training: *Three recruit classes have been completed and two are scheduled to finish before the end of FY87.*

■ Provide timely analysis of crime evidence by maintaining average turn-around times for analyzing various types of evidence—fingerprints in four days; photographic evidence in three days; trace evidence (hair, blood, etc.) in twenty days; firearms, tool, and treadmarks in twelve days; questioned documents in twelve days; and drug evidence in ten days: *Fingerprints were processed in five days; photographic evidence in five days; trace evidence in twenty-five days; firearms, tool, and treadmarks in twenty-eight days; questioned documents in seventeen days and drug evidence in sixteen days.*

■ Deploy Crime Scene Search Units so that 90 percent of calls for service are responded to within one hour: *87 percent of 5,768 calls were answered within one hour.*

- Provide a level of follow-up investigation of total Part I offenses that will allow for successful case closure of 30 percent of those cases investigated: *Adam Patrol Division provided successful follow-up to 38 percent of investigated cases; Baker Patrol Division provided successful follow-up to 35 percent of investigated cases.*
- Increase the number of arrests for prostitution-related offenses during FY87 to a level 5 percent higher than arrests for prostitution-related offenses during FY86: *Through the first eight months of FY87, arrests for prostitution-related offenses have increased 75 percent over the same period in FY86.*

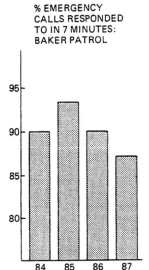

% EMERGENCY CALLS RESPONDED TO IN 7 MINUTES: BAKER PATROL

Note that although the box gave some output indicators, this table primarily gives process (workload) indicators for each program element. This makes the budget a hybrid between a program and performance budget.

Program Elements of the Charlotte FY89 Police Budget.

	Positions	Budget
a. Patrol	538	$15,719,573
Provide emergency response and directed patrol to 8 patrol districts, 24 hours per day, 7 days a week. Protect persons and property; serve 376,000 citizens and property valued at $17.5 billion.		
b. Recruitment and training	13	703,504
Provide recruitment, recruit training, in-service, and firearm training to departments' 686 sworn officers.		
c. Youth services	25	1,012,182
Coordinate all criminal investigations involving juveniles as a victim or suspect (2,923 were processed		

Program Elements of the Charlotte FY89 Police Budget *(cont.)*

	Positions	Budget
in FY87); provide in-school programs and act as liaison with public and private schools; operate the Police Athletic League and organize all youth sporting events; coordinate school-crossing guard program.		
d. Crime laboratory	32	1,041,777
Provide crime scene searches, evaluate and collect evidence (8,649 calls for service were received last year); 853 microanalysis of criminalistic evidence were conducted in FY87; provided 2,778 analyses of drug evidence in FY87; processed 4,009 crime analysis photographic searches in FY87.		
e. Felony investigation	68	2,018,558
Investigate all felony offenses, including auto theft, fraud, and arson; 5,459 cases were investigated in FY87.		
f. Vice and narcotics	25	973,017
Investigate all narcotics and dangerous drug offenses, gambling, and prostitution.		
g. Special services	15	754,408
Coordinate all specialized services for public safety, including the helicopter program, crime prevention, noise control, and tactical operations.		
h. Administration	31	1,400,157
Coordinate all administrative functions of the Police Department including Internal Affairs, Staff Inspections, Police Attorney's Office, Police Counseling, Fiscal Affairs, and Planning and Research.		
i. Civilian programs	2	83,359
Coordinate the Police Reserves and all civilian volunteer programs.		
j. Dispatch	63	2,646,985
Receive and dispatch all calls for service (198,808 were received in FY87); provide staffing to operate the enhanced-911 emergency dispatch system.		
k. Property control	23	3,788,551
Provide or monitor automotive use, custodial service, printing, and building maintenance.		
l. Information services	16	655,758
Provide department's data processing and word processing services; provide the public information function for the department.		
m. Records management	58	1,153,368
Process all fingerprint requests and latent fingerprint examination (4,042 requests for analysis were received in FY87); provide all polygraphing services.		
Total	909	$31,951,197

Box 7–2. ZBB: Three Packages. Senior Citizens' Nutrition Program: County Hot-Lunch Program.

STATEMENT OF PURPOSE

To maintain or improve the mental and physical health and living conditions of the elderly citizens of Mecklenburg County by providing proper nutrition and reducing isolation for as many residents over sixty years of age as possible; enabling the elderly to remain in their own homes instead of in nursing homes and mental facilities; coordinating services and information for the elderly so that they are aware of the services available to them; and providing area focal points for the senior citizens to come together and share common concerns.

SERVICE LEVELS

1. This level provides 940 meals per day to senior citizens at eight sites. The staff coordinates program activities; completes reports for federal, state, and county agencies; prepares, serves, and delivers meals; and provides transportation to and from sites for 150 elderly per day. Supportive services are also provided at this level. $891,943

2. This level adds four preparation sites providing 710 meals per day. Additional staff prepares food on site and performs the same activities listed in service level 1. $476,764

3. This level adds two preparation sites and one catered site that provide 500 meals per day for a total of fifteen sites and 2,150 meals per day, enabling 2,500 eligible elderly to be enrolled in the program. Additional staff prepares food on site and performs the same activities listed in service level 1. $311,510

   TOTAL $1,680,217

procedure, based on the Carter administration's instructions, is reproduced in this chapter's appendix.)

A ZBB system has a ravenous, almost unquenchable appetite for information. Thus one federal agency found that ZBB required it to triple its budget documentation, so that it had 90,000 pieces of paper prepared for 478 decision packages for 75 decision units.[10]

To operate correctly, ZBB must have figures on the output that could be expected from *each* program at *each* funding level. Although it demands much more detail than program budgets, ZBB theoretically has roughly the same emphasis—intermediate program outputs. In actual practice, though, most agencies understandably have difficulties in determining accurate output information for so many programs for so many funding levels. Therefore they often use process (workload) indicators with their ZBB packages.

ZBB requires far larger amounts of paperwork and analysis than program budgeting, yet it does not consistently provide any more usable information.[11] Most agencies have found that even when the ZBB process helped illuminate the choices involved in a program one year, it was not worth going through all the paperwork of levels and ranking again the second year; the first-year analysis was still basically valid. ZBB seems unlikely to maintain a permanent niche as a regular, annual budgeting approach, but it nonetheless can be very helpful when used periodically as an analytic tool for clarifying program choices.

Budget Formats and the Accounting System

To be meaningful, budgets must be tied to the accounting system. We can see why by considering a hypothetical program budget that is not so tied. A police department, very proud of its new program budget, sends the city council a budget request, with such program budget categories as $140,000 for crime investigation and $1,300,000 for crime prevention and control. The council, after much debate, slightly increases the amount for investigation and lowers the amount for crime prevention and control. However, the police department's accounting system utilizes only typical input categories such as supplies, travel, salaries, and pension. At the end of the year the police department can use its accounting system to tell how much money it spent in total, and how much of that total was spent on various objects of expenditure. But neither the police department nor the city council has any way of knowing whether the department has indeed spent exactly the appropriated amounts for crime investigation or for crime prevention.

Of course the department can estimate how much it spent in each program category, basing its estimates on the line-item accounting system. But as emphasized in Chapter Two, such estimates are next to useless because they never surprise; that is, they show only whatever assumptions the manager had to begin with. Only a bill-by-bill, expense-by-expense daily tracking system will actually reveal whether the department in fact spent the budgeted sums for its programs. Without such a system, neither the department nor the council knows how much was spent for each program category; and therefore the department's time in determining how much to ask for in each category and the city council's debate over the appropriation amounts were both meaningless. If the budget is to be an expression of real choices, the categories of the accounting system must replicate those of the budgeting system.[12]

When an accounting system maintains separate figures for performance or program budget categories, basically cost centers are being utilized. Chapter Two discusses the advantages of using separate sets of accounts to track the expenses of an organization's subunits or activities; it notes that these separate activities or units with their own accounts are usually called *cost centers*. Although we do not need a performance or program budget to have cost centers, they are complemented and strengthened by such budget systems. First we reflect the organization's programs or activities as categories in a performance or program budget. Then we use the accounting system to track the expenses of each such category in the form of a cost center. At the beginning of the year, the budget suggests what an activity (e.g., street paving) is budgeted to cost; then throughout the year a cost center built around that activity collects data on what it is actually costing.

An organization can track expenditures or expenses for more than one budget format. Accounts are building blocks that can be added together in different ways to provide different information. Accordingly it is possible to build an accounting system that codes each item with numbers that assign it both to an item of expenditure category and to a separate program or performance budget category. This system then enables the agency to maintain several types of budgets, and managers can easily *crosswalk*— track an item from one type of budget to another. When the legislature demands a line-item budget (as it often does), this multiple system may be the best way for the agency to meet the legislature's demand and still have the internal management advantages of a program or performance budget. But in all cases, the budget categories are meaningful *only* if the accounting system tracks the budget format(s).[13]

Choosing a System for Managerial Budgeting

The choice of budget formats sometimes lies outside the purview of the managers. Sometimes, the president, mayor, or governor may choose a particular budgeting system on the basis of political symbolism. New systems can be used to distinguish a new administration from an old one. Or the budget system choice can be used to send a political message to the public; the announcement of a ZBB system can symbolically strengthen a newly elected executive's promise that all government expenditures are "now going to be scrutinized from the ground up."

Even when the executive has not dictated a particular budget format, managers often just use the system that is used by the legislature because many managers do not wish to maintain two different systems—one for formulating and defending budget requests for the legislature, and the other for the month-to-month tracking of inputs and their results. However, this decision is often short-sighted, particularly if the legislature uses a line-item format, which provides little useful managerial information. As just noted, today's accounting software packages greatly simplify the maintenance of two systems.

Very often managers do have some influence in choosing internal budget formats. If they do, which of the four possible budgeting approaches is best for the manager? In selecting a useful managerial budgeting system, ZBB is rarely the strongest option. It demands too much time and analysis.

Its ranked categories (packages) lend themselves to one-time choices but not to month-to-month tracking of routine operations.

The three remaining types of budget systems all have strong points. Very low-ranking managers with few subordinates and small budgets will probably find a line-item budget sufficient. It will allow them to track individual items purchased, and that is the only information that they really need. High-ranking managers who are often involved in policy as well as management will find a program budget most useful. It displays strategic choices and emphasizes the intermediate and ultimate outputs of an organization. Most other managers will find the information in a performance budget the best because it provides the process and immediate output information that is most useful in the month-to-month monitoring of the organization's costs and performance. Performance budgets often closely connect with the types of information generated by output-oriented management systems. Box 7–3 summarizes the four types of budget systems.

Usage data indicates that many governments do not use just one system. For example, most states keep line-item budgets, especially because most legislatures seem to prefer them. Nonetheless, a mid-1980s survey of states found program budgeting also used in thirty-seven states, ZBB in twenty, and performance measures in thirty-one. Almost all the states rated such approaches as "effective" or "somewhat effective."[14]

The most extensive survey of local governments found that 78 percent use line-item budgets, but only about half use them exclusively. Fifty-two percent use program or PPB budgets, and 18 percent use performance budgets. (The performance budget figures are probably understated because some localities may claim "program" budgets while in fact using workload indicators, and therefore actually having performance budgets.[15]) ZBB was used by 11 percent of the jurisdictions. Over 60 percent use performance indicators in some way, and over 90 percent of those using performance indicators believed that they were useful in increasing productivity.[16]

All of these budget formats serve important organizational purposes. Many organizations operate from a basic program budget but keep supplementary information on line items and on organizational activities. Such hybrids are often the most practical of all approaches.

SHOULD MANAGEMENT SYSTEMS BE TIGHTLY LINKED TO THE BUDGET SYSTEM?

Most Existing Links: Loose and Informal

As discussed, legislative-level budgeting systems are not management systems; they are policy systems used to determine how to allocate future money. Management systems take effect after the annual budgeting decision

Box 7-3.

TYPE OF BUDGET	ALTER-NATIVE NAMES	PRIMARY FOCUS	PRIMARY CHARACTER-ISTICS OR COMPONENTS	MOST USEFUL TO
Line-item budget	Object-of-expenditure budget	Inputs	Structured by objects purchased	Very low-level managers; others seeking *economy*
Performance budget	Activity budget	Activities	Structured by activities	Middle-level managers seeking *efficiency*
Program budget	Planning programming budgeting system (PPBS or PPB) Also: mission budgeting	Outputs	Structured by programs (i.e., desired outputs)	Higher-level managers and policy-makers seeking *effectiveness*
Zero-base budget	ZBB or service-level budget	Activities or outputs (depending on the information used to rank packages)	Structured by a ranking of different program funding levels	Rarely useful as a continuing process; main use is as a one-shot analytic device focused on *effectiveness*

has been made, either to track the money itself, through the financial systems, or to track the effect of the money, through MBO and performance monitoring systems. But as noted earlier, some links between management systems and budgeting are inescapable. We will call these usually informal links *loose links.*

In most organizations, there are a great number of loose links. A financial management system tracks money that is allocated under budgeting, often using categories determined by the budget. An output-oriented system uses goals that were partially determined in the budget process to judge success. Moreover, the effect works in the other direction as well; information gathered by the management systems will be considered by budgetary decision makers before they decide on the best areas to commit next year's funds.

An additional, more informal link exists between budgeting and management systems because the subordinate manager usually realizes that the same top manager with whom he or she negotiates and tracks management progress has a substantial voice in budget decisions.

Formal, Tight Links Between Budgeting and Management Systems

Most organizations are content to keep the links at this informal level. However such informal links seem incomplete to some management system designers. MBO and especially performance monitoring systems, they argue, should be integrated completely with the budgeting system. Such a formally linked system would have two requirements:

1. The budgeting, analysis, and management functions would be combined in one office.[17] Such a combination does not guarantee that these systems are in fact integrated, but integration is impossible without it.
2. The principal budget decisions—who gets what—would be based almost entirely on the output figures generated by the management systems.

Thus about a year before a new budget would be in effect, subagencies would submit their budget requests to higher executives, just as they do now. But unlike now, they would defend their budget requests primarily in terms of how much output they could produce for the money they were requesting. These requests would be reviewed by the combined budget/analysis/management office, which would give its recommendation to the chief executive. After the legislature has acted on the request, the same combined office would be in charge of tracking the output figures, seeing if they measured up to the figures that were "promised" when the agency submitted its budget request. If such promises were not kept, the agency would receive less money in future years.

For most organizations, which use informally linked systems, the only link between budgeting and the management systems is that the information on output is available to all the actors, and some actors are involved in both processes. But in the formally linked process, both the management system process and the budget process are exactly the same, taking place at the same time and involving exactly the same actors.[18]

Advantages of a Tight, Formal Link

Advocates of such tight links cite a number of advantages. First, for all agencies, the budget cycle is immortal. The cycle is automatic, and its deadlines are inexorable. Because the budget cycle must continue with or without leadership at the top, anything tied to it may have a better chance of continuing as well. We have seen in the preceeding chapters that management systems often depend on fragile, personal motivations. Tying a management system to the budget is an attempt to institutionalize a system so that it does not rest on such a fragile foundation.

Second, money (i.e., a desire for an increased agency budget) is probably the strongest, most universal incentive for top line managers. Thus a system that links its incentives directly to the budget has powerful sanctions. This connection is very clear because a formal link means that the goals of each subunit become "bids" in an auction for agency funds. This approach makes the "contract" metaphor of MBO much more realistic. In a system without a formal link, subordinate managers promise to deliver a certain amount of output if they are given a certain level of resources (budget and personnel). This fact is reflected by the space on most MBO forms for budget and personnel figures. But in fact MBO objectives are usually set after the budget process is well along, and the amount of money and the personnel available are fairly well set. The contract is therefore somewhat one-sided because only the subordinates have much range in their responses; the options of the agency head are restricted. -

However, if the output-oriented management system is formally linked to budgeting, both the superior and the subordinate begin the process uncommitted. The budget has yet to be submitted to the legislature when the top manager bargains with his or her subordinates. Thus the subordinate managers are to some extent "bidding" for slices of the upcoming budget because they are promising to deliver so much additional output for additional budget funds. If some other subordinate manager can promise more output for the money, he or she will receive the funds. And the tracking process, while serving its traditional managerial role, is also a way of holding the "winning" managers to their output promises.

Application of the Tight Link System.   Tight link systems are in the minority, but a number do exist. Sunnyvale, California, a part of whose budget was shown earlier, has perhaps the most extensively linked of all municipal systems. Phoenix, too, tightly links its budget and management system.

At the federal level, the U.S. Forest Service has used such linked systems, and it is pleased with the results. Output data are tracked by both the budget office and the superior managers; incentives are extremely powerful because the budget is so important to managers; and the system is institutionalized to the extent that discontinuing the management system would require a strong effort from the top of the department, not just neglect.[19]

Disadvantages of a Tight, Formal Link

Although the link to budgeting gives management systems the advantage of increased sanctions and institutionalization, there are substantial disadvantages. First, goals must be set much earlier in systems with formal budget links because the goals must precede the budget decisions. This requirement forces a lag of at least a year between the time objectives are set and the time tracking begins. For example, in many states as well as in the federal government, an agency must finish developing its fiscal year 1994 request as it is simultaneously defending its 1993 request before the legislature and executing the final months of its 1992 budget. Such a long lead time greatly reduces the management system's timeliness and flexibility. It cannot respond quickly to changes in the environment.

Second, if MBO or a performance monitoring system is to be the basis of the budget process, as in the Forest Service, it must cover all organizational outputs so as to lead directly to budget figures. There are a number of problems with this requirement. A federal MBO official emphasized the diversion of attention: "We'd like to tie MBO closer to the budget. But we wouldn't want it to be like [pure] PPB; every dollar shouldn't be in a category. That way you spend a lot of time trying to figure out what program the Secretary's trip to Denver should go under."[20]

A designer of an MBO system defended the avoidance of tight budget links for related reasons:

> We only have a small staff. Some of the really important things that we should focus our attention on, that we feel need close watching, don't address the major part of the budget.
>
> They tend instead to concern high-impact items. We had goals more for bellwether items than for things that cost a lot. . . . For example, determining a national coal policy—these things have extremely important ramifications, maybe concerning billions of dollars. So they should be the focus of some MBO objectives. But what does it cost to determine a coal policy? Maybe the salaries of twenty-five or thirty people. That's nothing in the departmental budget.

A final potential cost of such a budget and management system link is the subordination of management. A series of management reports have for two decades criticized the federal Office of Management and Budget (OMB) for neglecting management in favor of budget.[21] Many government managers and agencies understandably think first and foremost about budget because money is power. The danger of totally uniting management systems with a budget system, then, is that when management and money are put next to each other, management can get lost in the budget's shadow.

In Conclusion: Should Links Be Loose or Tight?

How then should this trade-off between the advantages and disadvantages of a tight link between the budget and management system be decided? Of course, managers have more than just the two choices of either a "tight" or a "loose" link. These two categories are ends of a continuum, and agencies may choose to split the difference, moving partway toward tight links without totally unifying their budget and management systems. But "tight" and "loose" are useful labels for two broad types of budget and management system links. In which general direction should an agency with new management systems move?

The experience of a large number of agencies seems to suggest that managers should use caution before opting for the sophisticated, unified system implied by tight links. Generally, the experience of agencies such as the Forest Service, which maintains tight links, should not be taken as typical. The Forest Service has unusually tangible outputs, such as board feet cut, trees planted, and miles of road paved. It is much easier to link output measurements tightly to the budget when the agency's production function is clear—when it is known that a certain amount of money produces a particular amount of additional output. This system may be possible only if the organization's outputs are as unusually discrete and tangible as those of the Forest Service. Promising a certain amount of output for a certain input would clearly be much more difficult for managers in a school system or health clinic.

The Forest Service successfully implemented its system because its output is tangible, because it had a tracking and reporting system for many years, and because it has a very strong esprit de corps. These characteristics minimized resistance during the switchover by those who were adversely affected, and they also minimized cheating on the system during its regular operation.

Most government agencies have few or none of these characteristics, and thus extensive budget and management system links seem inappropriate. They would need so much paperwork and such a huge staff that the system would resemble the unlamented federal ZBB of the 1970s, and a similar fate—slow death—would probably await it.

Although tight links increase managerial incentives for performance, they produce incentives for less positive behavior as well. The "rewards" for cheating become much greater if the organizational budget will be directly and automatically affected by the reported performance measures. Other problems of management systems, such as goal displacement, will similarly be exacerbated. The more direct the link, the greater the incentives for cheating and/or displacement.

In response, the organization must develop and deploy equally strong counterincentives, such as increasing the number of indicators to fight displacement and increasing the amount of double-checking and parallel reporting to fight cheating. But most of the time, this extensive network of counterincentives is simply beyond the capabilities of public organizations. The extensive management system necessary to keep the figures from leading to displacement or misreporting would require a great deal of time and money. Money and personnel for setting up such a strong managerial system is likely to look like unnecessary managerial layering to the legislature, which controls the funding. Civil service systems and political considerations may also prevent much sanctioning.

The extremely high mortality rate of sophisticated management systems in the public sector makes the conclusion clear. It is best to begin with loose links and then proceed cautiously toward tightening. For most organizations, it is usually better to use the system information as one important input to be considered in all types of managerial decision making, without tying the system exclusively and directly to the budget. This approach lowers the time and personnel necessary to run the systems and the level of expertise necessary from all participants. It also lowers the incentives for misreporting and displacement to a level where counterincentives are more easily deployed.[22]

INTERNAL POLITICAL EFFECTS OF BUDGETING SYSTEMS

The *external* political effects of budgeting are clear; budgeting is without doubt the most political organizational process because it determines which outside groups win or lose. But *internal* political implications also suffuse budgeting, starting with even such a seemingly technical matter as the choice of a budget format. Traditionally, budgeting has been a *bottom-up* process. The lower levels of the organization decide their staffing and supply needs and send the request to the next level up, which considers it with other requests, makes changes, and sends it up to the next level. When all the requests finally reach the top level of the organization, the top administrators pool the requests, adjust them, and draw up a line-item budget. A line-item budget gives a great deal of power to the lower levels of the organizations since only they have the detailed information about their needs for supplies and other line items.

In program budgeting, in contrast, the top officials of the organization first draw up overall organizational priorities and then express these in the program categories and objectives. Only then are lower levels of the organization asked for their budget requests, which must be expressed in terms of these objectives.[23] Program budgeting is thus a *top-down* process, which gives much more power to the top of the organization. If politics is "who gets what," then the choice of a budgeting system is political because different parts of the organization gain or lose power in the choice. The top wins with program budgets; the lower levels win with line-item budgets.

Last-Minute Spending.   Other aspects of budget systems also have internal effects that are ultimately political. For example, almost all jurisdictions structure their budget systems so that unspent money must be returned at the end of the fiscal year. This requirement leads to a great deal of goal displacement. Agencies are often terrified of having funds left over because the legislature might begin to suspect that they did not really need all the money they were given, and future appropriations might be cut. Accordingly the last few weeks of the fiscal year are often marked by haphazard spending as inflated contracts are let and unneeded objects bought in a mad rush to avoid any unencumbered funds.

For example, the Federal Maritime Administration assigned 42 percent of the year's procurement contracts in the final forty-eight hours of one fiscal year. The Interior Department once even awarded a contract to an outside consulting firm to determine why the department did so much contracting at the very end of the year. Not surprisingly, the contract was awarded in the final three days of the fiscal year. In similar end-of-year splurges, Fort Riley, Kansas, bought eighty color TV sets, then kept fifty of them in storage for almost a year; the Army paid $187,000 for redecoration and new construction on a base scheduled to be closed; and an Interior Department Young Adult Conservation Corps camp in Missouri bought 1,000 pairs of chaps, 4,000 pairs of gloves, lawn mowers worth $120,000, 10,000 fence posts, and 181 chain saws for the use of fewer than 300 enrollees.[24]

Top managers who wish to discourage this behavior in their subunits can personally review all large contracts and purchases made during this period, or they can control the amount of money, allowing perhaps only one-twelfth of the subunit budget to be encumbered in the last month. Congress has passed a law, for example, that limits Defense Department spending on maintenance and operations procurement during the final two months of the fiscal year to 20 percent of the year's total.[25]

As suggested by just these few examples, the choice of budget procedures and rules, seemingly a technical matter of efficiency, can have a great behavioral impact internally. Managers wishing to implement new budgetary systems must be aware of the internal effects in choosing and selling their systems.

SUMMARY

At the highest levels, budgeting is primarily a policy (strategic planning) function, not a managerial function. But managers must allocate the resources within their organization on a monthly or quarterly basis in a managerial budgeting process as well. Of the four types of budgeting systems, line-item budgeting is input oriented and is most useful to managers as a control device. Performance budgeting is oriented toward activities and immediate outputs; it often connects easily with a management system. Both program and zero-base budgeting are clearly output oriented, focusing on intermediate outputs if possible. Although they are primarily directed toward policy, they also have important management uses. With currently available accounting software, agencies can (and should) use more than one of these budget formats. To be meaningful, a budget system must be directly linked to the accounting system.

In most organizations, output-oriented management systems are linked to the budget system through loose, informal ties. The information generated by the output system is generally known to the budget managers, who consider it in their decisions. Often, some of this information is reported in the budget documents. Moreover, sometimes the same actors (e.g., top managers) are involved in both systems.

However, some system designers wish to make these links much tighter and more formal by making goal setting and output measurement so important that they drive the budget process. Under this tight system, budget requests and decisions are based almost entirely on promised output performance, as measured by the management system. This system can be used successfully by a few agencies with concrete outputs and strong discipline, but most agencies will lose more than they gain by trying to unite totally two complex systems. A tight budget link often requires the management system to move to very long lead times, decreasing flexibility; to cover all items, diffusing attention from priority concerns; and to administer budgeting and management jointly, raising the likelihood that management will be eclipsed by the more immediate concerns of the budget.

Budgeting has a great number of political implications. At the megalevel, of course, its very nature—the decision over who gets what—puts it at the heart of politics. But even when viewed from a middle manager's perspective, it also has important internal political effects. The choice of a budgeting system can move power up an organization (as does program budgeting) or down (as does line-item budgeting). Manipulating budgeting figures—by going on spending sprees at the end of the year, for example—can affect whether or not an agency receives full funding the following year.

REVIEW QUESTIONS

1. What types of information are most useful to each level of a public organization? Which type of budget provides this information?

2. Give three examples of information about a city's recreation department that could be learned from a line-item budget, from a performance budget, and from a program budget.

3. Give three examples of information about a state's department of corrections that could be learned from a line-item budget, from a performance budget, and from a program budget.

4. Why do agencies engage in year-end spending sprees? What remedial measures can be taken?

5. In what ways are budgets political?

6. What problems arise in connecting the budget to the accounting system? What are the advantages of such a connection?

7. What does a "loose" tie between the budget and the management system entail? What are its advantages and disadvantages?

8. What does a "tight" tie between the budget and the management system entail? What are its advantages and disadvantages?

Case 7-1

A training division operates four training programs located in different places, each aimed at different groups of the general population. The division has been told that it will be given a lump sum for the next fiscal year's budget. Since its resources are limited, the division wants to allocate those resources to the most efficient programs. Thus the division will use cost and performance information to make the allocation decisions.

The department has collected the following information. The administrative and coordination costs incurred by the division's management office have been calculated and proportionally allocated to each program under the heading "General administration."

COSTS	PROGRAM 1	PROGRAM 2	PROGRAM 3	PROGRAM 4
General administration	$12,000	$10,000	$14,000	$12,000
Training personnel	40,000	35,000	38,000	45,000
Clerical support	20,000	18,000	15,000	16,000
Advertising	5,000	7,000	6,000	7,000
Placement	2,000	3,000	3,000	2,000
Supplies	4,000	5,000	4,000	6,000
Utilities	6,000	6,000	5,000	7,000
Telephone	3,000	3,000	2,000	3,000
Maintenance	20,000	22,000	16,000	25,000
Evaluation	10,000	10,000	8,000	12,000
Total	$122,000	$119,000	$111,000	$135,000

RESULTS

Trainees per year	125	115	130	120
Percentage of trainees keeping job over 6 months	40%	60%	35%	50%
Savings on unemployment compensation and increased income	$180,000	$140,000	$160,000	$200,000

1. Organize the data into line-item, performance, and program budget formats.
2. What data are more important for each budget format? What additional data should be gathered to make each more complete?
3. What questions are best answered *for this agency* by each type of budget?
4. How can the given data be used to justify budget requests?
5. Very specifically focusing on this agency, which data on performance should be linked to budgeting, and how should they be linked?

SUGGESTED FURTHER READING

DONALD AXELROD. *Budgeting for Modern Government.* New York: St. Martin's Press, 1988. A first-rate introduction. Among its many strengths is its documentation of the extent that each aspect discussed is actually implemented in the real world.

FREMONT J. LYDEN and ERNEST G. MILLER, eds. *Public Budgeting: Program Planning and Implementation.* Englewood Cliffs, NJ: Prentice-Hall, 1982. Collection of twenty-five essays on budgeting. Most of the essays emphasize the use of budgets as strategic plans, but there is a section devoted to management.

Appendix—A Detailed Example of ZBB

The following pages illustrate ZBB in greater detail. The example shows four decision packages for a mental health program, and a final ranking that includes these four packages after they have been combined into a larger package, and then compared to other government programs. They are reproduced from the examples distributed to federal agencies by OMB during ZBB's government-wide federal installation in the late 1970s.

Decision Package 1

Federal Support of Community Mental Health Services

Mental Health Administration

Mental Health: 75-0001-0-1-550

Activity Description. Continue grants only to the 450 CMHC's currently receiving Federal support, until each CMHC's eight-year grant cycle is completed

Resource Requirements: Dollars (in thousands)

	1977	1978	This Package	Cumulative Total
Planning grants ($)	1,000	1,000	0	0
Operating grants ($)	97,000	147,000	120,000	120,000
Total obligations	98,000	148,000	120,000	120,000
Budget authority	98,000	148,000	120,000	120,000
Outlays	97,000	145,000	119,000	119,000

	yr3	yr4	yr5	yr6	1983
Five-year estimates					
Budget Authority	120,000	100,000	80,000	60,000	40,000
Outlays	119,000	98,000	79,000	59,000	40,000

Short-term objective. To ensure in 1979 access to qualified comprehensive mental health services to 45% of the population (this results in treatment of about 2 million patients)

Impact on major objectives. The major objective of 1200 qualified CMHC's by year 12 would not be met if this short term objective were continued. It is unlikely that *any* net increase in qualified CMHC's would result at this level because few communities have the resources to develop a qualified program. It is estimated that for each community that would develop a qualified CMHC, an existing qualified CMHC would cease to qualify because of cutbacks in service provided due to tight funds. The impact of continuing this level objective follows:

	1977	1978	1979	1980	1981	1982	1983	1984
Number of public and nonprofit CMHC's	700	710	720	730	740	750	760	770
Number of CMHC's providing comprehensive services, as now defined	550	600	600	600	600	600	600	600
Number of CMHC's receiving grants	400	450	400	350	300	250	200	150
Percent of population covered	43	45	45	45	45	45	45	45
Percent of probable patients covered	45	50	50	50	50	50	50	50

Other Information. Continuing grants to the 450 CMHC's currently receiving Federal support until each CMHC's eight-year cycle is completed is the minimum level because (a) the government has an eight-year contract with each CMHC and (b) no new CMHC's will receive any grants. If zero-funded, the government would be subject to legal action brought by CMHC's. This level would cease to encourage communities to develop CMHC's because of the (a) lack of planning grant funds and (b) lack of operational grant funds thus negating the potential growth in the number of qualified CMHC's. Only 57% of the high priority catchment areas would receive qualified CMHC coverage.

Decision Package 2

Federal Support of Community Mental Health Services

Mental Health Administration

Mental Health: 75-0001-0-1-550

Activity Description. Continue grants to a total of 450 currently funded CMHC until the end of its eight-year cycle for eligibility, provide an eight-year grant to a newly qualified CMHC.

Resource Requirements: Dollars (in thousands)

	1977	1978	1979 This Package	1979 Cumulative Total
Planning grants ($)	1,000	1,000	0	0
Operating grants ($)	97,000	147,000	20,000	140,000
Total obligations	98,000	148,000	20,000	140,000
Budget Authority	98,000	000	20,000	140,000
Outlays	97,000	145,000	19,000	138,000

Five-year estimates	1979	1980	1981	1982	1983
Budget authority	140,000	142,000	143,000	145,000	146,000
Outlays	138,000	141,000	142,000	144,000	145,000

Short-term objective. To ensure in 1979 access to qualified comprehensive mental health services to 49% of the population (this results in treatment of about 2.1 million patients)

Impact on major objectives. Even without the planning grants, many communities will be encouraged to develop CMHC's because of the possibility of receiving the operating grants. However, the major objective would not be met at this level of funding. It would take until about 1990 to establish 1200 qualified CMHC's. The impact of continuing this level follows:

	1977	1978	This Package	1979 Cumulative	1980	1981	1982	1983	1984
Number of public and nonprofit CMHC's	700	710	40	750	800	850	900	950	1,000
Number of CMHC's providing comprehensive services, as now defined	550	600	50	650	700	750	800	850	900
Number of CMHC's receiving grants	400	450	50	450	450	450	450	450	450
Percent of population covered	43	45	4	49	58	65	75	80	85
Percent of probable patients covered	45	50	4	54	64	69	80	84	88

Other Information. By 1982, 70% of the high priority catchment areas will have a qualified CMHC. Assuming the objective of CMHC's is desirable even by 1990, stretching out the program past the major objective date of 1984 will increase total program costs from $3.6 billion to $4.3 billion due to estimated increases in service costs.

Decision Package 3

Federal Support of Community Mental Health Services

Mental Health Administration

Mental Health: 75–0001–0–1–550

Activity Description. Fund 50% more newly qualifying CMHC's. That is, for every two CMHC's whose eight-year eligibility period ends, fund three newly qualifying CMHC's.

Resource Requirements: Dollars (in thousands)

	1977	1978	1979 This Package	1979 Cumulative Total
Planning grants ($)	1,000	1,000	0	0
Operating grants ($)	97,000	147,000	10,000	150,000
Total obligations	98,000	148,000	10,000	150,000
Budget authority	98,000	148,000	10,000	150,000
Outlays	97,000	145,000	10,000	148,000

Five-year estimates	1979	1980	1981	1982	1983
Budget authority	150,000	162,000	172,000	183,000	194,000
Outlays	148,000	161,000	171,000	182,000	193,000

Short-term objective. To ensure in 1979 access to qualified comprehensive mental health services to 51% of the population (this results in treatment of about 2.2 million patients)

Impact on major objectives

	1977	1978	This Package	1979 Cumulative	1980	1981	1982	1983	1984
Number of public and nonprofit CMHC's	700	710	25	775	850	925	1,000	1,075	1,150
Number of CMHC's providing comprehensive services, as now defined	550	600	25	675	750	825	900	975	1,050
Number of CMHC's receiving grants	400	450	25	475	500	525	550	575	600
Percent of population covered	43	45	6	51	65	75	80	85	90
Percent of probable patients covered	45	50	6	56	66	77	83	87	90

Other Information. By 1982, 95% of the high priority catchment areas will have a qualified CMHC. If stretched out from 1984 to 1986, total program costs for establishing 1200 CMHC's will increase from $3.6 billion to about $3.8 billion.

Decision Package 4

Federal Support of Community Mental Health Services

Mental Health Administration

Mental Health: 75-0001-0-1-550

Activity Description. For every CMHC whose eight year eligibility periods ends, fund two newly qualifying CMHC's.

Resource Requirements: Dollars (in thousands)

	1977	1978	1979 This Package	1979 Cumulative Total
Planning grants ($)	1,000	1,000	0	0
Operating grants ($)	97,000	147,000	10,000	160,000
Total obligations	98,000	148,000	10,000	160,000
Budget authority	98,000	148,000	10,000	160,000
Outlays	97,000	145,000	10,000	158,000

Five-year estimates	1979	1980	1981	1982	1983
Budget authority	160,000	172,000	183,000	193,000	204,000
Outlays	158,000	170,000	182,000	192,000	203,000

Short-term objective. To ensure in 1979 access to qualified comprehensive mental health services to 53% of the population (this results in treatment of about 2.3 million patients)

Impact on major objectives

	1977	1978	This Package	1979 Cumulative	1980	1981	1982	1983	1984
Number of public and nonprofit CMHC's	700	710	25	800	900	1,000	1,100	1,200	1,300
Number of CMHC's providing comprehensive services, as now defined	550	600	25	700	800	900	1,000	1,100	1,200
Number of CMHC's receiving grants	400	450	25	500	550	600	650	700	750
Percent of population covered	43	45	2	53	75	80	84	93	100
Percent of probable patients covered	45	50	2	58	77	82	85	93	100

The major objective will be met at this level of funding.

Other Information. By 1982, 100% of the high priority catchment areas will have a qualified CMHC. Total program cost by 1984 will be $3.6 billion.

Ranking Sheet

Department of Government
Fiscal Year 1979

(Other identifying information)   BULLETIN NO. 77–9
                                                                        EXHIBIT 4

Rank	Decision Package	Budget Authority	Outlays	Cumulative BA	Cumulative Outlays
1	A1	924	901	924	901
2	B1	800	785	1,724	1,686
3	A2	121	121	1,845	1,807
4	C1	0	0	1,845	1,807
5	B2	30	30	1,875	1,837
6	A3	0	0	1,875	1,837
7	B3	30	30	1,905	1,867
8	C2	0	0	1,905	1,867
9	C3	0	0	1,905	1,867
10	A4	22	22	1,927	1,889
11	B4	11	11	1,938	1,900
12	C4	0	0	1,938	1,900
13	B5	30	30	1,968	1,930
14	C5	0	0	1,968	1,930
15	C6	0	0	1,968	1,930

ENDNOTES

1. Gloria A. Grizzle, "Does Budget Format Really Govern the Actions of Budget Makers?" *Public Budgeting and Finance,* Spring 1986, pp. 60-70. By observing the behavior of legislative committees that have been given different budget formats, Grizzle empirically establishes that format does make a difference; it substantially changes the types of questions asked by the committee members. This is an important study that deserves wider attention.

2. The formats discussed are primarily operating budget formats. Most states (thirty-seven) and most localities maintain separate capital budgets for fixed assets. Such budgets will not be examined in this chapter, but the integration of such capital expenditures into any calculations of total program costs would be very desirable. Only thirteen of the fifty states combine their capital and operating budget totals, which suggests that there is a great deal more to be done in this area. U.S. General Accounting Office, *Budget Issues: Capital*

Budgeting Practices in the States (Washington, DC: GAO, July 15, 1986), p. 2.

A note on terminology: Different formats imply different systems, as we will develop. Thus it seems a close call between calling this section "budget systems" or "budget formats." I have opted for the latter because formats are the most clearly distinguishable feature. Nonetheless we will attempt to emphasize that different formats do entail different associated tools, and thus different systems.

3. For example, all federal agencies must use the following line-item categories: personnel compensation and benefits; travel; transportation of things; communications, utilities, and other rent; printing and reproduction; other services; supplies and materials; equipment; land and structures; investments and loans; grants, subsidies, and contributions; insurance claims and indemnities; interest and dividends; and refunds undistributed. Donald Axelrod, *Budgeting for Modern Government* (New York: St. Martin's Press, 1988), pp. 38–39.

4. Allen Schick, "The Road to PPB: The Stages of Budget Reform," *Public Administration Review*, 26 (December 1966), 243–58.

5. Donald Axelrod, *Budgeting for Modern Government* (New York: St. Martin's Press, 1988), p. 266, uses *program budgeting* as a synonym for *performance budgeting*. For an example of the more common approach adopted here of using *program budgeting* as a synonym for *PPB*, see the Introduction to Fremont J. Lyden and Ernest G. Miller, eds., *Public Budgeting*, 4th ed. (Englewood Cliffs, NJ: Prentice-Hall, 1982), p. 4.

6. Joseph A. Ferrara and Daniel J. Dunmire, "Bureaucratic Influence on Budget Preparation: A Practitioner's View of Pentagon Budgeting," *Management Science and Policy Analysis*, 5, no. 2 (Winter 1988), 1–13. An analysis that is highly critical of how the Reagan administration treated the Defense Department's PPB is Lawrence J. Korb, "Ordeal of PPBS in the Pentagon," *The Bureaucrat*, 17, no. 3 (Fall 1988), 19–21.

7. Program budgeting's structure replicates the chain of outputs in reverse. Its broad categories—called functions, and then programs—are united by their long-range goals. Programs are then broken down into subprograms whose goals are expressed in terms of outputs further left on the chain. Subprograms are broken down into elements (also called activities) that are directed at immediate outputs and even processes.

8. One of the most famous state PPB systems later formalized its intention to lower its aspirations and focus more on the early links of the output chain. See David Sallack and David N. Allen, "From Impact to Output: Pennsylvania's Planning-Programming-Budgeting

System in Transition," *Public Budgeting and Finance,* Spring 1987, pp. 38–50.

9. ZBB is described by its primary developer in Peter A. Pyhrr, "The Zero-Base Approach to Government Budgeting," *Public Administration Review,* January/February 1977, pp. 1–8. ZBB's nomenclature is somewhat confusing: One would normally expect "packages" to contain "units," but the reverse is true.

10. U.S. General Accounting Office, *Streamlining Zero Base Budgeting Will Benefit Decisionmaking* (Washington, DC: GAO, September 25, 1979), p. 31. Cited in Axelrod, *Budgeting for Modern Government,* p. 297.

11. Allen Schick and Harry Hatry, "Zero Base Budgeting: The Manager's Budget," *Public Budgeting and Finance,* Spring 1982, pp. 72–87. After a four-state, four-city study, the authors find that ZBB raises participation in the budget process but that "ZBB does not appear to have significantly improved the information available in making resource allocation choices. Most systems continued to rely on workload units as indicators of the output of the programs. . . ." (p. 87).

12. One of the first (and still among the clearest) of all discussions of tying accounting systems to the budget format is Francis E. McGilvery, "Program and Responsibility Cost Accounting," *Public Administration Review,* 28, no. 2 (March/April 1968), 148–54. McGilvery makes an argument for putting responsibility cost accounting ahead of program accounting. Modern software makes such either-or choices less relevant.
    A discussion of how multiple systems can be run off the accounting system is in Alan Walter Steiss, *Management Control in Government* (Lexington, MA: Lexington Books, 1982), pp. 256–61.

13. The federal government uses an eleven-digit code. Axelrod, *Budgeting for Modern Government,* p. 241.

14. Stanley B. Botner, "The Use of Budgeting/Management Tools by State Governments," *Public Administration Review,* 45, no. 5 (September/October 1985), 616–22.

15. This is a common finding when investigating "program budgets." The inclination to use workload measures as substitutes for outputs is also discussed in Thomas P. Lauth, "Performance Evaluation in the Georgia Budgetary Process," *Public Budgeting and Finance,* Spring 1985, pp. 67–82. Lauth also finds that the legislature does not seem inclined to learn about or use the measures (also common) and that the measures are feared by agencies, who think they will be used only to cut funds.

16. All the local government figures are from Glen Hahn Cope, "Local

Government Budgeting and Productivity," *Public Productivity Review*, Spring 1987, pp. 45–57.

A roughly contemporaneous survey found slightly higher percentages for ZBB and program budgeting. Roughly 15 percent of the responding cities said they used ZBB citywide, and about 18 percent said they used it in selected areas. Sixty-six percent said they used program budgeting, and about two-thirds of that total said they used it citywide. Gregory Streib and Theodore H. Poister, "Established and Emerging Management Tools: A 12-Year Perspective," *The Municipal Yearbook 1989* (Washington, DC: International City Managers Association, 1989), pp. 47–48.

17. A combined agency can take many forms. Sometimes the management analysis and budget agency are one, as with the federal OMB. More often, both management analysis and budgeting may report to a single head in a broader "department of administration." The tighter link is of course the first.

18. How to generate data and build ties between the budget and performance measurement system is discussed in Gloria A. Grizzle, "Linking Performance to Funding Decisions," *Public Productivity Review*, Spring 1987, pp. 33–44.

19. The Forest Service system is called "ends results" budgeting, and it represents the most sophisticated link between management and budgetary systems of any federal agency. Useful examples of the new budgetary categories as well as a good description of the overall system are given in U.S. General Accounting Office, *Forest Service: Evaluation of 'End-Results' Budgeting Test* (Washington, DC: GAO, March 1988).

The current system is the culmination of almost twenty years of Forest Service experience with output-oriented budgeting. For a discussion of an earlier system, see Lee L. Gremillion, James L. McKenney, and Phillip J. Pyburn, "Program Planning in the National Forest System," *Public Administration Review*, 40, no. 3 (May/June 1980), 226–30.

20. This and the following quotation are from my interviews with federal managers, as noted in Chapter Three, note 10.

21. Most articles on the management side of OMB judge it to be a failure, primarily because the importance and short time frame of budgetary decisions have eclipsed management. See Peter M. Benda and Charles H. Levine, "OMB and the Central Management Problem: Is Another Reorganization the Answer?" *Public Administration Review*, 46, no. 5 (September/October 1986); and Eric Wiesenthal, "Congress Targets OMB in Management Reform," *Public Administration Times*, May 1, 1986, p. 1.

22. One article calling for what we are terming "loose" ties between budgeting and performance measures is Thomas P. Lauth, "Budgeting and Productivity in State Government," *Public Productivity Review,* Spring 1987, pp. 21–32.

23. The top-down process involved in the Defense Department's PPB is described in Ferrara and Dunmire, "Bureaucratic Influence on Budget Preparation," pp. 1–13.

24. All examples are from Tom Dowling, "How the September Spending Surge Was Stopped," *Fortune,* March 22, 1982, p. 152.

25. Ibid., p. 150. OMB has attempted to counteract one cause of this problem by proposing that agencies be allowed to keep up to half the "savings" of unspent money that results from productivity increases. *National Journal,* May 30, 1987, p. 1431.

chapter eight

Connecting Rewards
to Management Systems

INTRODUCTION

In Chapter Seven we discussed tying budget shares to management systems, and of course that is a type of reward. But now we focus more explicitly on how management systems can be tied to *individual* rewards such as praise, promotions, bonuses, and salary increases. Once managers begin considering rewards, the topic of personnel systems inevitably arises because they are the most common way of determining who does and does not receive a reward. Accordingly, this chapter could also have been entitled "Connecting Management Systems to Personnel Systems."

The two purposes of management systems—providing information for decisions and influencing workers' behavior—are never completely separable. Nonetheless, one or the other becomes more important at different times or in different systems.[1] Because it focuses on rewards, the primary emphasis of this chapter will be on ways that management systems are used to influence employees' behavior. To understand behavior, managers must consider how incentives affect motivation, which is the topic of the next section.

BEHAVIOR AND MOTIVATION

Intrinsic Motivators

There are two reasons why a worker may change his or her behavior in response to a management system: intrinsic and extrinsic motivators.[2] As the name suggests, *intrinsic motivators* are psychological drives within an individual that are activated simply by performing the job. *Extrinsic motivators* are outside punishments or rewards such as bonuses or promotions.

Intrinsic motivators are based on self-image and on attitudes toward work, attitudes often formed in childhood. Intrinsic motivators can be elicited by a management system simply if the worker perceives that the standards are fair and that the information fed back on achievement is accurate. Sometimes workers respond to intrinsic motivators. When the management system indicates that workers have fallen short on some output category, they may react by increasing their effort or changing their behavior even though there is no external reward or penalty linked to the management system. If one were to ask the workers why they had changed their behavior, the explanation would be "pride" or "I'm a professional; I want to do my best." The management system measurements lead such workers to improve for reasons of self-esteem or self-satisfaction.[3] Therefore the system does not need to be tied to anything else to produce changes in behavior.

Unfortunately for designers of management systems, not all workers have such strong internal motivators. Many workers are not bothered by falling short on some output measures if they are sure that their performance will not cost them any rewards or cause any punishments. As an extremely broad generalization, it seems that workers with rural backgrounds or higher education levels are more likely to respond to intrinsic motivators. Motivation is shaped by culture, and rural workers tend to be brought up with more traditional strictures on achievement; education, too, produces people who view work as a chance to express talent and show ability.[4] Unfortunately the categories of rural-raised and highly educated are small enough to leave great numbers of workers who are less likely to respond in this way.

Extrinsic Motivators

Extrinsic motivators are rewards or punishments tied to a management system. Everyone responds to extrinsic motivators, but again unfortunately, it is not clear which particular rewards or penalties will affect the behavior of different individuals. There are a number of theories on the topic.[5]

To take just one example, Frederick Herzberg's theory holds that there are two types of incentives.[6] Some, such as money and working conditions, can make employees unhappy and drive down productivity. But once they reach a certain level (e.g., once workers feel fairly paid) they produce no greater effort. These rewards and punishments are termed *hygiene factors*. Generally, hygiene factors can hurt, but not help. A second group of factors, such as prestige and interesting tasks, are real motivators that can produce greater effort and job performance as they are increased.

Herzberg's theories are far from universally accepted,[7] and other theorists have proposed other categories of job motivators. It seems safe to conclude that although virtually everyone will change their behavior in response to some extrinsic motivators, different workers respond to different ones. Some are more highly motivated by increased leisure; others would prefer more money. Some look primarily to the approval of their bosses, while others value the approval of their co-workers; some prefer individual recognition, while others want more tangible rewards.[8] This disparity argues for tying management systems to a wide variety of rewards.[9]

Two Basic Principles of Motivation

In all this uncertainty about the best rewards for affecting behavior, there are two widely accepted guidelines for tying incentives to management systems.

First, the workers must perceive the system as fair. If the workers believe that a system is producing data that are distorted, incomplete, or irrelevant, they will resist the system. The only change in behavior likely to occur is sabotaging or cheating. This is one more argument for the strong involvement of workers in establishing a system and in setting performance measures.[10]

Second, the workers must also believe that they can affect the measures for which they are rewarded or penalized.[11] For example, some huge business corporations are very proud of their profit-sharing plans, in which all workers are rewarded with bonuses when corporate profits increase. Despite this pride, such systems are probably not very useful as motivators. Although most workers may desire the bonus, they will rightly perceive that their own behavior is not going to increase or decrease the profits of a huge corporation. Accordingly they will perform no better because of the announced reward.

AT WHAT LEVEL SHOULD PERFORMANCE BE REWARDED?

The preceding two guidelines provide some help in deciding which of the three possible organizational levels should be the focus of the management system's rewards in order to best affect employees' behavior.

First, the system can monitor the output and performance of each *individual* and tie rewards to these individual measures. MBO sometimes comes close to this type of system, and as discussed in Chapter Six, many performance monitoring systems build their organizational data by combining data on individual workers. This individual level is also almost always the focus of personnel systems.

Second, the system can base rewards on the performance of the *organizational subunit,* such as the office or branch. Here the system measures the office's output, without using individual measures. Rewards and sanctions are tied to this subunit level, and so if the subunit performs well, all its workers share in the reward.

Third, the system can tie rewards to the performance of the *organization as a whole.* Any rewards are based on total organizational output and go to all employees, perhaps numbering in the thousands.

Which of the three choices is most likely to affect employees' behavior positively? We will examine each level in some detail. But, generally, tying rewards to the subunit's performance may be the most practical and effective motivational approach.

It is often difficult to monitor the output of a single individual. In many government organizations each worker is part of a team, which together conducts a survey, processes applications, or audits an agency. Thus tying rewards to individual performance may offend the principle about fairness since any division of credit would be somewhat arbitrary. Moreover, if individuals view themselves as competing with their close co-workers, displacement is likely. Operations-level workers in a social services agency, for example, may fight for the easiest cases, resist taking hard cases, and denigrate the performance of each other when speaking to the boss. Thus for most agencies that require close group cooperation, awards for individual performance can be counterproductive. In rarer cases where individual cooperation between equals is less important—for example, at the very top of an agency—individual awards may be more applicable.

If basing rewards on individual performance is often difficult or nonproductive, we may look to organization-wide awards. But as discussed earlier, it is also usually not productive to tie rewards to the performance of a huge organization because workers realize that their own efforts will have little effect on year-end performance. Accordingly, the reward system does not motivate their behavior.

Therefore, basing rewards (or punishments) on the performance of offices or other subunits, totalling perhaps twenty to one hundred employees, is often the best compromise. A reward system focused on such subunits meets the twin principles of relevant, fair measures, on the one hand, and control over the outcome by the individual employee, on the other hand. Nonetheless some organizations will monitor and reward performance at all three levels. Accordingly, we will now examine each level in greater detail.

FOCUSING ON THE INDIVIDUAL: MANAGEMENT SYSTEMS AND PERSONNEL SYSTEMS

If an output-oriented management system focuses on the individual, it becomes part of (or a substitute for) the organization's personnel system. There are three types of systems for evaluating employees. Traditionally, most organizations have used trait-based evaluations. More recently, some organizations have moved to behaviorally anchored rating scales (BARS). But only MBO-type personnel evaluation systems (sometimes termed *assessment by objectives,* or ABO) emphasize outputs; and therefore only these personnel systems can be directly tied to the agency's overall management systems. We will begin by examining the first two systems and then look at how ABO systems differ.[12]

Trait-Based Personnel Appraisals

The most traditional personnel approach is trait-based appraisal. In such a system, a manager rates a subordinate on such traits as initiative, personal appearance, drive, and honesty. Trait-based systems are widely used because they are relatively easy to understand, design, and use. Nonetheless, trait systems have several very substantial flaws. They depend entirely on the perception of the supervisor, and the terms are so ambiguous that even fair-minded supervisors interpret them in very different ways. Because trait-based systems are so ambiguous, they can be distorted by "halo effects," in which very high or very low ratings on one trait affects the ratings on other traits. Moreover, the system's subjective basis can lead to more pernicious distortions, including various forms of personal bias. Finally, trait-based performance systems have little relationship to job performance. Such traits as "personal appearance" or "mixes well with co-workers" may have no effect on how well the worker performs the job.

Because of these problems, experts in the field of personnel have long argued for replacing trait-based personnel evaluations with more objective rating systems.[13] Recently a series of court decisions have also ruled against organizations that make important personnel decisions on the basis of such systems. The courts have required the appraisal to be shown to relate directly to job performance.[14] Despite such developments, however, trait-based appraisals are still very common.

Behaviorally Anchored Rating Scales (BARS)

Behaviorally anchored rating scales (BARS) are a second form of appraisal system, which asks managers to state whether a subordinate carries out certain behaviors related to a particular job. Thus the BARS for a secretary ("checks for misspellings without being asked"; "greets visitors politely") will differ from those for a painter ("aids co-workers when done with own job"; "is careful with detail work"). This job-specificity makes BARS different from trait-based appraisals. Moreover, the BARS categories are developed and weighted statistically to capture the most important behaviors involved in each job. Finally, the specificity of the categories lessens the ambiguity that allows ratings to be affected by bias.

However, for all its improvement in job specificity and objectivity, the BARS approach has at least two major problems. First, it is expensive to apply to a large organization with a large number of tasks because scales must be developed for each job description. Second, the BARS system is still usually unilateral; that is, the superiors rate subordinates without any subordinate participation. Such unilateral ratings necessarily involve a great deal of subjectivity. (Figure 8–1 shows two pages of a BARS for Coast Guard officers.)

Appraisal by Objectives (ABO)

Performance-based personnel appraisals are the third and final form of appraisal system. Such performance standards can be set by engineered standards (standard times); thus a line worker could be judged on whether he or she processed as many forms as an industrial engineering study indicated was possible. In fact, however, most performance-based standards are jointly set by the supervisor and employee, and they seem to be very similar to MBO. Most organizations accordingly use the term *MBO*, but we wish to save this term for an organizational measurement system; thus we will call personnel-oriented MBO by a term only occasionally used: *assessment by objectives (ABO)*.[15]

MBO and ABO are distinguished only by their focus: MBO goals are all directed at the performance of an organization under a manager; ABO goals may include personal goals, such as greater promptness. However, if MBO goals are used for personnel appraisal, the difference between MBO and ABO dissolves.

The advantages of tying personnel appraisal to objective performance indicators are clear. Because the standards are objective, the possibility of ratings being affected by the bias of superiors is much less. Because the subordinate has a role in setting the standards, they will be perceived as fair and job-related. But perhaps the most important advantage of ABO is the advantage of all output-oriented systems: They focus on results. Focusing on results is good for the organization, but it is also good for the individual because it involves fewer restrictions on the individual's freedom and creativity. Most individuals would prefer to be given a destination and then allowed to reach it any way they wish. The alternative—specifying each process or action rather than the goal—discourages autonomy and creativity. Because there are so many possible actions, specifying procedures necessarily requires specifying all types of permissible and nonpermissible actions in great detail. (An extreme example of this approach, the *Federal Personnel Manual,* has 8,814 pages.[16]) Output control is simply much less intrusive than process control. Yet output control is ultimately more effective because it allows the organization to hold the worker accountable for achieving the goal.[17]

ABO is far from perfect, however; there are a number of problems. Often an individual is part of a team, and it is difficult to determine whether the individual was responsible for the success or failure of the team project. One way of circumventing this problem is to use process-type goals ("miss only five days"; "answer all reports within ten days"), but this is generally not a good approach because such goals invite displacement through misdirection of effort. Another problem is that when some individuals are working on different projects, ABO goals will differ from person to person. This fact makes it difficult to defend salary increases or other rewards on the basis of comparability. However, the gains in ease of operation, perceived fairness, and output orientation all outweigh these disadvantages, and greater use of ABO is both likely and useful.

Personnel Systems and the Chain of Outputs

Personnel systems can easily be related to the organizational chain. An individual brings his or her own inputs (personality traits) to an organization. Utilizing these traits, the employee engages in a series of processes or activities within the organization, and these processes in turn produce immediate and intermediate outputs. Trait-based evaluations focus on the beginning of the organizational chain, on inputs. BARS moves along the chain, focusing on processes. And ABO moves further to the right, focusing on immediate and intermediate outputs.

In Chapter Five we discussed the difficulty in connecting programs

TRANSPORTATION
U.S. COAST GUARD
CG-5311 (Page 1) (Rev. 8-84)

COMMANDER
OFFICER EVALUATION REPORT (OER)

THE REPORTED-ON OFFICER WILL COMPLETE SECTION 1, ADMINISTRATIVE DATA

a. NAME (Last, First, Middle Initial)

	b. SSN		c. GRADE	d. DATE OF RANK
				YR	MO	DAY
			05			

e. UNIT NAME

| f. DIST | g. OPFAC | h. OBC | i. STATUS INDICATOR | j. DATE SUBMITTED |
| | | | | YR | MO | DAY |

k. DATE REPORTED PRESENT UNIT

| YR | MO | DAY |

l. TYPE REPORT
☐ Regular ☐ Special ☐ Concurrent

m. OCCASION FOR REGULAR REPORT
☐ Semi-Annual ☐ Detachment of Reporting Officer ☐ Detachment of Officer ☐ Promotion of Officer

n. PERIOD OF REPORT

| YR | MO | DAY | TO | YR | MO | DAY |

o. DAYS NOT OBSERVED
PCS   TAD   LV   OTHER

p. REPORTED-ON OFFICER SIGNATURE

THE SUPERVISOR WILL COMPLETE SECTIONS 2-7. In Section 2, describe this officer's job including primary and collateral duties, resources available and relationship to unit or Coast Guard missions. Then for each of the rating scales in Sections 3-4, compare the officer's performance during the reporting period against the standards shown and assign a mark by filling in the appropriate circle. In the area following each section, describe the basis for the marks given, citing specifics where possible. Use only allotted space. Complete Section 7.

2. DESCRIPTION OF DUTIES

☐ Documentation Reference:

3. PERFORMANCE OF DUTIES: Measures an officer's ability to get things done.

a. BEING PREPARED:						
Demonstrated ability to anticipate, to identify what must be done, to set priorities, and prepare for accomplishing unit and organizational missions under both predictable and uncertain conditions.	Gets caught by the unexpected. Appears controlled by events/crises. Sets vague or unrealistic goals, if any. Sets wrong priorities. Tends not to follow existing operating procedures, plans or systems. Not always prepared to meet responsibilities or missions.		Takes prompt positive action to meet changing or unexpected situations. Rarely caught, unprepared. Sets high and realistic goals. Uses existing operating procedures, plans, or systems well. Uses good basic management tools and ideas. Does homework to stay well prepared for responsibilities and missions.		Anticipates extremely well. Looks beyond the immediate events/problems. Sets the "right" priorities and controls events. Sets realistic and specific goals well in advance. Utilizes people, operating procedures, plans, systems to achieve the highest state of preparation for accomplishing responsibilities and missions. Turns potential adversity into opportunity.	N/O
	①	②	③	④	⑤	⑥	⑦	⊗

Figure 8-1.

	①	②	③	④	⑤	⑥	⑦
b. USING RESOURCES: Demonstrated ability to utilize people, money, material, and time efficiently, to delegate, and to provide follow-up control.		May over/under allocate resources, concentrate on unproductive areas, or overlook some critical demands. More effective managing a narrow range of activities. Over/under manages; doesn't delegate wisely. Under-utilizes people or "burns" them out. Doesn't follow-up.		Successfully manages a variety of activities simultaneously with the resources available. Is cost conscious. Delegates; gets job done well through others. Uses follow-up control effectively; requires some of subordinates.		Unusually skillful at bringing scarce resources to bear on the most critical demands while managing a spectrum of activities. Constantly "does more with less." Delegates whenever possible. Has the "big picture." Always knows what's going on; "stays on top of things."	
c. GETTING RESULTS: The quality/quantity of the officer's work accomplishments. The effectiveness or impact of results on the officer's unit and/or the Coast Guard.		Usually obtains results, though sometimes at the cost of extra resources or lost opportunities. In routine situations will meet specified goals. Results usually maintain the status quo.		Gets the job done well in all routine and unusual situations. Fulfills identified goals and requirements even when resources are scarce. Produces finished, quality work and requires same from subordinates. Results have a positive impact on unit and/or Coast Guard.		Gets results which far surpass your expectations in all situations. Always finds ways to do more and do it better in spite of resource constraints. Own work and that of subordinates is consistently of high quality; never needs redoing. Results have significant positive impact on unit and/or Coast Guard.	
d. RESPONSIVENESS: The degree to which the officer responds, replies, or meets deadlines in a timely fashion.		Needs reminding; doesn't report back. Tends to miss due dates/deadlines without justification. Slow or late responding to requests, memos, letters, or calls. Resists changes in policy, direction, or responsibilities.		Reports back; keeps you informed. Dependably completes projects and meets deadlines. Makes timely response to requests, memos, letters, or calls. Takes changes in policy, direction, or responsibilities in stride.		Highly conscientious in keeping you well informed. Adept at finding ways to complete projects early. Unusually prompt in responding to all requests, memos, letters, or calls. Readily adjusts to major changes in policy, direction, or responsibilities; extremely flexible.	
e. PROFESSIONAL EXPERTISE: The level of service knowledge and technical skills the officer demonstrates in the present job. (Includes seamanship/airmanship, engineering, commercial vessel safety, SAR, law, etc., as appropriate.)		Basically qualified. Demonstrates minimal technical skills. Completes routine assignments but requires some supervision and technical guidance. Has shown little or no effort to broaden knowledge or skills.		A professional officer who knows the job. Demonstrates needed technical expertise for assigned duties. Needs no supervision for technical assignments. Seeks new experiences to learn; has shown steady growth in knowledge and skills. Shares experience and knowledge		An expert. Demonstrates superior technical competence under a variety of circumstances. Recognizes and resolves complex issues/problems. Never needs guidance or supervision. Sought after for experience and knowledge. Advice is always "on the mark." Develops better ways to do things.	

f. COMMENTS (Performance of Duties):

Figure 8–1. Continued

10. REPRESENTING THE COAST GUARD: Measures an officer's ability to bring credit to the Coast Guard through looks and actions.

a. APPEARANCE:

The extent to which an officer appears neat, smart, and well-groomed, in uniform or civilian attire, conforms to prescribed weight standards, and uniformly requires subordinates to do the same.

①	②	③	④	⑤	⑥	⑦	N/O
	May not always meet uniform or grooming standards. Civilian attire may be inappropriate at times. May not present a physically trim appearance. Does not hold subordinates to service standards.		Appears neat, smart and well groomed in uniform and civilian attire. Presents physically trim appearance. Requires subordinates to conform to grooming/uniform standards and maintain a physically trim appearance.		Always presents an impeccable appearance. Clearly meets grooming standards. Demonstrates great care in wearing and maintaining uniforms and civilian attire. Has a smart physically trim military appearance. Fosters excellence in grooming, dress and physical appearance of subordinates and others.		

b. CUSTOMS AND COURTESIES:

The degree to which an officer conforms to military traditions, customs, and courtesies and uniformly requires subordinates to do the same.

①	②	③	④	⑤	⑥	⑦	N/O
	Occasionally lax in observing basic military customs, courtesies, and traditions. May not show proper respect when dealing with others. Tolerates lax behavior on part of subordinates.		Correct in conforming to military traditions, customs, and courtesies. Conveys their importance to others and requires subordinates to conform. Treats people with courtesy and consideration; ensures subordinates do the same.		Always precise in rendering military courtesies. Inspires subordinates to do the same. Exemplifies the finest traditions of military customs, etiquette, and protocol. Goes, out of way to insure police, considerate, and genuine treatment is extended to everyone. Insists subordinates do likewise.		

c. PROFESSIONALISM:

How an officer applies knowledge and skills in providing service to the public. The manner in which an officer represents the Coast Guard.

①	②	③	④	⑤	⑥	⑦	N/O
	May be misinformed/unaware of Coast Guard policies and objectives. May bluff rather than admit ignorance. Does little to enhance self-image or image of Coast Guard. May be ineffective when working with others. May lead personal life which infringes on Coast Guard responsibilities or image.		Well-versed in how Coast Guard objectives, policies, procedures serve the public; communicates these effectively. Straightforward, cooperative, and evenhanded in dealing with the public and government. Aware of impact/impression actions may cause on others. Supports CG Ideals. Leads a personal life which reinforces CG image.		Recognized as an expert in Coast Guard affairs. Works creatively and confidently with representatives of public and government. Inspires confidence and trust and clearly conveys dedication to Coast Guard ideals in public and private life. Leaves everyone with a very positive image of self and Coast Guard.		

d. DEALING WITH THE PUBLIC:

How an individual acts when dealing with other services, agencies, businesses, the media, or the public.

①	②	③	④	⑤	⑥	⑦	N/O
	Appears ill-at-ease with the public or media. Inconsistent in applying Coast Guard programs to public matter. Falters under pressure. May take antagonistic, or condescending approach. Makes inappropriate statements. May embarrass Coast Guard in some social situations.		Deals fairly and honestly with the public, media and others at all levels. Responds promptly. Shows no favoritism. Doesn't falter when faced with difficult situations. Comfortable in social situations. Is sensitive to concerns expressed by public.		Always self-assured and in control when dealing with public, media and others at all levels. Straightforward, impartial, and diplomatic. Applies Coast Guard rules/programs fairly and uniformly. Has unusual social grace. Responds with great poise to provocative actions of others.		

e. COMMENTS (Representing the Coast Guard):

Figure 8-1. Continued

256

to outputs that are well down the chain of outputs because the further down the chain, the more likely the output is affected by outside events and forces. This problem recurs in personnel evaluation. The manager and subordinate may lack confidence in a system that ties all rewards to output indicators because these outputs may be affected by so many outside forces—other agencies, the legislature, even the economy.

As discussed in Chapter Six, this problem is strongest for programs for which we have only an incomplete understanding of the technology or production function by which outputs are produced. Thus we may be quite willing to make outputs the primary basis of a personnel system for highway construction, water filtration, or sanitation. However, at the same time we may be more reluctant to base the personnel evaluations *entirely* on outputs for individuals working in programs to reduce teen pregnancies, adult drug addiction, or crime because we have only a partial understanding of the technology for producing better outputs in these areas. Many organizations have attempted to mitigate this concern while preserving a results focus by developing combination systems that mix some BARS or other process measures with ABO-type output measures.[18]

Combination Appraisal Systems

There are a number of advantages to employing an appraisal system that incorporates both ABO and BARS. With this combination, an individual who works very hard and very thoughtfully is recognized (through BARS) even if bad luck, unskilled co-workers, or outside events prevent the goal from being achieved. Yet output *is* the most important thing, and a strong focus on results is maintained through ABO. Such combinations of BARS and ABO draw from the strengths of both types of systems.

Such systems can be combined in several ways. The simplest and most used approach is to cover an individual under both systems, with the understanding that, say, 60 percent of the overall performance rating will be based on ABO and 40 percent on BARS. The weight given to ABO will differ, with higher weights given to workers with more individual control over their outputs, more easily measurable outputs, or more stable organizational environments. Whatever the starting percentage, it is likely that the ABO percentage will grow as the organization gains skill and confidence in specifying outputs and setting standards.

A variation on this combination involves a more formal linking of ABO and BARS. ABO output goals are chosen first; then a BARS is developed for each goal, specifying different levels of behavior that might be expected to lead to that goal. In this more formal link, no ABO goal exists without a corresponding BARS scale, and vice versa.[19] Because developing BARS scales is often time-consuming, this direct link requires a great deal of time if the ABO goals are constantly changing, requiring the development of new BARS each time. Accordingly, the direct ABO-BARS link is best used in stable work situations where the ABO goals (and thus the BARS scales) remain relatively constant. Other types of organizations often choose to employ BARS and ABO at the same time but without the formal links. All such combinations can strengthen the appraisal process.

MONEY AS AN EXTRINSIC MOTIVATOR: INDIVIDUAL REWARDS

Should ABO Results Be Tied to Rewards?

Even if the ABO system is not tied to rewards and punishments, it may nonetheless be useful. It could be used to counsel employees, helping them to improve job-related skills. Moreover, the system might influence employees' behavior by directing and strengthening the workers' own internal motivators.[20]

However, if the primary goal of the system is to increase the level of individual performance, it is often preferable to tie the system to extrinsic motivators rather than rely on internal motivators, which are sometimes absent. There are a number of potential extrinsic motivators. For example, symbolic rewards such as plaques, titles, and corner offices can often have a surprisingly large impact on performance.[21] However, the extrinsic motivator that has gained by far the most attention, and which remains the center of the most controversy, is money.

Advantages of Tying Monetary Rewards to the Personnel (ABO) Systems

Beginning in the late 1960s, many academics in the area of personnel administration began to emphasize the need to link performance and rewards in the public sector. Academics and practitioners alike were heavily influenced by Victor Vroom's "expectancy theory," which in the broadest terms reaffirms the commonsense belief that individuals will change their behavior in response to anticipated rewards and punishments.[22] Money is an extremely important potential reward for a number of reasons. First and most obviously, it is very highly valued by most individuals for what it can buy. Second, it is also important because it is very flexible (unlike, say, promotions, which can be given only to a few). Finally, for many people, a monetary reward represents more than extra dollars to spend. It also serves a series of important symbolic and psychological purposes because it is generally seen as a sign of respect and appreciation within the organization.[23]

Disadvantages of Tying Monetary Rewards to the Personnel (ABO) Systems

At first glance, it might seem that a vast majority of states and localities already tie monetary rewards to performance. Almost all of these governments have provisions for "merit pay," which is a salary increment that is technically distributed on the basis of job performance. A number of studies have shown, however, that government agencies generally do not even attempt to use merit pay to reward performance.[24] In fact, for most governments, merit pay is automatic, going to all employees without consideration of job performance. Thus at the federal level, 99.7 percent of all operations-level workers used to receive a merit increase each year.[25] Even jurisdictions that limit the percentage of employees who can receive such pay do not tie it to performance. Such provisions are usually evaded by rotating merit increases: One group gets it one year, another group the next year; then the cycle starts again. In sum, very few government agencies actually use money to reward outstanding performance.

Why this neglect of the most obvious of all extrinsic motivators? There are a number of defensible, understandable reasons. One is that many agencies have trait-based appraisal systems, which are so subjective that they cannot be used to distribute rewards fairly. Most government unions oppose tying pay to performance, perhaps because of their reluctance to see some members treated differently from others. But their opposition to putting increased salary discretion in the hands of top managers is defensible when inaccurate, subjective appraisal systems are widespread. Also, merit pay is distributed evenly because government workers often do not receive pay increases that keep pace with inflation. This increases the pressure to use merit pay as an across-the-board cost-of-living adjustment. Certainly regular salary increases for government workers should at least keep pace with inflation.

As discussed earlier, in government it is often difficult to isolate the achievement of one worker in a group. The group often works together and thus succeeds and fails together; rewarding some individual performances but not others often leads to perceptions of unfairness and to lower morale.

A final reason for the neglect of money as a reward is the reluctance of superiors to differentiate among employees. Most superiors will give the same rating to all or almost all the employees under them. This reluctance is understandable: Studies show that most workers have an inflated view of their performance. One study found that 80 percent of workers surveyed considered themselves to be in the top third of their agency in performance. Another typical survey found that 86 percent of research engineers ranked themselves in the top 25 percent in excellence of performance; the other 14 percent saw themselves in the top 50 percent.[26] Obviously a large number of workers mistakenly believe they are performing well above average, and they accordingly would be disappointed and even angered if they were given lower raises than fellow employees.[27]

Although it is of course true that low-performing workers cannot improve unless they recognize that there is a problem, many supervisors see such potential gains as being far in the future. In the short run, superiors understandably prefer to avoid friction; they do so by providing merit increases to everyone.

Linking Money to Individual Performance—Merit Pay Vs. Bonuses

If money is in fact tied to individual performance, there are two possibilities. High-performing workers can be given raises (i.e., increases in salaries) or they can be given one-time bonuses. Of the two choices, bonuses seem likely to provide more flexibility.[28] Once given, a salary increase continues year after year. Thus an employee may receive an increase for good performance in 1991, fall to low levels of performance thereafter, and yet still be receiving that added salary increment in 1998. The cost to the organization in rewarding 1991's outstanding performance is very high; it would be much lower if each year's performance was rewarded by bonuses. Bonuses are also more flexible because they can be given in the middle of the year or tailored to specific projects.[29]

However, legislatures and political executives have shied away from instituting bonus plans. Much of the reluctance stems from the problems with all individual monetary rewards already cited, but there are political reasons as well. Bonuses are difficult to justify to the tax-paying public, who rarely believes that *any* government worker is performing in an outstanding manner. This problem is illustrated by the great timidity legislators and executives have shown in dealing with the related but much less dramatic area of rewarding suggestions. Most government agencies reward suggestions that save money by giving the author of the suggestion a percentage, such as 10 percent, of the first-year savings. However, almost all governments put a ceiling on the amount that can be awarded, seldom allowing more than a few thousand dollars to be distributed. This restriction is very shortsighted. If the employee newsletter could run occasional stories on the worker whose suggestion saved $1 million and who was therefore awarded $100,000 (and can be reached in Tahiti!), employee efforts to find ways to save money would increase enormously. This result would save taxpayers far more money than they would lose for the hefty rewards.

Political considerations inevitably outweigh managerial ones, however. Legislatures put ceilings on the rewards that can be offered because they fear the wrath of voters who pick up their newspaper on a wintry morning and read about a bureaucrat who's vacationing in Tahiti on their tax money. Although it might be far more rational and efficient to lift the cap on awards, explaining large bonuses is beyond the courage of most legislators; the cap remains.

A similar situation prevailed at the upper levels of the federal Senior Executive Service. Congress originally offered bonuses of up to $50,000 to these top managers for outstanding accomplishments. Although $50,000 sounds like (and is) a great deal of money, it shrivels when compared to salaries of a half million dollars (or more) that the private sector awards executives with budgets and personnel responsibilities that are equivalent to those of top federal managers. Nonetheless Congress responded to a budget crunch by cutting back the top bonus to $20,000.[30] This move clearly costs the taxpayers far more money than it saves because it greatly lowers the retention rate for the most experienced managers, who now have less incentive to remain active and are retiring in great numbers.[31] Moreover, those that remain have reduced incentives to perform at the extra level of effort that might have opened up such a reward. Cutting back on the bonuses was clearly inefficient in the long run; but the political world (and elections) pivot on the short run.

Current Patterns in Government Personnel Practices

Much of this chapter has examined types of personnel systems and some empirical findings about their effectiveness, but it has not examined the extent of their use in government. We can divide this brief examination into two parts: the use of different types of appraisal systems, and the use of monetary rewards tied to those systems.

Use of Appraisal Systems. Recent surveys of different types of appraisal systems in municipal governments have found that the typical city does not appraise its upper-level managers in the same way as its operations-level workers. Perhaps the most surprising finding is that only 59 percent of major U.S. cities formally appraise upper managers. The remainder appraise them through various informal means or, in the case of 12 percent of all cities, do not appraise managers at all.[32]

For just the 59 percent of cities that do appraise upper-level managers, by far the most used tool was ABO (or synonymously, MBO). Thirty-five percent of cities used ABO alone; another 30 percent used it in combination with other techniques. Thus roughly two-thirds of the cities used ABO for evaluating managers. Trait-based scales and BARS followed in a near tie for second place, each far behind ABO. Cities that were more professionalized—that had council-manager forms of government—were most likely to use ABO and least likely to use trait-based scales.

When researchers looked at the pattern of municipal appraisal practices for lower-level (nonmanagerial) employees, they found many differences.[33] As might be expected in dealing with large numbers of employees, most cities used formal appraisal systems. Almost 87 percent reported such systems—far more than the 59 percent who used them for upper managers. As also might have been predicted, ABO was less used. It was used alone or in combination with other techniques about 35 percent of the time; so was BARS. Trait-based scales were the most popular approach; they were used alone in 30 percent of the cities (primarily smaller cities) and in combination with other techniques another 45 percent of the time. (The numbers total to more than 100 percent because techniques were often combined; thus BARS might be used with a trait scale.) BARS and ABO tended to be used more by larger cities and council-manager cities.

In terms of municipal appraisal systems, then, we see a two-tiered approach: ABO is most common for upper managers, and trait scales for lower managers. Compared to earlier surveys, however, ABO and BARS are growing substantially at all levels, and trait systems are in retreat.[34]

Connecting Money to Systems.   The debate about how closely money can be tied to individual performance ratings received an important, if unscientific, empirical test during the 1980s. There was a strong renewed emphasis on linking pay to performance, and not just in the public sector; large numbers of businesses revamped their compensation plans to tie pay to performance more tightly.[35] In the public sector, career ladders and merit pay for schoolteachers were a symptom of a new concern for measuring and rewarding the performance of the best teachers.[36]

The most extensive public sector change was at the federal level, where the 1978 Civil Service Reform Act set up ABO-type evaluation systems and tied them to bonuses and salary increases.[37] These reforms had a rocky career. In their early years, the new appraisal systems were wildly unpopular for a whole variety of reasons, including congressional meddling (which lowered the amount of bonus and merit money available), hasty implementation, and the widely varying systems and standards that made many participants feel the system was unfair.[38] Some of the worst problems were eliminated as the system matured, and eventually, the new personnel systems moved from unqualified failure to a more ambiguous state, succeeding in some agencies but not in others.[39]

State and local experiments in tying monetary rewards to personnel systems has been similarly mixed.[40] Experience at the state and local levels seems to reinforce the lessons of the federal experience: Tying monetary rewards to appraisals will work only if strong, trusted appraisal systems are already in place and if the amount of money for solid but average performance at least keeps up with the rate of inflation. If solid workers receive no rewards and fall behind inflation because the system directs all awards to star workers, the negative impact on the morale of numerous solid employees is likely to outweigh the positive impact on the fewer star employees.[41] A final requirement for success is that employees have a voice in setting up and maintaining the system. Unfortunately but understandably, it is rare to find all three of these prerequisites present.

Summary of Individually Oriented Monetary Rewards

Let us briefly recap the discussion. We began with the question of how to appraise individual performance and concluded that ABO systems are almost always superior to trait-based systems, and often superior to BARS because ABO focuses on outputs and because it enlists employees' participation. However it is sometimes difficult to link individual behavior to outputs, especially for low-level managers and nonmanagerial employees. Thus a combination of ABO with BARS may be the best solution for such workers. This combination allows top management to emphasize output (through ABO) while still employing a reasonable person approach since BARS allows the organization to reward performance that was not specified or captured through ABO.[42]

Once they have chosen their appraisal system, top managers must then decide whether to tie the system directly to individual monetary rewards. In general, such direct ties work best for top managers who can be reasonably held accountable for the output of their unit. They are also applicable to some operations workers who turn out a very tangible output. For most other employees, however, organizations should proceed very cautiously in installing such tight links between rewards and individual measures because problems of goal displacement, increased competitiveness with co-workers, and resentment are likely to outweigh the advantages. For such workers, organizations should consider using ABO-oriented personnel systems for promotions and counseling and tying monetary rewards to the more easily measured outputs of larger groups. This is the topic of the next section.

MONEY AS AN EXTRINSIC MOTIVATOR: GROUP AND ORGANIZATION-WIDE REWARDS

As noted at the beginning of this chapter, management systems rarely track individual performance; they usually track the performance of subunits or the organization as a whole. Thus we are now returning to pure management systems as we consider how rewards can be tied to the output measures for subunits or the total organization.

Private Sector: Profit Sharing

The private sector has long experimented with profit-sharing plans, whereby each employee of a business gets a share of all profits that are above a certain baseline. In its most basic form, if a management system indicates a 10 percent increase in profits, employees get 10 percent of their salary as a bonus at year's end.

There are a number of positive things to say about this approach. Perhaps most important, it gives employees the same perspective as managers. Both have a stake in how well the company will do in the marketplace. A possible flaw, however, is that annual profit is very far down the chain of outputs for a operations-level employee. Because profit is affected by so many outside forces, the typical worker may not feel that he or she has much effect on it. This belief has caused some companies to move to a second approach: gainsharing.

Public and Private Sector: Gainsharing

Gainsharing is rewarding employees for exceeding an output target, when the target is expressed in terms other than profit.[43] Thus a lawn mower company may give annual monetary rewards to employees for turning out 50,000 high-quality lawn mowers—whether or not the lawn mowers produced a profit. The advantage of this approach is that employees feel more control over the number of high-quality lawn mowers produced than over the company's profits for the year. An additional advantage is that gainsharing can be used for smaller groups. A corporation with 100,000 workers would have to reward all of them equally under a profit-sharing plan, but it can reward or not reward small groups on the basis of whether they met a gainsharing objective.

In the public sector, literal profit sharing is of course impossible because there is no profit. Thus all unit or organization-wide rewards must be based on gainsharing. A substantial number of agencies are currently implementing gainsharing at both the local level and at the federal level, especially in the Department of Defense.[44]

We suggested earlier that gainsharing may well work better if it is not used for an overall large organization because a reward is most likely to affect workers' behavior when the workers believe that they can actually affect the outcome. Thus if rewards are tied to the output of a very large group, there will be little or no impact on the productivity of each worker. But as noted, a good compromise may be to tie rewards to the output of a small group, such as an office or branch of several dozen people.

This approach avoids some of the subjectivity of individual ratings, arouses less union ire, and does not require superiors to distinguish among individual subordinates, and yet at the same time it encourages productive behavior.[45]

As noted in earlier chapters, the primary goal when using a management system to affect behavior is to produce *goal congruence* between individuals and the organization. That is, incentives should be structured so that when individuals do what is best for themselves, they are also doing what is best for the organization. Tying rewards to subunit performance seems the most promising way to produce such goal congruence.

In the next chapter we will discuss result centers, relatively self-contained units in which employees produce a common product. Such structures maximize the benefit of group-based reward systems such as gainsharing because then the office or branch actually controls its inputs and outputs. Its actual performance is accordingly much easier to judge, and thus tying rewards to it is much fairer.

AN OVERVIEW: LINKING MANAGEMENT SYSTEMS TO OTHER SYSTEMS

In this chapter we considered tying performance measures of the management system directly into the organization's personnel system, and then rewarding individuals on the basis of that unified system. Ultimately, we concluded that this approach is rarely possible. It asks too much of the personnel system's measurements to determine accurately what each individual added to the group's output. It overtaxes both the personnel and management system. Instead, it seems better to settle for a less ambitious plan—to move the personnel system more closely to management systems by emphasizing output measures through ABO. At the same time, the reward system should be kept somewhat separate, some of the rewards (e.g., promotions) being allocated through the personnel system and some of them (especially bonuses) through management systems for subunits. This prevents all rewards from being tied to a single measurement or group of measurements, and it allows room for the unmeasurable as well.

The discussion in this chapter of linking personnel systems to management systems and in Chapter Seven of linking budget to management systems raises the broader question of how tightly the management system should be tied to other systems. Both chapters suggested that usually loose links work best. Is this a generalizable prescription? In other words, to what extent should management systems be linked to other systems? Perhaps, at the most extreme, an agency could have just one "super system," of which finance, personnel, budgeting, and output-oriented management systems would be tightly integrated components. At the other extreme, each system could be completely independent.

The last option can be rejected easily. All management systems must be linked to ongoing organizational processes or they are meaningless. If a management system truly stands alone, and its information is not considered when making salary, budget, promotion, and program decisions, then it has no use and should be eliminated. The whole purpose of a management system is to generate information that is useful for decision making and motivation. Therefore the question is not really whether a system should be linked to organizational processes but instead whether the links should be highly formal, leading to a tightly integrated, almost single super system or whether the links should be informal and partial. In this chapter we have again concluded that for many organizational outputs, the link must have a "fudge factor," usually achieved through a reasonable person approach, because not *all* relevant information can be captured by the systems and thus the incentives for displacement can become overwhelming.[46] The more rewards are tightly and automatically connected to the system readings, the more the system must fight incentives for displacement and misreporting. This statement suggests the broader point: The fact that incentives in government are rarely as harmonious as system designers would wish.

The Inevitability of System Imbalance in Government Administration

The discussion of budget and personnel links makes an important point: The need to keep management systems simple and balanced is far greater in government than in private industry. By its very nature, government forces all management systems to develop unevenly. Important incentives in such systems, that private industry simply develops in unison, are often the properties of two independent government suborganizations. Most decisions about program money, perhaps the most powerful unit incentive, will be in the hands of the legislature and the executive, rather than the agency head who uses the management system; and many decisions about promotions, salary increases, and other personnel-directed incentives will be controlled by the Civil Service or political considerations.[47]

Moreover, in public organizations, management systems must often be installed piece by piece, with a much longer installation period than for similar systems in private organizations, because of several reasons. First, resistance to new systems is likely to be stronger in public organizations than in private ones because the whole idea of an output orientation is less familiar (and thus more threatening). Second, those who feel threatened by such systems have more resources for fighting than they do in private organizations: Civil Service systems, legislative committees, interest groups, and others are often available to protect organizational members who resist changes. Third, and most important, it is simply harder to design and install an output-oriented system in the service-oriented, nonprofit world of government than it is in the private sector.

Thus there is often an incremental pattern of management system installation in government: The system is installed over a long period, in stages, as resistance weakens. Therefore, barring perfect cooperation, all government management systems will develop unevenly, with aspects controlled by one unit maturing ahead of those controlled by other units. Battered by variable environmental factors—in the form of changing legislative dictates, subcommittee oversight, yearly budget shifts, pressure groups, and so forth—the management systems of political organizations can never be as complex or delicate as some of the systems used by private organizations.

Dealing with the Problem

There are a number of guidelines for attacking the problems presented by these stresses. First, because wide-reaching management systems that include large numbers of organizations must depend on all of them to cooperate, the chances of failure are increased proportionately; thus beginning systems are often best kept localized. Second, because the public sector buffets the hardiest of systems, the system should be kept simple— a requirement that dictates against setting up a super system with complex, tight links to budgeting and personnel. Third, managers should be particularly vigilant at those times when the risks of system failure are at their greatest, that is, when systems are beginning or especially when existing systems are given new emphasis or importance.

One of the primary causes of system failures is the lack of consciousness—on the part of program designers and on the part of individual managers—of the great vulnerability of public management systems and the resulting need for constant vigilance.

SUMMARY

System designers who wish to use management systems to affect workers' behavior face a large number of choices. The first choice is whether or not to tie the system to rewards such as salary increases and promotions. Systems that are not so tied will still affect the behavior of some workers, those who respond to intrinsic motivators. However only extrinsic motivators will affect the behavior of all workers.

If the system designers opt to connect their system to rewards, there are two major choices:

1. The level of connection: Should outputs be monitored and sanctioned at the level of the individual worker, the subunit, or the organization?
2. The choice of sanction: Should outputs be rewarded only by symbolic means or by money and other tangible motivators?

Two basic principles can guide system designers in making these choices. First, behavior is most positively affected when the system's standards and its rewards are perceived as fair. Second, the more that workers believe that they personally can control the outputs being monitored, the greater the system's impact on their behavior. The first principle suggests that workers should participate in setting standards. The second principle suggests that rewards should be tied to outputs monitored at a low organizational level so that workers will feel control over the measured output.

It is possible to stipulate how a well-working system at the level of the individual worker would be designed. It would replace trait-based appraisals with objective MBO-type goals, and it would use monetary bonuses as extrinsic motivators. Nonetheless such systems are usually infeasible for a number of reasons: unions oppose them; superiors are uncomfortable in rating employees; output indicators tend not to track individuals; many government tasks are jointly performed, precluding any evaluation of each individual's contribution; and politicians are unwilling to authorize individual bonuses.

A system that is based on subunit performances, rather than individual performances, is a plausible compromise that would still greatly advance organizational efficiency. Moreover, nonmonetary rewards—formal recognition, titles, and even praise—are very important and should not be neglected.

This discussion suggests the question, To what extent should management systems be integrated with other systems such as personnel and budgeting? As just discussed, integration with personnel is often very difficult. In addition, tight formal integration with other systems often increases the incentives for cheating and displacement beyond the management system's limited capabilities to police these problems. Thus organizational systems are often best integrated informally. Most public sector systems cannot and should not pursue the level of sophistication and integration that characterizes the best business systems; their environment and their tasks are too different.

REVIEW QUESTIONS

1. What are four examples of extrinsic motivators?
2. What are the two basic principles about the effect of management systems on workers' behavior?
3. What do the principles in question 2 suggest about using engineered standards for a public management system? About using past performance standards?
4. What do the principles suggest about the organizational level to which rewards should be connected?
5. What are the advantages of trait-based systems? Disadvantages?
6. What are the advantages of BARS systems? Disadvantages? For what types of jobs are they best suited?
7. What are the advantages of ABO systems? Disadvantages? Suggest several jobs for which they are well suited. For what types of jobs are they ill suited?
8. How does each of the major types of appraisal systems relate to the chain of outputs?
9. What are combination appraisal systems? What are their advantages? For what types of jobs are they best suited?
10. What are the obstacles to tying rewards to individual-level measurements? Suggest several jobs for which these obstacles are least important and most important.
11. How does profit sharing differ from gainsharing?
12. Which appraisal and reward systems are most likely to produce goal congruence? Why?
13. Why are public management systems generally less likely to succeed when tightly integrated with other systems? For what types of programs is this generalization most likely to be wrong?

Case 8–1

Robert Clary has recently been appointed head of a state agency that enforces alcohol regulations. His 190-employee agency is charged with checking bars, to ensure that minors or inebriated customers are not served, and checking retail stores that sell alcohol, to ensure that untaxed liquor is not sold. Clary has decided to discuss the new appraisal and management systems that he is considering with his five line subordinates, each of whom heads an agency section. The five sections cover five geographic areas of the state.

The meeting was surprising to Clary. The five all supported their current appraisal system, which rated individuals on a trait scale and was used only for individuals below themselves. They opposed gathering data on unit performance. They maintained that measuring output across agents was unfair because some worked in cities and made many arrests; others worked in less populated rural areas and did not. Moreover, often the most important thing about an agent was his or her courage in investigation and in backing up partners; this trait can only be captured in trait systems. Also some agents worked in two- or three-member teams, whereas others worked alone. Some agents were involved in long-range investigations that would not produce arrests for months, whereas others scouted bars and made weekly arrests.

Subunit performance data were similarly useless, they argued, because each geographic area of the state was so different. Given that output information would be so flawed, connecting rewards to such measures would only lead to frustration on the part of agents who did not receive rewards because of geographic location.

Clary argued but did not change their minds. After the meeting, he tentatively decided not to push the issue for a year or so. He saw no advantage in confronting them; he had to work with them in the year ahead. He did not wish to implement a system they could not agree to, although he remained dissatisfied with the current system.

1. What types of individual appraisal systems would be best for such an organization?
2. What types of management system data should be gathered on subunit and organizational performance? How could they be used?
3. What types of rewards, if any, should be attached to the data gathered by the appraisal system and the management system?
4. How should Clary handle the system design stage?

Case 8-2

Margaret Fairly heads the department of revenue for a city of 200,000. Her twenty-seven employees include her deputy, seven clerical workers, five secretaries, five property appraisers, seven accountants, an economist, and a lawyer. The city depends entirely on a property tax, and Fairly's office accordingly appraises property, hears the preliminary appeals of property appraisals, sends out bills, collects the tax money, invests it in short-term accounts, and (to aid the city council) also tracks and predicts all revenue.

Other executives in the city government view the department of revenue as competent but rarely innovative or impressive. The city has a plan by which four outstanding employees are honored with a plaque and a bonus each year. Fairly has nominated three of her employees in the past, but they were never chosen by the citywide screening panel.

Fairly has traditionally evaluated her employees through a trait-based appraisal system but is considering adopting a different approach. She has no other clear rewards to give her top performers but believes that the city manager would listen to her if she proposed some reward system.

She is generally satisfied with her employees' performance, but there are occasional problems. For example, one secretary has been performing at a very low level. Her immediate superior reports that he spoke to her without results. Fairly believes that the superior is unskilled in handling employees and is accordingly reluctant to blame totally (and fire) the secretary. Fairly wonders what performance measurement changes, if any, might help her with this problem when it recurs with future employees.

1. How should Fairly measure individual and unit performances? How does the small number of employees and their widely varying educational levels affect Fairly's choices?
2. Should she suggest some type of reward system? What are the advantages and disadvantages?
3. If she does receive permission to institute a reward system, does the work in the revenue office lend itself to group rewards or would individual rewards provide greater incentives?
4. Once her new system has been working for a year or two, what criteria should Fairly use to decide whether it has been a success?

SUGGESTED FURTHER READING

PETER M. BLAU. *The Dynamics of Bureaucracy*, rev. ed. Chicago: The University of Chicago Press, 1963. A ground-breaking study of behavior in two government agencies; one of the emphases is the effect of management systems on behavior.

MICHAEL CROZIER. *The Bureaucratic Phenomenon.* Chicago: University of Chicago Press, 1964. Employee behavior in two French government organizations. How process-oriented rules affect power relationships and productivity.

JOHN M. GREINER. *Productivity and Motivation: A Review of State and Local Government Initiatives.* Washington, DC: The Urban Institute Press, 1981. Thorough (470+ pages) examination of government productivity experiments at the state and local level. Gathers together empirical results that had been scattered throughout the literature. Very useful.

EDWARD E. LAWLER, III, and JOHN GRANT RHODE. *Information and Control in Organizations.* Pacific Palisades, CA: Goodyear Publishing Company, 1976. A fine summary of the research on many management system topics. Written with an expectancy theory focus, it particularly emphasizes employees' behavior.

ANDREW D. SZILAGYI, JR., and MARC J. WALLACE, JR. *Organizational Behavior and Performance,* 4th ed. Glenview, IL: Scott, Foresman, 1987. A well-balanced overview of motivation theory.

ENDNOTES

1. For an interesting argument that U.S. private industry tends to use management systems for information for top-level decision making, whereas the Japanese send the same information down to affect behavior (and decision making) at lower levels, see Robert E. Cole, "Target Information for Competitive Performances," *Harvard Business Review,* May/June 1985, pp. 100–12.

2. There are several useful summaries of theories of motivation and management approaches. Two texts with well-balanced overviews are Andrew D. Szilagyi, Jr., and Marc J. Wallace, Jr., *Organizational Behavior and Performance,* 4th ed. (Glenview, IL: Scott, Foresman, 1987), chapters 4 and 5; and Judith R. Gordon, *A Diagnostic Approach to Organizational Behavior,* 2nd ed. (Boston: Allyn & Bacon, 1987), chapter 3.

   A well-written overview that this chapter draws on and that is primarily based on expectancy theory is Edward E. Lawler, III, and John Grant Rhode, *Information and Control in Organizations* (Pacific Palisades, CA: Goodyear Publishing Company, 1976).

3. There are, of course, other related internal motivators. Embarrassment at failure is one. How managers sometimes employ self-embarrassment as an intrinsic and extrinsic motivator is discussed in my "Publicizing Organizational Performance Goals: Self-Embarrassment as a Management Strategy," *American Review of Public Administration,* Summer 1983.

4. Supporting studies for this assertion are cited in Lawler and Rhode, *Information and Control in Organizations,* p. 66. Among them are A. N. Turner and P. R. Lawrence, *Industrial Jobs and the Worker* (Boston: Harvard University School of Business Administration, 1965); and J. R. Hackman and E. E. Lawler, "Employee Reactions to Job Characteristics," *Journal of Applied Psychology,* 55, no. 3 (June 1971), pp. 259–86.

5. Two well-written texts that recap the theories and indicate current thought are Dennis W. Organ and Thomas Bateman, *Organizational Behavior: An Applied Psychological Approach,* 3rd ed. (Plano, TX: Business Publications, 1986), chapters 4, 7–12; and the already-mentioned Szilagyi and Wallace, *Organizational Behavior and Performance,* chapters 3, 4, and 5.

6. Frederick Herzberg, B. Mausner, and B. B. Snyderman, *The Motivation to Work* (New York: John Wiley, 1959).

7. One text concludes that "evidence refuting Herzberg's theory is almost as extensive as evidence confirming it." See Organ and Bateman, *Organizational Behavior,* p. 113. The literature testing the theory is extensive; most of it dates from the 1965–1975 period. Two articles casting doubt are B. L. Hinton, "An Empirical Examination of the Herzberg Methodology and Two-Factor Theory," *Organizational Behavior and Human Performance* (February 1968), pp. 286–309; and Robert J. House and L. Wigdor, "Herzberg's Dual Factor Theory of Job Satisfaction and Motivation: A Review of the Evidence and Criticism," *Personnel Psychology,* 20 (1968), 369–89.

8. This discussion partially echoes a contingency theory approach. In general, however, this chapter implicitly assumes that the battles of motivational theorists are important but somewhat misleading. There are a surprising number of shared assumptions even among warring motivational theorists, and these shared assumptions provide a sufficient basis for most management system choices.

9. These include increased intrinsic rewards gained by job enlargement and job enhancement, which will be covered in Chapter Ten rather than here, however. When we tie rewards to goals, we have moved from what Judith Gruber terms "control by authority" to "control by exchange." Judith E. Gruber, *Controlling Bureaucracies* (Berkeley: University of California Press, 1987), pp. 211–12.

10. Thus the work standards must be objective, the rewards proportionate, and the procedures fairly applied. See the discussion in U.S. General Accounting Office, *Ways to Improve Federal Management and Use of Productivity Based Reward Systems* (Washington, DC: GAO, December 31, 1980).

    In one study, participation in setting budget targets was very important in motivating effort: D. G. Searfross and R. M. Monczka, "Perceived Participation in the Budget Process and Motivation to Achieve the Budget," *Academy of Management Journal,* 16, no. 4 (December 1973), pp. 541–54. A good overview of the literature on such fairness is contained in Robert Folger and Mary A. Konovsky, "Effects of Procedural and Distributive Justice on Reactions to Pay Raise Decisions," *Academy of Management Journal,* 32, no. 1 (January 1989), 115–32.

11. See Edward E. Lawler, III, *Pay and Organizational Effectiveness: A Psychological View* (New York: McGraw-Hill, 1971); and Raymond A. Katzell and Daniel Yankelovich, *Work, Productivity and Job*

Satisfaction: An Evaluation of Policy Related Research (New York: Psychological Corporation, 1975).

12. The following discussion relies heavily on John M. Greiner et al., *Productivity and Motivation: A Review of State and Local Government Initiatives* (Washington, DC: Urban Institute Press, 1981), chapters 13–17; Dennis L. Dresang, *Public Personnel Management and Public Policy* (Boston: Little, Brown, 1984), chapter 8; Donald E. Klingner and John Nalbandian, *Public Personnel Management*, 2nd ed. (Englewood Cliffs, NJ: Prentice-Hall, 1985), chapters 10 and 14.

There are appraisal tools other than the three listed here, including forced choice and critical incident approaches. But these three are by far the most used; and the others, with some broadening of categories, can be subsumed within them.

13. For example, see the chapters cited in each of the three books in note 12.

14. See Lawrence S. Kleiman and Richard L. Durham, "Performance Appraisals, Promotions and the Courts: A Critical Review," *Personnel Psychology* 34, no. 1 (Spring 1981), pp. 103–22; Shelley R. Burchett and Kenneth P. DeMeuse, "Performance Appraisal and the Law," *Personnel*, July 1985, pp. 29–37.

15. This term is used by Grenier et al., *Productivity and Motivation*.

16. National Association for Public Administration, *Revitalizing Public Management* (Washington, DC: National Academy of Public Administration, 1983), p. 37. The same study also calls for OMB and OPM to "emphasize results or performance objectives and avoid detailed procedures which attempt to structure the means by which the objectives are achieved" (p. 17).

17. An interesting empirical study of employees' attitudes toward ABO is Dennis Daley, "An Examination of MBO/Performance Standards Approach to Employee Evaluation: Attitudes Toward Performance Appraisal in Iowa," *Review of Public Personnel Administration*, 6, no. 1 (Fall 1985), 11–28. Daley finds that employees under such a system give it a qualified vote of approval, with the largest complaint about once-per-year feedback. Not surprisingly, the highest-rated employees rate the system most positively. Similarly, a positive view of merit evaluation was found among Washington State employees: Nicholas P. Lovrich, Jr., et al., "Do Public Servants Welcome or Fear Merit Evaluation of Their Performance?" *Public Administration Review*, 40, no. 3 (May/June 1980).

18. Hybrid systems are discussed in Gary B. Brumback and Thomas S. McFee, "From MBO to MBR," *Public Administration Review*, 42, no. 4 (July/August 1982), 363ff. A related discussion of the difficulty of setting output standards with employees is U.S. General Account-

ing Office, *A Two Year Appraisal of Merit Pay in Three Agencies* (Washington, DC: GAO, March 26, 1984).

19. See Craig Eric Schneier and Richard W. Beatty, "Combining BARS and MBO: Using an Appraisal System to Diagnose Performance Problems," *The Personnel Administrator,* September 1979, pp. 51–60.

20. A substantial body of thought argues that this is the only way such systems should be used because combining compensation decisions with counseling is undesirable. For a call to keep the two processes separate, see Klingner and Nalbandian, *Public Personnel Management,* chapter 14; Arie Halachmi and Marc Holzer, "Merit Pay, Performance Targeting, and Productivity," *Review of Public Personnel Administration,* Spring 1987, pp. 80–91.

21. For a discussion that strongly advocates reliance on such nonmonetary incentives as formal recognition, job rotation, advanced training, and consultation, see Gerald T. Gabris and William A. Giles, "Improving Productivity and Performance Appraisal Through the Use of Noneconomic Incentives," *Public Productivity Review,* 7, no. 2 (June 1983).

22. Expectancy theory has generated an explosion of articles and books in the past twenty-five years. Among the basic works that precipitated the explosion are Victor H. Vroom, *Work and Motivation* (New York: John Wiley, 1964); and L. W. Porter and Edward E. Lawler, *Managerial Attitudes and Performance* (Homewood, IL: Dorsey Press, 1968).

23. One survey of research indicated that goal setting resulted in a median performance improvement of 16 percent. However, when goal setting was combined with monetary incentives, the median performance increase was 40 percent. Edward A. Locke, D. Feren, V. McCaleb, K. Shaw, and A. Denny, "The Relative Effectiveness of Four Methods of Motivating Employee Performance"; cited in Organ and Bateman, *Organizational Behavior,* p. 117.

    Expert opinion agrees: In a survey, municipal personnel officers ranked rewarding superior performance through pay as the most important potential contributor to productivity and conversely ranked the lack of such possibilities as the greatest barrier. Charles E. Davis and Johnathan P. West, "Adopting Personnel Productivity Innovations in American Local Governments," *Policy Studies Review,* 4, no. 3 (February 1985), 546–47.

24. This is the conclusion drawn from an extensive survey by Greiner et al., *Productivity and Motivation,* chapter 5.

    This problem is not confined to the public sector. A 1983 survey of both business and government workers found that only 22 percent of workers say there is a direct relationship between how they work and how much they are paid; only 23 percent say they are performing to full capacity; 61 percent identify pay tied to performance as a feature they most want from their work. New York Times Syndicate, "Desire of Workers to Do a Good Job Hurt by Management, Study Says," *Raleigh News and Observer,* September 6, 1983, p. 4d.

But if not confined to the public sector, the problem is worse there. See Hal G. Rainey, "Public Agencies and Private Firms: Incentives, Goals, and Individual Roles," *Administration and Society,* 15, no. 2 (1983), 207–42. Rainey finds that compared to private managers, government managers are less likely to believe that there is a link between good performance and higher pay. They also have less job satisfaction, which Rainey attributes at least in part to this lack of pay for performance.

25. Greiner et al., *Productivity and Motivation,* chapter 5. The Civil Service Reform Act of 1978 attempted to change this system, but it has had difficulties. On the change, see the discussion in notes 37, 38, and 39.

26. The 80 percent figure is from James T. Brinks, "Is There Merit in Merit Increases?" *Personnel Administrator,* May 1980, pp. 59–69.

The figure on engineers comes from A. Mikalachki, "There Is No Merit in Merit Pay," *Business Quarterly,* Spring 1976, p. 178; cited in George W. Downs and Patrick D. Larkey, *The Search for Government Efficiency* (New York: Random House, 1986), p. 198.

There are many other examples. A survey of New Jersey high school principals found that 74 percent ranked themselves in the top 10 percent of all state principals. Not one ranked himself or herself in the bottom half. Craig E. Richards and Robert Height, "Accountability and Performance Incentives for School Principals," *Public Productivity Review,* 12, no. 1 (Fall 1988), 20.

27. One is reminded of Lake Woebegone, where author Garrison Keillor notes that "all the children are above average."

28. For a clear discussion of the use of bonuses instead of salary increases, see John S. Piamonte, "In Praise of Monetary Motivation," *Personnel Journal,* September 1979, p. 624.

29. This is generally the conclusion of Greiner et al., *Productivity and Motivation.* The discussion that follows is partially derived from that book, especially chapters 4 and 7.

30. Alan Campbell offers the interesting theory that the cut arose because congressional staff members, jealous that they were not eligible for bonuses, were hostile to the bonus provision of the SES. Alan Campbell, "A Frame for Three Faces," *Journal of Policy Analysis and Management,* 2, no. 4 (1983), 526–30.

31. Patricia W. Ingraham and Carolyn R. Ban, "Models of Public Management: Are They Useful to Federal Managers in the 1980s?" *Public Administration Review,* 46, no. 2 (March/April 1986), 154.

32. The discussion of managerial appraisal systems is from David N. Ammons and Arnold Rodriguez, "Performance Appraisal Practices for Upper Management in City Governments," *Public Administration Review,* 46, no. 5 (September/October 1986), 460–67.

33. The discussion of nonmanagerial appraisal practices is from Robert E. England and William M. Parle, "Nonmanagerial Performance Appraisal in Large American Cities," *Public Administration Review,* 47, no. 6 (November/December 1987), 498–504. They used the same questionnaire as Ammons and Rodriguez, so their results are directly comparable.

34. The earlier survey, showing much less ABO and BARS, is Kenneth J. Lacho, G. Kent Stearns, and Maurice F. Villere, "A Study of Employee Appraisal Systems of Major Cities in the United States," *Public Personnel Management,* March/April 1979, pp. 111–25.

35. "Santa's Golden Handcuffs: At Many Companies, Pay for Performance Is Taking the Measure of Management," *Newsweek,* December 24, 1984, pp. 28–29. Public and private comparisons of this trend are briefly discussed in Constance Horner, "Managing and Moving the Executive Agenda," *The Bureaucrat,* Winter, 1985–86, p. 8.

    Cindy Richards, "Productivity-based Pay Plans on the Rise," *Chicago Sun-Times,* January 5, 1987, p. 42, reports on a poll by the American Productivity Center, which finds that the use of such systems had doubled in the preceding five years.

    Cindy Skrzycki, "Linking Wages with Performance," *Washington Post,* May 24, 1987, p. H1, finds that 75 percent of private sector firms use some form of pay for performance. They have grown dramatically in recent years, with gainsharing growing the most. Small-group incentives are also growing rapidly.

    An important pro-pay-for-performance article by one of the most respected contemporary organizational theorists is Rosabeth Moss Kanter, "The Attack on Pay," *Harvard Business Review,* March/April 1987, pp. 60–67.

36. One of the few empirical examinations of the results of using a merit pay system for teachers is David K. Cohen and Richard J. Murnane, "The Merits of Merit Pay," *The Public Interest,* Summer 1985, pp. 3–30. They find it to be a limited success, with some interesting qualifications.

37. The 1978 reforms are a very complicated topic, in part because they had several distinct parts. One aspect attempted to establish pay for performance for both middle managers (GS13 to GS15) and for

supergrades. Another aspect that received a great deal of attention but will not be emphasized here was the establishment of a Senior Executive Service (SES) for the very top federal managers. Although it involved the bonuses already discussed, many of its approaches are somewhat tangential to this chapter, including increased job rotation and greater ease of both promotion and demotion. Such SES-type systems have spread to a number of states. On this topic, see Mark A. Abramson, "Executive Personnel Systems in Government: How Are They Doing?" *Public Administration Review,* 47, no. 4 (July/August 1987), 360–63; Frank A. Yeager, "Assessing the Civil Service Reform Act's Impact on Senior Manager Work Priorities," and Frank P. Sherwood and Lee J. Breyer, "Executive Personnel Systems in the States," *Public Administration Review,* 47, no. 5 (September/October 1987).

38. For an extensive symposium that reviews this trouble and for the most part concludes that the reforms have failed, see *Review of Public Personnel Administration,* 7, nos. 1 and 2 (Fall 1986 and Spring 1987). Among the useful and very critical articles in the symposium are Frank Sherwood and Barton Wechsler, "The HAD-ACOL of the Eighties: Paying Senior Public Managers for Performance," Fall 1986, pp. 27–41; Frederick C. Thayer, "Performance Appraisal and Merit Pay Systems: The Disasters Multiply," Spring, 1987, pp. 36–53; Gerald T. Gabris, "Can Merit Pay Systems Avoid Creating Discord Between Supervisors and Superordinates? Another Uneasy Look at Performance Appraisal," Fall 1986, pp. 70–89; Dennis Daley, "Merit Pay Enters with a Wimper: The Initial Federal Civil Service Reform Experience," Spring 1987, pp. 72–79.

     See also William J. Lanovette, "SES—From Civil Service Showpiece to Incipient Failure in Two Years," *National Journal,* July 18, 1981, pp. 1296–99.

39. As noted and as indicated by the preceding citations, my judging the reforms a mixed success is a controversial statement. For a generally positive view of the 1978 reforms see Judith Havemann, "More Civil, More Serviceable," *Washington Post National Weekly Edition,* May 26, 1986, pp. 31–32.

     See U.S. General Accounting Office, *Pay for Performance: Implementation of the Performance Management and Recognition System* (Washington, DC: GAO, January 1987). GAO generally finds that the 1978 linkage of pay and performance is working in federal agencies but that there are continuing difficulties, in part because of agency-to-agency differences in rewarding the same performance. Earlier, GAO concluded that SES has achieved some of the goals set for it: *Testimony of the Comptroller General on the Impact of* the *Senior Executive Service* (Washington, DC: GAO, December 30, 1983), pp. 12–14. On blue-collar pay, see General Accounting Office, *Blue Collar Workers: Appraisal Systems Are in Place, But Basic Refinements Are Needed* (Washington, DC: GAO, June 1987).

For OPM's overview, see U.S. Merit Systems Protection Board, *Performance Management and Recognition System: Linking Pay to Performance* (Washington, DC: December 30, 1987).

Also guardedly positive is Gilbert B. Siegel, "The Jury Is Still Out on Merit Pay in Government," *Review of Public Personnel Administration,* Summer 1987, pp. 3–15.

40. See Peter Allen and Stephen Rosenberg, "An Assessment of Merit Pay Administration Under New York City's Managerial Performance Evaluation System: Three Years of Experience," *Public Personnel Management,* Fall 1986, pp. 297–309; Nicholas P. Lovrich, Jr., "Merit Pay and Motivation in the Public Workforce: Beyond Technical Considerations to More Basic Considerations," *Review of Public Personnel Administration,* Spring 1987, pp. 54–71; Greiner et al., *Productivity and Motivation,* chapters 2–7.

41. Linda C. McNish, "A Critical Review of Performance Appraisal at the Federal Level: The Experience of the PHS," and James L. Perry, "Merit Pay in the Public Sector: The Case for a Failure of Theory," *Review of Public Personnel Administration,* Fall 1986, pp. 42–69.

42. For a good discussion of the way that objective systems may fail to capture many important personal attributes, see John Nalbandian, "Performance Appraisal: If Only People Were Not Involved," *Public Administration Review,* 41, no. 3 (May/June 1981), 329–33.

43. Like most management terms, *gainsharing* is not always defined the same way from article to article. Occasionally it is used as an umbrella term that includes both profit sharing and non-profit-based rewards. The definition here, I think, is more common.

44. For a very elaborate form of gainsharing, see Neal Q. Herrick, "Co-operative Self-Interest: Learning from Joe Scanlon," in Marc Holzer and Arie Halachmi, *Strategic Issues in Public Sector Productivity* (San Francisco: Jossey-Bass, 1986). This work has a very good example of how bonuses could be calculated and applied.

For an overview of other experiments, see U.S. General Accounting Office, *Gainsharing: Department of Defense Efforts Highlight an Effective Tool for Enlarging Federal Productivity* (Washington, DC: GAO, September 1986). It calls for combining gainsharing with employee participation systems such as quality circles and suggestion systems. In contrast to our discussion, this study calls for relatively large-scale approaches to simplify record keeping and work standards.

45. Gainsharing approaches are treated positively in Greiner et al., *Productivity and Motivation,* pp. 88–93. Gainsharing is also found to be the most promising incentive approach in Gary W. Florkowski and Donald E. Lifton, "Assessing Public Sector Productivity Incentives: A Review," *Public Productivity Review,* no. 43 (Fall 1987), 53–70.

46. Displacement is of course a constant problem, even with group awards. For example, a federal/state program has established incentive awards for local job-training programs that are successful, but it does not regulate the definition of "success." Although the federal government provides a uniform list of competencies to be achieved, it allows each program to decide how many competencies must be achieved before deeming it a "success." Not surprisingly, one program required attainment of only one of fifteen skills. GAO concludes that this problem necessitates national uniform standards or the "incentive awards could discourage, rather than encourage, the provision of the training many youths need." U.S. General Accounting Office, *Youth Job Training: Problems Measuring Attainment of Employment Competencies* (Washington, DC: GAO, February 1987), p. 3.

47. This section draws from my article "Unbalanced Incentives in Government Productivity Systems," *Public Productivity Review,* 7, no. 1 (March 1983).

chapter nine

Structure as a Management Tool: Links to Management Systems

INTRODUCTION

An organization's structure will have a direct and substantial impact on its management systems. Like management systems, structure also affects information for decision making and incentives for employees' behavior. Different organizational structures produce different organizational information and different patterns of behavioral incentives. Two organizations, similar in every way except structure, will need quite different management systems. Accordingly, management systems and structural arrangements must be developed in unison.

This chapter will first focus on how structure is viewed from the top—from the office of the president, governor, or mayor. At such high, megalevels, questions of efficiency often take a back seat to politics. After examining these political ramifications of structure, we will then move on to structure from the vantage point of the upper- and middle-level manager. At this level, efficiency considerations are often more important (although of course politics is never completely absent). We will examine ways that managers can manipulate structure to create more efficiency by producing different organizational decision-making and incentive patterns.

Finally, we will examine how management systems must be modified to fit these various types of structure.

THE VIEW FROM THE TOP: STRUCTURE AS A POLITICAL TOOL

Among public and politicians alike, reorganizing government has long been seen as the most important means of making it more efficient. The last president to emphasize this point was Jimmy Carter, who played on this belief in his 1976 presidential campaign by promising to compress the "1,900" agencies of the federal government into 200. In fact, the only way in which one could count 1,900 federal organizations was to include numerous boards and coordinating bodies that perform useful small services while costing virtually nothing and adversely affecting nobody. Thus to the lack of surprise of veteran observers, Carter proposed only a few important organizational changes once he was president, and he backed off from several of those proposals in the face of congressional resistance.

Such legislative resistance is common at all levels. Often legislative committees (or powerful individual legislators) have based their power on their relationship to the particular conglomeration of agencies that they oversee. They are thus likely to resist any proposals that will change the agency alignments and break up the existing patterns of power.[1]

Especially when viewed from the top level of governors or presidents, structure is not a neutral, efficiency-oriented tool; it is a major determinant of power. An agency that reports directly to the departmental secretary is likely to wield far more clout than one that is buried several layers down. Putting an agency into a larger organization that is hostile to its purposes can all but destroy it. Putting it in a friendly home organization can allow it to wield great influence. In almost any state the same loan program for the poor would look very different if it were housed in the state treasury department, dominated by bankers and auditors, rather than in the state department of human resources, dominated by social workers.

One of the most bitter reorganization battles of the 1980s arose when the Reagan administration proposed combining the Department of the Interior with the Department of Energy. The proposal was spiritedly opposed and ultimately defeated by environmentalists, who feared that in the new, combined department, the conservation-oriented Interior Department would be dominated by the more development-oriented Energy Department.[2] Both sides of the battle saw the reorganization proposal as the matter of politics and policy that it was.

Presidents, governors, and mayors recognize that structure affects both power and politics, and they often use structure for political purposes. For example, they may wish to emphasize their commitment to a particular group or program, and giving it its own agency is a costless symbol. Thus they move an office of civil rights to the governor's office as an expression of their concern, or they placate teachers by creating a separate department of education.

Chief executives also use reorganization to break the power of individuals or groups in the bureaucracy. Thus reorganizing a department may provide an excuse for demoting or transferring a political opponent or for inserting more political supporters.[3] Putting two bureaus together may prevent them from becoming too dependent on any one interest group because the new combined organization can play off the interest groups against each other.

Even if a reorganization is motivated by politics, it is usually defended in terms of efficiency. Claims of great prospective savings are often necessary to gain the political support needed to implement large reorganizations. In fact, reorganizations at all levels are usually accompanied by claims of substantial economies, usually based on "the elimination of duplications." Such economies are almost impossible to document,[4] but at the top level of government, whether or not money is saved is besides the point. Governors and presidents understandably wish to increase their control over "their" executive branch, and reorganizations are a means toward this policy (i.e., political) goal.

THE VIEW FROM THE MANAGER'S OFFICE: STRUCTURE AS A MANAGEMENT TOOL

Although political considerations will dominate structure at the top, many presidents, mayors, governors, and legislatures will give lower-level managers some lattitude in how they organize their agencies. As a general principle, the lower the agency is in the executive hierarchy, the more freedom it has to restructure (because any change has less political impact). This presents a great opportunity for many public managers because manipulating structure can be a highly useful managerial tool. Although we have noted the common legal and political constraints, many managers have surprisingly wide discretion in how they can arrange their organizational unit. Yet most managers do not use this power to give themselves the maximum amount of feedback and flexibility.

Structure has been a long-studied aspect of management. In fact, in the early part of this century most public management theorists considered structure to be the most important single aspect of an organization. Beginning with the Hawthorne experiments in the 1920s and 1930s, we have learned that formal structure is often far less important than informal structure—the informal relationship between individuals as expressed through friendships, group norms, and group sanctions.[5] However these important discoveries of the human relations school were too often interpreted to mean that formal structure did not matter.[6] Private businesses did not make this mistake, and they have reaped the benefits of treating structure as one more tool managers can use to accomplish their task.

ANALYZING STRUCTURE: CLASSICAL THEORY

In the first part of this century a body of administrative principles was developed by a group of theorists of whom the most famous is Luther Gulick.[7] These principles, often termed the *classical approach* to public organization, dominated public administration theory for several generations and are still important today. Among the most important principles of the classical orthodoxy are that power arrangements should be hierarchical, with each person responsible to only one superior, and that operating (line) personnel should be clearly separate from advisory (staff) personnel. We will examine several other tenets of the classical approach in greater detail.

Client, Place, Process, and Purpose

All agencies, said classical theory, had to be structured by one of four principles: place, clientele, process, or function (purpose). These venerable categories are still used in many analyses today and they are often useful, although they are imprecise and overlap substantially. We will consider each briefly.

Let us imagine that you have just been appointed the head of a state job-training agency. The purpose of the agency is to provide unemployed people with marketable skills so that they can get private sector jobs. You must decide how to divide up the agency's 900 employees.

One option is by *place*—four divisions, say, that handle all operations in the east, north, south, and west of the state. A second option is by *clientele*. For example, if you believed that women have significantly different experiences in the work force than men, you might have one division that trains women for all kinds of jobs and another that trains men. A third way of structuring the organization is by *process*—all the employees who handle forms are in one division; all those who provide classroom training are in another.

However, the fourth possibility—*purpose or function*—is by far the most common. In this case you would divide employees by the purpose they serve. One group might handle long-range training; another group might handle the short-range training of those who are briefly between jobs; a third group might handle graphics design and the writing of instructional materials; and a fourth group might handle placement for the workers once they are trained. Most public organizations choose a functional structure because it allows workers to specialize rather than being generalists, as they sometimes must be under clientele-based or geography-based structures.

For example, if a city's human resources department has a functional organization, there is likely to be a separate health bureau within it, with perhaps eight doctors. Each doctor can specialize, handling only cases involving the field of medicine in which he or she is expert. If the same organization were structured by place, however, the doctors would be divided among the four place-based bureaus—two to the eastern bureau, two to the western, and so on. Now each doctor must handle all types of diseases; the doctor must be jack-of-all trades. Functional arrangements encourage specialization; client- and geography-based structures demand generalists.

An organization need not choose just one of these categories for its structure. An agency could be first divided by function, and then each of these functional divisions could be divided by geography or clientele.

Hierarchies and Spans of Control

At roughly the same time that the classical analysts proposed purpose, place, process and clientele as the basis for all organizational structures, they also developed the concept of *span of control*—that is, the number of employees directly supervised by one manager. Clearly if a manager supervises a large number of employees (i.e., has a large span of control), each employee will not receive the same amount of individual attention as would members of a smaller group. At the same time, moving to a short span of control requires more managers, resulting in extra costs and inefficiencies.

A second concern of classical analysts was the number of levels in the organizational hierarchy. The larger the number of levels, the more difficult it would be to process information. Each level through which information must pass up or down increases the possibility of distortion and slows its ultimate receipt.[8]

Some early theorists went so far as to suggest that the span of control of each supervisor should be kept short to enhance personal supervision and that the number of organizational levels should also be kept small to facilitate the flow of information. Of course, the two principles are contradictory. For example, if there are 11,000 employees and the span of control is ten, there are *five* organizational levels; if the span of control is reduced to four, there must be *eight* levels to contain everyone (illustrated in Figure 9–1).

1

10

100

1,000

10,000

Span of control of ten; five levels required to contain 11,111 people.

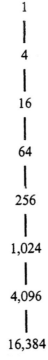

1

4

16

64

256

1,024

4,096

16,384

Span of control of four; eight levels required to contain 11,000+ people.

Figure 9-1.

"Cheek to Jowl"

A final principle of the classical orthodoxy held that efficiency was gained by *eliminating duplication* and overlap, and that therefore similar functions should always be grouped together in a single agency.[9] The first Hoover Commission, set up to apply classical principles to the federal government, added its own phraseology to this notion by noting that all related functions should be joined "cheek to jowl" in the same organization.[10]

Limitations of the Classical Orthodoxy

These orthodox principles have guided dozens of government reorganizational committees and commissions at various levels of government. Without exception, such bodies invariably recommend a relatively short span of control for the chief executive and his or her department heads, as well as the combination of similar functions in a single agency. These orthodox principles are useful as far as they go, but they do not go very far.

For example, let us focus on combining similar functions in one agency—the "cheek to jowl" principle. One problem is that sometimes duplication is useful. Duplication allows chief executives to receive two or more views on the same issue, and it also allows citizens to play off organizations against each other, making them more responsive.[11] However, a second, more universal problem with the cheek and jowl maxim has been noted by Peter Szanton: "Grouping some programs together means, inevitably, separating them from others to which they are also related. As Rufus Miles has pointed out, "all government is a complex of matrices: if work is divided on one set of principles or axes, it must be coordinated on another."[12]

Thus an education program for veterans could be put into the Defense Department, to be coordinated with other veterans' programs, or into the Department of Education, to be coordinated with other education programs. A state health program for low-income farmers could go into a health department or into an agriculture department. The cheek to jowl principle provides little guidance for such choices.

Management systems are involved in the wake of this dilemma. Whatever choice of organization is made, there will be outside agencies with which each agency must coordinate. Information generated by management systems plays a major role in enabling each agency to know what it is accomplishing and what other related agencies are doing, thus enhancing coordination.

Since the peak of the influence of the classical school in the 1930s there have been a number of attacks. Herbert Simon led the way in pointing out the ambiguities (such as the overlap between process, place, purpose, and clientele as a principle of organization, or the imprecision of the cheek to jowl principle) and the contradictions (such as the conflict between small spans of control and the small number of hierarchical levels).[13] The human relations school pointed out the importance of informal organizational structures. Contingency theorists have pointed out the folly of looking for a single best, "one size fits all" structure; they have shown how different organizational tasks and environments will require different structures. However, no overarching replacement theory of structure has been established. And thus when supplemented with these more recent insights, the tenets of the classical school can still provide useful, if very limited, guidelines.[14]

CENTRALIZATION VS. DECENTRALIZATION

Although rarely emphasized by the classical theorists, an important concern in structuring any organization is the choice between centralization and decentralization. *Centralization* is the concentration of power at the top or headquarters of the organization. *Decentralization* is the dispersion of power, so that many decisions can be made and actions taken at lower levels or field offices.

If a new executive has been given a free hand in running a nationwide job-training program, for example, he or she can centralize it by having all the major decisions and many of the training programs handled by the top people at central headquarters. On the other hand the executive could decentralize it by having the two hundred branch offices scattered around the country make most decisions and handle all the training. The test of decentralization is not whether there is a single central office vs. field offices. An organization can still have field offices and be centralized if the field offices do nothing but carry out detailed commands from headquarters. The test of decentralization is whether the field offices or lower levels have much independent power. The more autonomy they have, the more the organization is decentralized.

Both centralization and decentralization entail a different array of advantages and disadvantages, which affect management system needs.

Advantages of Centralization

One advantage of centralizing most of the job training decisions is *uniformity*. If all applications to the program are sent to headquarters for approval, an applicant from Maine is likely to be treated the same as an applicant from New Mexico because the same decision makers will review both applications. This is an advantage because it is likely to bolster people's sense of fairness (equity) if they are all treated the same.

Another advantage is that centralization is conducive to a *functional structure*, and thus to *specialization*. If applications from all over the country are sent to headquarters, there will be sufficient volume to support one reviewer, say, who will specialize in training the hard-core unemployed, and another one who is an expert in handicapped retraining. If all applications had been reviewed in the branch offices, on the other hand, each office probably could support only one reviewer, who would then have to be a jack-of-all-trades.

A third advantage of centralizing the program is *economy of scale*. If forms are reviewed by computer, the central office must buy only one computer. If each branch reviews all applications, each must buy a small computer. "Economy of scale" refers to the fact that large, centralized operations often cost less than small, scattered branch offices because many items do not have to be bought in quantity, and therefore do not sit idle much of the time.

A fourth advantage is *political control*. If a government program falters badly, it is very difficult for the legislature (or chief executive) to know who to hold responsible if there are dozens of independent field offices or lower levels. An organization with a single policy and program dictated from the central office, on the other hand, provides a clear focus of political accountability.

However, there are also substantial disadvantages to centralizing the agency's activities. Because the decisions are all made at headquarters, decision making is several layers removed from the "real world." A centralized organization responds slowly to the changing environment, which often causes clients to begin muttering about "red tape." Also, because people in Maine are treated the same as those in New Mexico, the agency often seems inflexible.

Advantages of Decentralization

If the field offices are empowered to make most of the decisions themselves (i.e., decentralization), there are again advantages and disadvantages. Not surprisingly, most of the advantages are the flip sides of the advantages of centralization.

Thus the field office decision-making mechanisms are likely to be *quick* (no waiting for headquarters to respond), *responsive* to changing conditions (they are right on the scene and ready to move), and *flexible* (New Mexico is likely to be treated differently from Maine). Morale of middle-level managers rises because they have real discretion.

There are disadvantages as well. One is the possibility of agency employees being *co-opted,* or as it is more colorfully termed, "going native."

If the U.S. ambassador to Lower Mauritania remains in that post for ten years or so, he or she is likely to begin thinking in terms of "we Lower Mauritanians." The process is a natural psychological one. When someone works with the same people for a large number of years, he or she naturally begins to see things as they see them. The trouble for the agency arises when its agents are more loyal to the viewpoint of the clients they serve than to their agency and its norms. They less and less represent the agency to outsiders and more and more represent the outside to the agency.

There are two ways for the agency to counteract this natural tendency. One is frequent rotation of employees, which prevents them from staying in one area long enough to internalize the local norms. The U.S. State Department, for example, requires employees to spend several years in the United States for every period abroad. A second way of counteracting co-option is strong control from the center. Then, even if the organizational workers in the field have internalized outside norms, they lack the discretion to do much about it because decisions are being made at headquarters.

Returning to the Question: Centralization or Decentralization?

It now seems that top managers are faced with an extremely difficult choice. On the one hand, they would like to decentralize their organizations because they would then gain the advantages of greater flexibility, speed, responsiveness to environmental change, and higher employee morale. But they would also like the advantages of centralization, such as coordination, accountability provided by central goal setting, uniformity, and economy of scale. As discussed when considering other managerial choices, managers must think in terms of contingent solutions; some tools work better under some circumstances than others, but no tool is *always* the best.

Decentralization is often most valuable when the organization must deal with complex, nonroutine tasks and environments. Thus it will be very valuable for a research institution, for example; a highly centralized research institution would be unable to process efficiently the constantly changing information necessary to maintain tight control from the top.

On the other hand, the more that uniformity is necessary (e.g., Internal Revenue Service regional centers), the less decentralization is desirable. In human services, offices that provide transfer payments, such as unemployment compensation or disability checks, must be centralized because their output must be uniform. Offices providing services such as counseling or training can work best if at least partially decentralized;

uniformity is less important, and responsiveness to complex, changing needs is more important.

The choice between centralization and decentralization, then, involves trade-offs that will be weighted differently by different types of organizations. However, these tradeoffs can sometimes be minimized. Decentralization would involve fewer trade-offs if the decentralized units produced very clear outputs; then it would be easier to hold them accountable for their results. This type of decentralized structure with clear outputs goes by a number of names in the public sector. We will call such structures *result centers*.

The topic is sufficiently complex that it is useful to examine the private sector first. Private sector structures are easier to understand because their output (profit) is much easier to track. In the business world, result-oriented subunits are called *profit centers* and have been used since the 1930s.

PROFIT CENTERS AND RESULT CENTERS

One of the earliest pioneers of profit centers was General Motors.[15] But to avoid some of the complications of real life, we will use the GM experience to invent an imaginary example of profit centers from the business world: Consolidated Motors.[16]

Consolidated's Functional Structure

The Consolidated Motor Company is one of the largest car companies in the country. It turns out compact cars, luxury cars, and trucks. It uses a functional structure, with four functional sections, each headed by a sectional manager: purchasing (which buys all the steel, vinyl, aluminum, and other materials necessary for the cars), manufacturing (which actually makes all the cars and trucks), sales (which runs the marketing and sales operations), and legal (which handles legal matters). The line chart for this organization is given in Figure 9–2.

The functional structure of Consolidated Motors allows specialization, but it has great disadvantages in terms of feedback, as illustrated by the following situation: Consolidated's sales and profits drop 30 percent for the quarter, while those of its competitors rise. As soon as the figures are presented, the president of Consolidated calls the sales section manager, demanding to know why sales have fallen so dramatically. "Don't blame us," says the sales head, "We could never get the hot selling models from the manufacturing section. They kept sending us the slow sellers."

The head of the manufacturing section is questioned; she blames the purchasing section: "We wanted to manufacture more of the high-

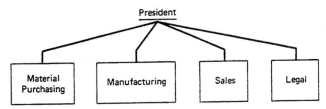

CONSOLIDATED MOTORS

Figure 9-2. A Functional Structure. Each component handles one aspect of the total process, which allows specialization and large economies of scale but obscures accountability and feedback on results.

selling models, but we could never get the particular material we needed from the purchasing section."

Not surprisingly, the head of the purchasing section blames legal for a mistaken opinion that hindered their operations, and the legal section head points the finger of blame elsewhere, too.

The president of Consolidated Motors realizes that the corporation is not doing well, but he cannot pinpoint the difficulty. The corporation is divided into functional sections, and no one section is responsible for its own costs and profits. Because each section is dependent on the others, the lapses of one affect the other, and pinpointing accountability—for good results or bad—is greatly hindered by the interrelatedness. Feedback, the heart of good management, is unclear.

Consolidated's Profit Center Structure

Consolidated Motors could turn out the exact same products by utilizing a profit center concept. A *profit center* is a self-contained subunit that controls both its own inputs and outputs (costs and revenues), and thus is responsible for its own profits. A private organization must structure itself along product lines to have profit centers.

Accordingly, Consolidated might have four different divisions: the compact cars division, the luxury car division, the truck division, and (retained from the old system) a legal division. Each car and truck division purchases its own materials, manufactures its own product, and sells the product. Thus each division controls its own costs and revenue (see Figure 9-3).

Now when the Consolidated president faces the same report of a 30 percent drop in corporation sales and profits, pinpointing the source of the difficulty is simpler because each division handles all the previously separate functions. It is possible to say which division incurred the loss (trucks down by 40 percent in sales and profits) and which are performing adequately (compact cars up by 8 percent). No longer must the president search all over the corporation for the difficulty; he has narrowed it down

CONSOLIDATED MOTORS

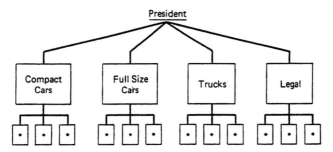

Figure 9-3. A Profit Center Structure. The third organizational level, marked here with asterisks, has two possibilities. The level can be divided on the basis of function again (e.g., the compact cars division divided into purchasing, sales, and manufacturing) or it can be a new level of profit centers (the compact cars division divided into family car and sport car subunits).

to the 25 percent of the corporation represented by the truck division. The use of profit centers has greatly increased the clarity of feedback about organizational performance.

The president may still not be satisfied, however; it is an extremely large corporation, and all he knows is that the difficulty lies within the 25 percent represented by the truck division. The idea of profit centers need not be restricted to just the first cut of an organization. Each of the profit centers mentioned can be divided further into smaller profit centers. Thus the truck division can have two semiautonomous profit centers within it—a heavy truck division and a pickup truck division—and both can handle their own purchasing, manufacturing, and sales. Thus the president of Consolidated can examine their profit statements to see which is responsible for the profit plunge. Feedback is yet more detailed and thus clearer.

Service-Oriented Profit Centers and Transfer Pricing

Until now, we have not discussed the legal department. How can it be made into a profit center since it only services the other divisions? The answer has been suggested in Chapter Two. The legal department should charge the other divisions of Consolidated Motors for its work. If these divisions would find it cheaper or more efficient to go outside to independent law firms, that choice is fine. If, at the end of the year, the legal division has lost money—indicating that it costs more to run than other divisions are willing to pay—it is a clear indication that the legal division's value is not as great as the money it costs. Perhaps the division will have to increase its efficiency. Or since it cannot maintain a profit even with all the advantages it has in handling only one type of law, perhaps it should be eliminated and outside firms used instead.

The new structure turns the legal division into a type of profit center, even though it sells its product not to outside customers but internally, to other divisions of the company. As we discussed in Chapter Two, the price that it charges other divisions for its legal services is termed a *transfer price*. A transfer price is a price charged for any service or product that is sold to other internal units rather than to outside customers.

Advantages of the Profit Center Structure

We have emphasized the clarity of feedback, but there are other advantages to a profit center structure. All of the profit centers of Consolidated Motors are free to band together to share an asset, such as a computer system, if that is cheaper than purchasing it separately. The parent corporation also provides the capital that any individual division may not be able to raise.

Thus the profit center structure, although a form of decentralization, also provides a number of advantages usually associated with centralization because an overall direction can be given from the top, with goals for each of the divisions. This ensures uniformity and coordination. (In the public sector, this setting of overall direction would also ensure greater political accountability.) The ability to share assets ensures economy of scale. All of these are the traits of a centralized organization.

However, a profit center structure imparts the advantages of decentralization as well. Because each profit center can pursue its goals for the year in any way it sees fit, it is likely to be more innovative, more responsive to changing conditions, and more flexible than if it had to await detailed directions from an isolated central office. The central office specifies goals such as profit, but these are well down the chain of outputs. It is up to the subunits to determine the means to achieve them. Moreover, because more power is given to lower organizational levels and there is less red tape, the morale of middle managers is likely to be higher.

Rarely can one have one's cake and eat it too, but the profit center structure is a close approximation. Through such centers, a decentralized organization can still retain many of the advantages that accompany centralization.

The Relationship of Profit Centers to Cost Centers

As discussed in Chapter Two, many public (and most private) organizations track their inputs by dividing their organization into cost centers. A cost center is any organizational activity or unit for which separate accounts are kept. For example, a private clinic can be broken into such cost centers as "patient intake" (which includes record-keeping and receptionist costs), "direct services," and "X-ray services." By keeping separate accounts for the costs incurred by each cost center, the clinic can better determine efficiency, plan budgets, and price services.

As we have noted, profit centers go one step beyond the concept of cost centers. A profit center is a cost center that also (1) tracks its own revenues and (2) has substantial autonomy. Thus, for the preceding example, "patient intake" is a cost center, but it probably cannot be turned into a profit center because attributing any revenues to it would be very difficult. But "X-ray services," by charging transfer prices, could easily be turned into an internal profit center. More radically, the clinic's structure (which now is somewhat functional) could also be changed. The clinic could be divided into such profit centers as "long-term care," "short-term care," "maternity services," "ambulance services," and "X-ray services." Each of these could be a profit center if separate accounts, tracking costs and revenues, were kept for each and if one person were clearly in charge of directing each center's activities.[17]

Profit centers (and result centers) can be "nested"—that is, profit centers can contain other profit centers, which in turn contain even smaller profit centers. Thus the clinic in the preceding example is a profit center, but it also contains smaller profit centers within itself.

Direct Application of Profit Centers to Public Organizations

The profit center concept antedates this century, but General Motors popularized it by pioneering its practical application in the 1930s. Today there are relatively few major companies that structure their operations entirely in terms of function; most use at least a modified form of the profit center concept.

The application of this concept to public organizations is less common. It is obviously more difficult to create profit centers in a nonprofit organization. We must distinguish two categories of public organizations: (1) those that sell their output, and therefore can directly utilize the profit center concept, and (2) those that cannot charge for services, and for whom profit centers present only indirect models. Let us look first at the first group.

Some public organizations charge for their services and receive revenues. Organizations that fall into this category include public colleges and universities, public hospitals, transit lines, housing projects, cafeterias and restaurants within public agencies, supply stores, and license bureaus. Their resemblance to private business profit centers is very strong. These organizations can be treated as profit centers, and both their costs and revenues can be monitored; often they can be broken into smaller, component profit centers as well. Of course, in government the goal is usually not to make a profit but to break even. However this difference is not crucial; turning these organizations into profit centers, with control over both their costs and revenues, will provide almost all of the benefits of enhanced goal setting and monitoring that are characteristic of a private sector profit center.

A number of public suborganizations could fall into this category if transfer pricing were introduced. For example, many large agencies have a motor pool. If the pool charged subunits for using vehicles, it would become an internal profit center. Many school districts maintain buses, used for field trips and other outings. Charging individual schools for the use of these buses would make them profit centers. (As discussed in Chapter Two, such charges at the local level are usually handled through internal service funds.)

Indirect Application of the Profit Center Concept: Result Centers

Most public agencies fall into a second category, however. They do not now sell their output and cannot begin doing so. Organizations such as public schools, defense departments, social service agencies and police forces cannot counterbalance costs with revenue because they receive no revenue. Thus the profit center concept cannot be used as a direct model. Nonetheless, the most important attributes of profit centers can be applied to these agencies as well: giving subunits clear control over inputs and outputs. We will term such cost centers with clear control over non-monetary outputs *result centers*.

Just as a profit center is built around a product, a result center is built around an output provided to clients. A result center has three characteristics: First, it is relatively *self-contained;* everyone charged with producing the output is within the result center. Second, it is given *autonomy* in deciding how to achieve its output. Third, its managers are held *accountable* because the output is monitored and reported back to headquarters.

Organizations structured primarily by purpose (function) or process have many advantages, but they usually cannot be divided into result centers. Functionally structured subunits, by definition, are built around narrow specializations. Such units must usually be centralized because only a strong center can put together all the specialized, narrow pieces. Accordingly, organizations structured by place or clientele are more likely candidates for result centers. If a management system is installed that provides the top of the organization with enough immediate and inter-mediate output data to hold these subunits accountable, and if the subunits are free to determine the means to reach their result-oriented goals, then they are result centers.

Many of the output measures we have discussed in the preceeding chapters can be used in a result center structure. For example a city police department might begin with a centralized, functional structure, with units for patrol, investigation, traffic, record keeping, and so forth. As the city grew larger, the department might move to a result center approach, with the department divided into four geographic districts, each one relatively self-sufficient. Each one would be responsible for all decisions in its area and would be held accountable only for results—such as crime rates, arrest and conviction rates, and citizens' complaints. Such units become result centers, and not just branches of the central administration, to the extent that they are given autonomy; but autonomy is possible only if the management system clearly tracks outputs so that the central administration can monitor overall achievements without specifying processes.

Because the output of result centers is measured in nonmonetary terms, such as students graduated, workers placed in new jobs, or felons convicted, output cannot be expressed as money and be directly compared to costs. Nevertheless, some of the advantages of a pure profit center remain under this approach: clear goals, clear lines of responsibility, clear accountability, and flexibility in the means of achieving the goals.

Moreover, result centers encourage goal congruence. Each individual's goal is more likely to be in accordance with the overall organizational goals if each individual is part of a relatively small unit, which does not have a narrow, functional goal but instead the more far-reaching goal of producing outputs for the organization's clients.[18]

When a public organization utilizes a result center structure, the top management can ask, "How well did you achieve your goals, using the resources we gave to you?" If the goals are not achieved, the subunit managers cannot obscure accountability by blaming others. There has been substantial interest and movement toward result centers in recent years; Florida, for example, has been a pioneer in decentralizing social services.[19] As management systems mature and better output measures are developed, more and more organizations will feel free to decentralize.

MATRIX ORGANIZATIONS

In many organizations, both public and private, it is impossible to use a permanent profit center or result center structure because the work of the organization changes rapidly, and therefore the outputs expected one month are different (and involve different organizational workers) from those of the previous month. This is especially characteristic of agencies that handle large changing projects, such as audit, legal, and research agencies.

It is sometimes possible to gain some of the advantages of a profit or result center structure nonetheless. Matrix organizations are a cross between a purely functional organization and one based on a result center. The permanent organizational structure of a matrix organization is function-based, with traditional sections for accounting, legal, research, and the various line activities. But the individual workers within these functional sections are assigned to official groups that focus on a single project that may last anywhere from weeks to years. Each project group has its own leader and its own budget. When the project is over the members of the group return to their "home" functional sections—the accountants to accounting, the lawyers to legal—until assigned to another project group. Each new project is likely to demand a different mix of skills, so members of one group are rarely reunited on the next project. When the project is ongoing, a central principle of the classical school is violated—that lines of authority should be clear, with only one supervisor per person. Members of a project group have two supervisors because they are formally responsible to the supervisor of their functional section and of their project.

If a major city employs such a project management approach, for example, it might set up a project group of thirty-one people to implement an important program to renovate the central business district. This project group of thirty-one would be headed by a planner and would include people from such functional divisions as the engineering, finance, planning, transportation, and zoning departments (see project A in Table 9–1).

The goal-setting stage of the management system—usually MBO for matrix organizations—is particularly important because of the two bosses. However, if handled correctly, the goal setting is clearer than under the pure functional lines of authority because everyone working together in the project has negotiated with the same boss, the project leader.

A matrix approach, like profit and result centers, establishes a clearly defined group, with clearly defined goals (i.e., output standards) and budgets (i.e., inputs) and clear lines of responsibility. All of these important feedback cues would be missing if the same city employees simply coordinated their work informally while all responsibility and budget control remained with the functional departments.

Profit and result centers allow comparison of performance from one year to the next because they are stable organizations. Because they are constantly changing, project groups within a matrix organization do not allow such year-to-year comparisons. But matrix organizations do provide clearly defined groups, each with its own clearly defined input and output, and so many of the coordination and feedback advantages of a profit or

TABLE 9–1 Example of a Matrix Organization: Number of Employees Assigned to Each Project

	Planning Department	Engineering Department	Legal Department	Finance Department	Transportation Department
Project A:					
Renovating central business district (2-year project)	2	22	1	2	4
Project B:					
New traffic laws/construction (6-month project)	1	6	2	—	8
Project C:					
Handling an annexation (3-month project)	3	—	1	1	—
Project D:					
(2-month project)	1	4	—	—	6
Unassigned: day-to-day operations	8	3	1	1	15

A matrix organization for a medium-sized city.

Every project member has two supervisors for the duration of the project. For example, the six members of engineering assigned to Project B are directed both by their functional superior (the head of the engineering department) and the project manager.

result center remain. It is not stretching too much, in fact, to characterize project groups as "temporary result centers."

TYING MANAGEMENT SYSTEMS TO STRUCTURE

As noted, management systems and structural arrangement both have many of the same effects. Manipulating structure can change information patterns and incentive patterns; the same results arise from manipulating management systems. The task, then, is to fit management systems and structures together in such a way that they complement each other.

Throughout this chapter we have discussed the types of information generated by different forms of structures. Thus our discussion here of the ties between management systems and structure can be short; we will simply explicitly connect some of the points made earlier.

The information generated by a management system reflects the structure of the organization. If the organization is functionally arranged, the management system will measure the output of the functional sections. Such functional information is usually found at the beginning of any chains of output for an organization. Because it is so early in the chain, the information is much more difficult to relate to the organization's overall success or failure. Information generated by result centers, on the other hand, is more often about outputs further down the chain.

Let us illustrate by using the example of a (very simplified) state job-training agency that is divided functionally. Within the agency are three functional sections:

1. *Training section,* which contains the dozens of trainers of all types who provide the classroom instruction
2. *Placement section,* which contains the many placement specialists who seek job openings and help place students once they have completed the classroom training
3. *Survey section,* made up of curriculum experts who survey the marketplace to learn job needs and then revamp courses to meet the ever-changing needs of area employers

Within each of these functional sections, employees can become highly specialized because they handle a high volume of cases. The management system would gather information on the performance of each functional section. For example, the training sections would be evaluated by such measures as number of pupils taught and student evaluations of courses. The section in charge of surveying market needs and changing curriculum would be evaluated by such measures as number of employers contacted and number of courses restructured. These measures for the trainers and the curriculum experts are important, but they are at the very beginning of the output chain and are not clearly connected to the desired ultimate outputs: placement of pupils into high-paying, long-lasting jobs. Even the functional section most closely connected to these long-range outputs—the placement section—could plausibly blame bad performance on the poor teaching of the trainers or the poor performance of the curriculum experts in responding to changing employer needs.

If the same organization were structured into result centers, each result center would handle a certain number of students, perhaps two or three hundred. Each center would include a number of trainers of all types, a curriculum expert who surveyed the marketplace to determine training needs, and one or more people who placed students after training was completed. The result center as a whole would be held responsible for attaining a series of immediate and intermediate output indicators, such as number of pupils initially placed, number holding jobs after a period of time, starting salary, and salary after one year. These are measures far further down the chain of outputs. The head of the result center could be held accountable in a way that the head of the functional sections could not because it is difficult to blame outsiders for any poor results. Coordination is enhanced, and the management system is delivering information less prone to displacement and more likely to reflect results directly.

CHOOSING AN ORGANIZATIONAL STRUCTURE

Because decentralized result centers are comparatively new in the public sector, we have emphasized their many advantages. They should be used more. But as noted, there are many reasons why some public agencies will and should continue to use functional structures. Some depend heavily on specialization. For example, most of us would prefer that a hospital remain functionally organized and that radiologists not dabble in surgery. Also, agencies might maintain functional, centralized structures to ensure political control. Especially if the agency deals with politically hot issues (such as city planning or any type of regulation) it would be undesirable to have each subunit making its own rules. Therefore functional arrangements continue to be the best approach when uniformity, specialization, or top control are especially important.

Once a structure is chosen, the management system must be designed to meet its particular needs. In a functional organization, top executives must adjust the management system by gathering more data (because the data will be fragmentary), sharing the data more widely (because coordination is a constant problem), and being especially vigilant for displacement (because functional units tend to focus on their specialization rather than the organizational end products).

Functional arrangements will continue to have a very important role in public sector organizations. However, managers should not routinely opt for functional arrangements without considering the alternatives, as many seem to do now. The gains in creativity, responsiveness and accountability all make result centers a choice too rarely taken.

SUMMARY

Especially at the highest levels, structural manipulation is often a political act, designed to emphasize symbolic commitment, to demote enemies, or to appear efficiency-minded. Structure is not politically neutral; it affects power. At middle and lower levels, structural manipulation is more often a tool of efficiency, although politics is never entirely absent.

Too often managers in public agencies treat organizational structure as an immutable constraint, even when the managers, in fact, have considerable power to change the structure to suit their needs. Instead of thinking about whether the organization is too centralized or decentralized to suit their particular needs for coordination, specialization, or flexibility, many managers take their structure as given and then attempt to work around it through their management systems. This approach is inefficient; managers should aggressively manipulate their structure, viewing it as one more tool for achieving their ends.

Classical organization theory suggests that organizations should be structured by place, clientele, process, or function. Of these four, function (purpose) is the most common choice. A functional structure allows specialization, but it often obscures managerial accountability.

A related choice facing managers is between centralization and decentralization. Functional structures are usually centralized because only a strong center can coordinate all the specialized subunits. On the other hand, decentralized structures often require organizational members to be generalists. A centralized organization has such advantages as easier political control, increased specialization, uniformity of procedure and rules throughout its service area, and economies of scale. But a decentralized organization has advantages of greater speed of response, more flexibility, and higher morale.

Most public agencies must continue to be structured along a more centralized, functional format because of requirements of uniformity, politics, or central control. But agencies that would profit from flexibility and a quick response time are increasingly decentralizing through a result center format.

A result center is a government subunit modeled on the private sector's profit center. Just as a profit center is a subunit built around a product, a result center is built around an output that is provided to the public. All those involved in producing that output are housed together in a single result center. The organization's headquarters gives each of its result centers a great deal of freedom of action but holds them accountable for results. Therefore, like several of the other tools discussed in this book, result centers are an example of "control by specifying outputs." On the other hand, many functionally based subunits do not produce clear, freestanding outputs that can be readily monitored; headquarters then is often forced to use "control by specifying processes."

Like a profit center, a result center is a decentralized unit that still retains some of the advantages of centralization. An organization divided into result centers has economies of scale, uniform goal setting, and clear accountability, like centralized agencies, but wide discretion at middle and lower levels, like decentralized agencies.

Organizational structure affects management systems in several ways. Often, different structures will change the raw data fed into management systems—for example, functional units will generate data that lie earlier on the output chain. Structure also affects the primary purpose of the management system. Different organizational structures will present different primary needs. For example, coordination will be more important to an organization with functional subunits, but maintaining uniformity will be more important to an organization divided into result centers. Management systems should accordingly be adapted to the structure in which they operate.

REVIEW QUESTIONS

1. Give examples of how each of the four traditional structural patterns could be applied to a
   a. state health agency.
   b. city department of streets and sanitation.
   c. county income maintenance (welfare) department.
2. Why does a functionally based organization allow more specialization than a clientele-based one? Give an example.
3. What are some of the basic principles of classical orthodoxy?
4. What problems arise in following the classical theory guidelines for determining how programs should be located within any organization? Use an example of an inoculation program for first-graders.
5. How can political goals be furthered by manipulating the structure of public agencies?
6. Indicate the ways in which the advantages of centralization are the

opposite of those for decentralization. Use a statewide group of free clinics as an example.

7. Define a profit center and a transfer price.

8. Which advantages of centralization and decentralization does a result center provide? Which does it not provide?

9. Name three organizations that could use a matrix organizational structure and two for which it would be inappropriate. Why?

10. In what ways will the choice of structure change the information generated by a management system? Why?

11. In what way will the choice of structure change the primary missions of management systems? Why?

12. Name several organizations for which a result center structure would be appropriate and several for which it would be inappropriate. Why?

SUGGESTED FURTHER READING

JAMES W. FESLER. *Area and Administration.* University: University of Alabama Press, 1949. A classic analysis of how government bureaucracies can reconcile functional and areal considerations.

LUTHER GULICK and L. URWICK, eds. *Papers on the Science of Administration.* New York: Institute of Public Administration, 1937. Definitive statement of the classical approach to organizational structure.

CHRISTOPHER HOOD and ANDREW DUNSIRE. *Bureaumetrics.* University: University of Alabama Press, 1981. A very ambitious, ground-breaking attempt to establish the methodology for measuring qualities of public organizations, especially their structure.

HAROLD SEIDMAN and ROBERT GILMOUR. *Politics, Position and Power,* 4th ed. New York: Oxford University Press, 1986. Description and analysis of the interaction of politics and structure at the federal level.

HERBERT SIMON. *Administrative Behavior,* 3rd ed. New York: Free Press, 1976. Latest edition of the famous attack on the classical approach to administration.

PETER SZANTON, ed. *Federal Reorganization: What Have We Learned?* Chatham, NJ: Chatham House Publishers, 1981. Essays on structure and organizational design.

Case 9-1

The state department of natural resources oversees forty-eight large lakes, a 100-mile ocean shoreline, and twenty major state parks in a large eastern state. Its duties include issuing boating, fishing, and hunting licenses; policing the lakes, parks, and ocean front, particularly for license violations; dredging old lakes and creating new ones; and offering tours and protecting wildlife.

The department has more than 1,900 employees and is divided into six bureaus:

Administration (100 employees): Handles computer processing, information systems, budgeting, and other staff functions.

Biology and Wildlife (200 employees): Studies wildlife on location and through laboratories; protects declining populations; stocks lakes with fish.

Safety (600 employees): Teaches firearm safety and water safety; gives firearm training to hunters; hires and trains lifeguards; marks trails.

Enforcement (500 employees): Issues licenses; patrols all recreation areas for license violations and for all legal offenses.

Engineering (450 employees): Designs and builds new recreation areas; maintains existing areas; builds access roads; dredges lakes.

Tourism (100 employees): Gives tours; designs and posts directional signs; handles advertising for tourists.

Robert Townes has recently been appointed head of the department, and he is dissatisfied with its performance. In particular, Townes believes that the current organizational structure is cumbersome. Part of the problem, he believes, is that the employees located in one park area must report to six different bureaus in the state capital. This system, he believes, hinders day-to-day cooperation.

Townes is unclear about how he might improve this situation. He is also unclear about whether he should counterbalance any move toward more decentralization of structure by increasing the number of instructions in the department's 200-page manual that is meant to guide day-to-day operations in the field.

1. Suggest an alternative, result center structure for the organization. Illustrate your new structure through an organizational chart, showing at least two organizational levels below Townes. Indicate the strengths and weaknesses of the new structure in comparison to the existing one.

2. What type of information reported back to headquarters is generated by the current structure? How will the information generated be different under the new suggested structure? Illustrate by examples.

3. Should Townes draw up tighter instructions in the department's manual to counterbalance the changes in your new structure?

ENDNOTES

1. Harold Seidman and Robert Gilmour, *Politics, Position and Power,* 4th ed. (New York: Oxford University Press, 1986), chapter 2.

2. A. Peter Grier, "Interior Department Shuffle," *Christian Science Monitor,* January 10, 1985, p. 1.

3. Jimmy Carter ran for the presidency in 1976 by emphasizing how, as governor of Georgia, he had used reorganization to increase efficiency. Yet here, too, power was a major motive. One of the primary purposes of Governor Carter's reorganization in Georgia was to increase his own power by lessening the power of bodies, such as the state board of health, that could be expected to oppose him. Laurence E. Lynn, Jr., *The State and Human Services* (Cambridge, MA: MIT Press, 1980), p. 30. Carter's federal reorganization attempts are discussed in Seidman and Gilmour, *Politics, Position and Power,* chapter 5.

   A number of interesting illustrations of the way that organizational structure responds to (and in turn, shapes) politics is contained in Jack H. Knott and Gary J. Miller, *Reforming Bureaucracy: The Politics of Institutional Choice* (Englewood Cliffs, NJ: Prentice-Hall, 1987).

4. One of the very strongest studies to go beyond anecdote and really attempt to find managerial gains in megareorganization is James Conant, "Reorganization and the Bottom Line," *Public Administration Review,* 46, no. 1 (January/February 1986), 48–56. Conant's study of New Jersey is useful for its careful methodology in attempting to document the always slippery "cost avoidance." He tentatively finds some modest savings from the reorganization. The same author provides a good, fifty-state overview of recent reorganization efforts in "In the Shadow of Wilson and Brownlow: Executive Branch Reorganization in the States, 1965 to 1987," *Public Administration Review,* 48, no. 5 (September/October 1988), 892–902.

5. Hawthorne studies are covered in F. J. Roethlisberger and William J. Dickson, *Management and the Worker* (Cambridge, MA: Harvard University Press, 1939).

6. Formal structure can affect informal structure, of course. See, for example, Stephen Maynard-Moody, Donald T. Stull, and Jerry Mitchell, "Reorganization as a Status Drama: Building, Maintaining and Displacing Dominant Subcultures," *Public Administration Review,* 46, no. 3 (July/August 1986), 301–10. The term *human relations school,* as used broadly here would include such researchers as Elton Mayo, Abraham Maslow, Douglas McGregor, and Chris Argyris.

7. Luther Gulick, "Notes on the Theory of Organization," in Luther Gulick and L. Urwick, eds., *Papers on the Science of Administration* (New York: Institute of Public Administration, 1937), pp. 1–45.

   Other important works in this tradition include Frederick W. Taylor, *The Principles of Scientific Management* (New York: Harper

& Row, 1911); and Henri Fayol, *General and Industrial Management* (London: Pitman, 1949; first published in 1919).

8. There has been some recent interest in this topic. For example, one of the most famous contemporary management consultants has suggested that there be no more than six levels in a business organization. See Tom Peters, "Why Small Staffs Do Better," *New York Times,* April 21, 1985, p. 1F.

9. An intriguing attempt to develop an objective series of rules for determining which agencies should be grouped together is John M. Boyle, "Reorganization Reconsidered: An Empirical Approach to the Departmentalization Problem," *Public Administration Review,* 39, no. 5 (September/October 1979). Boyle utilizes factor analysis in determining the amount of interdependence among government agencies, with the idea of combining the most interdependent.

10. U.S. Commission on the Organization of the Executive Branch of Government, *General Management of the Executive Branch* (Washington, DC: U.S. Government Printing Office, February 1949), report No. 1, pp. 34–35.

11. Martin Landau, "Redundancy, Rationality and the Problem of Duplication and Overlap," *Public Administration Review,* 29, no. 4 (July/August 1969), 346–58.

12. Peter Szanton, "What Are We Talking About, and Why?" in Peter Szanton, ed., *Federal Reorganization* (Chatham, NJ: Chatham House Publishers, 1981), p. 28.

13. Herbert Simon, "The Proverbs of Administration," *Public Administration Review,* 6 (Winter 1946), 53–67; also Herbert Simon, *Administrative Behavior,* 3rd ed. (New York: Free Press, 1976; first published in 1947).

14. What we do know about how structure can improve organizational efficiency and effectiveness is surprisingly sparse. See Dan R. Dalton et al., "Organization Structure and Performance: A Critical Review," *Academy of Management Journal,* January 1980, pp. 49–64.

    See also Barry Bozeman, "Organizational Structures and The Effectiveness of Public Agencies," *International Journal of Public Administration,* 4, no. 2 (1982). After a review of representative sections of the literature, Bozeman concludes that we have far less knowledge than the amount of research about structure's effects should have produced. He goes on to suggest reasons for our ignorance. His extensive reference section lists 159 relevant works.

15. The classic work on how profit centers were established in American businesses is Alfred D. Chandler, Jr., *Strategy and Structure: Chapters*

in the History of the American Industrial Enterprise (Cambridge, MA: MIT Press, 1962).

16. Although I do not know any specific work beyond Chandler that originated this example (and that could be cited here), variations of this example appear widely in business texts.

17. An interesting discussion of how cost centers within large market bureaucracies often lack feedback (like nonmarket organizations) and how they can be revitalized by becoming profit centers is Frances Gaither Tucker and Seymour M. Zivan, "A Xerox Cost Center Imitates a Profit Center," *Harvard Business Review*, May/June 1985, pp. 168–70.

18. For a related but distinct argument for keeping organizations small and self-contained, see Leonard R. Sayles, "Organizational Size, Effectiveness, and Human Values," *Administration and Society*, November 1987, pp. 328–45.

19. Florida's Department of Health and Rehabilitative Services (HRS) began the reorganization effort in 1975 and worked on it for over a decade. The department moved from "a conventional, hierarchical structure with nine politically independent divisions into a unified, functionally integrated, geographically decentralized structure under the control of generalist managers." C. Allen W. Imershein et al., "Service Networks in Florida: Administrative Decentralization and Its Effect on Service Delivery," *Public Administration Review*, 46, no. 2 (March/April 1986), pp. 162ff.

    Although the Imershein article is generally positive, a more negative evaluation of the same experiment is Les Garner, "Managing Change Through Organization Structure," *The Journal of State Government*, 1988, pp. 191–95. Garner concludes that the experiment did not succeed because the Florida result center managers were never given sufficient authority. He calls for better management systems as a first step toward improvement.

chapter ten

Connecting Productivity Improvement Efforts to Management Systems

INTRODUCTION

Productivity Defined

As discussed in Chapter Six, *productivity* is defined differently by different authors. Technically, it is a measure of immediate output compared to input; in other words, it is a measure of efficiency. Chapter Six examined the most commonly used quantitative measure of productivity: output divided by input and compared to a base year.

But the term *productivity* is also used more broadly. Most managers will speak of "productivity improvement efforts," using the term *productivity* as a synonym for *efficiency,* with some overtones of *effectiveness* as well. Adopting that broader definition here, we will discuss ways of improving organizational productivity—that is, increasing the quantity and quality of the organizational output.

Most government managers wish to increase their organization's productivity. Some earlier chapters, particularly Chapter Eight on rewards, primarily looked at how management systems affect workers' behavior; this can of course raise productivity. Now we will focus primarily on the second way of increasing productivity—managers making productivity-improving *decisions* in response to a problem indicated by the system's readings.

We have had less to say about such specific decisions than about the management systems that inform them. There is a good reason for this. Because *productivity* is a single term, it is easy to fall into the trap of treating it as a single, real object that can be pursued in the same way at different government levels and in all types of agencies. But there are no specific approaches to improving productivity that apply to all agencies at all levels because productivity is not a single, isolated attribute. Productivity simply means doing the job better and, not surprisingly, ways of doing the job better differ with the jobs involved; productivity improvements for delivering the mail often have little in common with those for delivering health services.

Therefore, we have concentrated on ways of monitoring organizational input and output; monitoring systems share similar characteristics across even very different government programs. Specific remedial actions, on the other hand, are not shared across different programs, and so they are more difficult to discuss; each manager is often the best judge of action if there are shortfalls. However, although many of the improvements must be job-specific, there are nonetheless some useful broad guidelines.

In response to a management system that indicates an unsatisfactory level of productivity, managers should look toward innovations that can be grouped within three broad categories: capital investment, personnel factors, and methods improvement.[1] These categories, which can act as a type of checklist for a manager interested in improving productivity, will very briefly be surveyed in this chapter.

INCREASING PRODUCTIVITY: CAPITAL INVESTMENT

The major part of all recent government productivity gains stems from improved equipment and facilities—in other words, from capital investment. In particular, the computer has produced a real revolution in the handling of paperwork; and many recent productivity gains have resulted from the computerization of formerly manual record-keeping activities.[2] However, as the number of uncomputerized record-keeping activities diminishes, other forms of capital investment have gained more attention.

A large number of innovations have been successful:

- Word processing equipment has greatly expedited clerical tasks.
- Scanning machines can now read and sort for filing tasks, and such machines are already used heavily by the post office to read addresses automatically.

- Robotics handles private sector manufacturing tasks and seems close to public sector adaptation.
- Larger, high-pressure hoses and "slippery" (chemically treated) water have greatly improved the efficiency of fire departments.[3]
- New forms of trucks have enabled sanitation departments to achieve large gains, in part because the trucks require fewer people to run.[4]

Disincentives to Capital Investment

All these innovations, and most others, require a substantial initial outlay of money. Despite the fact that capital investment has proven to be the quickest, surest way to productivity improvement, it is probably the productivity path most blocked by red tape and other structural disincentives.

A major problem at the federal level, for example, is the lack of a separate capital budget. Thus all capital investments, even those paying for themselves quickly, must be financed out of current funds.[5] All such investment options compete with (and generally lose to) regular operating expenses. A manager with a tightly stretched budget of $400,000 usually cannot carve out $80,000 for a capital expenditure, no matter how much it would save in future years. Because there are almost no provisions for spreading the costs of capital investment over time, this "lumpiness" problem makes capital investment very difficult. These disincentives lead to the economically irrational use of funds, such as repairing old equipment over and over rather than spending a little more just once to buy new equipment.

A second problem that plagues all levels of government is long lead times. Because the budget process is usually very slow, eighteen to thirty-six months often elapse between the recognition of a capital investment opportunity and the actual appropriation approval and purchase. The request for a capital investment must make its way up through at least several levels of the executive branch to final approval. Then it must be submitted to the legislature, and hearings must be held. Finally, if approved, the funds must be released to the agency and the procurement process begun. During the elapsed time many capital investments could pay for themselves several times over.

Ways of Overcoming Investment Obstacles

Ways to overcome these disincentives to capital investment have been tried experimentally in a number of jurisdictions. These solutions share a common approach: The money for productivity investment is made available to the agency outside the normal budget process in order to move quickly; the agency must then pay it back.

For large projects one option is the establishment of *productivity banks,* under the control of the state budget office. Agencies can apply to the bank for loans for capital improvements that would increase productivity. The bank would screen loan applications like a private bank, looking at the amortization potential of the projects proposed. The bank's operating costs are paid out of interest on the loans, with a lien on the agency's future appropriations as collateral. This proposal is self-policing because the agency must pay back the amount borrowed. Therefore it is unlikely that the agency will "cheat" by using productivity-increasing funds for other purposes. Once established, a productivity bank is capable of handling large projects if the legislature gives it enough initial funding.

Such a bank could not be used for smaller agency projects because of procedural costs, but these projects could be handled by a second capital investment option—*productivity funds.* Productivity funds are lump sums carved out of existing appropriations and set aside for small capital investments. Project approval is decentralized to quite low management levels, lowering application approval time to thirty days or less. This is an easily implemented approach, although the necessity of carving the fund out of existing appropriations means that it is probably limited to small investments. A combination of productivity banks with productivity funds, however, provides the necessary flexibility for large or small capital investments.[6]

Because capital investments—in both the public and private sectors—have produced the lion's share of all productivity improvements, *public managers should look first to capital investment possibilities when pursuing productivity improvement.* Such investments are likely to continue to be the single most important path toward increased efficiency. They often return dramatic improvements; moreover, they are permanent and cannot be reversed by changes in organizational or political climate.[7]

INCREASING PRODUCTIVITY: PERSONNEL FACTORS

Structuring work to meet the psychological needs of workers (sometimes called "human factors") is a second important pathway to increased productivity. This area has undergone a number of semantic changes over the years. By the 1990s it was often subsumed within discussions of "organizational culture."[8] We will return to the topic of organizational culture shortly, but first it is useful to look at some discrete approaches to meeting the psychological needs of organizational members.

We must begin by separating two concepts that many managers mistakenly intertwine: workers' happiness and workers' productivity. Many popular treatments of the 1950s and 1960s tightly linked personal satisfaction and job performance. As one expert told a management seminar about these popular beliefs, often spread by consultants,

> [It] was broad and diffuse, but, if it had any definable core, it was a faith best expressed in the slogan "the happy worker is a productive worker."
>
> The only trouble with this simplistic faith is that, like a lot of such simple principles, it turns out not to be true. Happy workers are not always productive and productive workers are not always happy. Although there is a modest positive correlation between the two, it is all too modest to guide us in designing jobs, organizations, or our own behavior as managers.[9]

However, job satisfaction is not a completely isolated attribute; if it does not affect the quantity of output, it does modestly affect the quality. Some private industry experiments have indicated that generally satisfied workers engage in less sabotage and have lower output rejection rates. Moreover, there is less absenteeism and lower turnover in plants with satisfied workers. Since hiring and training new employees requires both time and money, there are real economic savings from greater job satisfaction, although such economic benefits are neither as direct nor as dramatic as was once hoped.[10]

Fragmentary evidence suggests that government employees may have somewhat less job satisfaction than their private sector counterparts.[11] Thus there is a lot of work to be done. There are at least several dozen widely tried approaches to improving workers' environment to improve productivity.[12] We will examine three of the most important: flextime; job enrichment; and participative management, including quality circles.

Flextime

Already adopted by many private businesses, flextime allows employees to set their own working hours. Some units allow four days of ten hours (called 4/40); most insist that the workers put in eight hours per day, but they are allowed to choose any eight hours from, say, 6:00 A.M. to 6:00 P.M. Such guidelines provide a core period (10:00 A.M. to 2:00 P.M.) during which all workers are present to facilitate meetings and cooperation, while still providing a great deal of discretion in choosing hours. Flextime greatly eases the problems of coordination for two-worker households, and it all but eliminates work lost through tardiness because the worker's day starts when he or she arrives. But most important, it gives workers more control over their lives; not surprisingly, questionnaires indicate an overwhelmingly positive reaction to flextime, so it seems a successful experiment even if measured only in terms of employees' satisfaction.[13] Many states and localities employ some form of flextime (also called *flexitime*), and the federal government has allowed it on an "experimental" but still widespread basis for more than a decade. Currently 20 percent of the federal work force (and 13 percent of private sector workers) are covered by flextime.[14]

Job Enrichment

Job enrichment is an old idea whose time, seemingly, has come again. It holds that the undeniable mechanical advantages derived from splitting work processes into small, repeatable actions are outweighed by the psychological disadvantages, because such repetitive tasks create boredom, which leads to more mistakes and workers' discontent. Under job enrichment programs, workers are assigned wider tasks, involving a larger number of steps, so that they can more easily see the results of their efforts.

Job enrichment attempts to improve the job in at least one of three dimensions:

a. autonomy, or freedom in carrying out the task;
b. diversity, or variety of tasks; and
c. wholeness; or the worker's ability to gain a sense of closure by seeing both the beginning and end of the task.[15]

Some private industries have attempted to enrich jobs by creating work team arrangements, under which one group may assemble an entire car from beginning to end, for example. In government, one worker may process the same application through four of five steps, rather than a different worker processing each step. Job-enrichment programs are primarily designed to increase workers' satisfaction, and thus they are often considered successful if satisfaction increases while productivity remains at its preprogram level.[16] However, Civil Service regulations may discourage some such programs because job enrichment often forces up the Civil Service classifications of each employee slot (from GS3 to GS5, for example), thus costing the agency more wages for the same output. Despite these obstacles, more than half of all local governments report using job-enrichment approaches, especially team-based methods.[17]

Job Participation

In job-participation approaches, workers take an active part in shaping job procedures. MBO is a form of participation management, although it has other aspects (e.g., goal tracking) as well. Theory Z and other nonhierarchical approaches are also implemented under this category.[18]

Quality circles are one of the most recent and widespread forms of job participation. A *quality circle* (QC) is a voluntary group of workers who have a shared area of responsibility.[19] The workers meet regularly, usually for an hour per week, to discuss quality problems in their work area and to jointly work toward solutions. These meetings are voluntary, on company time, and unsupervised by management.

The QC approach originated in Japan, but it seems to work well in other cultures.[20] When QC has been instituted in American companies, results have often been impressive.[21] In the public sector, it is widely used at all government levels; at least nineteen state governments report such programs, for example.[22] Because QCs are new, they do not have a long-term government record by which to judge their effects, but rigorous studies do seem to indicate real benefits.[23] Quality circles draw their strength from the intimate, hands-on work knowledge of their members. In Missouri, for example, printing press operators spent a half hour each day searching for printing materials in unorganized storage areas. The QC's solution was to purchase shelves to store and organize the material. The shelves cost $2,100, but the benefit in time (salary) saved was $26,400 per year.[24]

At a federal shipyard, workers had to wait at different locations to pick up different types of tools. The QC changed the process so that all tools were available at all tool distribution locations. Average waiting time was reduced from twelve minutes to five, with an estimated savings (in lost time) of $200,000 annually.[25]

The voluntary nature of QCs is very important. Some Japanese firms have put so much pressure on workers to join and use quality circles that misreporting has become widespread. Twenty percent of Japanese companies have reported such practices as fabricating ghost QC meetings and inflated reports of QC activities.[26] Quality circles work only if the workers are *willingly* coming together to improve their jobs for themselves as well as their employers.

Research in this broad area of personnel factors is very difficult. Two problems hinder any confident assessment of experiments in this field: (1) the lack of rigorous measurements and controls and (2) the difficulty of neutralizing the Hawthorne effect, which leads personnel to react positively to *any* nonthreatening changes in their routine.

However, as noted, the large numbers of studies that have been done consistently indicate that, counter to the intuition of most managers, a happier employee is not necessarily a more productive one. Nonetheless, pursuing increased workers' satisfaction is very important. It is important in its own right because people should be satisfied with their jobs, but it is also important for its instrumental effects. Increased satisfaction can reduce job stress, absenteeism, and turnover.

Can Organizational Culture Be Changed?

Such techniques as quality circles or job enlargement are attempts to change the way that a worker interacts with the rest of the organization. In recent years, these and similar approaches are often thought of as part of the broader topic of organizational culture. The concern with culture began in the business world, and each year dozens of articles on the topic appear in business magazines, and large numbers of consultants are kept busy analyzing and attempting to change the culture of companies. More recently, government agencies have also begun to focus on their culture.

Organizational culture comprises the collective *values* and *beliefs* of an organization's members. The culture develops over a number of years and is passed on to new organizational members. The culture of an organization is reflected in its symbols (e.g., its most respected and talked-about past leader) and its institutional rhetoric ("If there is one thing we stand for here, it is . . ."). But most importantly, an organization's culture is reflected in the actions of both management and workers. Some organizations have cultures that are not conducive to success; they encourage rigid patterns of behavior and distrust between managers and workers, for example. Other private and public organizations have cultures that encourage success, with such components as a clear sense of mission, strong commitment to the organization, trust between levels, and flexible responses to the environment.

Organizational culture is a very useful concept, but at the same time it is not a dramatically new idea. Most of the concerns that are covered under the topic of culture are simply different aspects of matters that have concerned managers for decades: participation, internal communication, morale, and commitment.

The best-known treatment of organizational culture is a book by Thomas J. Peters and Robert H. Waterman, Jr., *In Search of Excellence.* Although the treatment of the topic was aimed at nonscholars, the authors drew a number of their basic concepts from academic research, and their own ideas on the topic in turn led yet other researchers into the area.[27]

Many of the approaches considered in this and previous chapters can be fitted within the organizational culture framework. To return to Peters and Waterman as useful synthesizers, they emphasize keeping staffs lean and decentralizing to self-contained units (e.g., result centers). They emphasize that managers should not base their decisions entirely on data generated by formal reports. Instead, they say, managers should gather additional, nonformal data through MBWA (management by walking around), which echoes the reasonable person approach to gathering and evaluating reports. They call for an overall "loose-tight" approach, that is, holding managers accountable for broad goals but providing a great deal of freedom on details, much as a good MBO system would do.

Above all, they call for generating intense commitment to the organization as the single greatest path to success, and they view participation as one important way of generating it.

Can organizational culture be changed? Yes, but managers at the same time must be wary of accepting oversimplifications,[28] often on the part of unscrupulous consultants. These consultants, although a small minority, often have gained the most publicity by overselling the benefits of each new approach in the human factors area. This initial overpromising in turn led to inevitable disappointment and disillusionment.

Organizational culture fits into this unfortunate historic pattern. As it became more popular, the concept of culture was oversimplified by some consultants, who promised quick cures for ailing organizations. Improving the morale and commitment of an agency's workers is a difficult task. Such attitudes are often the result of patterns, personalities, and symbols that have a long organizational history. Accordingly it often takes a long time to change them completely.

At the same time, however, problems caused by overselling should not be allowed to obscure real, if often undramatic, results. Organizational culture can be changed. Goal setting, with rewards tied to the goals, is an important part of this change. The new goals signal the new values of the organization, and the rewards encourage members to excel. Similarly, participation-enhancing approaches such as MBO and decentralization, and autonomy-increasing approaches such as flextime, quality circles, and job enlargement, can play very important and useful roles in increasing the morale and commitment of organizational members.

INCREASING PRODUCTIVITY: METHODS IMPROVEMENT

Work methods improvement involves analyzing a job or procedure, step by step, and then determining whether performance could be improved through such means as changing the physical layout, eliminating unnecessary steps, or combining some steps. Methods improvement can raise the specter of New Taylorism, with time-and-motion studies and "one best way" of accomplishing tasks. Although this level is occasionally approached by isolated programs in some blue-collar areas, for the most part practitioners in this field are more sophisticated; they help simplify work procedures and eliminate needless paperwork or other procedural steps. Nonetheless, this is the most job-specific category. Although it is often important, few things can be said about methods improvement in general. Each task must be separately evaluated to eliminate unnecessary steps or to find new ways of handling the job.[29]

Methods improvement often begins with the development of a pro-

cess chart, which is simply a record of each step of a work process. For
example, a process chart for a university registration office might be
developed for the procedure of submitting a course change. It would track
each step (fill out form, get form approved, enter form in computer,
receive hard copy, file hard copy, etc.). A process chart can be developed
by workers who actually perform the function or by an outside observer.
A process chart is very standardized, with conventional symbols for each
type of action, such as inspection, transport, delay, and storage. (Chart
symbols are shown in Figure 10–1.)[30]

Once a process chart has been developed, the analysts try to determine
whether any of the steps could be eliminated, shortened, or perhaps
handled by lower-skilled (and lower-paid) personnel. In the preceding
example, if secretaries in the university's registration office carry material
to different offices several times an hour, the analyst would try to determine
whether some of the trips could be replaced by a phone call, or if not,
whether some of them could be routinely combined.[31]

One of the more notable methods improvement developments has
been in federal procurement. The amount of paperwork and time spent
on buying small items for the federal government has been cut dramatically
by the use of government-issued credit cards. The federal government
now requires that all purchases under $2,500 be made by credit card
instead of using the purchase orders, invoices, and separate payments of
the old system. This new procedure is expected to save over $100 million
annually in time and vendor discounts.[32]

As noted earlier, most improvements in work methods are extremely
job specific. Accordingly, methods improvements must usually be considered on a case-by-case basis. See Table 10–1 for some examples of
potential areas of improvement.

IMPROVEMENT METHODS IN PERSPECTIVE

Although we have examined separately each of the three types of productivity improvement actions, they can and should be considered together. San Diego has gone one step further by having the same people
who handle human relations (organizational development) simultaneously
handle work methods improvement.[33] This system greatly increases the
likelihood that work methods improvement will be handled sensitively,
and that employees will be viewed as people as well as workers. New
York's and New Jersey's successful productivity efforts did not combine
the techniques as formally as did San Diego, but they too were careful
to use approaches borrowed from all three fields of capital investment,
personnel, and work methods.[34]

Unfortunately, although there are numerous success stories, they are

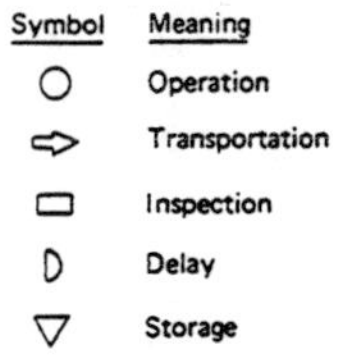

Symbol	Meaning
○	Operation
⇒	Transportation
□	Inspection
D	Delay
▽	Storage

The five distinct symbols of a process flowchart.

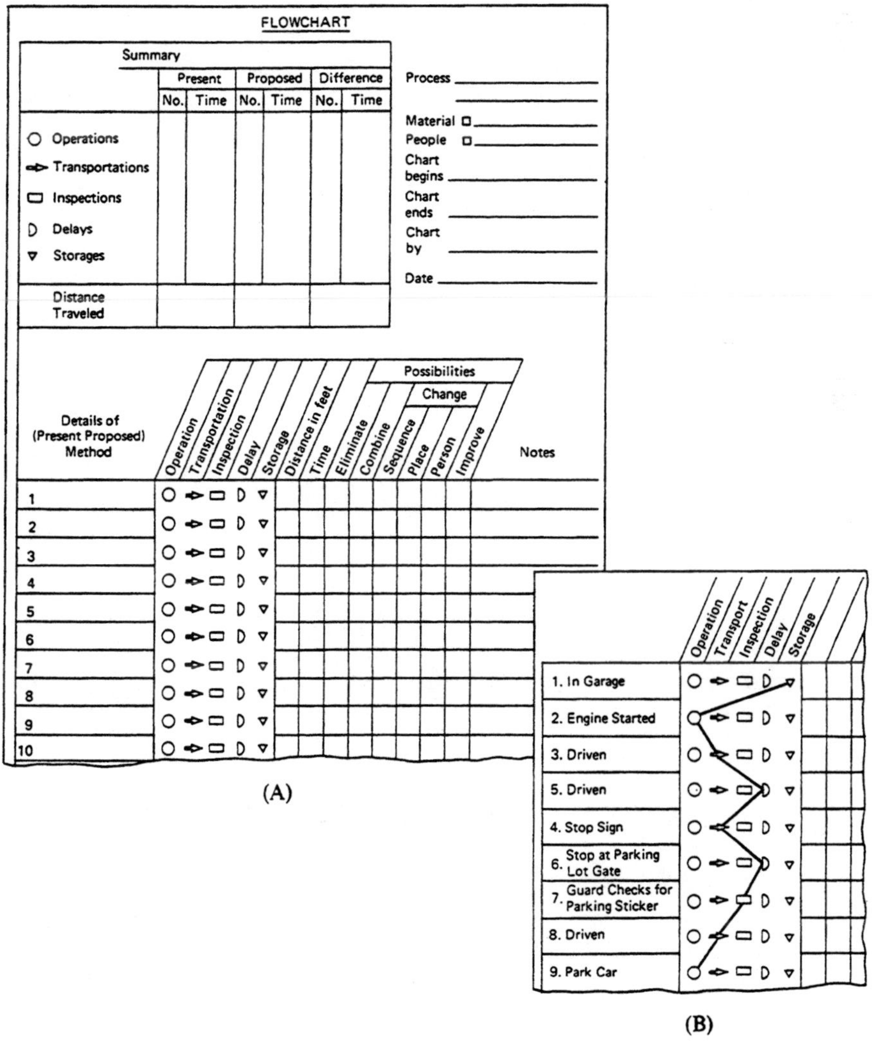

(A)

(B)

Figure 10–1. (A) A preprinted flowchart format. (B) Flowchart of a car being driven to work in the morning. Source: David Bain, *The Productivity Prescription* (New York: McGraw-Hill, 1982) pp. 96–97.

TABLE 10-1 Common Problems of Low Productivity and Suggested Corrective Actions: Some Specific Examples

Problem	Possible Corrective Action	Illustrative Examples
Sufficient work not available or workloads unbalanced	Reallocate manpower	Housing complaint bureau schedules revised and temporary help employed during peak winter season.
	Change work schedules	Mechanics rescheduled to second shift when equipment is not in use.
	Reduce crew size	Collection crew size reduced from 4 to 3 men.
Lack of equipment or materials	Improve inventory control system	Inventory reorder points revised to reduce stock-out occurrences.
	Improve distribution system	Asphalt deliveries expedited to eliminate paving crew delays.
	Improve equipment maintenance	Preventive maintenance program instituted.
	Reevaluate equipment requirements	Obsolete collection trucks replaced.
Self-imposed idle time or slow work pace	Train supervisors	Road maintenance foremen trained in work scheduling, dispatching, and quality-control techniques.
	Use performance standards	"Flat rate" manual standards adopted to measure auto mechanics' performance.
	Schedule more work	Park maintenance crews mobilized and work scheduling system installed.
Too much time spent on non-productive activities	Reduce excessive travel time	Permit expiration dates changed to reduce travel time of health inspectors.
	Reevaluate job description and task assignments	Building inspectors trained to handle multiple inspections.
Excessive manual effort required	Mechanize repetitive tasks	Automatic change and toll collection machines installed and toll collector staffing reduced.

Response or processing time too slow	Combine tasks or functions	Voucher processing and account posting combined to speed vendor payments.
	Automate process	Computerized birth record storage and retrieval system installed.
	Improve dispatching procedures	Fire alarm patterns analyzed and equipment response policies revised.
	Revise deployment practices	Police patrol zones redefined to improve response time.
	Adopt project management techniques	Project control system installed to reduce construction cycle.

SOURCE: Published by The Center for Productive Public Management, John Jay College of Criminal Justice, 445 West 59th Street, New York, N.Y. 10019. From "So, Mr. Mayor, You Want to Improve Productivity," National Commission on Productivity and Work Quality.

not the norm. A recent survey of centralized productivity improvements in state government found a number of interesting efforts but in general concluded that they are scattered and fragmented.[35] The survey finds that statewide productivity efforts need support from the governor's office, and this support is often missing.[36] Moreover, management systems to measure performance—which are necessary to determine whether output has improved or not—are weak in most of the states surveyed. As noted earlier, productivity improvement efforts are difficult to design, evaluate, or defend without an accurate management system to register the results.

In the next chapter we will examine how management systems—for whatever purposes—can be implemented.

SUMMARY

Managers have a number of options when they find organizational productivity unsatisfactory. The three principal approaches to improving productivity are capital investments, work methods improvement, and personnel measures.

Perhaps the most attention has been focused on personnel actions. Among the approaches in this category currently being tried are flextime, job enlargement, and participative management through quality circles. The research on quality circles is still incomplete, but job enlargement and flextime have been shown to have more effect on workers' *satisfaction* than on short-term *productivity*. However, satisfaction is very important, and so these techniques are valuable nonetheless.

Historically, most gains in productivity in both the private and public sectors have sprung from capital investment. Although the budget process presents many obstacles to increased capital investment in the public sector, such measures as productivity funds and productivity banks can be used to surmount these obstacles.

REVIEW QUESTIONS

1. How is productivity-oriented capital investment discouraged by common government procedures? In what ways can these obstacles be surmounted?

2. If most research seems to indicate that increased job satisfaction does not cause increased performance, what are the arguments for pursuing it?

3. For what types of organizations would flextime be most easily implemented? Least easily implemented?

4. What attributes are likely to contribute to a successful quality circle?
5. What characteristics of a job are affected by job enrichment? Give examples of how job enrichment could be applied to three different public sector jobs.
6. Once a process chart is completed, how can it be used?
7. Name a number of possible productivity improvement approaches that might be explored by a newly named manager of a police department. How would his or her approach probably differ from that of a newly named manager of a city planning department?

SUGGESTED FURTHER READING

DAVID N. AMMONS. *Municipal Productivity: A Comparison of Fourteen High-Quality-Service Cities.* New York: Praeger, 1984. As suggested by the subtitle, a scholarly, methodologically sound examination of what factors can cause productivity differences. Only two prove to be statistically significant—raising one's own revenue and using performance indicators for guidance rather than punishment—but the background and the methodology are both very interesting.

PAUL D. EPSTEIN. *Using Performance Measurement in Local Government.* New York: Van Nostrand Reinhold, 1984. Particularly strong on detailed case studies of successful local government productivity improvement efforts.

INTERNATIONAL CITY MANAGERS ASSOCIATION. *The Guide to Management Improvement Projects in Local Government.* A quarterly periodical, primarily sold through annual subscriptions, that provides executive summaries of local projects. It comes with a three-ring binder in which to keep the reports. (Address: 1120 G St., NW; Washington DC, 20005.)

JOHN MATZER, JR., ed. *Productivity Improvement Techniques: Creative Approaches for Local Government.* Washington, DC: International City Managers Association, 1986. Like most collections, the quality varies from article to article. A number of very useful, practical guidelines are given by the authors, who are usually managers.

ELAINE MORLEY. *A Practitioner's Guide to Public Sector Productivity.* New York: Van Nostrand Reinhold, 1986. A number of good sections, including a very strong one on process charts.

GEORGE J. WASHNIS, ed. *Productivity Improvement Handbook.* New York: John Wiley, 1980. As mentioned in the notes of several earlier chapters, this 1,400-page collection allows managers to focus on the particulars of a narrow functional area that they wish to improve.

ENDNOTES

1. These three productivity areas are distinguished and discussed in several federal productivity documents, including Joint Financial

Management Improvement Program, *Productivity Programs in the Federal Government:* FY 1974 (Washington, DC: Joint Financial Management Improvement Program, 1975), vol. 1 and succeeding volumes in the same series.

2. Useful guidelines for using computers are provided in John A. Worthley, "Computer Technology and Productivity Improvement," in Marc Holzer and Arie Halachmi, eds., *Strategic Issues in Public Sector Productivity* (San Francisco: Jossey-Bass, 1986), pp. 205–14.

3. Fire department innovations are briefly described in Elaine Morley, *A Practitioner's Guide to Public Sector Productivity Improvement* (New York: Van Nostrand Reinhold, 1986), pp. 204–205.

4. The substantial gains from moving to new types of sanitation trucks are discussed in Norman Steisel, "Productivity in the New York City Department of Sanitation: The Role of the Public Sector Manager," *Public Productivity Review,* 8, no. 2 (Summer 1984).

5. This discussion closely follows General Services Administration, *Enhancing Productivity Through Improved Acquisition and Management of Capital Equipment* (Washington, DC: U.S. Government Printing Office, 1975).

6. Four different variations on these types of funds are discussed in Panel 4, "Financing Productivity Investments," *Public Productivity Review,* Spring 1985, pp. 83ff.

This discussion applies to all levels of government. For example, the federal Department of Defense has used both productivity funds and productivity banks to finance capital expenditures, with great success. See U.S. General Accounting Office, *Productivity: Selected DOD Capital Investment Projects* (Washington, DC: GAO, December 1986): for omnibus funds, see U.S. General Accounting Office, *Incentive Programs to Improve Productivity Through Capital Investment Can Work* (Washington, DC: GAO, April 1981). A good overview of the Environmental Protection Agency's use of a similar approach is Larry Hubbell and John Sandy, "Productivity Investment Funds," *The Bureaucrat,* 16, no. 4 (Winter 1988), 51–54.

7. This conclusion is reached by the director of a major facet of the 1970s New York City productivity drive:

Once installed, new hardware inevitably produces improvements; put a caseworker's files into a centralized terminal digit system, and he has no choice but to use it.

Improvements depending on management control are considerably less effective than technical improvements. The existence of a telephone service does not guarantee that employees will answer the phones. Performance measures will not work when the supervisors themselves take hour-long coffee breaks.

Arthur H. Spiegel, III, "How Outsiders Overhauled a Public Agency," *Harvard Business Review,* January-February 1975.

8. The conceptual groupings are of course not synonymous, but they overlap so substantially that they are often treated together.

9. Robert L. Kahn, "Organization and Design of Jobs: Job Enrichment, Quality of Working Life," *Human Factors in Organizational Productivity* (Washington, DC: U.S. Civil Service Commission, 1973), p. 35.

    Research since the Kahn statement has reinforced his conclusion. See, for example, M. M. Petty, Gail McGee, and Jerry W. Cavender, "A Meta-Analysis of the Relationship Between Individual Job Satisfaction and Individual Performance," *Academy of Management Journal,* 1984, pp. 712–21.

    For an interesting discussion of why managers seem to believe so resolutely in a strong link between workers' satisfaction and performance, in the face of all the disconfirming evidence, see Dennis W. Organ and Thomas Bateman, *Organizational Behavior* (Plano, TX: Business Publications, 1986), pp. 360–64.

10. These relationships are discussed in Organ and Bateman, *Organizational Behavior,* pp. 356–60.

11. Among workers in the private sector, 74 percent rated their work as good, compared to only 64 percent in a sampling of public sector agencies (both federal and local). Additionally, 80 percent of the private sector people rated their supervisor as technically competent in human relations skills; only 65 percent of the government people did so. A question asking whether the supervisor was "doing a good job" elicited similar responses. National Center for Productivity and Quality of Working Life, *Employee Attitudes and Productivity Differences Between the Public and Private Sectors* (Washington, DC: U.S. Government Printing Office, 1978).

12. A federal survey of practices found sixty-one ongoing human-resource-oriented productivity practices. Besides the three considered in this chapter, the list includes such approaches as dual career paths, pay-for-knowledge, work sharing, futuring, and stress management programs. U.S. General Accounting Office, *Human Resource Management: Status of Agency Practices for Improving Productivity* (Washington, DC: GAO, July 1987).

13. Glen W. Rainey, Jr., and Lawrence Wolf, "Flex-Time: Short-Term Benefits; Long Term . . .?" *Public Administration Review,* 41, no. 1 (January/February 1981), 52–62. Rainey and Wolf conclude that flextime produces positive subjective (survey) reactions, but objective indicators show mixed results, particularly for blue-collar workers.

    After reviewing the literature, two other authors reach a generally (but cautiously) positive conclusion about flextime: Robert T. Golembiewski and Carl W. Proehl, Jr., "Public Sector Applications of Flexible Work Hours: A Review of Available Experience," *Public Administration Review,* 40, no. 1 (January/February 1980), 72–83.

14. Judith Havemann, "Alternative Work Schedules: Good for the U.S. Government?" *Washington Post,* October 13, 1987, p. A4.

15. John M. Greiner et al., *Productivity and Motivation: A Review of State and Local Government Initiatives* (Washington, DC: Urban Institute Press, 1981), p. 233.

16. Ibid., pp. 234–35, 243.

17. Charles E. Davis and Johnathan P. West, "Adopting Personnel Productivity Innovations in American Local Governments," *Policy Studies Review,* 4, no. 3 (February 1985), 545. The authors find that use of such techniques has substantially risen since the Greiner survey (notes 15 and 16).

18. See Ronald Contino and Robert M. Lorusso, "The Theory Z Turnaround of a Public Agency," *Public Administration Review,* 42, no. 1 (January/February 1982), 66ff.

19. This definition is taken from Ed Yager, "Examining the Quality Control Circle," *Personnel Journal,* October 1979, p. 682.

20. A good overview of quality circles in government is Joyce L. Roll and David L. Roll, "The Potential for Application of Quality Circles in the American Public Sector," in Holzer and Halachmi, eds., *Strategic Issues In Public Sector Productivity,* pp. 119–32.

    An interesting combination of quality circles with quality-oriented performance measures is profiled in Clarence Thomas, "Improving Federal Work Quality," *The Bureaucrat,* 15, no. 2 (Summer 1986). A good case study of the successful use of QCs in a state department of transportation is James S. Bowman and Jane I. Steele, "Quality Teams in a State Agency," *Public Productivity Review,* 11, no. 4 (Summer 1988).

21. John Simmons, "Letter," *Harvard Business Review,* May/June 1985, p. 200.

22. James E. Jarrett, "An Overview of Productivity Improvement Efforts in State Governments," *Public Personnel Management,* 14, no. 4 (Winter 1985), 388.

23. For research on the effectiveness of the QCs, see S. A. Mohrman and L. Noveli, Jr., "Beyond Testimonials: Learning from a Quality Circles Program," *Journal of Occupational Behaviour,* 6 (April 1985), 93–110. See also M. L. Marks et al., "Employee Participation in a Quality Circle Program: Impact on Quality of Work Life, Produc-

tivity, and Absenteeism," *Journal of Applied Psychology,* 71 (February 1986), 61–69.

24. Robert B. Denhardt, James Pyle, and Allen C. Bluedorn, "Implementing Quality Circles in State Government," *Public Administration Review,* 47, no. 4 (July/August 1987), 304–309.

25. Stephen Bryant and Joseph Kearns, "Workers' Brains as Well as Their Bodies: Quality Circles in a Federal Facility," *Public Administration Review,* 42, no. 2 (March/April 1982), 144–50.

26. Robert E. Cole, "Target Information for Competitive Performance," *Harvard Business Review,* May/June 1985.

27. Thomas J. Peters and Robert H. Waterman, Jr., *In Search of Excellence* (New York: Harper & Row, 1983). One attempt to relate the Peters and Waterman suggestions to government is Harold W. Williams, "In Search of Bureaucratic Excellence," *The Bureaucrat,* 15, no. 1 (Spring 1986). Williams finds that most of the Peters and Waterman suggestions violate government rules and practices and thus could not be implemented, although he makes suggestions for implementing the spirit of some of their arrangements.

A good overview of how the concept of organizational culture developed through a dialogue between business practitioners and academics is Stephen R. Barley et al., "Cultures of Culture: Academics, Practitioners, and the Pragmatics of Normative Control," *Administrative Science Quarterly,* 33 (March 1988).

28. An analysis that looks at theories of organizational culture and maintains that too many have been oversimplified is Guy S. Saffold, III, "Culture Traits, Strengths, and Organizational Performance: Moving Beyond 'Strong' Culture," *Academy of Management Review,* 13 (October 1988), 546–59.

29. As noted in Chapter Five, the single best source for activity-specific performance measures and for activity-specific productivity improvement suggestions is the 1,400-page volume by George G. Washnis, ed., *Productivity Improvement Handbook* (New York: John Wiley, 1980).

30. The symbols are from David Bain, *The Productivity Prescription: A Manager's Guide to Increased Productivity and Profits* (New York: McGraw-Hill, 1986), pp. 96–97.

31. This process is well described in Morley, *A Practitioner's Guide,* pp. 89–117.

32. President's Council on Management Improvement, *1987 Annual Report to the President: Government Excellence Through Partnership* (Washington, DC), p. 9.

33. Paul D. Epstein, *Using Performance Measurement in Local Government* (New York: Van Nostrand Reinhold, 1984), pp. 68, 117–20.

34. A short review of the New York State productivity program is Jeanette S. Whitbeck, "Improving Management in New York State," *Public Administration Review*, 45, no. 4 (July/August 1985).

New Jersey's effort went on throughout the 1980s; it was particularly notable for employing a number of very different approaches simultaneously. For an examination of the effort's beginnings, see Richard F. Keevey, "State Productivity Improvement: Building on Existing Strengths," *Public Administration Review*, 40, no. 5 (September/October 1980), 451–59.

35. Theodore H. Poister et al., "Centralized Productivity Improvement Efforts in State Government," *Public Productivity Review*, 9, no. 1 (Spring 1985).

36. As we will discuss again in the next chapter, commitment of the managers involved, as well as of the chief executive, is necessary for productivity improvement actions. For a study that shows that productivity improvement is often crowded out of the agenda of local managers by other concerns, see David N. Ammons and Joseph C. King, "Productivity Improvement in Local Government: Its Place Among Competing Priorities," *Public Administration Review*, 43, no. 2 (March/April 1983).

chapter eleven

Installing a Management System

The best-designed management system is worthless if it is not actually used, and a system's use is often determined by the way it is installed. The initial stages are crucial for a public management system. More systems fail than succeed, and most often this failure occurs either when the system is first beginning or after the leadership of the agency changes, when the system must begin again.

This chapter examines the problems of installing a public sector management system. We begin by surveying the environment for potential outside support (and find little); we then look at outside, systemic disincentives (and find many) and at internal sources of resistance (again, many). But there are ways around these very sizable obstacles, and in the final sections we consider ways of alleviating the negative aspects and creating positive incentives for a management system.

POTENTIAL SOURCES OF OUTSIDE SUPPORT

The tasks of top administrators who wish to install a management system would be greatly eased if they could find important outside actors who would support and reward such efforts. One potential outside power source is the interested legislative committees; a second is the general public.

Legislative Committees

In seeking a powerful actor to support efficiency efforts, one of the most obvious possibilities is the involved legislative committees. Certainly they have legitimacy since they are enjoined to oversee the departments; and they have the greatest of all powers, control of the purse strings. If such committees would reward efficiency and punish inefficient organizations, they would greatly strengthen the hands of those attempting to install management systems. Steps have been made in this direction, particularly with sunset programs, but with very little success. There are two approaches to using legislative committees to oversee efficiency, each with nearly intractable problems.[1]

One approach (adopted by a number of states) is to use a "super" committee with jurisdiction over the entire executive branch. The difficulty is that such committees lack the specialization and expertise that allow detection and correction of any but the most blatant inefficiencies. Because they lack the ability to specialize, such committees are often at a disadvantage vis-à-vis the executive branch, with its control of information.

The second approach attempts to surmount this difficulty by having those committees with expertise—the authorization and budgetary subcommittees most directly connected to the bureaucracy—perform the oversight function. But although such committees have the ability to interpret technical information and (through the budget) to apply sanctions, there is an understandable reluctance to do so. Such committees are often closely tied to the interests they are supposed to be supervising—agencies and their allied interest groups. When these ties are tight, the alliances are called *iron triangles;* when they are looser, they are called *issue networks.* Agriculture committees, for example, are part of an iron triangle. Such committees have little inclination to call the attention of a wider public to the inefficiencies of "their" bureaucracy, thus undermining public support for it. They are even less likely to cut its budget, which usually means budget cuts in their districts.[2]

Public Attention

A second outside actor that might be enlisted to back efficiency efforts is the general public. But although the public registers substantial concern with eliminating government waste when it is polled, it has very little interest in the details of management or administration. This is understandable. Certainly the claims of many other problems—from tax rates to personal concerns such as paying the mortgage—preclude citizens from spending large amounts of time and effort to learn about the efficiency of particular organizations.[3] Although this inattention is understandable, it nonetheless eliminates mass public monitoring as a strong incentive for increased government efficiency.

An administrator or politician can gain what few benefits of public approbation are available simply by announcing a program. Thus a president who announces zero-base budgeting or a reorganization or a governor who announces MBO may be rewarded with a modest story on page 11 of the newspaper. There is no further gain, however, to be reaped from the hard work of installing, running, and repairing this system. Even a sham system will produce the same symbolic effect. The public has neither the interest nor the ability to make the highly technical determination of whether a system is in fact improving an organization's operations.

SYSTEMIC DISINCENTIVES TO EFFICIENCY

Not only are there no outside bodies that can provide strong incentives for efficiency measures, but also there are numerous systemic disincentives.

Administrators' Backgrounds

At the local level, many top department heads are professionals, such as engineers heading public works departments and doctors heading health departments. At the state and federal level, there are still many professionals, but they are often outnumbered by lawyers and politicians. Unfortunately, none of these careers provides the type of background needed to manage a large organization. Most members of these groups have received no management training, and one suspects that management is not a primary interest for most of them simply because they did not choose managerial careers.

Tenure of Top Administrators

The typical top administrator in a state or federal bureaucracy remains in his or her post for a very short time. At the assistant secretary level for federal departments, where most of the detailed managerial work is handled, the average tenure is twenty-two months.[4] Since it takes at least twelve months to get acclimated to a bureaucracy, this type of turnover can only hurt management systems, which require year after year of continuous operation to return the best results.

Moreover, most management systems require a long start-up period. The typical MBO or performance monitoring system requires at least three years from inception to routinized operation. During the early years, resistance is at its greatest because the system is perceived as new and threatening, and organizational disruption is at its height because managers do not yet know how to use the system. Thus a top administrator pays a heavy price in disrupted organizational operation, suspicion, and resistance during the early years. From an organizational viewpoint, this is usually a price well worth paying because the advantages of having a functioning management system are so great.

However, an administrator who realizes he or she will be gone from the job in two or three years has few incentives to install such a system. Managers see little reason to labor for two or more years, bearing up under the problems of disruption and resistance, in order to find the system functioning just as they head out the door. Someone else will reap the benefits of their pain; worse yet, that future administrator may be a member of the other party. Not surprisingly, many top government administrators do not have the heart for such self-sacrifice for the greater good of the organization. When combined with the lack of public ability to distinguish real efficiency improvements, short tenure means that administrators have incentives to encourage efficiency actions that are short term, flashy, and symbolic.

"Lost" Savings

As discussed in Chapter Seven, a major disincentive to efficiency is the fact that an agency that spends less because it has increased its efficiency generally loses its savings. When agency administrators appear before the council or legislature the following year, they are asked, "Why should we give you the full amount you're asking for this year if you couldn't use all that we gave you last year?" Their budgets are cut back, and adding insult to injury, additional money often goes instead to agencies that are so inefficient that they have overrun their budget. Efficiency is punished, inefficiency rewarded. As noted earlier, this phenomenon creates the legendary last quarter spending spree, when agencies try to commit their funds in any way possible so that they will have spent all of the money before the year ends.

Across-The-Board Actions

Ironically, the very techniques that politicians use to show their support for greater government efficiency destroy all real incentives to be efficient. The two favorite actions of politicians looking for bold symbolic efficiency actions are across-the-board personnel freezes and spending cuts. A personnel freeze means that agencies cannot hire new people to replace those who resign or retire. Budget cuts mean that all agencies lose the same percentage of their funds for the year.

Governors, presidents, or mayors are often hailed by both voters and editorial writers for their commitment to efficiency when they announce that they are going to freeze hiring or slash 5 percent from the budgets of all agencies. Yet if an agency has exerted great effort to become more efficient, working itself into fighting trim, then ceilings and across-the-board cuts slice into the agency's bone and muscle. It must cut people who are needed and money that is well spent. On the other hand, an inefficient organization merely lops off some of its organizational fat. Administrators who have worked hard to trim their agency's fat find themselves punished for their efficiency. All but the most masochistic administrators remember the pain of cutting into muscle, and in future years they build some fat into their agency in preparation for the inevitable time when a new governor or president decides to take a symbolic action.

This disincentive will remain until the public realizes that such across-the-board actions are those of a poor executive who is actually encouraging waste in the long run. Good executives use scalpels rather than meat cleavers; they prune inefficient agencies a great deal and leave efficient agencies alone. However, this approach takes effort and attention to detail; few political leaders will spend their time on it as long as the public continues to applaud and reward them for taking across-the-board actions.

INTERNAL RESISTANCE TO MANAGEMENT SYSTEMS

In addition to these systemic disincentives to improving efficiency through management systems, there are also internal obstacles, particularly resistance. To install such systems successfully, managers must be able to anticipate the sources and forms of resistance in order to allay the hostility.[5] All three levels of an organization—the upper-level managers, middle managers, and operations-level workers—are potential opponents of a new management system.

Resistance from Top Managers

Many upper-level managers, those right below the top administrator, are likely to fight a new system because it forces them to adopt an entirely new management style. A well-working system requires top managers to give up control over process details and instead to exercise their authority by setting policy guidelines and specific objectives, and then monitoring periodically to be sure that those objectives have been achieved.

For many old-school, career managers, this approach requires a wrenching rethinking of their role. They take great pride in their mastery of details and process, seeing it as a symbol of their competence. They have always made it a point to know when someone three levels down has an out-of-town assignment or who is making the most long-distance phone calls. To many of these top managers, devolving this concern with detail in favor of simply setting standards seems like an abdication of power. The idea that giving subordinates greater discretion over processes will lead to greater efficiency seems like doubletalk. When a new management system is installed, they are likely to want to continue to intervene many levels down and to specify the details of processes instead of setting goals, thus negating many of the benefits of the new system.

Resistance from Operations-Level Workers

Resistance is likely to come also from the opposite end of the organizational hierarchy. Changes originating from above are likely to be viewed with suspicion by those workers who actually carry out the activities of an organization, such as the police officers on the beat, teachers in the classroom, and clerks at the intake desk. Such operational-level workers often resist MBO and performance monitoring systems because they perceive them as "speed-up" systems. These workers often view themselves (correctly) as the backbone of the organization and view top administrators (usually incorrectly) as natural enemies who want more work out of subordinates without being willing to do much work themselves. Because they see these systems as schemes to wring more work out of them, or to lay off fellow workers, they will often initially oppose them. If the work force is unionized, this resistance may in fact prevent any system from being installed.

Resistance from Middle Managers

The fiercest resistance of all is likely to come from the group between the top and the operations level, the middle managers. These managers often fight hardest because in many ways they are the most insecure. Unlike lower-level workers, they do not have clear task definition nor unions or employee associations. Unlike top managers, they have no strong power base. Given their ill-defined job definition and relatively powerless positions, middle managers are often highly insecure and sensitive to new developments that could knock them from their tenuous perch. They often perceive management systems as ways of holding them accountable for standards they did not set, and thus as attacks on them and their judgment.

Middle managers also have the most tools at their command for fighting a management system. They can delay its installation by not cooperating with the designers of the system, raising objections to every suggestion, and reopening the fight with every change of top administrators. Once the system is installed, they can refuse to feed it information. Without prompt and accurate input and output figures from every unit, a system cannot provide guidance. Middle managers can ignore the system's information in making their decisions or attempt to keep alive the old information sources that the new system is meant to replace. If enough managers actively resist the system, even managers who wish to use it will find it incomplete and inaccurate and begin drifting away. Because middle managers are both the principal suppliers of "raw" information that feeds into a system and the principal users of the "massaged" information that comes out of it, they have the power of life and death over the system.

All of this paints a bleak picture of the external and internal obstacles facing a new management system. But although these obstacles are substantial, they are certainly not insurmountable. Many excellent management systems function at all levels of the public sector. Of the 62 percent of American cities that employ MBO, for example, a large majority reported that the systems are performing well.[6] A top administrator who is aware of the likely sources of problems and who takes steps early to overcome them has an excellent chance of installing a functioning system.

OVERCOMING SYSTEMIC OBSTACLES

The obstacles hardest to overcome are the systemic ones. They are most often rooted in the legislature or even in the culture of society at large, and thus are not very amenable to action by administrators. Nonetheless, there has recently been a few encouraging signs. For one, as discussed in Chapter One, the public's demand for efficiency has gained in strength, which provides an environment of support for efficiency initiatives.

More concretely, as discussed in Chapters Seven and Eight, some governments have begun experimenting with incentives for agencies to save money. These efforts are still rare and often short-lived, but they represent a beginning. Allowing agencies to retain a percentage of "saved" funds for expanding existing programs or beginning new ones provides an incentive for agency-wide efficiency. Providing bonuses or salary increases that are keyed to productivity encourages individual and subunit efficiency.

Unfortunately there is less movement toward overcoming other systemic obstacles. Fighting the disincentives of across-the-board freezes and budget cuts would require a massive reeducation of the public, which currently applauds such moves. Government managers must become opinion leaders in instructing the media and others about the counterproductive effects of such freezes and cuts.

Systemic obstacles show no sign of a dramatic turnaround, but this need not determine the fate of management systems. A canny administrator can provide enough internal incentives to override both internal opposition and external obstacles. The first step is to remove the negative aspects by alleviating some of the natural internal resistance, and the second is then to add positive reasons for agency members to support the system.

OVERCOMING THE NEGATIVE: ALLEVIATING INTERNAL RESISTANCE

Resistance to threatening change is common to all people, and each level of an agency will also have particular reasons for opposing a system. Administrators cannot hope to alleviate all this resistance before the system is installed, but they can reduce it to levels that can be handled. Two important approaches toward alleviating resistance are providing extensive early information and arranging widespread involvement.

Early Information

Large bureaucracies are in some ways like small towns. In both, rumors fly from one end to the other, gaining in drama and losing in accuracy as they are passed along. This process can poison the ground for a new management system before it is even begun. Top administrators must seize the opportunity to inform and reassure all members of the organization at the very moment they tentatively decide to begin a new system. This step prevents inaccurate rumors from causing panic and keeps the initiative with the prosystem people. This information should be frank and extensive; organizational members may not read it at all, but they will be reassured by the fact that it is there.

Early reassurance should also include promises of no layoffs, often the greatest employee fear. If there are any personnel gains to be realized from the new system, they can be secured from attrition.

Involving All Levels

As noted, it is often three years from the time a management system is begun until it is routinely operating. In the early stages a great number of decisions must be made, including what units will be covered, what output measures will be used, what procedures will determine changes in the system, and what links the system will have to budgeting and personnel systems.[7]

Even if outside consultants are brought in to help with system's design and installation, these decisions must be made by the agency, not the consultants. Within the agency, these questions should be decided by a group process that includes the suggestions of all levels. If the work force is unionized, union leaders must be an integral part of this process.[8]

Sometimes the early and complete involvement of all organizational levels runs counter to the inclinations of top administrators. "We're already spending large sums on an outside consultant to design and install this system," they think. "Why should we run up additional costs by releasing employees from their regular jobs to take part? Besides, they'll just delay the system with questions, suggestions, and objections."

A rough but usually accurate test of the quality of consultants is whether they are willing to go along with this approach. Although it certainly simplifies their lives to be able to design and install a system by dealing only with top administrators, the best consultants will not agree to such an arrangement. They realize that unless the people who are going to have to use the system on a day-to-day basis are involved in designing and installing it, its long-term prognosis is poor. A management system is designed to bring the most usable information to bear on the most pressing problems facing managers. Only the managers of each agency can say what their most pressing problems are and what form of information would be most useful in attacking them.

Managers can be involved in a number of ways. Initial questionnaires can be sent to all organizational members; these will suggest areas to be pursued at greater length. Personal interviews can then provide this in-depth information. But perhaps the most important form of involvement is "spinning off" staff and managers between the system design group and line management. That is, some line managers are brought into the group that is designing the system right from the beginning, and some remain during the entire year or two during which the project is designed and installed. Other managers may be brought in for only a few months, just enough time to learn the system and to provide advice. Both groups of managers can serve as envoys to other line managers, explaining procedures and allaying fears. Finally, at or near the end of the installation stage, some staff people from the design and installation group may be spun off to line positions, again because it is useful to have people who understand and support the system scattered throughout the agency. This highly porous, in-and-out structure of the design and installation group lessens the number of inaccurate rumors and prevents the rest of the organization from developing any "us against the outsiders" attitude.[9]

Both of these approaches—quick, early information that includes promises of no layoffs or speed-ups, and extensive interaction—are meant to defuse the hostile reaction to a new system. Although they are absolutely necessary, they are not enough by themselves. If a management system is to overcome the very substantial external obstacles that have been discussed, it is not enough that agency personnel do not strongly oppose the system. They must have positive reasons to support it.

INSTALLING MANAGEMENT SYSTEMS: PROVIDING POSITIVE INCENTIVES

Each level of the organization has different needs and fears, and therefore incentives must be tailored to each level. The heart of system installation is first to determine the incentives for each level and then to provide them. We can begin, however, by dismissing one approach as having little effect on any level.

The Futility of Selling Efficiency

One common mistake is trying to sell the system to members of the organization almost entirely as a way to increase efficiency. At worst, *efficiency* seems a code word for speed-ups, layoffs, and budget cuts. It suggests that more work will be expected with less time and money and fewer people to get it done. Even when discussions of efficiency do not evoke such fears, they do not provide much motivation, either. Why should workers undergo all the discomforts and extra efforts involved in installing a new system for a benefit as abstract and indefinite as "greater efficiency"? Efficiency is something that may affect society at large, sometime in the future. Government employees, being human, are often reluctant to suffer current discomfort for such nebulous future gains.

Of course, most government workers do like to take pride in their agency's efficiency and effectiveness. In the rare cases in which this pride can be evoked without raising all the unpleasant connotations, efficiency is a fine secondary argument. It is not a strong enough attribute, however, to be a major selling point for a new management system. Only level-specific inducements can perform that role.

Convincing the Top Level

Often the top level of an agency has already been convinced or there would be no question of even installing the system. It is they who call in the consultants and they who often try to sell the system to the other levels. One major reason why top managers are often sold on management systems in general was suggested in Chapter Four. In large departments that have very restrictive civil service systems and tenured subordinate managers with strong ties to the legislature, the top manager often has surprisingly little influence over the department. (Such departments can be found in many places, particularly in the federal government and some of the largest industrial states.) In such cases, management systems can give some power to the top managers. Their wishes are clearer because their choice of outputs to be tracked and performance goals indicate their priorities; information is forced up because performances are clearly documented. This shift in power is useful to society, too, because as argued in Chapter Four, it means that those officials over whom the public has the most control are those who are really directing an organization. Of course, using these arguments to sell a system to the top level requires that the top official or officials want power, or perhaps for ideological reasons, greater efficiency. Fortunately, it seems that one or both of these motives is usually present.

In many agencies at the state and local level, the top manager already has sufficient power. But in these cases there is an additional incentive that applies to all types of agencies: increased autonomy. Top government executives consistently note that a record of organizational effectiveness buys "breathing room" from outside overseers. Says one former government executive,

> If the head of an organization appears to be an excellent manager, he will be left relatively free in his choice of means to carry out the organization's programs. He is likely to be entrusted with additional responsibilities and additional resources to carry them out. The price of appearing biased, indifferent, ineffective or wasteful is more rigorous oversight, specific mandates from the legislature or superiors, and personal attacks that will undermine influence in the smoke of political battle. The programs will suffer. . . . Support for the manager by those who carry out the programs, or must cooperate in the execution of the programs, will diminish rapidly.[10]

A former state executive comes to a similar conclusion: "Where agencies have strong management systems and clearly control their programs, projects, and costs, they achieve considerable credibility with administrations and legislatures and, in general, gain more flexibility in controlling their funds."[11]

Top officials, then, can be convinced of the advantages of the system on the basis of increasing their internal influence within the agency and also on the basis of greater freedom from external interference and control.

Convincing the Bottom Level

Perhaps the best way to sell a new system to operating personnel is by tying material rewards to increased efficiency. Gainsharing, discussed in Chapter Eight, is one way in which a management system can be shown to lead to real benefits, promising the carrot instead of the stick. Workers must be convinced that new approaches are not disguised speed-up campaigns, that the system will increase productivity by allowing them to work (in a favorite slogan of consultants) "smarter, not harder."

In the private sector, operational-level workers often are given a share of the gains of a new system; this step should be taken in the public sector too. Gainsharing, personal bonuses, increased rewards for money-saving suggestions, and other monetary and nonmonetary rewards discussed in Chapter Eight are important incentives for operating-level efficiency.

Convincing the Middle Level

As noted earlier, middle managers comprise the group that is most likely to feel threatened by new management systems, and thus to oppose them. Unfortunately, this group is also often the hardest to convince about the advantages of a new system.

One benefit that should be emphasized is the tangible, monetary rewards that were sold to lower-level workers as well. Such rewards and bonuses might be tied to subunit performance or to particular individual accomplishments. Again, only a management system that tracks and documents unit and individual performances allows such rewards.

A second benefit is also provided by MBO-type management systems. As discussed in Chapter Four, middle-level managers often have a frustrating lack of access to their superiors, who are constantly on the road or in meetings. When middle managers do get to meet with their superiors, the meetings have usually been prompted by an immediate crisis. MBO systems give middle managers regular, guaranteed access to their superiors to discuss ongoing operations, before crises can arise. Especially near the top of the largest government organizations, such access is rare and highly valued.

However, the greatest gain for this level, and the one that should be emphasized, is increased certainty. Middle managers operate in a nebulous world of unmeasurable outputs, unclear expectations, and little security. Output-based management systems can provide a foothold on the slippery slope of uncertainty. MBO and performance monitoring systems give managers a voice in selecting the standards by which they will be measured and provide a clear indication of what is expected. No longer are managers vulnerable to the whims and caprices of superiors, and no longer are their careers based only on process measures and subjective evaluations. Management systems, then, provide middle managers with a means of getting control over their own destiny.

This is a difficult concept to sell. It is true and important, but it sounds too abstract to most middle managers, who fear a new system will eliminate their jobs or hold them ransom to unreasonable, unilaterally established performance standards. Convincing these managers that the gains of a new system will outweigh the losses is one of the largest challenges facing system installers. (These approaches are summarized in Table 11–1.)

AFTER THE SYSTEM IS ESTABLISHED

Once the management system is installed and working, the battle is not over. For one thing, the system must be periodically evaluated. Certain indicators will cease to be important because of shifts either in the organizational task or in the environment, and new ones will be necessary. Moreover, procedures and approaches will sometimes begin to atrophy simply because they are taken for granted as the years pass; they need to be changed and rejuvenated.

Finally, it is important to realize that with each change of top political leadership the system will have to be sold again. The immediate reaction of a new party or administration is to view all existing procedures as "their" way of doing things, which "got us into all these problems in the first place." Continuing managers must convince the new top administrators that the system will work to their advantage. And if the system is discontinued, career managers must renew the fight to reestablish it when agency leadership changes again in two or three years.[12] Because procedures are refined during the system's initial period, and many fears are proved groundless, reinstallation is often relatively quick and uneventful.

Both the need for constant revision and for the occasional resurrection of agency systems emphasize that it is essential for agency personnel to support the system strongly, rather than merely to tolerate it. Only supporters will have the motivation to repair it continually and to sell it to succeeding agency heads.

SUMMARY

Even a management system with a superb technical design will soon falter and die unless it is used and supported by the members of the organization. Enlisting this support requires overcoming substantial obstacles because most of the incentives acting on the agency as a whole and on the workers at each level are not conducive to efficiency.

The agency itself usually loses the funds that it saves, and its efficiency is further punished by across-the-board personnel freezes and budget cuts.

Top levels of the organization have incentives toward policy making, not administration; middle levels are often the most insecure; the lower levels have unions that remain suspicious of efficiency drives.

TABLE 11–1 Summary: Likely Resistance and Counterbalancing Side Benefits in Installing Management Systems

Organizational Level	Potential Reasons for Resisting Management Systems	Side Benefits that Encourage Support for Management Systems
Top managers	1. Fear of loss of authority by giving up control over details and procedures 2. Change in operating style caused by giving up control over details and procedures	1. Greater control of the largest, most tenured-in agencies 2. Record of efficiency that causes outside supervisory bodies to grant greater autonomy 3. Greater efficiency for those who value it for personality reasons
Middle managers	1. Fear of being held accountable 2. Fear of being held accountable to unreasonable standards 3. Fear of loss of power	1. Greater control over criteria by which they will be evaluated 2. With MBO, guaranteed access to top decision makers 3. Greater environmental certainty, and thus greater security 4. Monetary rewards: bonuses, gainsharing; nonmonetary rewards
Supervisors and operating-level workers	1. Fear of speed-ups 2. Fear of loss of jobs 3. Fear of loss of existing level of autonomy	1. Monetary rewards—bonuses, gainsharing; nonmonetary rewards

In addition, all levels must be brought into the planning process for the new system, consulted and involved at all stages of installation, and promised no system-generated job loss.

System designers should enlist the cooperation of all levels, beginning with the very first decision to explore a new system. The suggestions of all organizational members should be solicited and incorporated. *Efficiency* is often perceived as a code word for regimentation or speed-up and therefore is not a useful argument. Instead, the designers should emphasize the specific day-to-day management benefits that the new system will provide to each level of the organization. One incentive for the top officials of large agencies with very restrictive Civil Service systems is increased control. For top managers in all types of public organizations, management systems also build a record of efficiency that causes outside overseers to give the officials greater freedom of action. For middle- and lower-level managers, specific bonuses could be connected to productivity gains through gainsharing. Moreover, middle managers will have more control over the pattern of expectations by which they are judged.

System designers must consciously build in such side benefits to any contemplated management system. Even with these benefits, systems often face a tough fight, but the large number of success stories provides strong ground for optimism.

REVIEW QUESTIONS

1. What potential sanctions do legislative committees have to reward and punish agencies for efficiency? Drawing on your own reading and experience, does it seem that there are particular circumstances in which committees are more likely to become effective watchdogs?

2. What would be the best background and the best personal characteristics for a top administrator of a large federal or state bureaucracy? Do these attributes seem common? Why?

3. Why are across-the-board personnel and budget cuts so often used? What are their disadvantages?

4. For what reasons do top managers resist new management systems? Middle managers? Operating-level workers? Could we expect these patterns of resistance to differ in a predictable way between agencies that are different in size? In professionalization?

5. What techniques can be used by installers of management systems to alleviate resistance?

6. What incentives can be given to each organizational level to support management systems? Do any of these incentives apply to more than one level?

7. What symbolic import does *efficiency* have for many government workers? Should this effect vary between organizations with very different organizational cultures?

8. Why must the battle for management systems be continually re-fought?

SUGGESTED FURTHER READING

PHILIP B. HEYMANN. *The Politics of Public Management.* New Haven, CT: Yale University Press, 1987. An interestingly written, example-filled book on how top government managers must also be good politicians in order to succeed.

LAURENCE E. LYNN, JR. *Managing the Public's Business: The Job of the Government Executive.* New York: Basic Books, 1981. A good discussion of the incentives acting on government managers.

JAMES L. PERRY and KENNETH L. KRAEMER, ed. *Public Management: Public and Private Perspectives.* Palo Alto, CA: Mayfield Publishing Company, 1982. A collection of essays about the differences between government and business management. Many of the authors have served in both sectors. The problem of incentives is central to many of the articles.

Case 11–1

After years as a management consultant, Carmen Prionte has been asked by the new governor to put his preaching into practice. He has been named the head of the department of revenue. The department is divided into two sections that are independent from each other to an extent unusual for most public organizations; they are even housed in separate buildings about one block apart.

The record-keeping and information section is in charge of updating withholding records, sending out late notices, opening tax returns, and providing routine information to citizens' tax queries. Except for a few managers, most of the 800 people in this section have high school educations or less. Their work is repetitive and primarily clerical.

The audit/legal services division audits tax returns, interprets tax legislation, and adjudicates tax cases that go to court. Of the 450 members in this division, two-thirds are either lawyers or accountants. Their work is primarily professional and it changes on a day-to-day basis. They have a great deal of discretion in choosing cases to audit or prosecute.

Neither section has ever had a formal management system, and management records are rudimentary. Twelve years ago the head of the department attempted to install a system; resistance caused it to fail within a year.

1. Suggest the output categories that might be included in a system for each section.
2. Which section's system is most likely to change employees' behavior? Managerial decision making? Why?

3. Should Prionte vary his installation strategy for the two sections? If so, how? Might this appear unfair to employees who learn of the different approach in the other section?

Case 11–2

When Jill Tomlinson received her mid-career MBA, the textbook on management change emphasized that change agents—whether outside consultants or new administrators—must work through the managers on hand. Thus when she received her first top position, as administrator of a 140-person office, Tomlinson was determined not to impose change unilaterally. She sought the opinions of her three top subordinates and tried to incorporate their ideas as she developed the new output measurement and personnel system.

One of these managers, Gordy Jones, was the most enthusiastic and interested; he also worked the hardest. Accordingly, she used him more and more to call the meetings with other managers, to make suggestions, and to run system development on a day-to-day basis.

Once the system was operating, she gave Jones the task, on top of his other duties, of formally overseeing the information flow, gathering new figures, and so on. Tomlinson believes he has done a thorough, highly competent job. Even after the system had been operating for a year, however, it was not performing to Tomlinson's satisfaction. Managers clearly resented it and maintained their previous sources of information. Tomlinson heard disparaging comments about the system in the halls.

One of her immediate subordinates explained, "Of the three of us, Gordy has always been the least liked by the rank and file. Most people think he is a climber, who'll say and do anything to please the boss. Of course, I don't think that. When Gordy began to handle more and more of the details of the system's installation, people began to think of it as Gordy's system. They think he's trying to use it to build a record and get your job when you move up. And they resent the fact that he, of all people, is looking over their shoulder and studying their units' records."

Tomlinson realizes that this analysis is correct, and she remains disturbed by the lower morale caused by the system, of the slow feed of information, and of the other managers' reluctance to use the results of the new system. She ponders her next steps. Tomlinson is reluctant to remove Jones from his job of running the system for several reasons. First, he has done an excellent job and should be rewarded, not removed. Second, she realizes that the system will be connected to Jones in most people's minds even if he no longer runs it. Third, she doesn't wish to look as if she's bending to pressure.

1. One of Tomlinson's options is to wait until time and force of habit has made the system a standard piece of the agency's management, in other words, to do nothing now. Is this a good idea?

2. Tomlinson wishes to draw lessons from her experience that she can apply to her next job. Are there any?

Case 11-3

After installing a productivity improvement system in the 600-person printing department of a large city, the consultant was very pleased. She had instituted both unit and individual measures of performance, set up negotiated work standards, compared tasks on the basis of standard times, and installed a bonus system for workers who exceed their work standards. In addition, she instituted quality circles, where workers and managers could discuss possible work changes and improvements.

Although there was some grumbling during the eight-month installation period, and although several dozen of the older employees were still refusing to cooperate with the changes, most workers seem satisfied with the new system. The consultant considered the changes a success, and a modest rise in productivity seemed to bear out her assessment.

Next month she is to oversee a team to institute very similar changes in another city's print shop. The major difference is that this shop, unlike the first one, is strongly unionized.

The consultant wonders whether she should modify either the changes she wishes to install or the way she installed them. Discuss.

ENDNOTES

1. See Neil R. Pierce and J. Hagstrom, "Is It Time for the Sun to Set on Some State Sunset Proposals?" *National Journal,* June 18, 1977, pp. 937–39; "Survey Shows Sunset Legislation Benefits," *Public Administration Times,* April 1, 1982, p. 8. The survey indicated that thirty-five states had sunset laws. Ten states reviewed just regulatory agencies; ten reviewed all agencies; the remainder were in the middle. This was the high-water mark for sunset laws; they became less important in the ensuing years, partially because of the limitations suggested here.

A good overview article is Harry S. Havens, "Congressional Oversight: Reality and Reform," in Jerome B. McKinney and Michael Johnston, eds., *Fraud, Waste and Abuse in Government* (Philadelphia: ISHI Publications, 1986), pp. 118–26.

This discussion of systemic disincentives draws from my "Holding Agencies Accountable for Efficiency: Learning from Past Failures," *Administration and Society,* February 1983.

2. Issue networks and iron triangles are closely related concepts. Issue networks are loose-knit, changing groupings of involved citizens, interest groups, experts, and agencies that are all concerned with an issue. The concept was originally developed in Hugh Heclo, "Issue Networks and the Executive Establishment," in Anthony King, ed., *The New American Political System* (Washington, DC: American Enterprise Institute, 1978). Even though issue networks are marked by shifting alliances, and legislative committee members may find themselves torn between opposing interest groups interested in the same issue, such conflicts would rarely disturb their loyalty to the involved agency and its programs.

    Not all areas of American politics are marked by issue networks. In some areas, including agriculture, highways, and (often) defense, the alliances among interest groups, agencies, and involved committees are firm and long lasting. In such alliances, usually termed *iron triangles,* legislative committees are, of course, even more reluctant to criticize or sanction "their" agency for inefficiency. Two of the most notable explorations of the role of iron triangles in American policy making are Theodore Lowi, *The End of Liberalism,* 2nd ed. (New York: W. W. Norton & Co., 1979); and Grant McConnell, *Private Power and American Democracy* (New York: Vantage Press, 1966).

3. Although the public cannot be rallied behind overall efficiency drives or management systems, occasionally a particular segment of the public can be enlisted in a very specific productivity effort. For example, the U.S. Postal Service received a great deal of resistance when it tried to close small rural post offices. It greatly helped its cause when it released salary figures: Townspeople were dismayed to learn that postmasters were making so much for what was, in these communities, not a full-time job. John T. Tierney, *Postal Reorganization: Managing the Public Business* (Boston: Auburn Publishing House, 1981), p. 76.

    The same theme of enlisting small groups or interest groups on narrow issues underlies Amitai Etzioni, "The Fight Against Fraud and Abuse: Analyzing Constituent Support," *Journal of Policy Analysis and Management* 2, no. 1 (Fall 1982), 26–38. The author concludes that the general public is not a useful ally in efficiency drives, but that interest groups can be helpful in specific narrow areas. For example, the Grey Panthers and social worker associations can be enlisted in the fight to monitor nursing homes and to curb abuses.

For an account of how business people were brought into one efficiency effort, see Patrick J. Dolan, "State Land Management and Productivity Improvement: A Public-Private Sector Approach," *Public Productivity Review,* Winter 1985, pp. 353–68.

4. Such time estimates vary only slightly from work to work. For example, see Hugh Heclo, *A Government of Strangers: Executive Politics in Washington* (Washington, DC: Brookings Institution, 1977); Dean E. Mann and Jameson Doig, *The Assistant Secretaries: Problems and Processes of Appointment* (Washington, DC: Brookings Institution, 1965), pp. 6–7, 277–81; Dick Kirschten, "Reagan Gets Unsolicited Advice on His Personnel Appointments," *National Journal,* December 14, 1985, p. 2869.

5. There are many good articles on system implementation. A comprehensive, practical series of suggestions are provided by Mary Wagner, "The Role of Policy Analyst in Implementing Performance Measurement Methods," *Policy Studies Review,* 6, no. 1 (August 1986), 121–36. Similarly interesting is David R. Braunstein, "Productivity: NASA's Nine Themes," *The Bureaucrat,* 15, no. 1 (Spring 1986).

Looking at the other side, an implementation that failed, is G. David Garson and D. S. Brennan, "Incentive Systems and Goal Displacement in Personnel Resource Management," *Review of Public Personnel Administration,* 1, no. 2 (Spring 1981), 1–12.

6. Gregory Streib and Theodore H. Poister, "Established and Emerging Management Tools: A 12-Year Perspective," *The Municipal Yearbook 1989* (Washington, DC: International City Managers Association, 1989). MBO was rated either "somewhat" or "very" effective by over 95 percent of those using it. It was more likely to be rated as "very effective" (by 57 percent) if it was installed citywide rather than just in selected areas. See also Perry D. Moore and Ted Staton, "Management by Objectives in American Cities," *Public Personnel Management Journal,* Summer 1981, pp. 223–32.

Although not based on such comprehensive surveys, there are also numerous individual stories that also tend to support the fact that these systems are very often a success. For example, the federal Department of Labor began an MBO-type system in fall 1985. When questioned by the General Accounting Office one year later, 92 percent of all managers wanted the system to continue. U.S. General Accounting Office, *Department of Labor: Assessment of Management Improvement Efforts* (Washington, DC: GAO, December 1986). Five different case studies illustrating successful system implementation and use are in Theodore H. Poister, ed., "Symposium: Success Stories in Revitalizing Public Agencies," *Public Productivity Review,* 11, no. 3 (Spring 1988), 27–104.

7. A good call for involvement is Richard E. Walton, "From Control to Commitment in the Workplace," *Harvard Business Review,* March/April 1985, pp. 77–84.

8. Union opposition to productivity improvement is often overestimated by managers and outsiders. For a short but useful overview of the literature see David N. Ammons, *Municipal Productivity: A Comparison of Fourteen High Quality Service Cities* (New York: Praeger, 1984), pp. 130–33.

    For an interesting case study of how the New York City sanitation unions, which are very strong, became a constructive part of productivity improvement, see Vincent P. Whitfield and Howard N. Apsan, "The Hardest Part: Implementation," *The Bureaucrat,* Fall 1985, pp. 13ff. Advance consultations and continuing discussions through labor-management committees were crucial to the development.

9. This approach was used with great success by a group of outside analysts brought in to improve New York City's welfare delivery system. Arthur Spiegel, III, "How Outsiders Overhauled a Public Agency," *Harvard Business Review,* January/February 1975.

10. Philip B. Heymann, *The Politics of Public Management* (New Haven, CT: Yale University Press, 1987), p. 47.

11. Donald Axelrod, *Budgeting for Modern Government* (New York: St. Martin's Press, 1988), p. 178.

12. Sometimes managers do not realize that installation is a continuing process, one that must be renewed year after year. A continuing survey of state productivity efforts concluded,

    > . . . the programs did not appear to become "institutionalized." Rather than a sustained trend of more states creating, nurturing and maintaining centrally coordinated productivity improvement programs, as might be expected in theory, actual experience has followed more of an "up and down" pattern. While additional states do establish new initiatives . . . other states have de-emphasized or eliminated their productivity efforts—especially when personnel at the top have changed.

    Theodore H. Poister et al., "Centralized Productivity Improvement Efforts in State Government," *Public Productivity Review,* 9, no. 1 (Spring 1985), 18.

    Another author has compared management improvement efforts to the torment of Sisyphis: Robert P. McGowan, "Improving Efficiency in Public Management: The Torment of Sisyphis," in Marc

Holzer and Arie Halachmi, eds., *Strategic Issues in Public Sector Productivity* (San Francisco: Jossey-Bass, 1986), pp. 17–32. Harold Geneen has compared it to writing in the snow; one must retrace the letters again and again or they disappear.

Afterword: The Future of Management Systems

THE FUTURE OF MANAGEMENT SYSTEMS

Criticisms of Management Systems

As management systems have become more important in the public sector, they have drawn increasing fire. One of the strongest attacks has been led by Russell Stout, Jr. Referring to the approaches considered here by their common name of "management control systems," he asserts that "to control is not to manage."[1] He adds that management systems emphasize control, which is reactive, routinized, and concerned with processes. *Real* management, on the other hand, is creative, aggressive, and concerned with people.[2]

Although greatly overstated, such attacks on management systems may serve as a useful warning for those few who would see a management system as the equivalent of an automatic pilot—set it and it takes you where you want to go. Obviously, management systems are only one component of the complex and creative task of managing; but they are an extremely essential component. Without setting goals and tracking progress toward them, an organization is rudderless. Creativity and "people" orientations can produce results only when management systems or their equivalents set the course and register the progress. An organization without management systems that is directed only by intuition and creativity evokes the dialogue of Alice in Wonderland:

> "Would you please tell me which way I ought to go from here?"
> "That depends a good deal on where you want to get to," said the Cat.
> "I don't much care where—" said Alice.
> "Then it doesn't matter which way you go," said the Cat.
> "—so long as I get *somewhere*," Alice added as an explanation.
> "Oh, you're sure to do that," said the Cat. "If you only walk long enough."[3]

Management systems are for managers who want to know where they and their organizations are going.

Factors Fostering Increased Use of Management Systems

Output-based management systems seem to have a secure future because of a number of systemic and societal factors. For one, the public continues to support political figures of both parties who promise increased government efficiency and effectiveness. For another, most government budgets will remain tight long into the foreseeable future. At the federal level, continuing increases for so-called "uncontrollable" outlays (particularly for programs tied to rocketing healthcare costs and to the pension needs of the ever-growing over-sixty-five population) will cause discretionary funds to remain scarce. In a chain reaction, this scarcity causes state and local governments to assume more of the burdens of social programs, greatly tightening their budgets. This development forces government decisionmakers at all levels to emphasize improved program implementation, for which management systems are a prerequisite.

In addition to the traditional use of systems within organizations, there are at least two changing patterns of service delivery that increase the need for better output measures:

1. Intergovernmental administration. The amount of money raised at one government level and spent at another has increased over time. Although federal funds spent by states and localities has plateaued at slightly under 20 percent of their budgets (still a large number), the percentage of local funds derived from the states has continued to increase. Accountability for such funds requires output measures

that enable the funder to see that the money is being used for good purposes without restricting the freedom of action of the local community.

2. Contracting out. As mentioned in earlier chapters, privatization experiments depend on the ability to hold the private contractor responsible for certain outputs, and on the ability to compare the outputs of privatized service delivery to government service delivery. Only well-developed management systems provide these requirements.

Conclusion

All this is not to say that matters will continue exactly as they are. As has been true since at least the 1920s, each new administration in Washington or the state capitals will certainly bring with it enthusiastic reformers who will be armed with new (or recycled) administrative techniques and who will be certain that government need only be shown their own, more "rational" system for it to be adopted.[4] And just as certainly, these reformers will be in retreat after two or three years, expressing surprise about how "political" the bargaining-based decision-making process of government really is and about how little interest most participants seem to have in changing it.

However, these potential events are unlikely to change the major, current administrative trends. Performance-oriented management systems such as MBO or performance monitoring systems have the characteristics necessary to function in a political environment because they are simple, flexible, incremental, and nonstrategic. The growing importance of these systems is being fostered by such factors as the increased formal training of career public managers, the increased importance of intergovernmental and privatized service delivery, the penurious public mood, and the unavoidable budgetary constraints. Because these systems meet the needs of public managers functioning in a political environment, performance-oriented management systems will continue to play an important role far into the future.

SUGGESTED FURTHER READING

MARTIN J. SCHIESL, *The Politics of Efficiency: Municipal Administration and Reform in America: 1880–1920.* Berkeley: University of California Press, 1977. Emphasizes the political motives underlying the efficiency-oriented reform movement that battled the urban political machines.

RUSSELL STOUT, JR. *Management or Control?* Bloomington: Indiana University Press, 1980. An attack on management control systems. Stout diffuses his argument somewhat by not distinguishing between operational control systems and management systems.

ENDNOTES

1. This is actually the title of a jointly written article: Martin Landau and Russell Stout, Jr., "To Manage Is Not to Control: Or the Folly of Type II Errors," *Public Administration Review,* 39, no. 2 (March/April 1979), 148–56. The argument is developed at greater length in Russell Stout, Jr., *Management or Control?* (Bloomington: Indiana University Press, 1980).

2. Another interesting critique of management systems that we have discussed in earlier chapters is George W. Downs and Patrick D. Larkey, *The Search for Government Efficiency* (New York: Random House, 1986). However, although the authors' criticism is sharp, it seems less directed at management systems themselves than at the overpromising and misuse that can often accompany them. Although Downs and Larkey criticize "excessive faith" in such systems and note that they are "not a magical cure-all" (pp. 59–60), the authors also indicate that these systems "have a potentially important role to play" (p. 91).

3. Lewis Carroll, *Alice's Adventures in Wonderland,* in Martin Gardner, ed., *The Annotated Alice* (New York: Bromhall House, 1960), p. 88.

4. We considered ideological reasons for change in Chapter One. A few of the other, less important forces acting for and against change of management approaches can be listed:

TOWARD CHANGE

1. Declining benefits (because of institutionalization and goal displacement) of old system
2. Changes in academic theories or emphases in business practices
3. Desire of new administration to distinguish itself from its predecessors

AGAINST CHANGE

1. Ingrained habits of bureaucracy
2. Pressure from
   a. Clientele/special interests who did well under the old system
   b. Legislative committees that have become accustomed to the old system

      c. Professional groups that benefit from the old system (economists in planning-based ones; MBAs in management-based ones)

Underlying all of these motives is the desire to avoid uncertainty by retaining the existing degree of control over bureaucratic points of potential contact with the environment. Thus there is resistance if an entrenched professional group is threatened by a system that will increase "political" overview (as with productivity measures) or control (as with MBO).

The constant tug-of-war between all these forces is yet another reason that public management continues to change in interesting ways.

Glossary: Key Management System Terms Defined

account. The smallest category for which financial figures are kept. By adding accounts together in different ways, managers can gain different types of information.

accountability. The process of imposing sanctions if there is a shortfall from agreed-on levels of performance. Citizens in a democracy must be able to hold public agencies and public managers accountable truly to control government.

accrual accounting. One of the three major ways of registering resource flows for an organization. Accrual accounting registers both expenses and revenues when they are incurred, without regard to when they are paid. Accrual is the form of accounting that provides the most useful managerial information. See also *cash accounting* and *modified accrual accounting.*

achievement point. Any clear measure that allows the attainment of a goal or objective to be ascertained. Most achievement points are quantitative measures; these are also called *indicators.*

activities. The internal actions of an organization, such as interviewing clients, teaching students, or distributing supplies (also called *organizational processes*). Activities link inputs to outputs.

aggregation. Combining smaller units into a whole. For management systems, this term usually refers to combining individual measures into one overall measure.

assessment by objectives (ABO). The use of MBO purely as a technique for personnel evaluation.

average times. One form of standard time. Individual or organizational operations are often judged by the yardstick of *standard times*—that is, expected time of performance. If these standard times are based on the average performance of all employees, they are *average times*. This approach is often misleading.

base year. A year whose output is used as the standard against which all future outputs are compared in calculating an organization's performance. For productivity measurement systems, for example, the base year is the arbitrarily chosen year that is valued at 100 and against which all future productivity scores are compared.

behaviorally anchored rating scales (BARS). A personnel appraisal device by which different types of behaviors desired in a job are aligned along a continuum, and job evaluations are made in terms of the explicit behavioral patterns described.

benefit assessment. Procedure whereby the outputs of a program are turned into an equivalent monetary figure based on the consumers' inferred "willingness to pay" for the program's benefits. Benefit assessment, also called *monetizing,* is often an important part of cost-benefit analysis.

budget. An authoritative spending plan.

bureaucracy. Any large, hierarchical organization.

bureaucrat. Any person who works within a large, hierarchical organization.

capital budget. A spending plan for capital projects—that is, projects that are large, tangible, and return benefits well into the future. Many public organizations split their overall budgets into an operating budget and a capital budget.

capital expenditures. Spending on projects that are large, tangible, and return benefits well into the future, for example, buildings or large pieces of equipment.

capital investment. Investment in large, tangible products—usually equipment—that returns benefits over a long period of time.

cash accounting. One of three ways of registering organizational resource flows. Cash accounting registers transactions only when money changes hands. It is the least informative of the three accounting systems for purposes of managerial information. See also *accrual accounting* and *modified accrual accounting.*

centralization. The location of more organizational power at the organization's top. The directives come from the top, in contrast to decentralization, where more power lies with the lower levels and the field offices.

chain of outputs. Also called *hierarchy of outputs.* Categorizes outputs as an implicit causal chain, starting with immediate, localized outputs and proceeding to broader, more important societal impacts: "*A* leads to *B*, which leads to *C*, which leads to *D*," and so on. Usually the initial outputs are easier to track, but management systems that focus on them exclusively are prone to displacement. See also *immediate outputs* and *intermediate outputs*.

classical theory. The traditional approach to organizational structure, which emphasized "principles." Current approaches emphasize the limitations and contradictions of classical theory, but it remains an important, if flawed, guide to managers.

clientele. Those to whom an agency directs its programs.

contingent approaches. Usually applied to management tools. Unlike the more universalistic prescriptions of the 1930s, today most analysts prescribe virtually all management tools and management approaches on a contingent basis—applicable in some (specified) circumstances but not in others.

contracting out. See *privatization*.

co-optation. Psychologically enlisting outside parties. Thus members of regulatory bodies are often co-opted by the very industry they are meant to regulate, and they become advocates of the industry.

cost accounting. See *cost analysis*.

cost analysis. The process of assigning costs to units of service or output (for example, "Each mile of road paved costs $491,000"). In the private sector this is usually called *cost accounting*, but the term *cost analysis* is sometimes used in the public sector to denote the somewhat more relaxed standards that are used in public cost analysis. Also called *managerial accounting*.

cost-benefit analysis. Comparing an organization's inputs to its outputs, with both expressed in monetary terms (e.g., "On the margin, program A returns $5 in benefits for every dollar spent"). See also *cost effectiveness analysis*.

cost center. An organizational activity (e.g., paving streets) or unit (e.g., the print shop) for which there is a separate account or group of accounts. Direct cost centers actually deliver the organization's output; support cost centers provide services to the direct cost centers.

cost effectiveness analysis. Comparing an organization's inputs to its outputs, with inputs expressed as money and outputs expressed in nonmonetary terms (e.g., "On the margin, job-training program A will produce one trained worker for every $600 spent"). See *cost-benefit analysis*.

cost-plus pricing. A contract, common in defense, health care, and a few other public functions, which guarantees the supplier full costs plus a percentage. Such an arrangement removes most incentives for efficiency. See *prospective pricing*.

crosswalking. Relating items in one budget system to the same items in another budget system. Thus by crosswalking we can trace how a salary listed in a line-item budget recurs as part of a program element in a program budget for the same organization.

cycle of failure. Pattern whereby the clear objectives in the first year of a management system can document the shortcomings of a poorly performing subunit. This documentation in turn provides the subunit's superiors with the leverage to ask for clearer, more comprehensive objectives in the future, which may document yet more shortcomings. As the cycle continues, the superiors can gain enough influence to lead the subunit to improved performance.

decentralization. The location of organizational power at a number of points rather than one central location. The term is used both when organizational power is moved from a central headquarters to field offices and when it is moved from top- to lower-level managers.

decision packages. A term used in zero-base budgeting. Packages are marginal funding levels and their expected outputs for a program, called a *decision unit.* These packages are then ranked in order of policy priority. See also *decision units.*

decision units. The basic analytic unit in zero-based budgeting. An organization's functions are divided into decision units, which are usually programs. Decision units are in turn divided into funding levels, called *decision packages.* See also *decision packages.*

depreciation. Charging off the costs of fixed assets over a number of years as the assets are "used up." Accrual accounting utilizes depreciation; cash accounting and modified accrual accounting do not.

direct costs. Costs that are not shared and that therefore are directly and unambiguously attributable to a particular program or agency.

discounting. A technique for analyzing costs and revenues that are incurred in the future. Because current funds can be invested, future money is not worth as much as the same amount in today's (investable) funds. Discounting is the analytic technique for determining the worth of tomorrow's money in terms of today's dollars.

displacement. See *goal displacement.*

economy. As an organizational goal, economy emphasizes saving money over such potential alternative goals as producing more immediate output (efficiency) or more and better intermediate output (effectiveness).

economy of scale. Denotes the concept that increases in volume often lead to lower cost-per-unit prices because slack resources are utilized, which spreads the fixed cost over more units. In other words, sometimes "bigger is cheaper."

effectiveness. The extent to which a program achieves its goals, that is, a measure of the extent to which actual intermediate and ultimate outputs approximate the desired outputs.

efficiency. In managerial terminology, a measure of waste that indicates how many units of immediate output were produced for a given input. (The term is used differently in economics.)

encumbrance. Earmarking funds that have been committed but not paid. If an agency enters a $1 million contract in June for a product that will be delivered and paid for in November, it may "encumber" $1 million now to prevent it from being spent in the interim.

evaluation. See *program evaluation.*

execution. Implementation, that is, carrying out a program.

expenditure. The payment or disbursement of money. Cash accounting systems track expenditures, whereas accrual systems track expenses.

expense. The consumption or using up of a good or service. Accrual accounting systems track expenses rather than focusing on expenditures, as do cash accounting systems.

extrinsic motivators. Money, promotions, plaques, punishments, and other ways of providing workers with incentives for good performance. Extrinsic motivators are external to the job itself. See also *intrinsic motivators.*

feedback. Information that an organization receives on its own performance.

feedback system. Any process by which an organization gathers information on its own performance in a structured, routinized way.

fixed assets. A relatively expensive, tangible good that returns benefits over a period longer than one year. A large computer system is an example of a fixed asset.

fixed costs. Costs that remain the same within any expectable range of organizational volume. For example, building rental is a fixed cost for most social service organizations; it does not rise and fall within normal volume swings. See also *variable costs.*

flextime. A system under which employees have discretion over the exact hours that they work.

full costs. The sum of a program's or organization's direct and indirect costs.

full factor productivity. See *total factor productivity.*

functional structure. Dividing an organization into smaller organizations on the basis of their purpose (i.e., function). Most government agencies are structured on a functional basis.

fund. A self-balancing group of accounts; in other words, a separate category of money. The concept of funds is unique to the public sector. Funds legally segregate money to help ensure that money that has been raised or appropriated for a particular legal purpose is used only for that purpose. For most governments, the most important fund is the general fund.

gainsharing. A term with a wide variety of meanings in the public sector. Sometimes it is used to mean any organizational system that shares monetary benefits with the employees, for example, suggestion box rewards. The term is used in this book in a more limited sense of a monetary reward given to workers for meeting or exceeding certain standards.

goal. A specified, desired outcome toward which effort is directed. Although some systems use *goal* as a broader term than *objective,* this book treats them as synonyms.

goal congruence. Alignment of individual and organizational goals, such that an individual worker, pursuing his or her own goals, thereby advances the organization's goals as well. Managers attempt to design the organization's structure and reward systems to foster goal congruence. The opposite term is *goal displacement.*

goal displacement. Process by which an organizational worker pursues individual goals that are not in accordance with organizational goals. (The opposite term is *goal congruence.*) Some authors expand the term to cover an *organization* that pursues goals other than the "correct" one. This use involves the problem of defining "correct" organizational goals.

hybrid systems. *Hybrid* can refer to any combination that retains some characteristics of both components. The term is used in this book to refer to management systems that combine some characteristics of MBO with some of performance monitoring systems.

hygiene factors. The central concept underlying the motivational theories of Frederick Herzberg. Such job-related rewards as salary increases are hygiene factors, said Herzberg. They can reduce productivity if they are inadequate, but they do not increase it if they are increased.

immediate outputs. The initial outputs of an organization. Immediate outputs usually lead to outputs that are longer range, with wider social effects. These are termed *intermediate* and *ultimate outputs,* for which immediate outputs can be used as surrogate measures.

impact. A term used by some authors to designate longer-range outputs that have widening social effects. These authors often speak of organizational *outputs* leading to *impacts,* which in turn lead to *outcomes.* This book speaks instead of *immediate outputs* leading to *intermediate outputs,* which in turn lead to *ultimate outputs.*

implementation. Carrying out a program. A synonym is *execution.*

incentive. A reason for acting. Management, in part, is the process of manipulating organizational incentives to produce desired actions.

incrementalism. Step-by-step approach to policy making and implementation. The emphasis in incrementalism is on small steps and feedback rather than bold, preplanned initiatives. Most political scientists believe that government processes in the United States are usually incremental; whether this is good is more controversial. As originally presented, program budgeting was a nonincremental system, which accordingly went against traditional government processes; management systems are more comfortably incremental.

indicators. See *performance indicators.*

indirect costs. Costs that a program or agency incurs with other programs or agencies. To determine full costs, a program must add its direct costs to its indirect costs, that is, its fair portion of shared costs.

informal organizational structure. The patterns of interaction and power within an organization that spring from interpersonal relations and are not captured on any line chart.

input. All societal resources that a program or agency uses to produce its outputs. Inputs are varied—people, supplies, and so on—but they can usually be expressed as a single money figure indicating cost.

intermediate outputs. For any program, outputs can usually be viewed sequentially, arranged in order of broadening import—output *A* leads to *B*, which leads to *C*, which leads to *D*, and so on. Outputs in the middle of such a chain are termed *intermediate outputs.* These outputs are longer range and have a wider social effect than immediate outputs.

internal service unit. A subagency within an organization that produces a good or service for the rest of the organization and charges for it. At the local level, such an organization is given its own fund, termed an *internal service fund,* which uses accrual (rather than modified accrual) accounting.

intrinsic motivators. Psychologically based incentives for good job performance that come from the job alone. Thus workers who perform well because they enjoy their work are responding to intrinsic motivators. See also *extrinsic motivators.*

iron triangles. A term in political science denoting a very close, stable working arrangement among a legislative committee or subcommittee, affiliated interest groups, and the executive agency, for example, the Veterans Affairs committee (legislature), the Department of Veterans Affairs (executive), and the Veterans of Foreign Wars and the American Legion (interest groups).

issue network. A broad, often shifting pattern of interactions among interest groups, legislative committees, executive agencies, experts, and others, all of whom are interested in a single issue. This is a more inclusive, permeable, and transitory type of relationship than that of iron triangles, and it characterizes such national issues as health care, the environment, and civil rights.

job enlargement. A move away from the assembly-line approach. Under the assembly-line system a project is divided into small tasks, each of which is performed by a different person. Job enlargement expands the tasks handled by a single worker, usually allowing an individual to follow a project from start to finish. The rationale is that the loss in task efficiency is balanced by the gain realized from the employee's higher morale and interest.

life-cycle costing. Examining the costs that a purchase will incur over its entire lifetime—operating costs as well as initial purchase costs. Life-cycle costing ensures that low purchase costs do not disguise higher future operating costs.

line. See *line managers.*

line-item budget. A budget in which the primary categories are based on inputs, such as equipment, salaries, fringe benefits, and travel. A synonym is *object-of-expenditure budget.*

line managers. Managers directly involved in producing the organization's output. This term is usually used in contrast to *staff,* who engage in activities that feed into, but do not directly produce, the organization's output. See also *staff.*

longitudinal measures. Measures of organizational performance that extend over a number of years.

management. The link between strategic planning (policy making) and operations. Management is the process of turning the broad policies that are produced by the strategic planning process into the on-the-street delivery of service (operations).

management by exception. A style of management that focuses on the exceptional events (i.e., variances) rather than expending effort on events that are proceeding satisfactorily. Usually this term is used positively, but at the extreme it can denote a completely reactive, uncreative style of management.

management by objectives (MBO). A management system characterized by negotiated goal setting between supervisor and subordinate and regular face-to-face meetings to track progress toward those goals.

management conferences. The regular meetings between supervisor and subordinate to track progress toward MBO goals.

management control system. The term used in business texts for the systems considered in this book. Denotes any feedback-based organizational system that focuses on management (rather than operations or strategic planning).

management information system. A system that gathers and structures data for decision making. As the term is usually used, it implies electronic data processing. Most often, the data are meant to be used for the operations-level as well as management-level decisions.

management system. Like many managerial terms, used differently by different authors. Some authors use it to denote any administrative system—personnel, budgeting, and even operations-level systems like inventory control. The term is used in a much more limited sense in this book: a tool for monitoring the performance of an organization on a regular, short-term basis. A synonym is *management control system.*

market organization. An organization that buys and sells its products for a profit. See *nonmarket organizations.*

matrix organization. An organization that actually has two cross-cutting structures. The permanent structure is usually a function-based one. However, members of different functional units also join temporary work teams to accomplish short-term (e.g., eighteen months) tasks. These work teams cut across functional lines and often have their own budgets and leaders.

merit pay. A compensation procedure whereby employees' raises for a given year depend on performance rather than seniority or across-the-board approaches.

merit system. A government personnel system that bases hiring and promotions on objective indicators, usually tests, and which requires very substantial evidence of poor performance before the employee can be terminated. Merit systems were designed to replace patronage (sometimes called "spoils") systems, which used subjective, usually political, grounds for hirings, firings, and promotions.

micromanagement. Managing by specifying the details of processes that subordinates must carry out. The term carries negative connotations; the executive branch often accuses the legislature of "micromanaging." Within the executive branch, management systems (which specify outputs and leave great freedom on the choice of processes to achieve the outputs) are an important move away from micromanagement.

milestones. Subgoals connected to completion dates that are used to track progress toward major performance goals in a management system.

misreporting. In a management system, providing figures on performance that are not true. In this book, also called *cheating.*

modified accrual accounting. One of the three ways of registering the flow of resources for an organization; the other two are accrual and cash accounting. The three techniques differ primarily by the time at which they register transactions. Modified accrual accounting accrues expenditures (rather than expenses, like accrual accounting). It accordingly lacks any depreciation measures. It is used by most local governments and many state governments.

monetizing. See *benefit assessment.*

nonmarket organizations. Organizations that do not sell their product for a profit. Most government agencies are nonmarket organizations but a few (e.g., Tennessee Valley Authority) are closer to being market organizations.

objectives. Targets of a program or manager. Some authors distinguish intermediate targets (objectives) from long-range ones (goals); this book treats the terms as synonyms.

object-of-expenditure budget. See *line-item budget.*

operating expenses. Many local communities and some states divide their overall budgets into a capital budget and an operating budget, which covers operating expenses. Operating expenses are those consumed in day-to-day operations such as salaries, rent, and maintenance.

operations. One of the three broad functions of all large organizations. It denotes the actual production or delivery of the organization's product. Operations for a high school would involve classroom teaching; for income maintenance, client interviews and check delivery. See also *strategic planning* and *management.*

organizational culture. The underlying values of an organization, especially as those values are expressed and fostered by institutional symbols and rhetoric. Different organizational cultures provide incentives for different patterns of behavior.

outcomes. Used by some authors as a term for ultimate outputs. See also *impact.*

output. Anything produced by an organization.

PPB. See *planning programming budgeting system.*

paired attributes. Refers to types of outputs that should be measured by a management system. Management system measures sometimes lead to goal displacement. Much of this displacement can be alleviated by measuring contrasting attributes such as quantity and quality (e.g., speed and errors) that offset each other. Such contrasting attributes are called *paired attributes.*

performance budget. A budget that focuses on the internal activities (and occasionally, the most immediate outputs) of an organization. Also termed an *activity budget.* Performance budgets often utilize cost accounting data, such as "cost per patient seen" or "cost per applicant interviewed." Performance budgets are in contrast to line-item budgets, which focus on inputs, and program budgets, which focus on intermediate outputs.

performance indicator. A measure, usually quantitative, that captures some aspect of organizational output. Most public programs need numerous indicators to give a full picture of their performance.

performance monitoring systems. Any output-oriented management system that is not MBO. Most performance monitoring systems focus on lower-level routine tasks and produce regular, often computer-processed reports. Neither goal setting nor tracking are face-to-face.

planning programming budgeting system. Also called *program budgeting, PPB,* and *PPBS.* A budgeting system that focuses on organizational (and cross-organizational) outputs. It has a program-based structure; a series of goal statements (called *program memoranda*); a five-year future projection; and connected special analyses, which are forms of program evaluation. PPB has a strong planning orientation, and it is most useful for top managers and analysts.

policy making. The setting of broad goals. Also termed *strategic planning.* Policy-making guides management, which in turn directs operations; however, all three functions blend and interactively influence one another.

privatization. The process whereby activities that were formerly carried out by government agencies are assigned to nongovernment, for-profit agencies, usually under contract with the government.

processes. Internal organizational activities.

process charting. The diagramming of all the steps involved in a particular job, usually on a preprinted flow chart. The chart is then used to determine whether some steps could be shortened, combined, or eliminated.

production function. In economics, a quantitative expression of the outputs that can be expected for a given amount of inputs. Outside of economics it is used more broadly, as a synonym for the relationship between a program's inputs and processes, on the one hand, and its output, on the other hand. Some government programs (e.g., social intervention with delinquent youths) have very unclear production functions, making it more difficult to hold them accountable for performance.

productivity. Technically, an efficiency measure of outputs divided by inputs. Traditionally, inputs have been measured by labor years; such an input measure is prone to distortion. See also *total factor productivity.* The term *productivity* is often used in a nontechnical sense as well, meaning any increase in effectiveness or (especially) efficiency.

productivity banks. A funding unit that loans money to agencies that apply for funds to finance capital investments to improve productivity. Agencies must then repay the productivity bank, using money they saved because of their higher productivity. Productivity banks allow agencies to avoid the long lead times and red tape endemic to the regular appropriations process.

productivity funds. A small pot of money carved out of appropriations and set aside to support purchases of productivity-improving equipment. This fund is used for projects too small for a productivity bank loan.

productivity system. A term that varies widely from author to author. It is used in this book to denote performance monitoring systems that express their results as a single number contrasted to a base year.

profit centers. A structural arrangement in which organizational components both control and track their own costs and revenues. This is often called a *divisional structure* in business. In the public sector, real profit centers are rare because few subunits can charge for their services, although organizational subunits can be given greater control over their own costs and outputs and held responsible for performance. Such an approach uses profit centers as a model and is termed a *result center*.

program. A grouping of organizational activities directed toward a single group of outputs.

program budgeting. See *planning programming budgeting system.*

program evaluation. Also called *evaluation,* a systematic analysis of a program's outputs, usually looking at before and after data and contrasting them to a control group. The significance of any differences are then interpreted by using statistical measures.

prospective pricing. Setting prices for a service before it is delivered. See *cost-plus pricing.*

proxy measures. See *surrogate measures.*

public goods. A term used in economics to denote outputs that are nonrivalous in consumption and, more important, are nonexcludable in use, so that nonpayers (sometimes called *free riders*) cannot be prevented from enjoying the benefits. Defense and pollution control are two examples of public goods.

quality circles (QC). A group of workers in a unit who meet regularly to discuss ways of improving their work or work processes.

reasonable person approach. A "fudge factor" in interpreting the results of management systems, meant to alleviate the goal displacement characteristic of linking rewards directly and exclusively to quantitative indicators. This approach says that the *spirit* of the law will be employed in interpreting the employee-superior contract, not just the *letter* of the law. Accordingly, management system results will be interpreted in light of unmeasured performance outputs as well if such outputs would be expected by a "reasonable person."

reliability. One of two important ways of characterizing the accuracy and usefulness of a measure. (The other is validity.) Reliability evaluates the degree of random error associated with a measurement procedure. If a measure is reliable, its scores do not significantly fluctuate from moment to moment. For a measure to be truly useful, it must first be reliable (the basic necessity) and then also valid. See *validity.*

responsibility structure. Grouping accounts according to actual organizational arrangements (i.e., agency by agency).

result center. An organizational subunit that has been designed to be relatively autonomous—that is, in control of some outputs for the clientele. In the public sector, result centers are usually based on place or clientele and headed by a generalist. Because it includes many functions within itself, it is thus the opposite of a subunit based on function. By definition a functional subunit includes only narrow specialists and therefore cannot stand alone.

scanlon plans. An arrangement by which workers share in an organization's profits.

senior executive service. At the federal level, one product of the Civil Service Reform Act of 1978. The SES is a separate group of very senior administrators who are not under some of the tight strictures characteristic of most merit or civil service systems. The SES members give up some job security in return for eligibility for bonuses for outstanding performance. Similar plans have been adopted by a number of states.

span of control. The number of employees directly supervised by a manager.

staff. Organizational employees who handle auxiliary functions such as legal affairs, accounting, or computer services. Staff members do not directly produce the organizational output but help those who do. See also *line managers.*

standard. Any goal against which performance is judged.

standard times. A measure used to evaluate the performance of an individual or unit. A commonly used standard time (also called *time standard*) is the time that it takes one well-trained worker to produce a unit of output. See also *work standard.*

strategic planning. One of the three broad functions found in all large organizations. Also called *policy making,* strategic planning is the determination of overall organizational goals and directions. See also *management* and *operations.*

sunset law. A law that states that the authorization for a program or agency must end after a specified period of time. For example, a state sunset law might require all programs to be reauthorized every seven years. The rationale is that the reauthorization forces a reexamination, and inefficient programs will be discovered and eliminated. Widely adopted in the late 1970s and early 1980s, it did not seem to produce major gains in efficiency and fell out of favor.

surrogate measures. A stand-in or proxy indicator used when the desired organizational output cannot be measured directly. For example, a program may use the indicator "number of client complaints" as a surrogate measure for quality of services. Often immediate output measures are used as surrogates for desired ultimate outputs.

technology. In management, the term refers to the specific organizational process by which outputs are produced. Thus a new teaching method that improves students' performance is an improvement in the schools' technology.

theory x. A management approach that assumes that employees do not like to work and that therefore managers must maintain tight control and wield substantial punishments to achieve organizational goals. See also *Theory Y.*

theory y. A management approach that assumes most employees enjoy expressing themselves through meaningful work. Therefore managers can best attain organizational goals by working with employees in a nonautocratic, supportive way. Both Theory X and Theory Y are the analytic creations of Douglas McGregor.

time standards. Standard times.

total factor productivity. Productivity is a measure of output to input. Total factor productivity measures are the most accurate productivity measures because they capture *all* input, expressing it in the form of monetary costs. See also *productivity.*

trait-based appraisals. The traditional form of personnel appraisal, which evaluates employees on such personality-based qualities as "presents good appearance," "cooperates well with fellow workers," or "is hard working."

transfer prices. Prices charged one organizational subunit by another. Transfer pricing encourages efficient use of organizational resources and allows subunit efficiency to be tracked more accurately.

ultimate outputs. The final links in a chain of organizational outputs, which can be viewed as a sequential chain: *A* causes *B,* which causes *C,* which causes *D.* The ultimate targets, the hoped-for final links in the chain, are the ultimate outputs. Often, the ultimate output is too nebulous (e.g., greater happiness for all) to track directly, and intermediate outputs are used as proxies.

user charges. Charges imposed on those who benefit from a service. Sometimes the charges are a form of directed tax (a tax on all automobiles as a user charge for roads). Other times it looks more like a private sector price; thus a public swimming pool may install a user charge in the form of an admission price.

validity. One of two important ways of characterizing the accuracy and usefulness of a measure. (The other is reliability.) Validity reflects whether a particular measure actually measures what it purports to. For example, a manager may need to consider whether "number of complaints" is a valid measure of "client satisfaction."

variable costs. Costs that change (on a total, not cost-per-unit, basis) as organizational volume changes. For example, the total costs for employee salaries will increase as the client volume in a social services office increases (and more employees are hired). Salaries are thus a variable cost for the welfare office. See also *fixed costs.*

variance. The difference between a goal or target and actual performance. Variances alert a manager to unexpected gains and possible problems.

weighting. Treating some output measures differently from others by adjusting them quantitatively. For example, a police department's productivity system may weight a drinking-while-driving arrest as being three times as important as a regular speeding arrest. Weighting is most used for combining a number of different measures into a single measure.

workload measures. Measures of the performance of an organization, based on processes or activities that the organization has performed. Common workload measures are people seen, forms filled out, calls taken.

work standards. A quantitative measure of the amount of output that is expected to be completed in a given time. For example, the work standard for auditing simple tax returns may be four forms per day. Work standards are the flip side of standard times: Standard times specify how much time it takes to produce one unit of output; work standards specify how much output can be produced in one unit of time.

zero-base budgeting (ZBB). One of four types of budgeting systems, ZBB ranks alternative spending levels for different programs. ZBB is more useful for strategic planning than for management. See also *decision units* and *decision packages.*

Index